DARI

KIT CARSON

AND

FRÉMONT,

AMONG

BUFFALOES, GRIZZLIES AND INDIANS,

BEING A SPIRITED DIARY

OF THE MOST DIFFICULT AND

WONDERFUL EXPLORATIONS EVER MADE,

OPENING, THROUGH YAWNING CHASMS AND OVER PERILOUS PEAKS,

THE GREAT PATHWAY TO THE PACIFIC

1887

COPYRIGHT 2014 BIG BYTE BOOKS

Get more great reading from BIG BYTE BOOKS

Contents

KIT CARSON: 4
ADVENTURES AND EXPLORATIONS 48
OREGON AND NORTH CALIFORNIA....................................158

KIT CARSON:

A FULL NARRATIVE

OF HIS

MOST DARING AND ADVENTUROUS CAREER

The Man and the Hour appear simultaneously. When the astronomers and geographers of the Middle Ages were growing dissatisfied with the dubious responses of their doubtful charts and imperfect instruments, Columbus came to prove the existence of a New World.

It was at that period of the existence of the United States when the vast acreage of fertile lands, through which the Missouri and the Mississippi cut their channels to the Gulf of Mexico, came into our possession, that "Kit"—as he was always endearingly called—came into this world. The whole wild West was in a state of transition, and all the more daring population of Kentucky and Missouri were making tracks into the vast river bottoms, displacing the "injuns, b'ars, painters " and other "varmint." This was just the dawn of the period that called for a hunter and a hero, and "Kit" responded to the call, and filled the requisition.

The precise date and place of Kit Carson's birth is not exactly told by his biographers. But the most reliable data which we can find places the date about Christmas, 1809, and the place in Old Kentucky, in the County of Madison.

The family of Kit took up land in the new territory obtained from France. It was a perfect hunter's paradise, while the land fairly teemed with the best agricultural products. Indians, it is true, were both plentiful and ferocious; but rifles were not sparse, and men to sight them were generally to the fore when wanted.

In a half fortified house, such as was the dwelling of the elder Carson, the young lad readily acquired the woodcraft that was to be learned by a sharp boy; and very soon he became familiar with the use of the deadly rifle and the hunting knife.

Disdaining the sedentary trade, which his father wanted him to learn, Kit, after a brief trial, turned his whole attention to what was already the delight, and was henceforth to be the principal employment, of his life: trading, hunting and trapping.

At this time, about 1826, the principal trade between the region about Santa Fe, then belonging to Mexico, and the extreme Western States was by means of wagons, from Missouri over the plains.

This business was much liked by daring spirits, fond of excitement; and they generally had their fill of danger before their return. Many would be fully satisfied with one trip of this sort, but to Kit it was pure amusement and he very soon became an expert, and a very valuable aid to any party about to make the passage. So he kept on to El Paso, some three hundred Miles further.

The Conquest of California, has accustomed many of our citizens to the sight of the adobe houses, built entirely of sundried bricks. Which, bye-the-bye, are as mean looking as they are lasting. The oldest house in the new world being one of these houses erected by the early Spanish visitors.

Our people have since become tolerably familiar with the appearance, products and trade of Santa Fe, but at the time of young Carson's visit, little was known about it, except to the traders, and their guards, and drivers. Indeed, instead of furnishing the "States" with any descriptions of the place and its people, they generally mystified about it in their occasional descriptions, as they wished for as few interlopers as possible, in what was really a very profitable business.

For some months Kit Carson traveled about this region in very humble capacities, but after a time he formed a situation much to his liking. He had picked up enough Spanish to act as translator for a dealer, whom he accompanied to Chihuahua, and started out on a journey to that remote place, at one time quite a town of importance, but now dwindled to a place of a few thousand inhabitants. The life that he now lived was entirely too slow for a person of his ardent temper and restless habits, and he soon found employment to drive a team to the Gild, and back. Now fortune favored him. He found a chance to engage properly in the life of a hunter and trapper.

Mr. Ewing was engaged in the fur business on quite a large scale. He was on friendly terms with Carson, and very readily engaged him for an expedition. The party started as if to punish Indians for their depredations, but the band, formed of about forty active, brave, and resolute men, without a poor shot in their ranks, really intended before their return to enrich themselves with not a few packs of beaver skins. When they did fall in with their Indian enemies they did not waste any ammunition; but soon put all the band to flight, less than about a dozen of their number. The Indians gone, the party went to work systematically to take as many of the highly prized beaver skins as possible in short metre.

The business of a trapper has always had a fascination for boys and young men, brought up in the neighborhood of any of the rivers or lesser streams that gently flow or madly dash in most parts of the American Continent. On the great affluents of the North, such as the Niagara and many mighty streams that empty into Hudson Bay, are found the Canadian voyagers, and their half breed conjeners; while in the Southern and Western waters flowing from their native fountains in the primeval clefts of the Rocky Mountains, the hunters and trappers were generally descendants of the old Virginia settlers, running through and over the Western States, with a slight sprinkling among them of Danes and Norwegians. From the latter race Kit Carson sprang, and he was well gifted with all the best attributes of that hardy and persevering people. From his childhood he had been accustomed to roam about the little log cabin, with no other companion than his faithful dog, no timepiece save the sun, and no chart but the barks of trees, the mosses of the rocks, and the narrow lanes made by deer and lesser animals, in their way to water, or to their chosen pastures or nut trees. Untaught except by the example of his father and their few friends, he soon mastered all the learning of the woods, of which they were masters. Constant exercise and frequent privation hardened his muscles and inured him to scanty fare, so that Kit had scarcely passed from boyhood ere he was in all respects a fully developed man. Often being brought in contact with the red men, who were still quite numerous near his paternal home, he eagerly studied all their ways, habits and tricks, and in many of their best qualities he was more Indian than the Indians themselves. He little cared whether night found him under a native's tepee, or merely sheltered by an overhanging rock, curtained by the drooping branches of a gloomy hemlock. So it will be seen that Kit was exactly the "boy" to baffle and circumvent the blanketed thieves that kept prowling about the camp, making free sometimes with the empty traps (of great value to the redskins), and occasionally seizing them, beaver and all, if the vigilant scouts slumbered on their posts.

After a brief stay in the section watered by the San Francisco river a part of the company started for a very long and toilsome journey. To the number of about twenty, in the employment of Young, they wended their way toward distant California. Passing through many regions of arid desolation, where water was hardly to be obtained in sufficient quantities to quench their burning thirst; at other times encountering Indian tribes inhabiting pleasant tracts of land, through which clear streams danced and glanced in the pleasant sunlight, they managed to pass through all these varied scenes without meeting with any serious mishaps, Kit proving able on all occasions to fully "keep up his end of the log," continuing daily to gain more and more the good will of his comrades by his unshrinking devotion to all that tended to the general good. In California they were much interested by that peculiar phase of settlement —"the missions." Each of these places, known by the name of some eminent Saint, was a very large domain granted by the government, in perpetuity to a certain number of priests and lay brothers, in consideration of their devoting their lives to the bettering of the condition of the Indians, and their conversion to Christianity. The native California Indian was but poor stock to operate upon; but in many of the missions they had been comparatively civilized; they were well fed and housed, and were taught the simple truths and many of the rights of the church. Certain it is, that they were far better off under the mild rule of the simple Padres, than they have been since the gold fever stampeded the Indians to the hills and gullies, and the missions have been mostly gobbled up by millionaire land grabbers under false patents and other formal frauds. The priests themselves have long since slept their long sleep beneath the crumbling walls of their quaint old adobe chapels.

But Kit Carson was not one to trouble himself with such sad reflections; indeed, at this period plenty—and its proper companion, hospitality—still happily welcomed the wayfarer.

The party to which Carson was attached, as much by choice as by agreement, brought up on the banks of that grand stream, the Sacramento, destined afterward to have its oft submerged borders graced by the capitol of California.

This river ran through a very rich country, and, what was of most consequence to Kit, wild animals, good for food and furs, thronged its forests and tulle swamps. Here roamed almost unmolested the gamboling antelope and almost every species of the deer kind. While on the banks of the Sacramento, Kit Carson was one of several of his comrades who were employed to assist the Padre of the San Gabriel mission in reducing his Indian peons to submission. They had risen in one of those half frenzied fits common to all half savages, and deserted the walls and work of the fathers. Before they were thoroughly subjugated, over one fourth of the mountaineers were slain and they returned to a sulky vassalage.

About this time Cap. Young, the leader of the expedition, traded off a lot of furs, and thereby came into possession of nearly half hundred horses. These steeds had barely been tethered out, before, under cover of darkness, the wily Indians sneaked into their neighborhood, and spirited away a number of the best animals. It shows the estimation in which Carson was held when we see him selected to lead a chosen band of his comrades in an attempt to recover them. The marauders had a long start, and although by wading in streams and making some detours they tried to mask their course, Kit skillfully led his band until they came up with them. Snugly ensconced in a deep hollow, far remote as they believed from any pursuit, the large band of Indians were regaling themselves on a portion of the stolen animals, which they had killed and roasted. Quietly surrounding the savages, Kit and his daring comrades burst in upon them, slaying eight of their number, and forcing the remainder into headlong flight. They left a few little pappooses behind them; which, together with the recaptured horses were triumphantly paraded into their forest home.

Cap. Young's band of trappers, including Kit Carson, turned their faces homeward in the Fall of 1829, leaving their pleasant hunting grounds on the margin of the Sacramento, with regretful feelings. On their return they made a brief stoppage at Los Angelos—well worthy of Goldsmith's panegyric of another "loveliest village of the vale." Its delicious surroundings of leaves and flowers marking it out truly as a "terra angelica." But it was not in such tranquil scenes that Carson took delight—his was not a disposition to be lapped in Elysium. So, after a few pleasant hours spent mostly in the refined family of a wealthy Spanish land owner and cultivator, Kit was once more on his route for wilder scenes and deeds of a more adventurous nature than he was likely to meet with in this luxuriant valley, teeming with the grape, the pear, and the orange. While Cap. Young's company got along very nicely among the mountain slopes and river bottoms of the uncultivated and unpeopled regions, they easily yielded to the seductions of the winecup and the dance, and in the ready movements of the fandango, they quickly lost all that coolness that they always evinced in the midst of the most appalling dangers. As if to prove the truth of the old adage, "when the wine is in the wit is out," some of the best men made the biggest fools of themselves, and got into several disgraceful brawls with the dwellers and workers in the neighboring ranches. A native, it happened, was slain in one of those unfortunate affrays, that often occurred between the Californians and the Americans, and it was not easily that Cap. Young got off scot free with his men, just escaping at least a temporary stay in the caboose, a very slight improvement upon Dante's Inferno.

Hardly a dozen days passed before Young, Carson, and the rest were "working like beavers" to entrap these intelligent animals and such other furbearers as could be induced to "walk into their parlor."

One day, when most of the band was afar in various directions, he had a most unexpected visit from apparently a whole tribe of redskins. The fellows swaggered into the purlieus of the encampment with a great display of insolent familiarity. As they appeared to be unarmed, and as they could see that Carson and the few men with him had their rifles in reach, Kit was a little surprised at their conduct, but by careful observation he became convinced that most of them had hidden weapons of some sort upon their persons.

These Indians, having been brought in contact mostly with Mexicans, and felt that their superior number would probably appall so few white men as Carson had to support him. But Kit was made of sterner stuff, and resolutely ordered them out of the camp when they became insolently familiar. Carson calmly looked around him, and was greatly pleased to observe that his men had anticipated his unspoken wishes. They had without any hurry or bravado, closed around him. Each rifle was in the exact position to come to "the present, aims!" at a slight motion. Yet each man looked as cold and as firm as a block of ice. Carson strode up to their spokesman (who had addressed him in Spanish) and looking him fixedly in the eye, bade him at once to withdraw, adding that, if necessary, his men carried the lives of half dozen Indians to each one of their rifles. For a second the old chief appeared to be calculating whether it would pay "to bring on a fight;" but Kit's firm demeanor had won. Frowning and grumbling, the old Indian said a few words to his followers, and they slowly retreated to the neighboring ravine. It will be seen that in this case, as in all others where Carson was brought to the test, his unswerving firmness conquered. Had he shown but the extreme tip of the "white feather" the Indians would have doubtless become emboldened, and uttering their fearful war cry, would have rushed on the whites, knives and tomahawks in hand. But Kit's indomitable bearing may have induced them to think that a force of white's might be handy, and that they would pay too dearly for their whistle if they began the fight.

It was while Young and Kit was on this hunting expedition about the wild banks of the Colorado, that they introduced, by way of a little spice, some of the Indian tactics into their style of doing up things. As a lot of Indians passed their camp one day, they perceived that they were leading and driving a drove of horses, and their critical sight told them at once that in the drove were many very superior steeds; indeed some of them had not yet been despoiled of the elegant accoutrement with which a Mexican loves to adorn his favorite riling animal. Following the Indians silently until they reached a suitable spot, they suddenly rushed upon them, yelling and discharging rifles. The surprised Indians fled leaving the vast drove of horses to Cap. Young's trappers as their lawful spoil. The thieving Indians had evidently thought a Mexican force had overtaken them, and "as the thief doth think each bush an officer," they did not stop to see his warrant, of arrest. The lot of fine horses brought them in several doubloons (a 16 dollar gold coin).

There were very few spots favorable for hunting and trapping about the banks of the Gila and the Colorado that had not reached to the report of some of their rifles, and they had diligently trapped and hunted. A goodly lot of pelts rewarded them for their hard service, and when they were "paid off," as sailors would phrase it, each man was several hundred dollars to the fore. These men earned their few hundred dollars by passing through many hardships and some dangers, but a few months on the borders of civilization soon emptied purses of all their coin.

Kit Carson had now attained his majority, and it was just after this time that he became acquainted with Mr. Fitzpatrick, and with him and quite a party started on another expedition. This time the Salmon river was settled upon as the headquarters of their trapping business. Here they were a good deal plagued by the devilish tricks of the Blackfeet (at that time a powerful tribe), Carson was for raiding them, but more prudent counsels prevailed. The Spring found Kit in the neighborhood of Salt Lake. It will be noticed that a few degrees of latitude and longitude didn't trouble his calculation much. The winter found him and his priests busily engaged with rifles and traps about the source of the Arkansas. Quite a large party of Crow Indians made a foray on their camp, during the Winter, and ran off a lot of their horses. These animals were of great service to the trappers in enabling them to carry traps and skins to the caches, where they were securely stowed away till wanted. It was therefore necessary to recover the horses, but it was desirable to punish the thieves to prevent further purloining.

Kit was chosen as the fitting leader of the little band of twelve sent on this hazardous service. For there was over half hundred crows in the marauding party. The Indians had sought shelter in one of their cunningly contrived fortresses. Kit lost no time in storming it, killing many of its defenders, releasing his fettered horses and returning without the loss of a man.

On another occasion he started after some deserters; he pressed them so hard that they fled into the wilderness, and were never heard of after.

For many months Kit and a comrade remained guarding an old fort where a cache of furs had been left by Capt. Gaunt. They remained here till a party of regular soldiers, which had been despatched to aid Capt. Gaunt, joined them. Kit went with them towards the Captain's rendezvous. On the way they repeatedly had to give a wandering Indian a rifle shot; but they kept at a safe distance. On one occasion Kit and his fellow trapper were surprised by some fifty Indians. They escaped by flight under a rain of bullets.

The year 1832 found Carson, with two companions, hunting in the high-up mountain streams. They took their furry spoils to Taos for sale. His friends recklessly spent the rewards of their hard toil, but Kit, although a lover of good cheer, carefully saved his money. In October, Carson started off with Capt. Lee, at Bent's fort, on a long trip. Before the start a very skillful Indian hunter had run off with half dozen of Mr. Robideau's horses. Carson was solicited to follow and try to capture the thief and the horses. Taking with him an agile and athletic young Utah fighter, he went in pursuit on a rather difficult trail. Ere they had passed over a hundred miles, the brave's horse gave out. He declined to pursue on foot. Kit determined not to back down, and went it alone. In a couple of hours he had got sight of the pursued, who had also detected him. As the Indian sought cover, Carson, whose horse was at the gallop, sent a ball with such unerring aim, that in a second a dead. Indian fell from his animal, his gun going off as he touched the grass. Carson came back to camp, where he was warmly welcomed, with the six stolen animals and the dead Indian's horse, all in good form. Soon after Lee and Kit traded off all their furs to a party camped near them. After a little rest, Kit joined three others, and successfully trapped about the Laramie. It was at this time that Carson had his famous encounter with the two, grizzles. One of these bears is a mighty hard " critter" for any man to grapple; but when it comes to two, few men care for the job. The instant he spied them, he broke for the nearest young tree. With the grizzles a good second and third. Shinning and dragging himself up with his heels just beyond reach of their strong claws, he had succeeded in getting a stout limb cut as one of the bears (for they could not both climb the tree together) got to close quarters, Kit would give him a smart rap on the nose, a particular tender part of their anatomy. At this he would drop, and grizzly No. 2 would try his chance. They kept it up till near daylight, when they left disgusted, and savagely grumbling. As soon as Kit was sure they had gone for good, he dropped to earth and hastened to camp.

During the Fall and Winter months Kit and some companions trapped with varying success. Being much troubled by Blackfoot Indians, who stole some eighteen of their horses, at the end of the Winter it was deemed necessary to punish the Indians and get back the horses. After some fruitless attempts to make the thieves, quietly return their plunder, both parties sprang to their rifles. Kit, to save a companion from instant death, sent his own bullet into an Indian's heart, regardless of the fact that an Indian had him spotted, the consequence was that he was hit, and the ball injured his shoulder blade. Although they had sent several Indians to grass, and Kit was the only one wounded on their side, they determined to return to camp. A party afterwards set out to pursue the Indians, but failed to find them.

Before Carson had got fully well, the time of the Summer assemblage had come. A wide clear space, with plenty of feed for the horses, and wood and water for all hands was chosen; then each of the principal traders selected a site for his particular adherents, and they would proceed to make all shipshape and comfortable for business and pleasure. Then begins a "fair," such as is still found in the wildest regions of Russia. The business is mainly trafficking. The various furs are examined closely, not only as to their peculiar kind, but as to the condition in which they have been kept. Then all the little nicknacks of civilization are exposed, and the trade is briskly carried on in the style in which old Mr. Astor drove his bargains in "ye olden time." Few that have ever seen these primitive trading places will ever forget them. The wide spreading trees, screening from the too fervid heat of the sun, the streams meandering in each depression, stealing away in glittering ribbands to the nearest river; rude tables bearing much that is good to eat, and not a little, sad to say, that was not equally good to drink.

Around these posts camped friendly Indians, trading like the rest, and many a Canadian voyager, generally with a good looking Indian squaw wife. Many of these, marriages turning out quite happily, by the way.

Kit Carson had by this time become quite a power in the vast region that he had so often roved. Men of his stamp get talked about in the lofty tepe, or the rude log hut, much as the ironclad wanderers of the middle ages had their deeds of dauntless prowess chaunted of by troubadours in hall and camp. Nearly all men instinctively admire a brave man, but when a man is at once valiant in battle and gentle in camp he is doubly admired. Such a man was Kit Carson, a kind of backwoods Bayard, "without fear and without reproach."

He naturally acquired great influence over his fellow hunters, not merely by his skill and courage, but by his calmness in all cases that led to displays of "mad" in ordinary men. While at this encampment, a coarse, burly chap of French descent, Shuman by name, made himself an object of dislike and terror to white and Indian. No one was secure from his insolence and bluster. It happened that he at one time caught a Tartar running foul of our friend Kit in one of his drunken sprees. "Americans," shouted he, "why they are only fit to be trounced with switches." Kit heard him and determined to make "him hold his horses." "I am an American, and not a prize specimen; but I can take you down without sweating." Shuman was on his horse, fully armed. His rifle was ready. Carson threw himself upon his horse, pistol in firm grip, and both dashed together. Almost before one could wink, they both drew trigger; but Kit's was a second before his opponents; and his bullet ripped up Shuman's arm, disabling him. The Frenchman's ball only took, away a lock of his hair from Carson's head. He was in Kit's power. He begged for mercy. It was accorded him, and afterwards he was the quietest man to be found in that section. Roving about with different bands, their success was not equal to their deserts. At length he found himself upon the Humboldt, after wandering about some time longer, occasionally meeting with squalid specimens of the Digger Indian, the most forsaken specimen of the redmen. Hereabouts fur animals were scarce, and Kit's men suffered many privations. At last they had to bleed their horses, and imbibe the precious draught. Some Snake Indians next day made their appearance. From them Kit bought a horse in fine condition and they had something to eat.

But here good news reached them, at no great distance vast herds of buffalo were feeding. They were soon in their midst, slaying, dressing and drying the Meat, and got back to the fort laden down with luscious food.

But some of the Blackfeet had been trailing Ahem, and before they had fully rested, the subtle foe had perpetrated one of their usual cunning thieveries. Watching when the Indian retired, thinking he was relieved, two of the Blackfeet took down the bars and the horses were at a distance before their flight was known. As but a few days had passed since the like trick had been successfully played, they had no horses to send in pursuit.

They could do nothing till Capt. McCoy got back. He had gone to Walla Walla, and it was four weeks before he returned from an expedition to the Kiowas. Quite a superior people were these Indians at that time. They owned an immense number of fine horses, and dwelt in what has since become Oregon. These Indians readily parted with enough good horses to mount Kit and his men.

Once more the whole party were in good condition and spirits, and started to keep engagements upon Green River. While waiting the arrival of other parties, they lost no time in oganizing to trap in the waters that first feed the Missouri. The Blackfeet it Vas surmised would start upon a similar expedition, and the hope of encountering them added another zest to the setting out. But a more fell destroyer had been busy with their enemies, and the smallpox had decimated their ranks. These Winter encampments proved rather uneventful.

With the Spring trapping gave them lots of employment. The Blackfeet recovering their courage with the cessation of the fell scourge, were once more in a condition for a fight. Carson returned from a scout to inform his men that the Indians, either to attack them or to fly, were removing their tents and sending off their families. Carson picked out about forty tried men, and rushed after the Indians. At the first onset ten Indians fell, and the trappers pressed them hard. Then the Indians fell back before the firery charge and the trappers pressed on. The Blackfeet acting warily; but as the Americans began to slacken in their efforts, the Indians rightly judged that they had run out of ammunition. On their part they began to advance, and with loud shouts they charged in turn. But now Kit and his men drew their pistols, and again drove the Blackfeet. At this time, Carson, by a swift and desperate act of courage, interposed between one of his men, who was pinned down by his fallen horse, and kept at bay half dozen warriors thirsting for his blood. Trappers flew to Carson's assistance, the man was saved, but many of his red foes had gone down never to rise again.

Both sides drew off, as if to rest. But afterwards Kit being reinforced by Fontenelle and his party, they once more attacked the Blackfeet, who never flinched until they had sustained very severe losses. The American party had meanwhile had their strength but slightly reduced. Thenceforward they went to and fro through the Blackfeet country without molestation.

After journeying with Fontenelle and others to Mud River, where the trappers had come together, satisfactory sales and settlements of all accounts were made, and Kit organized a small party to join a company to trade with the Navajoe Indians. A satisfactory business was done with these very fine specimen of Indians, who still retained many evidences of a previous cultivation. Returning with a drove of splendid mules, Kit came to a pretty valley on the Colorado.

Kit now engaged himself to keep the garrison at this fort supplied with game. Many elk and antelope fell at the crack of his rarely missing rifle. The next year Kit followed pretty nearly the same routine. Trapping up and down the Yellowstone, and going to the customary rendezvous with the results of his skill and labor.

During the Winter the Blackfeet, undeterred by their former beatings, had gathered all their warriors together to try once again the mettle of their foe. After a preliminary skirmish in which the Indians lost heavily they brought every available warrior into the field. Both leaders placed their followers so skillfully, that it looked exceedingly dubious who would prove victors. The Indians at length charged up to the Americans' front—but finding that nothing would induce them to leave their defences, they discharged a few harmless shots and finally went slowly off.

Probably they had seen Kit's hand in the arrangement of the defences, and feared for the result.

Certain, though quite ready to molest other trappers, they gave Kit very little trouble afterwards. After trapping awhile in company with the Flathead Indians, Kit "betook himself the next Spring to the Utah region, where the streams mingle their waters with Great Salt Lake. Here he found furs abundant. Afterwards he went for awhile to a place designated New Fork. Eight years had now passed since Kit Carson had embraced the life of hunter, trapper and scout, and in each occupation he had proved himself fully the equal of anyone who had ever pursued the like vocation. During this period, he had often exerted his great influence with chiefs of many of the leading tribes to bring about truces, often leading to long intervals of peace.

Leaving for a time the record of hunting and fighting with which the days and nights of this incessantly active man were so plentifully chequered, we must for a time fall upon "a gentler method."

At the time during which Kit Carson had an engagement with Bent and' St. Vrain, Kit united himself to an Indian wife. The mother lived but a very little time after her baby daughter greeted Carson as papa. When his motherless child grew old enough Kit determined to take his child to St. Louis, that she might be properly cared for and suitably educated. So when all his engagements were honorably fulfilled, he started to St. Louis to carry out his excellent intentions.

Determining, also, at the same time to take a look at his "boyhood's home," from which he had now been absent for sixteen years.

Few of his old friends remained to greet him.

Some had moved to different places. Many were dead. But enough remained to give him a hearty welcome, and to convince him that his courage and capacity had not remained untold of in his native town.

At St. Louis he was received almost with an ovation. That city being the headquarters of the Southwestern trade, was of course oftener visited by the trappers, traders, and army officers, many of whom, in the course of their narratives, would often introduce the name of Kit Carson as the leader in some exploit calling for courage and capacity. But this was by no means a style of life that suited a man like Kit, who was as modest in company as he was foremost in the ranks of danger.

Carson succeeded in finding proper guardians for his little daughter, and was at once anxious to return to the forest and the prairie.

It was at this time that the two great men first met, whose names were to go down to posterity, eternally linked together, John C. Fremont and Kit. Carson. Two men widely dissimilar in many points, but alike in their indomitable perseverance and skill in overcoming what seemed insurmountable obstacles.

Both Carson and Fremont had every reason to be thankful that they had met, for each possessed qualities which were invaluable in conjunction. This was soon proved.

Fremont, then a lieutenant in the United States army, had been ordered to make a thorough exploration of the vast range of country, of which little was known, lying between the edge of the State of Missouri and the South Pass in the Rocky Mountains, with a careful survey of the Kansas and Great Platte Rivers. According to instructions they set out for Choleau's landing, near the mouth of the Kansas River. Here they encamped at a trading post. This force, to which Carson was attached in the capacity of guide, was composed of about thirty souls, all told.

Most of the scouts had been in the service of the great fur companies, and were, of course, good guides and rare hunters. There was little between them and the Rocky Mountains, once they should start, but an apparently limitless prairie, through which an Indian was to pilot them for the first thirty miles or so.

Strict discipline prevailed. A circle of nearly a hundred yards was surrounded by all the wheel vehicles. Here the tents were arranged with systematic regularity, and the horses so fettered as to make escape, in case of fright, next to impossible. They soon deemed it expedient to have guards mounted each night, who relieved each other every two hours. At sunrise every individual was on his feet, and the animals given a chance to graze and drink. Before seven they had partaken of a hearty breakfast, and were again on their route. Noon gave them a halt for a couple of hours, and then off they started again till near sundown. It was on the afternoon of the 4th instant, on which the ford of the Kansas was reached. Losing as little time as possible in preparations, they boldly crossed the river, now greatly swollen by the rains. Everything went well, except that a boat cart turned over and dumped the contents into the water. All at last safely reached the western bank, Carson getting thoroughly drenched, and it was deemed best to give all parties a chance to get over their hard work and exposure. Their next stopping place was a beautiful spot of finely grassed prairie land. Here they made all preparations for their long journey, practicing at target shooting, for it was important to "get their hands in," before they encountered the dangerous redskins. They next struck out on the Oregon trail—this would take them past Laramie, a well-known fort. Except that water was scarce, everything else needed was abundant. Flowers of every color were prolific and plants flourished luxuriantly in all depressions.

When they had reached the lands dominated by the Pawnees, they had to redouble their precautions at night, for this tribe was notorious for its horse stealing propensities. Here Kit began to astonish his followers by dashing with headlong speed over the prairies on a saddleless steed, and searching the vicinage if ought led to an alarm. When they had reached an elevation of the Platte valley some thousand miles above sea level, they unexpectedly met a party of about a dozen. They had been on boats for sixty days from Fort Lamarie. The water, however, became so shallow that they were forced to hide the bulk of their furs, and were footing it to St. Louis with all they could struggle under on their backs. From among them Fremont picked out an old soldier who had served under him. He quickly arranged his share in the furs, and stepped out once again in Fremont's service. Two or three days later they were in the midst of droves of buffalo. It was daybreak and the animals were munching the succulent grass, while in places clouds arose marking where some unwieldy bull was rolling, or a couple of them were furiously fighting. The prairie that night witnessed a jolly feast. The daintiest morsels of tongue and hump satiated the appetites, and song, and jest, and story gave a mental flavor to the grosser feed: Kit had led in the chase, and he was never backward at the feast. For some days they hunted to their heart's content. It was not all plain sailing, for both Kit and Fremont more than once bit the dust, and came near being trampled under the hoofs of the infuriated animals.

They had "a glorious old time," on the 4th of July, near the north fork of the Platte. A good dinner, plenty of toasts, and lots of salutes, made the desert as lively and noisy as the largest city.

At this point Fremont parted from the rest of the expedition, leaving the other portion to ascend the river up to Fort Laramie.

Here alarming reports reached them that the Sioux had drawn together in great force, and had joined to them portions of the warlike tribes who were feeling very hostile to the whites. Things looked so dark that many of Fremont's men began to express a desire to take the back track. Being reasoned with, and an offer having been made by Fremont to settle up with any of the discontented at once, the second sober thought overcame their suddenly awakened fears, and they expressed their wish to go on to the end.

They ascended the South Pass. The land rose so gradually that even Carson with all his experience could hardly tell when the summit was reached. They were now seven thousand feet above the sea and the traveller suddenly found himself slaking his thirst with waters that flowed towards the Pacific ocean.

They were now at a spot almost one thousand miles from the mouth of the Kansas. Following so stream up to a sheet of water in the mountains, they looked out upon a scene of more than Alpine grandeur and beauty. Mounted upon hardy mules, they ascended higher and higher, if there was a slight descent on one side of the hill, it towered up again on the face of the next, so that they ultimately kept rising. They climbed peak after peak to find them rise higher and higher in front of them, Carson ever in the van, till just as the extreme pinnacle was reached, when Carson stood aside to allow Fremont's foot alone to rest upon the mountain height. Kit Carson's engagement ended with Fremont when with his aid the persevering explorer had placed his foot upon the highest pinnacle of the Rocky Mountains.

The return to Fort Laramie was not noted by any marked or marvellous incidents. During the year 1843, Carson married for the second time. On this occasion, the lady he selected for his bride was of Spanish origin.

He continued off and on at Bent's Fort, helping at times his old comrade and employer, St. Vrain. But he was far too valuable a man for his services to be dispensed with by Fremont. So that officer being about to go on a second important expedition, secured Kit's invaluable aid. His first mission was to get a supply of mules and have them ready for the start of the proximate tripe Fremont's objective point was the then little-known Salt Lake. Since become so widely known and variously thought of throughout the world. Later the party was to meet Lieut. Wilkes who had been busy exploring and making charts of lands lying on the Pacific. Bear River, one of the most important streams flowing into the Lake was the place at which they embarked. It was on the 21st of August that they first floated upon the waters of this wondrous confluence of waters. Almost every geographical feature about it was veiled in a mystery. The few trappers who had sailed upon it, had filled every frontier camp with strange stories about its formation, and whence it drew its supply of waters and where they escaped—if they did escape, unless by sun absorption. No survey had been yet made by any scientific persons. Illiterate, but by no means ignorant, trappers gave many reasons for a belief that somewhere in its midst was a huge vortex into which the whelming waters were drawn to be expelled through one or more canons in the surrounding mountains. Every person in the expedition had an opinion of his own upon these oft-debated subjects, and each was panting for the progress of the expedition which was to dispel or confirm the different opinions or theories. The first place that attracted the attention of Fremont and Carson were the Beer Springs, which threw up a gaseous fluid, which the trappers asserted tasted exactly like beer. It hardly reached the description given of it. But still its constant effervescence and bitter taste rendered it sufficiently near the flavor and appearance of frothy and pungent beverages to account for travelers perceiving some resemblance to "beer" in it. As they progressed they continually passed hot springs throwing jets to quite a height. As they passed along through several deep valleys, here termed gates, their eyes were greeted with many wild and wonderful formations. In one place they encountered a column piercing some three thousand feet to the sky. But it was not until reaching the outlet of Bear River and ascending a bluff on its high banks, that they at length saw just at their feet the billows of the mountain enveloped sea, looking as grateful to their astonished eyes, doubtless, as did those of the vast Pacific to the wonderstruck orbs of the delighted Spaniard.

The vast expanse of water stretching out before them was quite a treat after they had been so long hemmed in by narrow walls, with wall like ramparts piled sometimes cloud high on right and left. Islands rose up out of the smooth area, but whether arid rocks or crowned with luxuriant forests they were too far away to be discovered. A rude storm put a quietus on their speculations, and they left their visionary dreams for some realistic duties. They fixed upon this as a proper site for the location of a permanent camp. A rude but strong fortification was constructed, to hold out if necessary against an attack of Utah Indians, supposed to be dwelling somewhere hereabouts. Their rubber boat was payed with gum and inflated. So, as provisions were running low, a Lajeunesse, an excellent scout and trapper, was sent off with half a dozen of the party, as their services could be no further utilized.

The plan now formed was that another Lajeuness (Basil) with Fremont and Carson, should start in the rubber boat, while Badeau, Jacob, and Derosier became custodians of the camp and the things that remained. The night promised fair for next day's expedition. The air was mild, the sky luminous, and all the surroundings very pleasant. A plain but nice supper sent them to bed good-humored.

A supply of water was not forgotten, for it had occurred to the voyagers that the islands might not furnish sweet streams flowing into the lake. The first night found the voyagers not very far advanced. After some hard labor, for their boat had proved to be illy constructed, they made their resting place amid some young willows. Game was superabundant, so they didn't want for plentiful rations. The next day they had to redouble their labor, as the river was at times very shallow, and they had to undress and drag their frail bark along. After toiling away in this manner for some time, they at length arrived at the verge of what was Salt Lake proper. Here they emerged from the unsalted water to float upon the saline water of the great lake itself. They coasted along, rather dubious about advancing far from shore, as their boat, though of good model enough, was anything but tight and true. As they neared the island shore, one of their pleasant delusions was swept away. What had appeared to be an array of white pelicans, turned out to be nothing but a row of rocks incrusted with salt from the dashing waves of the sea. Landing on an island, Fremont and Carson, scaled a high mountain and took several barometrical and other observations. Though strongly tempted to continue on, prudence dictated a return. Their boat was by no means strong, and the snow on the distant mountain tops warned them that Winter was near. The observations satisfied them that the Lake itself was over 4,000 feet above the surface of the Gulf of Mexico.

Although a storm came up in the night which made the island tremble, they managed to have a good sleep, thanks to a rude shelter which they constructed of driftwood. Returning to the mainland, one of their first tasks was to evaporate five gallons of the salt water of the lake, and found that it yielded fourteen pints of very pure fine salt. Carson shot some seagulls the next night, on which they supped. Continuing on up the river, they fired to let Fitzpatrick know of their approach, but heard no reply.

They bought a fat young horse, but Fremont was too dainty to partake of the good cheer which Carson and the others eagerly devoured.

They were next day gladdened by finding that at a camp a short distance off lots of rice and other good provisions awaited them brought by Fitzpatrick. Once more the party being found uselessly large was lessened by upwards of a dozen men, who readily returned, as the coming hardships were more than they could encounter. Carson stuck ty Fremont, and they journeyed slowly along, stopping to rest when a supply of water, grass and shelter was to be found. They had a dozen wheeled carriages, which though strong were light, and it often required the men to put their shoulders to the wheels to get aver bad places. Buffalo was scarce, but Carson contrived to kill a couple of bulls. Every night that they succeeded in getting a little game, with which to eke out their slender stock of provisions, they indulged in a mild sort of a feast. They crossed the Snake River with great difficulty. For a time it seemed that the passage would prove impracticable, but courage and ingenuity surmounted all obstacles. Thanks, in a great degree to the courage and resources of Kit, they soon reached one of the posts of the Hudson Bay Company, and the remainder of Fremont's trip to the coast did not need Carson's assistance, so he was at once employed with his men in getting all ready for their return. As this was to be done in the middle of Winter, the hardships that they would have to encounter could not well be overestimated. The party had improved in health and strength by their short rest, and numbered a quarter of a hundred of six different nationalities. They were, however, a wonderfully' homogenous lot of adventurers, from Fremont and Kit to the Indian guide and the colored cook. The company was rather imposing in appearance, constituted of over one hundred horses and mules, with their wagons and several

California cattle, on the hoof, to be slaughtered when needed for food.

With the beginning of the new year the full brunt of their sufferings began. They now travelled on foot, to help their four-footed friends as much as possible. For many days they struggled on finding very little feed for the animals and small rest and comfort for the men. On the 6th of January they found themselves in a valley, where the numerous hot springs kept the grass abundant and green. Soon after Kit and Fremont, travelling in advance of the party, struck a trail, showing they were on a travelled route. They also found a limited supply of feed for the cattle. The following party were directed by a preconcerted signal to rest here, and the two went on ahead again.

They had not proceeded far before they struck the central ridge of the Sierra Nevada, the greatest of California's mountains. They made a thorough examination and found that they had sustained small losses, considering the hardships which they had encountered. Sixty-seven of their animals remained sure-footed. Their firelight brought many Indians into camp, almost naked. One old man, who seemed the most intelligent of the lot, gave Kit Carson to understand that it was six sleeps between them and where the other whites were to be found that the snow was away over our heads.

If, however, we should follow the windings of the river it would bring us to a large lake where there was plenty of big fish. People lived there and we could stay till Spring. Much of this talk was only interpreted by the fact that Kit Carson was an adept in the sign language of the Indians. They were told, however, that the animals and people were strong, and that we should go on. But that if he would furnish a guide, we would make a way through the snow. Then was displayed some scarlet cloth and shining trinkets, and he was shown what would be given for a guide.

After a long consultation among themselves, the old man told us that if we could break through the snow we might come to some grass after three suns, where the horses could feed. He had been hunting, and he shut his eyes and shook his head to intimate that he could go no further. After thinking a while he left, and came back fetching quite an intelligent looking youth. He said that this young man had met with the whites and gave us by signs the most solemn assurance that what he was saying was the truth. A good present of cloth and other articles induced the youth to agree to go with us as guide. The young fellow was called "Milo," which in their tongue signified friend. The youth was very poorly protected from the cold, and his feet almost uncovered. He was kept in the lodge where Carson, rifle in hand, laid across the door, and given some skins to make some moccasins.

Fremont, Kit and the others then had a serious confab. In the course of it Fremont told them that he was certain by what he had learned from the Indians being compared with his own observations by instruments that they were within seventy miles of the Sacramento valley, whose manifold richness had been so Often and so truthfully told of by Carson. If we get through we shall in two or three days be in the midst of abundance. If we stay here we must perish, for our supplies are about exhausted. Kit and the rest expressed themselves content to make the attempt. Then every one went to work' with a will to get everything in order "to tempt the pass." Nor was their guide neglected. They had taken a liking to the young fellow, who had arrayed himself in his various colored clothes, and was highly charmed with his appearance. Besides, their own preservation depended on the life of their guide. It will show to what they were reduced, when we tell that they killed a favorite dog who had traveled with them from the Great Bear Country. He made a partial meal for all of them. The next day the cortege was set in motion, but it was a very slow motion. The strongest of the horses, without baggage, could just reach the top of the first ascent; weaker horses had to succumb. Two Indians, not seen before here, made their appearance. One of them, by signs and a few eloquently delivered words, managed to get Carson to understand that they never could cross those mountains. So frightfully did he depict the insurmountable' obstacles, that their guide, Milo, took the earliest opportunity to slope—they saw him no more—while the balance of the hands were resting to prepare for their hazardous crossing. Kit determined upon one more reconnoissance. Ascending a ridge and sending his piercing glance into the farthest distance, Carson pointed out a low range of mountains, far, far away. Pointing out a mountain of singular appearance, Kit assured Fremont that yon distant mountains on the far verge of the western horizon was the Coast Range, on the edge of the Pacific. Consequently the intermediate country must be the valley of the Sacramento. Scarce thirty miles away was the Sacramento River, where all their wants would be supplied. But, alas, between them and this paradise lay great snow prairies, and pine covered mountains with, all their hollows packed with snow. That night the men suffered much, some of them had never travelled on snowshoes before, and it required much care and attention to keep their feet unfrozen.

It was the 20th of February, 1844, before Kit and Fremont, and all the rest of their party, with their impediments, fairly stood on the immediate dividing ridge of the Pass. They had now traveled one thousand miles from the Columbia River. While the rest were making what headway they could, for the descent was by no means easy—though gravitation, was in their favor, Carson with Fremont pressed on to lay out their future routes. On one of these occasions Carson leaped a stream confined by rocky sides. Fremont, in attempting the same leap, caught the sole of his moccasin and fell into the icy current. Kit, thinking his partner was unable to help himself, leaped in and got him out. Fremont's gun was lost in the stream. The first thing was to kindle a big fire to warm them and dry their clothes. Soon as this was done they returned to the camp. The gun, was subsequently recovered. The wind blew keenly from the northeast, and it was two degrees below freezing point. After a little while we found a foot path, which enabled our animals to keep their footing. Now and then we saw a hill with new grass on it. Grand trees of the pine tribe began to appear in the forest. The river rushed along with terrific force and the sight of oak trees was warmly welcomed. The reverse side of the mountain was just the opposite in its characteristics. It rose abruptly, was not varied by any ravines, and pines and snowbanks occupied it entirely. It had none of the small rivulets that swiftly descended on our side. We were almost frantic with excitement as we saw the young fresh leaves dancing in the wind, while trilling and warbling birds dashed through the branches as joyously as if they, like the travelers, were filled with delight. We already, in imagination, felt ourselves basking in the eternal sunlight of the Sacramento Valley.

Just as February drew to a close it was deemed advisable that Carson and seven others should advance as quickly as possible. Fremont being with the party. They left the balance of the band to continue along slowly as the condition of their animals seemed to require. The object was to get to Mr. Sutter's without the unnecessary loss of a moment that fresh animals and food might meet the following party. Before night Carson sung out from a hill in advance that he had found a good camping ground. Several fine horses were missed this eventful day, and two of the men were still absent when they were compelled to camp for the night. While they made every effort to let the missing men know the route they had taken, they kept on moving with all practicable speed.

As they proceeded they met with an oak, new to them, having large elongated acorns; this being of the kind eaten in that region by the Indians, and sometimes by the whites as a substitute for bread. The whole appearance of the country was now so pleasant and propitious, that they all reclined on the rich grass to afford themselves and their animals needed rest, and to give a chance to the missing ones to appear. Their sufferings were by no means over, notwithstanding the favorable appearance of things at times. Deer swept by them, but they had no time to deviate from the forward march. Sutter's Fort opened its hospitable gates to them as it had to numbers before them, This gentleman can never be too highly extolled for planting the highest virtue of civilization amid barbarous Indians and some more barberous white men. Less than half their original complement of animals survived to crop the sweet herbage of the Sacramento's banks, and most of those had to be helped along, instead of helping the weary wayfarers. All through this terrible forced march, Kit Carson was the real, though not the ostensible leader, and again and yet again the party Would have been severed and then, probably, not a tittle, if any, would have survived to see the tules that bordered the then pellucid waters of this noble stream.

Carson, as soon as he could be spared, lost no time in getting back to his family in Taos, a pretty large town of New Mexico, possessing all the usual attractions of such places in that section of the State of Mexico. A church, a few fair houses, but the balance being only adobe houses or rather huts. Fortunately the dryness and general salubrity of the air does not call for any great efforts to "expel the Winter's fluid." But a small part of the land lying between the town and the surrounding mountains is under cultivation, but the scarcity of breadstuffs and other vegetable food is easily eked out by the cattle and sheep which throng the neighboring pastures. Although at the time of which we write the natives had but partially adopted the improvements of United States citizens in their agricultural and other implements, still the wedge had been inserted and every hour it was driven further into the log dividing the old from the new. Here Carson's family resided and followed the customs of Mrs. Carson's ancestors, for it must be remembered that the lady was of Spanish descent. That style of living probably suited Kit Carson far better than the polished artificiality of manners prevalent in the States.

Fremont, who was of a very adventurous nature, and fond of doing things out of the common way —as witness his successful carrying off of Miss Cass (the "Jessie" of one of the most famous Presidential years that the country ever passed through)—was at this very time putting things together for another, the third of his great expeditions. The announcement came upon Kit not altogether pleasantly, for he recollected that when he had last parted from Fremont, the latter had won a promise from him, that come what might he could " be counted in " whenever again his favorite commander and companion was in the saddle. Nevertheless Fremont had his pledged word that he would be "thar," and although in many ways it considerably incommoded him he never thought of going back on his plighted word.

So Kit, disposing of his farming ventures to the best advantage, and yet with no little loss, provided for his wife in the best manner possible, and was soon ready to turn his back on his pleasant home.

With him went away one Owens, who was not only a friend of his, proven on many a dangerous tramp through trackless forests, but more recently a partner in his farming operations.

They were again to meet not only old friends, but the scene of the meeting was to be at the quarters of old endeared associates by a hundred dangers, and any number of daring deeds by flood and field.

The rendezvous was fixed to be at Bent's Fort, a well-known post upon the Upper Arkansas. Here they had last shaken hands with the gallant Fremont. They spent some time in locating, measuring, and getting the depths of the immediate sources of those small brooks and half hidden brooklets which are the sources of these mighty rivers, which end their journey by augmenting the faraway waters of the two great oceans.

Maxwell and Walker, two good men, tried to the bone in former travel, had also agreed to accompany Fremont, when they were informed that our friend Kit was "to be one of 'em."

October found them already encamped on the shores of the Great Salt Lake, facing that hardly known country, of which only the edge had been yet entered, and which the few Indians described as being entirely without needed grass and water to support any party that dared to enter it.

Still to them it was not an entirely unknown land. At one time its eastern shore was occasionally visited by wandering tribes of Indians; but now only a single family lived to represent the vanished aborigines. They were so abjectly poor that they could not show one little well, of pure water; but had to quench their thirst from a brackish stream.

A bare, plain, dry clay, through which a few plants struggled hard to grow, was the first view that met their disappointed gaze. Afar off in the dim distance, uninviting peak of what seemed treeless mountains rose to no great height. A little apart from this range, some fifty miles away, a rather lofty peak appeared a little more promising, towards this they wended their way.

They started off four of their men, their guide being a naked Indian. A mule bore water enough to last them for four days. This little expedition was predicated on the Indian guide's assertion that in a little distance he could show them a place where grass grew and water ran plentifully. This was meant as a scouting party, before the bulk of the expedition was irretrievably committed to that route.

A column of smoke was to ascend from the summit of the mountain if they succeeded in finding water. As no signal was visible, Fremont began to fear that some ill had happened to his men, and to find out the worst at once the gallant explorer went ahead with the whole party, not waiting for daylight. In the morning one of the scouts was met on his back journey. The Indian had proved a sad failure, and he was sent to the right about the men, however, with more sense or more courage, kept on their " winding way, " and presently met with sufficient food and water to warrant the whole party in continuing on, which they did the next morning, after resting through the night. In the morning they continued their tramp, and after travelling, in all, some seventy miles they reached their refuge, which was duly welcomed. The lofty peak of the mountain, by which they so happily steered their course, was named by them Pilot Peak. It was always referred to when they recalled their first venturous launch into the desert.

Travelling thus for a few days, they then took a brief halt and divided the party into two. The larger section, commanded by Walker, a mountaineer of great skill and knowing as much as any one of the route they were now pursuing, skirted the Sierra Nevada, where he had before done good " scout " service, while Fremont's branch, under the leadership of the indomitable Kit, started to make a beeline through the centre of the desert. The latter section included ten persons, Delawares and whites.

A strange incident occurred one day. The route lay at a mountain's foot, and some one spied a column of smoke floating skyward from a depression. Drawing near noiselessly, they saw a solitary Indian on the bank of a little creek. He stood, naked as a new born babe, gazing pensively at a little fire on which stood an earthen pot, gently simmering. It was filled with the little ground squirrels of the locality. He was a fine, stalwart youth, perhaps twenty-three or thereabout. More squirrels, and his bow and arrows lay near the fire. Manifestly greatly alarmed, yet he made no offer to run away, but seemed disposed to put a good face on the matter, and offered some of his squirrels. Placing some attractive presents in his hands, the party kept on their way. His hunting equipment of bows and arrows were wonderful specimens of skill and industry, the arrows tipped with polished stone. They had not proceeded far ere Fremont discovered that the Delawares had appropriated the Indian's hunting stock. As soon as Fremont knew it, he told them to take it back, as by depriving the poor fellow of his bow and arrows they had possibly left him in a condition to perish, as he had no means left to continue his hunting. The Delaware's made no objection to obeying Fremont's desire.

Another curious trait of Indian disposition was afforded Kit and his friends a few days thereafter. At a lake abounding in fish, and at certain seasons much frequented by the Indians, it happened, one time, that some dozen Indians suddenly appeared in sight. They were progressing like a file of geese, one almost stepping in the tracks of the preceeding, their heads bowed and their eyes cast down. The whites and Indians passed each other without giving the least sign that they had been observed.

It was one of the strange freaks of these strange races now almost extinct in their old hunting grounds, who are observed at times to draw their lips close, as if they feared too much intimacy might lead them to reveal something of the dim past history of their people.

Just as had been planned, Fremont, Carson, and Walker fraternized again, at the point of the river designated. Once again they were caught under gloomy circumstances and without a guide. Worse still, provisions were just giving out, and it was now the middle of the Winter. It could not be many days before every available pass through the Nevada mountains would be choked with snowdrifts. After brief discussion it was settled that Walker, with most of the party, should make his way with all possible speed toward the South, getting into the San Joaquin valley by the readiest low pass that invited him through, where snow seldom appears but for a few hours.

Fremont and Kit, with a few men, were to make an effort to somehow manage to get over the Sierra Nevada, in the neighborhood of Sutter's Fort. There they knew they could get all they wanted, cattle and beef, with which to hasten to the assistance of Walker's detachment. Soon they were reminded of the beautiful parks of Europe of which they had often heard or read. They had left the Mercedes River, and were journeying through open clumps of oak among which beautiful brooks brawled along.

Travelling thus agreeably along, they were startled at meeting with strongly marked trails, which had shortly before been traversed by cavalcades of horses, apparently travelling into the interior from coastwise. They had evidently neared some villages of Horse Thief Indians, who no doubt were just coming back from one of their raids. To account for this state of affairs it is necessary to know that by the dispersion of many of the Indians, who had once dwelt at the various Missions, lots of them turned their knowledge of Spanish and their acquaintance with their mode of life to pass backwards and forwards from the coast to the mountains, and rarely was the journey accomplished without a goodly number of horses changing owners. This stealing of horses soon became as extensive as it was profitable. Hundreds of the Indians off the Southern Nevadas had little occupation but running off with the horses of the California rancheros. Occasionally they were pursued and, rarely, some of the horses recaptured, but generally the Indians got off scot free and feasted for weeks on the stolen horsemeat.

Carson and his friend had now reason for all their vigilance. These Indians were rough riders, and cared little who they attacked if the prospect of plunder bore any fair ratio to the danger to be encountered. They had not taken the alarm a moment too soon. Scouts were sent off on a newfound trail. Maxwell and Owens and two Delawares were speedily following it up. Following them the balance of the party jogged along as usual. This was but for a 'little while, however, as everything indicated a number of trails bearing toward the main one. They were evidently numerous, and the whole band was soon in rapid motion on the route of the four scouts. Coming to a capital camping ground, which had evidently been lately used, they began unsaddling and unpacking ready for a night's rest. But they were arrested at their work for the barking of dogs and the shouting of women and children were a certain indication that their friends had fallen into the hands of enemies, and that the battle was already raging.

Fremont and Kit dashed off to the rescue, leaving four men as camp guards; and well was it that they had taken such a hasty departure, for furiously galloping they had just topped a little ridge, when they came full in view of a very large number of Indians, evidently hundreds, advancing up each side of a rise, of whose summit were the men; having made a prime defence of the rocks and trees there clustered. It could at once be seen that like skillful old hunters, the moment they found themselves in the Indian village, they leaped from their horses, and had put themselves in first rate order to keep their assailants at bay. The ridge was on the point of being completely surrounded, when Kit, Fremont and their dauntless followers approached. Their loud ringing, well-known shout, as they were in the act of rushing up the hill, was replied to by the Delawares appalling yell, as they swiftly made for their animals, while Maxwell and Owens sent a death shot from each of their well aimed rifles. The bullet of Owens had found its billet in the heart of the leading Indian, and he fell tumbling down the hill.

Kit having accomplished the object without loss that brought them there, viz., the safety of their friends, now returned with all possible speed towards their other friends to whom they had entrusted the guardianship of the camp.

They found all safe. But they remained all the livelong night silently watching against any treacherous attack. There happened, however, no cause for any serious apprehension. At times would come on the night breeze the sounds made by the children and women returning into the fastnesses of the mountains. But no armed foe felt bold enough to seek another encounter. They took advantage of the first early light to regain the open plain where they could not be ambushed.

As our hero had already gone through a somewhat similar series of adventures in traversing this extensive region of wild country, to recount what took place on his present trip would be too much like telling an old story over again. As before they were obliged to substitute old tough mule for tender fatted calf, and like Nebuchednezzar they were occasionally glad to fill up with grass. Fremont often remarked that but for Kit's wonderful prescience in seeming to divine danger at some moments and a means of escape at others, none of them would ever have got through to record the many mishaps they had met with. Sutter's Fort was at length reached, and within its safe and hospitable walls the party soon regained health and strength. And the members much needed both, for already Fremont was chafing at inactivity, and anxious to get on in the direction of Monterey. Here he supposed, that the California officers would favor his recruiting and getting the various supplies he much needed to go on with his discoveries and scientific explorations. At first they gave him a formal permission to proceed, but to his surprise this was soon cancelled; for his onward march was brought to a halt by an officer escorted by cavalry. Fremont was handed a peremptory order from General Castro requiring him to leave the country at once.

Here Carson's counsels were found of invaluable service. He it was who led the force to a suitable place for throwing up strong defensive works, for neither Carson nor Fremont had any idea of being hounded out of a country which they had entered with the most peaceble intentions, and for a purpose shielded by the comity of nations.

Scarcely had the camp been put into a situation to receive an enemy—if such approached,—before General Castro, heading many hundred soldiers, put in an appearance. He put his force in martial array, evidently believing that the mere appearance of such a formidable body would strike terror into the hearts of the comparatively small number of Americans. What, indeed, were the few Americans—forty in all against so many? But the American camp contained Carson and Fremont, Maxwell and Owens, and the rest were only inferior to them in all that constituted the real soldier.

Let it not be supposed, however, that the rancheros, who carried lances and muskets in the array of Castro, were men to be despised. In the first essential of cavalrymen they could not be surpassed, they were perfect centaurs. They handled their lances with strange adroitness, and many were fair shots with their rude muskets. But for some never satisfactorily explained reasons they generally yielded to the prowess of the northern Americans. So it will be seen that Carson and Fremont had on hand a by no means easy job, even allowing for the excellence of the material filling up their little ranks. But then Kit Carson's strategy and finesse were worth whole squadrons in the peculiar tactics that had to be practiced in the more or less Indian fighting likely to take place between the Californians and Americans. Besides Fremont and his men felt that they were really the head and front of the United States citizens then in California, for express after express arrived to tell them of the almost certainty of a war with Mexico, in which case his flag would be the rallying nucleus for every one of his countrymen to join. In the council which it was deemed prudent to hold, Carson proved himself, as always, as prudent and cautious as he was prompt and resolute in action. The men were ready for any alternative, they would at once attack Castro or they would retire anywhere and at any time that Fremont and Carson might advise.

The party remained quiet at Lawson's post for more than a week, when reliable news was brought in that at the urging of the Mexicans parties of Indians were advancing, timing their arrival so as to make a general attack. Fremont and Carson, with a little party of five, set out with the design of anticipating the Indian attack. Where people are anxious for a fight they generally find it. Such was the case with the Indians and Carson's party. The latter went right in with a fierce rush. It was only by a surprise that they could hope to achieve success. The Indians, though for an instant paralyzed, hit back; but the certainty that every ball from an American rifle knocked over a savage, while their, own slack fire was mostly useless, soon led them to retreat in a panic, without being able to arrive at anything like a true estimate of the American force. After that these same Indians gave the Americans a wide berth, particularly if they knew Carson and Fremont were among their number. Having destroyed any force likely to prove troublesome, Kit and Fremont started North, as Oregon was likely to be "the pastures new " of any future explorations.

As usual, it was the unforseen that usually cropped up. Two white men most unexpectedly appeared at a spot where a chaise full of ladies was as likely to be found. The men were the avant couriers of Lt. Gillespie, of the U. S. Marine corps. He had somehow learned that Fremont and Carson was in that region, and had sent on these men in the faint hope that they might intercept the party, and inform the leaders that he was advancing with the rest of his little band, which consisted of six soldiers, all told. Of course Kit and Fremont sprang into their saddles. They would have hasted to any American's relief; but this man was an officer of their country, and entrusted with a mission, as they learned from one of the guards. Ten men followed the two, who were inseparable, as Castor and Pollux, when danger struck the gong. To expect to find a small party of men travelling where no beaten track had ever been made was quite as likely as meeting with the traditional needle in the haystack; but they were determined that if the thing was possible they would achieve it. Arriving one evening at a likely place for encamping, Carson stated his belief that if the party were alive they would certainly stop at this spot, so they encamped and waited. Just as the evening shadows were beginning to close in they saw their men. It was a moment of indescribable pleasure to both parties. Lt. Gillespie had been away from Washington since the preceding November. He had been entrusted with despatches to the U. S. Consul at Monterey, Upper California; that he was directed to go and search for Lt. Fremont, but where the latter was to be found doubtless exceeded the knowledge of the heads of the government. Probably all they knew was that he had Kit Carson with him and was bound to turn up safe and sound.

The events that followed the meeting of Lt. Gillespie and Fremont were deeply interesting. Though there was a lamentable loss of life, it looks as if Providence had brought Fremont and Carson to meet him just at the nick of time. He had traversed half a continent safely, and it appeared as if he had reached his place of doom. But we will let Carson in his own plain and effective language narrate what further took place on this eventful evening. We quote Kit Carson's letter from the Washington Onion, of 1847:

"Mr. Gillespie had brought the Colonel letters from home, the first he had had since leaving the States the year before, and he was up and kept a fire burning until midnight. The rest of us were tired out, and all went to sleep. This was the only night in all our travels, except the one night on the island in the Salt Lake, that we failed to keep guard; and as the men were so tired and we expected no attack now that we had sixteen in the party,' the Colonel did not like to ask it of them, but sat up late himself. Owens and I. were sleeping together, and we were waked at the same time by the licks of the axe that killed our men. At first I didn't know it was that; but I called to Basil, who was on that side—'What's the matter there? What's that fuss about?' he never answered, for he was dead then, poor fellow, and he never knew what killed him—his head had been cut in his sleep; the other groaned a little as he died. The Delawares (we had four with us) were sleeping at the fire, and they sprang up as the Flamaths charged them. One of them caught up a gun, which was unloaded; but, although he could do no execution, he kept them at bay, fighting like a soldier, and didn't give up till he was shot full of arrows —three entering his heart; he died bravely. As soon as I had called out, I saw it was Indians in the camp, and I and Owens together cried out Indians.' There were no orders given; things went on too fast, and the Colonel had men with him that didn't need to be told their duty. The Colonel and I, Maxwell, Owens, Godev and Stepp jumped together, we six, and ran to the assistance of our Delawares. I don't know who fired and who didn't, but I think it was Stepp's shot that killed the Flamath chief, for it was at the crack of Stepp's gun that he fell. He had an English half axe slung to his wrist by a cord, and there were forty arrows left in his quiver—the most beautiful and warlike arrows I ever saw. He must have been the bravest man among them, from the way he was armed and judging by his cap. When the Flamath's saw him fall they ran, but we lay, every man with his rifle cocked, until daylight expecting another attack. In the morning we found by the tracks that from fifteen to twenty of the Flamaths had attacked us. They had killed three of our men and wounded one of the Delawares, who scalped the chief, whom we left where he fell. Our dead men we carried on mules; but, after going about ten miles, we found it impossible to get them any further through the thick timber, and finding a secret place, we buried them under logs and chunks, having no way to dig a grave. It was only a few days before this fight that some of these same Indians had come into our camp, and, though we had only meat for two days and felt sure that we should have to eat mules for ten or fifteen days to come, the Colonel shared among them, and gave them several useful little articles, although to get at them we were obliged to take the pack from the mule. This was a terrible lesson to all hands, and thenceforth a guard was always carefully posted. As Fremont now proposed to get back to California as quickly as possible, he made arrangements for doing so. Ere he started, however, he determined to give the Flamath's a severe chastisement for their cowardly attack upon his sleeping men and the assassination of Lajeunesse, Crane and the Delaware. Carson set off with a few men to search for the Indians. They found a camp without much trouble. They judged it to contain about one hundred and fifty men with the usual proportion of women and children. Just as they were seen by the Indians Carson, with the ten scouts under him, made a sudden rush without stopping to count the great odds against them.

Notwithstanding that the Indians would be fighting for their homes and families, the rapidity of the attack drove all thoughts of defense out of their minds, and they fled empty handed, escaping with life alone., To strike terror into their hearts, and maybe prevent any more such ferocious attacks upon friendly travelers, Carson, although the village was the most comfortable and highly finished of any Indian place he had ever seen, determined to wipe it out with flame. Gathering inside the combustible wigwams all the valued household effects of the dwellers, he gave the whole to the blazing torch. And when Fremont and the rest of the party, guided by the smoke, joined Kit, it was only to find a few heaps of ashes to show where the lodges had stood a few hours ago, while the Flamaths were homeless and weaponless wanderers. Keeping right on toward. Sacramento, a few days after, they would have fallen into an ambush, but just as they were about to enter a deep canon, by Carson's advice they took a longer way, and sure enough Kit's foresight was justified for a band of Flamath's rushed out of the canon howling and cursing at the Americans. One Indian perhaps to revenge the death of a relative, followed from one sheltering rock to another, shooting arrow after arrow, too well aimed to be pleasant. At length Kit saw his chance and, quick as lightning, tumbled him over lifeless. For a day or two they journeyed through a tract with but little game, and came near starving; but just in time to save them they came to Lawson's, and after a few day's hunting and resting they pushed on. The more Fremont learned about the state of affairs, the more he became convinced that now inactivity was not "masterly." So he made a bold push and took General Vallejos with his little garrison out of the town of Sonoma. Just as Fremont had struck out into action General Castro, then at San Francisco, determined to expel all Americans from California by force of arms. But the leader of Castro's force, on finding that Fremont was anxious to meet him, weakened, and returned to San Francisco in a fright.

Nearly all the Americans in California were seized with a patriotic furore, and leaving every vocation in which they were engaged, drew together in small parties to place themselves under the lead of Fremont and his trusty friend Kit Carson. With this party Fremont made a rush to seize Monterey, at that time deemed of more consequence than San Francisco. But Commodore Stout had preceded him.

Sonoma has the honor of being the first place at which the freedom of California was openly declared. There the "Bear" flag, together with that of the United States, were flung to the wind amid the vociferous shouts of Fremont, Carson and their indomitable followers—the mountain men.

Soon after, Fremont, as ever closely seconded by his friend Carson, found himself in command of some hundred and fifty men, all of the same stamp as themselves. With these he started for Los Angelos, without the least hesitation, although the force of the enemy exceeded seven hundred. Here he found his force augmented by an auxiliary body. At once pressing forward to the attack, Fremont found that he had achieved a useful but bloodless victory. Castro had fled. Commodore Stockton hereupon appointed Fremont Governor of California, a just recompense for his intelligent bravery.

Now Carson realized that his courage, intelligence and patriotism were indeed appreciated, for he was selected from among all the brave men there to be found in the Bear State to convey the news to Washington that a little over a thousand men had added a noble realm to the soil of the Union.

Seldom has any man been the bearer of more valuable information, for, although gold had not yet been discovered, there had been many intelligent men roaming over the fertile valleys of California and had been struck by its possibilities to become a great country in the near future. How well the abilities of Carson were gauged is seen by the small space of time that he was limited to in order to reach Washington: sixty days!

Kit started and nothing special called his attention till he reached the copper mines abounding in parts of New Mexico, there he found himself close to an Apache village. He kept right on through their huts until he came to a wood just past their home. Here he demanded a "talk" with their chief men. He told them they were quiet travelers, who had stopped at their village in order to change their tired horses for fresh ones, for which favor they were willing to pay fairly. The Indians were so surprised at this strange method of dealing, by men well armed, that they immediately acquiesced. Carson after arranging his camp so that he could not be taken any advantage of, made a satisfactory trade, and started the next day without having had the least trouble with these pirates of the plains.

It took but a few more days to bring Carson in the neighborhood of his own family, they had meanwhile greatly suffered from hunger; but this was all soon forgotten, when they neared the abode of Kit. Whatever feelings the Mexicans might entertain towards the Americans generally, this particular American, Kit Carson, was like an adopted citizen, for had he not shown how much he liked them by taking one of their nation, as a wife? So they were all very kindly entertained by the people as he drew near home. But Carson was not a man to linger even among friends, so as soon as his party were fairly rested, there was another start toward home.

After the conquest of California had been accomplished, and as was generally acknowledged, no little part of its celerity was owing to Carson, the residents and many of the natives gave a series of entertainments to the men who had so largely contributed to what promised to be a prosperous result. Carson and Fremont were the most highly honored guests on these occasions. But there was too great a scarcity of such men for either Kit or his chief to be long spared for any pleasant glorification. So, accordingly, in the month of March, 1847, Kit started for Washington, having for a comrade Lt. Beale with despatches for the Navy. The latter was so much of an invalid that Kit had to lift him on and off his horse for some three weeks. But by great care he contrived to fetch him through all right.

At Taos they made but a brief stay, and then hastened on to Washington, accomplishing the long journey of two thousand five hundred miles in the saddle, and the remaining fifteen hundred miles by rail, inside of three months. Much as Kit loved the ever varying scenes of river, canon and mountain, he was too well-informed and thoughtful a man not to be, deeply impressed by the thickly populated cities of the East, and the rapid strides being made in all directions toward enormous wealth, education and power. At St. Louis Kit was met and welcomed by that sturdy old patriot, Col. Benton (father-in-law of Fremont), and on reaching Washington, Mrs. Jessie Fremont had a kindly welcome for the champion of her husband. She knew him directly from her husband's graphic description. Carson's stay was very short in Washington, where he was received with the friendship due to his unusual merits. His return was monotonously peaceful until a dangerous pass in the vicinity of the "Rockies" was reached. Here Carson found an encampment of U. S. Volunteers, where he stopped over night. The horses of the volunteers were stolen during the night, and the cattle broke for Kit's camp, whose skill with their ready rifles rescued them. The horses, however, were gone. Though many of the rogues of Indians had been sorely wounded they all escaped, thanks to the tribe's habit of lashing themselves to their horses before venturing into a fight, so that their scalps should not fall into an enemy's hand.

Continuing on his way Kit soon arrived at Santa Fe, where he replaced his soldier guard with sixteen men of his own selection, to go with him to Fort Leavenworth. Here, retreat was in store for him. He met his family. He hastened on through some of the customary privations to hand his despatches to his superior at Monterey. Resuming his duties as Lieutenant of Dragoons, he assumed charge of the Lejou Pass, where he proved himself the right man in the right place, intercepting Indian desperadoes leaving or entering California.

Next Spring he was once again en route to Washington, stopping on his way at Taos, giving himself double pleasure, as he remained some time with his family and gave his men needed rest. A slight was about this time given to Carson through some political feeling, meant through him to reach Fremont. Some friends advised him to resent it by declining to proceed with the despatches, but Kit was too levelheaded. He said as he had been chosen for so important a position he would do his duty if it cost his life.

On finding that a large body of Comanches was on his direct road to Santa Fe, he lessened his large escort down to ten men, and made a new trail of his own, encountering new dangers successfully, but reached Washington with his despatches as he had been ordered to do. Returning by the shortest possible route, he arrived at Taos in October. This time he intended that his homestay should, be a good long one.

But it seemed that there could be no permanent rest for Carson for he was pounced on by Col. Beale to lead his command to avenge upon the Comanches some cruel wrongs. Kit enabled the Col. to meet the Indians, and take some hostages.

Carson had the pleasure about this period to entertain Fremont at his house at Taos. With Fremont was the remnant of a gallant party who had been making a Winter exploration and suffered terribly besides losing many good men. It had, doubtless, been well for them if Kit had been their guide.

Col. Beale, who had as great faith in Carson as Fremont always displayed, applied to Kit for his assistance, in February, to effect the return of a number of Mexican prisoners held by the Indians who occupied territory recently ceded by Mexico to the United States.

They found several tribes assembled, aggregating many thousands. The agent told Beale that it would be impossible to effect enforcing the requirements of the treaty with the few armed men under his command, as they would be certain to make a determined resistance. More especially as the Indians were in no manner consulted by the two governments in making their treaty. So that for no fault on the part of either, Beale or Carson, the expedition was fruitless of results.

Carson had for a long time designed to make his home near Taos, pleasant but also profitable. With this intent, in partnership with his friend Maxwell, he took possession of one of the most finely located tracts of land in any part of the world. It was a valley through which always flowed a cool and transparent stream, the banks exceedingly fertile and gradually rising towards the adjacent mountains, clothed to the summit with a noble growth of forest trees. The village established by Carson and Maxwell soon flourished like the rose. The houses of the two principal owners only differed from those of their neighbor citizens by their superior amplitude. For they had not only to shelter their proper inhabitants but their doors were ever thrown open to the visitors on their long travels to and fro between Mexico and the United States. A pleased visitor to their almost princely domain must have readily recalled the days of the patriarchs, whose tents were surrounded by innumerable oxen, goats and sheep, and where game was so abundant as to make Esau infatuated with the pursuit of hunting. His children grew up delighted with their glorious surroundings, for the air is as healthful as the sky is clear and beautiful. The neighboring Indians placed the greatest faith in every promise that fell from the lips of Kit for, although pitiless in punishing deceit, he never swerved from any agreement that he made with man, red or white. He has tried most assiduously to get the Indians to adopt habits of industry and thrift, but with little more success than other friends of the fast disappearing race.

The valley in which Carson has made his abode has great attractions for the old trappers of that region, and although the profitable exercise of their special vocation is almost at an end, they find it easy to make an agreeable living by odds and ends of hunting, guiding and farming, besides they have eager auditors for all their stories about their hazardous trips under Kit and Fremont.

About the end of the Winter of 1849, soon after Carson had taken up his residence for good in his valley settlement, a party of ten dragoons had been stationed there to guard the infant village: Some thieving Apaches continued to run off the soldiers' horses, and the men specially in charge were wounded. Next morning a party of thirteen, led by Kit, went after them. Only nine of the pursuers besides Carson were up to the front when the Indians were come up with. The Indians, some twenty in number, made a stand with the result that five of their number were killed outright, several wounded and almost all the horses retaken.

When soon after Carson made a trip to Fort Laramie with a large lot of stock, he attracted great attention from the men who were now crowding into California by the various overland routes. Many of them owing their discovery to the skill and endurance of Kit Carson and Colonel Fremont.

The days now passed away peacefully. True, Kit found it as difficult to keep out of the saddle as many find to keep in it. But he never let the house want for a mess of venison or game birds. He kept his hand and eye always in order to grasp his rifle again should his country need his services. At this time Carson learned that a very large trading company, organized by Messrs. Breevort and Weatherhead, which was travelling through the lonesome roads of that country were likely to lose their property if not their lives by an intended crime. A portion of their employees had conspired together with the intent of falling upon the leaders and their most trusted friends and, after murdering them, they designed seizing all the property as their own. A deed quite possible in a country where there was no organized police or magistracy to inquire into such affairs.. The instant Carson learned of this plot, he organized a small band of volunteers, overtook the caravan, and informed the owners of the design of the thieves. Several things had happened to verify the information of Carson. So the honest members of the party, aided by Carson's men, ordered the guilty ones to quit instanter, without arms or provisions, retaining only the ringleader, but he was subsequently allowed to run, as he had actually committed no crime. Sometime afterward the owners of the concern presented Carson with a magnificent pair of pistols, suitably engraved. At this period Carson found a little leisure which he utilized by paying his married daughter a visit, at her residence in St. Louis. It need hardly be said here that some of the officers of the United States forces betray their incapacity for command by conduct at once brutal and stupid in their treatment of the Indians. Such a person had the lash applied to a Cheyenne chief but a few days before Carson and his party arrived in the vicinity. The Indians were frenzied with rage and were eagerly looking for any white men on whom to take revenge. Kit just appeared in time to fill the bill for a victim, as his party was the first to pass that way since the outrage was committed. Many years had passed by since Kit's name was familiar to the Indians. But as soon as 1e understood the state of affairs, after telling his men to be prepared for the worst, he started right in to the Indian council which had assembled to consider what should be done to the party of whites. The Indians, as is their custom, talk right on, especially as they had no idea that the white man understood a word that they were saying. The speaker spoke of the manner of destroying all the whites and dividing their goods. As soon as the last speaker had spoken, Kit coolly spoke to them in their own tongue, told them of his former friendliness to their tribe, how they had hunted and shared provisions together, and that he, seeing that they had been wronged, was willing to see them righted. His scalp and the scalps of his men were not to be taken under any circumstances. The Indians appeared astonished, and perhaps thought, owing to his cool audacity, that he had a large force somewhere within call. At any rate they made no attempt to injure or detain him, so they departed on their several ways; but Kit saw that they were not disposed to be friendly. They drew away to the adjacent hills, evidently in no friendly mood. As evening drew near Kit gathered his men together, in a defensible position, with the wagons making a wall around. Grass was silently gathered from outside, the mules fed, and every man that could be spared was placed on guard. As soon as every one was stowed away for the night, Kit quietly left the camp accompanied by a Mexican boy, telling him to make for the U. S. troops, encamped at some distance. The lad knew where. Kit told him to make a broad trail as he wanted it found. Off the boy started. Kit returned to camp. As the morning wore away, Indians began to hang, restless, round. Kit told them he was satisfied they were not friendly, and intended to attack him. He said they Might begin; before long his soldier friends would be there; he had sent for them and they might see the trail. They searched for it, and soon there wasn't an Indian in sight.

In fact Carson was looked upon as the chief manager of all the Indians in that section, and this protection he was able to give by the reputation he had so well earned of being the Father of the Children of the Prairie.

He rose to be Brigadier General.

Kit Carson remained in the employ of the United States Government until his death, which sad event occurred at Fort Lyon, Colorado. The immediate cause of his decease was the breaking of a blood vessel in the neck. Any one that has followed this narrative will need no formal eulogium upon a man who was the most perfect, specimen of a hunter, a scout, and a skillful partizan soldier that ever wore moccasins or filled the stirrups of a trooper.

ADVENTURES AND EXPLORATIONS

OF THE COUNTRY LYING BETWEEN

THE MISSOURI RIVER AND THE ROCKY MOUNTAINS,

ON THE LINE OF

THE KANSAS AND GREAT PLATTE RIVERS.

TO COLONEL J. J. ABERT,

CHIEF OF THE CORPS OF TOPOGRAPHICAL ENGINEERS.

Sir: Agreeably to your orders to explore and report upon the country between the frontiers of Missouri and the South Pass in the Rocky Mountains, and on the line of the Kansas and Great Platte rivers, I set out from Washington city on the 2d day of May, 1842, and arrived at St. Louis by way of New York, the 22d of May, where the necessary preparations were completed, and the expedition commenced. I proceeded in a steamboat to Chouteau's landing, about four hundred miles by water from St. Louis, and near the mouth of the Kansas rive:, whence we proceeded twelve miles to Mr. 'Cyprian Chouteau's trading house, where we completed our final arrangements for the expedition.

Bad weather, which interfered with astronomical observations, delayed us several days in the early part of June at this post, which is on the right bank of the Kansas river, about ten miles above the mouth, and six beyond the western boundry of Missouri. The sky cleared off at length and we were enabled to determine our position, in longitude 90° 25' 46", and latitude 39° 5' 57". The elevation above the sea is about 700 feet. Our camp, in the mean time, presented an animated and bustling scene. All were busily engaged in completing the necessary arrangements for our campaign in the wilderness, and profiting by this short stay on the verge of civilization, to provide ourselves with all the little essentials to comfort in the nomadic life we were to lead for the ensuing summer months. Gradually, however, every thing—the materiel of the camp—men, horses, and even mules—settled into its place; and by the 10th we were ready to depart; but, before we mount our horses, I will give a short description of the party with which I performed the service.

I had collected in the neighborhood of St. Louis twenty-one men, principally Creole and Canadian voyageurs, who had become familiar with prairie life in the service of the fur companies in the Indian country. Mr. Charles Preuss, a native of Germany, was my assistant in the topographical part of the survey; L. Maxwell, of Kaskaskia, had been engaged as hunter and Christopher Carson (more familiarly known, for his exploits in the mountains, as Kit Carson) was our guide.

In addition to these, Henry Brant, son of Col. J. B. Brant, of St. Louis, a young man of nineteen years of age; and Randolph, a lively boy of twelve, son of the Hon. Thomas H. Benton, accompanied me, for the development of mind ana body such an expedition would give. We were well armed and mounted, with the exception of eight men, who conducted as many carts, in which were packed our stores, with the baggage and instruments, and which were drawn by two mules. A few loose horses, and four oxen, which had been added to our stock of provisions, completed the train. We set out on the morning of the 10th, which happened to be Friday, a circumstance which our men did not fail to remember and recall during the hardships and vexations of the ensuing journey. Mr. Cyprian Chouteau, to whose kindness, during our stay at his house, we were much indebted, accompanied, us several miles on our way, until we me an Indian, whom he had engaged to conduct us on the first thirty or forty miles, where he was to consign us to the ocean of prairie, which, we were told, stretched without interruption almost to the base of the Rocky Mountains.

From the belt of wood which borders the Kansas, in which we had passed several good-looking Indian farms, we suddenly emerged on the prairies, which received us at the outset with some of their striking characteristics; for here and there rode an Indian, and but a few miles distant heavy clouds of smoke were rolling before the fire. In about ten miles we reached the Santa Fe road, along which we continued for a short time, and encamped early on a small stream—having traveled about eleven miles. During our journey, it was the customary practice to encamp an hour or two before sunset, when the carts were disposed so as to form a sort of barricade around a circle some eighty yards in diameter. The tents were pitched, and the horses hobbled and turned loose to graze; and but a few minutes elapsed before the cooks of the messes, of which there were four, were busily engaged in preparing the evening meal. At nightfall, the horses, mules, and oxen were driven in and picketed,—that is, secured by a halter, of which one end was tied to a small steel shod picket, and driven into the ground; the halter being twenty or thirty feet long, which enabled them to obtain a little food during the night. When we had reached a part of the country where such a precaution became necessary, the carts being regularly arranged for defending the camp, guard was mounted at eight o'clock, consisting of three men, who were relieved every two hours—the morning watch being horse guard for the day. At daybreak the camp was roused, the animals turned loose to graze, am breakfast generally over between six and seven o'clock, when we resumed our march, making regularly a halt at noon for one or two hours. Such was usually the order of the day, except when accident of country forced a variation; which, however, happened but rarely. We traveled the next de) along the Santa Fe road, which we left in the afternoon, and encamped late in the evening on a small creek, called by the Indians, Mishmagwi. Just as we arrived at camp, one of the horses set off at full speed on his return, and was followed by others. Several men were sent in pursuit, and returned with the fugitives about midnight, with the exception of one man, who did not make his appearance until morning. He had lost his way in the darkness of the night, and slept on the prairie. Shortly after midnight it began to rain heavily, and, as our tents were of light and thin cloth, they offered but little obstruction to the rain: we were all well soaked, and glad when morning came. We had a rainy march on the 12th, but the weather grew fine as the day advanced. We encamped in a, remarkably beautiful situation on the Kansas bluffs, which commanded a fine view of the river valley, here from four to five miles wide. The central portion was occupies by a broad belt of heavy timber, and nearer the hills the prairies were of the richest verdure. One of the oxen was killed here for food.

We reached the ford of the Kansas late in the afternoon of the 14th, where the river was two hundred and thirty yards wide, and commenced, immediately, preparations for crossing. I had expected to find the river fordable; but it had swollen by die late rains, and was sweeping by with an angry current, yellow and turbid as the Missouri. Up to this point the road we had traveled was a remarkably fine one, well beaten, and level—the usual road of a prairie country. By our route, the ford was one hundred miles from the mouth of the Kansas river. Several mounted men led the way into the stream to swim across. The animals were driven in after them, and in a few minutes all had reached the opposite bank in safety, with the exception of the oxen, which swam some distance down the river, and, returning to the right bank, were not got over till the next morning. In the mean time, the carts has been unloaded and dismantled, and an India rubber boat, which I had brought with me for the' survey of the Platte river, placed in the water. The boat was twenty feet long and five broad, and on it were placed the body and wheels of a cart with the load belonging to it, and three men with paddles.

The velocity of the current, and the inconvenient freight, rendering it difficult to be managed, Basil Lajeunesse, one of our best swimmers, took in his teeth a line attached to the boat, and swam ahead in order to reach a footing as soon as possible, and assist in drawing her over. In this manner six passages had been successfully made, and as many carts with their contents, and a greater portion of the party, deposited of the left bank; but night was drawing near, and, in our anxiety to have all over before the darkness closed in, I put ,upon the boat the remaining two carts, with their accompanying load. The man at the helm was timid on water, and in his alarm capsized the boat. Carts, barrels, boxes, and bales, were in a moment floating down the current; but all the men who were on the shore jumped into the water, without stopping to think if they could swim, and almost every thing—even heavy articles, such as guns and lead—was recovered.

Two of the men who could not swim came nigh being drowned, and all the sugar belonging to one of the messes wasted its sweets on the muddy waters; but our heaviest loss was a large bag of coffee, which contained nearly all our provision. It was a loss which none but a traveler in a strange and inhospitable country can appreciate; and often afterward, when excessive toil and long marching had overcome us with fatigue and weariness, we remembered and mourned over our loss in the Kansas. Carson and Maxwell had been much in the water yesterday, and both, in consequence, were taken ill. The former continuing so, I remained in camp. A number of Kansas Indians visited us today. Going up to one of the groups who were scattered among the trees, I found one sitting on the ground, among some of the men, gravely and fluently speaking French, with as much facility aryl as little embarrassment as any of my own party, who were early all of French origin.

On all sides was heard the strange language of his own people, wild, and harmonizing well with their appearance. I listened to him for some time with feelings of strange curiosity and interest. He was now apparently thirty-five years of age; and, on inquiry, I learned that he had been at St. Louis when a boy, and there had learned the French language. From one of the Indian Women I obtained a fine cow and calf in exchange for a yoke of oxen. Several of them brought us vegetables, pumpkins, onions, beans, and lettuce. One of them brought butter, and from a half breed near the river, I had the good fortune to obtain some twenty or thirty pounds of coffee. The dense timber in which we had encamped interfered with astronomical observations, and our wet and damaged stores required exposure to the sun. Accordingly, the tents were struck early the next morning, and, leaving camp at six o'clock, we moved about seven miles up the river, to a handsome, open prairie, some twenty feet above the water, where the fine grass afforded a luxurious repast to our horses.

During the day we occupied ourselves in making astronomical observations, in order to lay down the country to this place; it being our custom to keep up our map regularly in the field, which we found attended with many advantages. The men were kept busy in drying the provisions, painting the cart covers, and otherwise completing our equipage, until the afternoon, when powder was distributed to them, and they spent some hours in firing at a mark.

We were now fairly in the Indian country, and it began to be time to prepare for the chances of the wilderness. The weather yesterday had not permitted us to make the observations I was desirous to obtain here, and I therefore did not move today. The people continued their target firing. In the steep bank of the river here, were nests of innumerable swallows, into one of which a large prairie snake had got about half his body, and was occupied in eating the young birds. The old ones were flying about in great distress, darting at him, and vainly endeavoring to drive him off. A shot wounded him, and, being killed, he was cut open, and eighteen young swallows were found in his body. A sudden storm that burst upon us in the afternoon, cleared away in a brilliant sunset, followed by a clear night, which enabled us to determine our position in longitude 95o '38' 05", and in latitude 39° 06' 40".

A party of emigrants to the Columbia river, under the charge of Dr. White, an agent of the government in Oregon Territory, were about three weeks in advance of us. The' consisted of men, women, and children. There were sixty four men, and sixteen or seventeen families. They had a considerable number of cattle, and were transporting their house hold furniture in large, heavy wagons. I understood that there had been much sickness among them, and that they had lost several children. One of the party who had lost his child, and whose wife was very ill, had left them about one hundred miles hence on the prairies; and as a hunter, who had accompanied them, visited our camp this evening, we assailed ourselves of his return to the States to write to our friends.

The morning of the 18th was very unpleasant. A fine rain was falling, with cold wind from the north, and mists made he river hills look dark and gloomy. We left our camp at seven, journeying along the foot of the hills which border the Kansas valley, generally about three miles wide, and extremely rich. We halted for dinner, after a march of about thirteen miles, on the banks of one of the many little tributaries to the Kansas, which look like trenches in the prairie, and are usually well timbered. After crossing this stream, I rode off some miles to the left, attracted by the appearance of a cluster of huts near the mouth of the Vermilion. It was a large but deserted Kansas village, scattered in an open wood, along the margin of the stream, chosen with the customary Indian fondness for beauty of scenery. The Pawnees had attacked it in the early spring. Some of the houses were burnt, and others blackened with smoke, and weeds were already getting possession of the cleared places. Riding up the Vermilion river, I reached the ford in time to meet the carts, and crossing, encamped on its western side. The weather continued cold, the thermometer being this evening as low as 49o. but the night was sufficiently clear for astronomical observations, which placed us in longitude 96° 04' 07", and latitude 39° 15' 19". At sunset, the barometer was at 28.845, thermometer 64o.

We breakfasted the next morning at half past five, and left our encampment early. The morning was cool, the thermometer being at 45° Quitting the river bottom the road ran along the uplands, over a rolling country, generally in view of the Kansas from eight to twelve miles distant. Many large boulders, of a very compact sandstone, of various shades of red, some of them of four or five tons in weight, were scattered along the hills; and many beautiful plants in flower, among which the amorpha canescens was a characteristic, enlivened the green of the prairie. At the heads of the ravines I remarked, occasionally, thickets of sans; longzfolia, the most common willow of the country. We traveled nineteen miles and pitched our tents at evening on the headwaters of a small creek, now nearly dry, but having in its bed several fine springs. The barometer indicated a considerable rise in the country—here about fourteen hundred feet above the sea—and the increased elevation appeared already to have some slight influence upon vegetation. The night was cold, with a heavy dew; the thermometer at 10 P. as standing at 46o, barometer 28.483. Our position was in longitude 96° 14' 49", and latitude 39° 30' 40".

The morning of the 20th was fine, with a southerly breeze and a bright sky; and at seven o'clock we were on the march. The country today was rather more broken, rising still, and covered everywhere with fragments of silicious limestone, particularly on the summits, where they were small, and thickly strewed as pebbles on the shore of the sea. In these exposed situations grew but few plants; though, whenever the soil was good and protected from the winds, in the creek bottoms and ravines, and on the slopes, they flourished abundantly; among them the amorpha, still retaining its characteristic place. We crossed, at 10 A. m., the Big Vermilion, which has a rich bottom of about one mile in breadth, one third of which is occupied by timber. Making our usual halt at noon after a day's march of twenty-four miles, we reached the Big Blue, and encamped on the uplands of the western side, near a small creek, where was a fine large spring of very cold water. This is a clear and handsome stream, about one hundred and twenty feet wide, running with a rapid current, through a well-timbered valley. Today antelope were seen running over the hills, and at evening Carson brought us a fine deer. Longitude of the camp 96° 32' 35", latitude 390 45' 08". Thermometer at sunset 750. A pleasant southerly breeze and fine morning had given place to a gale, with indications of bad weather; when, after a march of ten miles, we halted to noon on a small creek, where the water stood in deep pools. In the bank of the creek limestone made its appearance in a stratum about one foot thick. In the afternoon, the people seemed to suffer for want of water. The road led along a high dry ridge; dark lines of timber indicated the heads of streams in the plains below; but there was no water near, and the day was oppressive, with a hot wind, and the thermometer at 900. Along our route the amorpha has been in very abundant but variable bloom—in some places, bending beneath the 'weight of purple clusters; in others without a flower. It seemed to love best the sunny slopes, with a dark soil and southern exposure. Everywhere the rose is met with, and reminds us of cultivates gardens and civilization. It is scattered over the prairies in small bouquets, and, when glittering in the dews and waving in the pleasant breeze of the early morning, is the most beautiful of the prairie flowers. The artemisia, absinthe, or prairie sage, as it is variously called, is increasing in size, and glittering like silver, as the southern breeze turns up its leaves to the sun. All these plants have their insect inhabitants, variously colored—taking generally the hue of the flower on which they live. The artemisia has its small fly accompanying it through every change of elevation and latitude; and wherever. I have seen the aseleptas tuberosa, I have always remarked, too, on the flower a large butterfly, so nearly resembling it in color as to be distinguishable at a little distance only by the motion of its wings. Traveling on, the fresh traces of the Oregon emigrants relieve a little the loneliness of the road; and tonight, after a march of twenty-two miles, we baited on a small creek which had been one of their encampments. ,As we advanced westward, the soil appears to be getting more sandy; and the surface rock, an erratic deposite of sand and gravel, rests here on a bed of coarse yellow and gray and very friable sandstone. Evening closed over with rain and its usual attendant hordes of mosquitoes, with which we were annoyed for the first time.

22d.—We enjoyed at breakfast this morning a luxury, very unusual in this country, in a cup of excellent coffee, with cream from our cow. Being milked at night, cream was thus had in the morning. Our midday halt was at Wyeth's creek, in the bed of which were numerous boulders of dark, ferruginous sandstone, mingled with others of the red sandstone already mentioned lyre a pack of cards, lying loose on the grass, marked an encampment of our Oregon emigrants; and it was at the close of the day when we made our bivouac in the midst of some well-timbered ravines near the Little Blue, twenty-four miles from cur camp of the preceding night. Crossing the next morning a number of handsome creeks, with water clear and sandy beds, we reached, at 10 A. nr., a very beautiful wooded stream, about thirty-five feet wide, called Sandy creek, and sometimes, as the Ottoes frequently winter there, the Otto fork. The country has become very sandy, and the plants less varied and abundant, with the exception of the amorpha, which rivals the grass in quantity, though not so forward as it has been found to the eastward.

At the Big Trees, where we had intended to noon, no water was to be found. The bed of the little creek was perfectly dry, and on the adjacent sandy bottom, cacti, for the first time, mule their appearance. We made here a short delay in search of water; and after a hard day's march of twenty-eight miles, encamped, at 5 o'clock, on the Little Blue, where our arrival made a scene of the Arabian Desert. As fast as they arrived, men arid horses rushed into the stream, where they bathed and drank together in common enjoyment. We were now in the range of the Pawnees, who were accustomed to infest this part of the country, stealing horses from companies on their way to the mountains; and, when in sufficient force, openly attacking and plundering them, and subjecting them to various kinds of insult. For the first time, therefore, guard was mounted tonight. Our route the next morning lay up the valley, which, bordered by hills with graceful slopes, looked uncommonly green and beautiful. The stream was about fifty feet wide, and three or four deep, fringed by cottonwood and willow, with frequent groves of oak, tenanted by flocks of turkeys. Game here, too, made its appearance in greater plenty, Elk were frequently seen on the hills, and now and then an antelope bounded across our path, or a deer broke from the groves. The road in the afternoon was over the upper prairies, several miles from the river, and we encamped at sunset on one of its small tributaries, where an abundance of prele (equisetum) afforded fine forage to our tired animals. We had traveled thirty-one miles. A heavy bank of black clouds in the west came on us in a storm between nine and ten, preceded by a violent wind. The rain fell in such torrents that it was difficult to breathe facing the wind; We_ thunder rolled incessantly, and the whole sky was tremulous with lightning—now and then illuminated by a blinding flash, succeeded by pitchy darkness. Carson had the watch from ten to midnight, and to him had been assigned our young compagnons de voyage, Messrs. Brant and R. Benton. This was their first night on guard, and such an introduction did not augur very auspiciously of the pleasures of the expedition. Many things conspired to render their situation uncomfortable; stories of desperate and bloody Indian fights were rife in the camp; our position was badly chosen surrounded on all sides by timbered hollows, and occupying an area of several hundred feet, so that necessarily the guards were far apart; and now and then I could hear Randolph, as if relieved by the sound of a voice in the darkness, calling out o the sergeant of the guard, to direct his attention to some imaginary alarm; but they stood it out, and took their urn regularly afterwards.

The next morning we had a specimen of the false alarms to which all parties it these wild regions are subject. Proceeding up the valley, objects were seen on the opposite hills, which disappeared before a glass could be brought to beat upon them. A man who was a short distance in the rear, came springing up in great haste, shouting "Indians! Indians!" He had been near enough to see and count them, according to his report, and had made out twenty-seven. I immediately halted; arms were examined and put in order; the usual preparations made; and Kit Carson, springing upon one of the hunting horses, crossed the river, and galloped off into the opposite prairies, to obtain some certain intelligence of their movements.

Mounted on a fine horse, without a saddle, and scouring bare headed over the prairies, Kit was one of the finest pictures of a horseman I have ever seen. A short time enabled him to discover that the Indian war party of twenty-seven consisted of six elk, who had been gazing curiously at our caravan as it passed by, and were now scampering off at full speed, This was our first alarm, and its excitement broke agreeably on the monotony of the day. At our noon halt, the men were exercised at a target; and in the evening we pitched our tents at a Pawnee encampment of last July. They had apparently killed buffalo here, as many bones were lying about, and the frames where the hides had been stretched were yet standing. The road of the day had kept the valley, which is sometimes rich and well timbered, though the country generally is sandy. Mingled with the usual plants, a thistle (carduus leucographus) nad for the last day or two made its appearance; and along the river bottom, tradescantia (virginica) and milk plant (as clepzas syriaca*) in considerable quantities.

This plant is very odoriferous, and in Canada charms the traveler, especially when passing through woods in the evening. The French there eat the tender sheets in the spring, as we do asparagus. The native' make a sugar of the flowers, gathering them in the morning when they are covered with dew, and collect the cotton from their pods to till thei beds. On account of the silkiness of this cotton, Parkinson calla the plant Virginian silk.—Loudon's Encyclopedia of Plants.

The Sioux Indiana of the Upper Platte eat the young pods of this plant oiling them with the meat of the buffalo.

Our march today had been twenty-one miles, and the as. Pronornical observations gave us a chronometric longitude of 980 21, 12", and latitude 40° 26' 50". We were moving forward at seven in the morning, and in about five mile reached ,a fork of the Blue, where the road leaves that river and crosses over to the Platte. No water was to be found the dividing ridge, and the casks were filled, and the animal here allowed a short repose. The road led across a high and level prairie ridge, where were but few plants, and those principally thistle, (carduus leucographus,) and a kind of dwarf artemisia. Antelope were seen frequently during the morning, which was very stormy. Squalls of rain, with thunder and lightning, were around us in every direction; and while we were enveloped in one of them, a flash, which seemed to' scorch our eyes as it passed, struck in the prairie within a few hundred feet, sending up a column of dust.

Crossing on the way several Pawnee roads to the Arkansas, we reached, in about twenty-one miles from our halt on the Blue, what is called the coast of the Nebraska, or Platte river. This had seemed in the distance a range of high and broker hills; but on a nearer approach was found to be elevations of forty to sixty feet into which the wind had worked the sand. They were covered with the usual fine grasses of the country, and bordered the 'eastern side of the ridge on a breadth of about two miles. Change of soil and country appeared here to have produced some change in the vegetation. Cacti were numerous, and all the plants of the region appeared to flourish among the warm hills. Among them the amorpha, in full bloom, was remarkable for its large and luxuriant purple clusters. From the foot of the coast, a distance of two miles across the level bottom brought us to our encampment on the shore of the river, about twenty miles below the head of Grand Island, which lay extended before us, covered with dense and heavy woods. From the mouth of the Kansas, according to our reckoning, we had traveled three hundred and twenty-eight miles; and the geological formation of the country we had passed over consisted of lime and sand stone, covered by the same erratic deposits of sand and gravel which forms the surface rock of the prairies between the Missouri ana Mississippi rivers. Except in some occasional limestone boulders, had met with no fossils. The elevation of the Platte valley above the sea is here about two thousand feet. The astronomical observations of the night placed us in longitude 98° 45' 49", latitude 40° 41' 06".

27th.—The animals were somewhat fatigued by their march of yesterday, and, after a short journey of eighteen miles along the river bottom, I encamped near the head of Grand Island, in longitude, by observation. 99° 05' 24", latitude 400 39' 32". The soil was here light but rich, though in some places rather sandy; and, with the exception of scattered fringe along the bank, the timber, consisting principally of poplar, (populus moniliefera,) elm, and hackberry, (celtis cras sifolia,) is confined almost entirely to the islands.

28th.—We halted to noon at an open reach of the river which occupies rather more than a fourth of the valley, here only about four miles broad. The camp had been disposed with the usual precaution, the horses grazing at a little distance, attended by the guard, and we were all sitting quietly at our dinner on the grass, when suddenly we heard the startling cry, "Du monde!" In an instant, every man's weapon was in his hand, the horses were driven in, hobbled and picketed, and horsemen were galloping at full speed in the direction of the newcomers, screaming and yelling with the wildest excitement. "Get ready, my lads!" said the leader, of the approaching party to his men, when our wild looking horsemen were discovered bearing down upon them—"nous allons attraper des coups de baguette." They proved to be a small party of fourteen, under the charge of a man named John Lee, and, with their baggage and provisions strapped to their backs, were making their way on foot to the frontier. A brief account of their fortunes will give some idea of navigation in the Nebraska. Sixty days since, they had left the mouth of Laramie's fork, some three hundred miles above, in carges laden with the furs of the American Fur Company. They started with the annual flood, and, drawing but nine inches water, hoped to make a speedy and prosperous voyage to St. Louis; but, after a lapse of forty days, found them selves only one hundred and thirty miles from their point of departure. They came down rapidly as far as Scott's bluffs, where their difficulties began. Sometimes they came upon places where the water was spread, over a great extent, and here they toiled from morning, until night, endeavoring to drag their boat through the sands, making only two or three miles in as many days. Sometimes they would enter an arm of the liver, where there appeared a fine channel, and, after descending prosperously for eight or ten miles, would come suddenly upon dry sands, and be compelled to return, dragging their boat for days against the rapid current; and at others, they came upon places where the water lay in holes, and, getting out to float off their boat, would fall into water up to their necks, and the next moment tumble over against a sandbar. Discouraged at length, and finding the Platte growing every day more shallow, they discharged the principal part of their cargoes one hundred and thirty miles below Fort Laramie, which they secured as well as possible, and, leaving a few men to guard them, attempted to continue their voyage, laden with some light furs and their personal baggage. After fifteen or twenty days more struggling in the sands, during which they made but one hundred and forty miles, they sunk their barges, made a cache of their remaining furs and property in trees on the bank, and, packing on his back what each man could carry, had commenced, the day before we encountered them; their journey on foot to St. Louis. We laughed then at their' forlorn and vagabond appearance, and, in our turn, a month or two afterwards, furnished the same occasion for merriment to others. Even their stock of tobacco, that sine qua non of a voyageur, without which the night fire is gloomy, was entirely exhausted. However, we shortened their homeward journey by a small supply from our own provision. They gave us the welcome intelligence that the buffalo were abundant some two days' march in advance, and made us a present of some choice pieces, which were a very acceptable change from our salt pork. In the interchange of news, and tree renewal of old acquaintanceships, we found where with to fill a busy hour; then we mounted our horses and they shouldered their packs, and we shook hands and parted. Among them, I had found an old companion on the northern prairie, a hardened and hardly set veteran of the mountains, who had been as much hacked and scarred as an old moustache of Napoleon's "old guard." He flourished in the sobriquet of La Tulipe, and his real name I never knew. Finding that he was going to the States only because his company was bound in that direction, and that he was rather more willing to return with me, I took him again into my service. We traveled this day but seventeen miles.

At our evening camp, about sunset, three figures were discovered approaching, which our glasses made out to be Indians. They proved to be Cheyennes—two men, and a boy of thirteen. About a month since, they had left their people on the south fork of the river, some three hundred miles to the westward, and a party of only four in number had been to the Pawnee villages on a horsestealing excursion, from which they were returning unsuccessful. They were miserably mounted on wild horses from the Arkansas plains, and had no other weapons than bows and long spears; and had they been discovered by the Pawnees, could not, by any possibility, have escaped. They were mortified by their illsuccess, and said the Pawnees were cowards, who shut up their horses in their lodges at night. I invited them to supper with me, and Randolph and the young Cheyenne, who had been eyeing each other suspiciously and curiously, soon became intimate friends. After supper we sat down on the grass, and I placed a sheet of paper between us, on which they traced, rudely, but with a certain degree of relative truth, the watercourses of the country which lay between us and their villages, and of which I desired to have some information. Their companions, they told us, had taken a nearer route over the hills; but they had mounted one of the summits to spy out the country, whence they had caught a glimpse of our party, and, confident of good treatment at the hands of the whites, hastened to join company. Latitude of the camp 40°. 39' 51"

We made the next morning sixteen miles. I remarked that the ground was covered in many places with an efflorescence of salt, and the plants were not numerous. In the bottoms were frequently seen tradescantia, and on the dry lenches were carduus, cactus, and amorpha. A high wind during the morning had increased to a violent gale from the northwest, which made our afternoon ride cold and unpleasant. We had the welcome sight of two buffaloes on one of the large islands, and encamped at a clump of timber about seven miles from our noon halt, after a day's march of twenty-two miles.

The air' was keen the next morning at sunrise, the thermometer standing at 440, and it was sufficiently cold to make overcoats very comfortable. A few miles brought us into the midst of the buffalo, swarming in immense numbers over the plains, where they had left scarcely a blade of grass standing. Mr. Preuss, who was sketching at a little distance in the rear, had at first noted them as large groves of timber. In the sight of such a mass of life, the traveler feels a strange emotion of grandeur. We had heard from a distance a dull and confused murmuring, and, when we came in view of their dark masses, there was not one among us who did not feel his heart beat , quicker. It was the early part of the day, when the herds are feeding; and everywhere they, were in motion. Here and there a huge old bull was rolling in the grass, and clouds of dust rose in the air from various parts of the bands, each the scene of some obstinate fight. Indians and buffalo make the poetry and life of the prairie, and our camp was full of their exhilaration. In place of the quiet monotony of the march, relieved only by the cracking of the whip, and an "avance done! enfant de garce!" shouts and songs resounded from every part of the line, and our evening camp was always the commencement of a feast, which terminated only with our departure on the following morning. At any time of the night might be seen pieces of the most delicate and choicest meat, roasting en appolo,s, on sticks around the fire, and the guard were never without company. With pleasant weather and no enemy to fear, an abundance of the most excellent meat, au: no scarcity of bread or tobacco, they were enjoying the oasis of a voyageur's life. Three cows were killed today Kit Carson had shot one, and was continuing the chase in the undo of another herd, when his horse fell headlong, but sprang up and joined the flying band. Though considerably hurt, he had the good fortune to break no bones; and Maxwell, who was mounted on a fleet hunter, captured the runaway after 2 hard chase. He was on the point of shooting him, to avoid the loss of his bridle, (a handsomely mounted Spanish one,) when he found that his horse was able to come up with him. Animals are frequently lost in this way; and it is necessary to keep close watch over them, in the vicinity of the buffalo, in the midst of which they scour off to the plains, and are rarely retaken. One of our mules took a sudden freak into his head, and joined a neighboring band today. As we were not in a condition to lose horses, I sent several men in pursuit, and remained in camp, in the hope of recovering him; but lost the afternoon to no purpose, as we did not see him again. Astronomical observations placed us in longitude 100° 05' 47", latitude 400 49'

JULY. 1st.—Along our road today the prairie bottom was more elevated and dry, and the river hills which border the right side of the river higher, and more broken and picturesque in the outline. The country, too, was better timbered. As we were riding quietly along the bank, a grand herd of buffalo, some seven or eight hundred in number, came crowding up from the river, 'where they had been to drink, and commenced crossing the plain slowly, eating as they went. The wind was favorable; the coolness of the morning invited to exercise; the ground was apparently good, and the distance across the prairie (two or three miles) gave us a fine opportunity to charge them before they could get among the river hills. It was too fine a prospect for a chase to be lost; and, halting for a few moments, the hunters were brought up and saddled, ana Kit Carson, Maxwell, and I, started together. They were now somewhat less than half a mile distant, and we rode easily along until within about three hundred yards, when a sudden agitation, a wavering in the band, and a galloping to and fro of some which were scattered along the skirts, gave us the intimation that we were discovered. We started together at a hand gallop, riding steadily abreast of each other; and here the interest of the chase became so engrossingly intense, that we were sensible to nothing else. We were now closing upon them rapidly, and the front of the mass was already in rapid motion for the hills, and in a few seconds the movement had communicated itself to the whole herd.

A crowd of bulls, as usual, brought up the rear, and every now and then some of them faced about, and then dashed on after the band a short distance, and turned and looked again, as if more than half inclined to fight. In a few moments, however, during which we had been quickening our pace, the rout was universal, and we were going over the ground like a hurricane. When at about thirty yards, we gave the usual shout, (the hunter's pas de charge,) and broke into the herd. We entered on the side, the mass giving way in every direction in their heedless course. Many of the bulls, less active and fleet than the cows, paying no attention to the ground, and occupied solely with the hunter, were precipitated to the earth with great force, rolling over and over with the violence of the shock, and hardly distinguishable in the dust. We separated on entering, each singling out his game.

My horse was a trained hunter, famous in the West under the name of Proveau; and, with his eyes flashing and the foam flying from his mouth, sprang on after the cow like a tiger. In a few moments he brought me alongside of her, and rising in the stirrups, I fired at the distance of a yard, the bail entering at the termination, of the long hair, and passing near the heart. She fell headlong at the report of the gun; and, checking my horse, I looked around for my companions. At a little distance, Kit was on the ground, engaged in tying hit horse to the horns of a cow he was preparing to up. Among the scattered bands, at some distance below, I caught a glimpse of Maxwell; and while I was looking, a light wreath of smoke aimed away from his gun, from which I was too far to hear the report. Nearer, and between me and the hills, towards which they were directing their course, was the body of the herd; and, giving my horse the rein, we dashed after them. A thick cloud of dust hung upon their rear, which filled my mouth and eyes, and nearly smothered me. In the midst of this I could see nothing, and the buffalo were not distinguishable until within thirty feet. They crowded together more densely still as I came upon them, and rushed along in such a compact body, that I could not obtain an entrance—the horse almost leaping upon them. In a few moments the mass divided to the right and left, the horns clattering with a noise heard above every thing else, and my horse darted into the opening. Five or six bulls charged on us as we dashed along the line, but were left far behind; and, singling out a cow, I gave her my fire, but struck too high. She gave a tremendous leap, and scoured on swifter than before. I reined up my horse, and the band swept on like a torrent, and left the place quiet and clear. Our chase had led us into dangerous ground. A prairie dog village, so thickly settled that there were three or four holes in every twenty yards square, occupied the whole bottom for nearly two miles in length. Looking around, I saw only one of the hunters, nearly out of sight, and the long, dark line of our caravan crawling along, three or four miles distant. After a march of twenty-four miles, we encamped at nightfall, one mile and a half above the lower end of Brady's Island. The breadth of this arm of the river was eight hundred and eighty yards, and the water nowhere two' feet in depth. The island bears the name of a man killed on this spot some years ago. His party had encamped here, three in company, and one of the number went off to hunt, leaving Brady and his companion together. These two had frequently quarreled, and on the hunter's return he found Brady dead, and was told that he had shot himself accidentally. He was buried here or, the bank; but, as usual, the wolves tore him out, and some human bones that were lying on the ground we supposed were his. Troops of wolves that were hanging on the skirts of the buffalo, kept up an uninterrupted howling during the night venturing almost into camp. In the morning, they were sitting at a short distance, barking, and impatiently waiting our departure, to fall upon the bones.

2d.—The morning was cool and smoky. Our road led closer to the hills, which here increased in elevation, presenting an outline of conical peaks three hundred to five hundred feet high. Some timber, apparently pine, grows in the ravines, and streaks of clay or sand whiten their slopes. We crossed, during the morning, a number of hollows, timbered principally with box, elder, (acer negundo,) poplar, and elm. Brady's Island is well wooded, and all the river along which our road led today, may, in general, be called tolerably well timbered. We passed near the encampment of the Oregon emigrants, where they appeared to have reposed several days. A variety of household articles were scattered about, and they had pros, ably disburdened themselves here of many things not absolutely necessary. I had left the usual road before the midday halt, and in the afternoon, having sent several men in advance to reconnoitre, marched directly for the mouth of the South fork. On our arrival, the horsemen were sent in and scattered about the river to search for the best fording places, and the carts followed immediately. The stream is here divided by an island into two channels. The southern is four hundred and fifty feet wide, having eighteen or twenty inches water in the deepest places. With the exception of a few dry bars, the bed of the river is generally quicksands, in which the carts began to sink rapidly so soon as the mules halted, so that it was necessary to keep them constantly in motion.

The northern channel, two thousand two hundred and fifty feet wide, was somewhat deeper, having frequently three feet water in the numerous small channels, with a bed of coarse gravel. The whole breadth of the Nebraska, immediately below the junction, is five thousand three hundred and fifty feet.

All our equipage had reached the left bank safely at six o'clock, having today made twenty miles. We encamped at the point of land immediately at the junction of the North and South forks. Between the streams is a low rich prairie, extending from their confluents eighteen miles westwardly to the bordering hills, where it Is five and a half miles wide. It is covered with a luxuriant growth of grass, and along the banks is a slight and scattered fringe of cottonwood and willow. In the buffalo trails and wallows, I remarked saline efflorescences, to which a rapid evaporation in the great heat of the sun probably contributes, as the soil is entirely unprotected by timber. In the vicinity of these places there was a bluish grass, which the cattle refuse to eat, called by the voyageurs "herbe salee," (salt grass.) The latitude of the junction is 41o 04' 47", and longitude, by chronometer and lunar distances, 100o 49' 43". The elevation above the sea is about two thousand seven hundred feet. The hunters came in with a fat cow; and, as we had labored hard, we enjoyed well a supper of roasted ribs and boudins, the chef d'oeuvre of a prairie cook. Mosquitoes thronged about us this evening; but, by ten o'clock, when the thermometer had fallen to 47°, they had all disappeared.

3d.—As this was to be a point in our homeward journey, I made a cache (a term used in all this country for what is hidden in the ground) of a barrel of pork. It was impossible to conceal such a proceeding from the sharp eyes of our Cheyenne companions, and I therefore told them to go and see whs.+ it was they were burying. They would otherwise have not failed to return and destroy our cache in expectation of some rich booty; but pork they dislike and never eat. We left our camp at nine, continuing up the South fork, the prairie bottom affording us a fair road; but in the long grass we roused myriads of mosquitoes and flies, from which our horses suffered severely. The day was smoky, with a pleasant breeze from the south, and the plains on the opposite side were covered with buffalo. Having traveled twenty-five miles, we encamped at six in the evening; and the men were sent across the river for wood, as there 'is none here on the left bank. Our fires were partially made of the bois de vache, the dry excrement of the buffalo, which, like that of the camel in the Arabian deserts, furnishes to the traveler a very good substitute for wood, burning like turf. Wolves in great number:, surrounded us during the night, crossing and recrosting from the opposite herds to our camp, and howling and trotting about in the river until morning.

4th.—The morning, was very smoky, the sun shining dimly and red, as in thick fog. The camp was roused by a salute at daybreak, and from our scanty store a portion of what our Indian friends called the " red firewater" served out to the men. While we were at breakfast, a buffalo calf broke through the camp, followed by a couple of wolves. In its fright, it had probably mistaken us for a band of buffalo. The wolves were obliged to make a circuit round the camp, so that the calf got a little the start, and strained every nerve to reach a large herd at the foot of the hills, about two miles distant; but first one and then another, and another wolf joined in the chase, until his pursuers amounted to twenty or thirty, and they ran him down before he could reach his friends. There were few bulls near the place, and one of them attacked the wolves and tried to rescue him; but was driven off immediately, and the little animal fell an easy prey, half devoured before he was dead. We watched the chase with the interest always felt for the weak; and had there been a saddled horse at hand, he would have fared better. Leaving camp, our road soon approached the hills, in which strata of a marl like that of the Chimney rock, hereafter described, made their appearance. It is probably of this rock that the hills on the right bank of the Platte, a little below the junction, are composed, and which are worked by the winds and rains into sharp peaks and cones, giving them, in contrast to the surrounding level region, something of a picturesque appearance. We crossed, this morning, numerous beds of the small creeks which, in the time of rains and melting snow, pour down from the, ridge, bringing down with them, always, great quantities of sand and gravel, which have gradually raised their beds four to ten feet above the level of the prairie, which they cross, making each one of them a miniature Po. Raised in this way above the surrounding prairie, without any bank, the long yellow and winding line of their beds resembles a causeway from the hills to the river, Many spots on the prairie are yellow with sunflower, ohelmthus.

As we were riding slowly along this afternoon, clouds of duel in the ravines, among the hills to the right, suddenly attracted our attention, and in a few minutes column after column of buffalo came galloping down, making directly to the river. By the time the leading herds had reached the water, the prairie was darkened with the dense masses. Immediately before us, when the bands first came down into the valley, stretched an unbroken line, the head of which was lost among the river hills on the opposite side; and still they poured down from the ridge on our right. From hill to hill, the prairie bottom was certainly not less than two miles wide; and, allowing the animals to be ten feet apart, and only ten in a line, there were already eleven thousand in view. Some idea may thus be formed of their number when they had occupied the whole plain. In a short time they surrounded us on every side, extending for several miles in the rear, and forward as far as the eye could reach; leaving around us, as we advanced, an open space of only two or three hundred yards. This movement of the buffalo indicated to us the presence of Indians on the North fork.

I halted earlier than usual, about forty miles from the junction, and all hands were soon busily engaged in preparing a feast to celebrate the day. The kindness of our friends at St. Louis had provided us with a large supply of excellent preserves and rich fruitcake; and when these were added to a macaroni soup, and variously prepared dishes of the choicest buffalo meat, crowned with a cup of coffee, and enjoyed with prairie appetite, we felt, as we sat in barbaric luxury around our smoking supper on the grass, a greater sensation of enjoyment than the Roman epicure at his perfumed feast. But most of all it seemed to please our Indian friends, who, in the unrestrained enjoyment of the moment, demanded to know if our "medicine days came often." No restraint was exercised at the hospitable board, and, to the great delight of his elders, our young Indian lad made himself extremely drunk.

Our encampment was within a few miles of the place where the road crosses to the North fork, and various reasons led me to divide my party at this point. The North fork was the principal object of my survey; but I was desirous to ascend the South branch, with a view of obtaining some astronomical positions, and determining the mouths of its tributaries as far as St. Vrain's fort, estimated to be some two hundred miles farther up the river, and near to Long's Peak. There I hoped tc obtain some mules, which I found would be necessary to relieve my horses. In a military point of view, I was desirous to form some opinion of the country relative to the establishment of posts on a line connecting the settlements with the south pass of the Rocky Mountains, by way of the Arkansas and the South and Laramie forks of the Platte. Crossing the country northwestwardly from St. Vrain's fort, to the American Company's fort at the mouth of the Laramie, would give me some acquaintance with the affluents which heading the mountain between the two; I therefore determined to set out the next morning, accompanied by four men—Maxwell, Bernier, Ayot, and Basil Lajeunesse. Our Cheyennes, whose village lay up this river, also decided to accompany us. The party I left in charge of Cement Lambert, with orders to cross to the North fork; and some convenient place, near to the Coulee des Frenes, make a cache of every thing not absolutely necessary to the further progress of our expedition. From this point, using the most guarded precaution in his march through the country, he was to proceed to the American Company's fort at the mouth of the Laramie's fork, and await my arrival, which would be prior to the 16th, as on that and the following night would occur some occultations which I was desirous to obtain at that place.

5th.—Before breakfast all was ready. We had one led horse in addition to those we rode, and a packmule, destined to carry our instruments, provisions, and baggage; the last two articles not being of great weight. The instruments consisted of a sextant, artificial horizon, &c., a barometer, spyglass, ana compass. The chronometer I of course kept on my person. I had ordered the cook to put up for us some flour, coffee, and sugar, and our rifles were to furnish the rest. One blanket, in addition to his saddle and saddle blanket, furnished the materials for each man's bed, and every one was provided with change of linen. All were armed with rifles or double bar relied guns; and, in addition to these, Maxwell and myself were furnished with excellent pistols. Thus accoutred, we took a parting breakfast with our friends, and set forth.

Our journey the first day afforded nothing of any interest. We shot a buffalo towards sunset, and having obtained some meat for our evening meal, encamped where a little timber afforded us the means of making a fire. Having disposed our meat on roasting sticks, we proceeded to unpack our bales in search of coffee and sugar, and flour for bread. With the exception of a little parched coffee, unground, we found nothing. Our cook had neglected to put it up, or it had been somehow forgotten. Tired and hungry, with tough bullmeat without salt, (for we had not been able to kill a cow,) and a little bitter coffee, we sat down in silence to our miserable fare, a very disconsolate party; for yesterday's feast was yet fresh in our memories, and this was our first brush with misfortune. Each man took his blanket, and laid himself down silently; for the worst part of these mishaps is, that they make people ill-humored. Today we had traveled about thirty-six miles.

6th.—Finding that our present excursion would be attended with considerable hardship, and unwilling to expose more persons than necessary, I determined to send Mr. Preuss back to the party. His horse, too, appeared in no condition to support the journey; and accordingly, after breakfast, he took the road across the hills, attended by one of my most trusty men, Bernier. The ridge between the rivers is here about fifteen miles broad, and I expected he would probably strike the fork near their evening camp. At all events he would not fail to find their trail, and rejoin them the next day.

We continued our journey, seven in number, including the three Cheyennes. Our general course was southwest, up the valley of the river, which was sandy, bordered on the northern side of the 'valley by a low ridge; and on the south, after seven or eight miles, the river hills became higher. Six miles from our resting place we crossed the bed of a considerable stream, now entirely dry—a bed cf sand. In a grove of willows, near the mouth, were the remains of a considerable fort, constructed of trunks of large trees. It was apparently very old, and had probably been the scene of some hostile encounter among the roving tribes. Its solitude formed an impressive contrast to the picture which our imaginations involuntarily drew of the busy scene which had been enacted here! The timber appeared to have been much more extensive formerly than now. There were but few trees, a kind of long leaved willow, standing; and numerous trunks of large trees were scattered about on the ground. In many similar places I had occasion to remark an apparent progressive decay in the timber. Ten miles farther we reached the mouth of Lodge Pole creek, a clear and handsome stream, running through a broad valley. In its course through the bottom it has a uniform breadth of twentytwo feet and six inches in depth. A few willows on the banks strike pleasantly on the eye, by heir greenness, in the midst of hot and barren sands.

The antorpha was frequent among the ravines, but the sunflower (helianthus) was the characteristic; and flowers of deep warm colors seem most to love the sandy soil. The impression of the country traveled over today was one of dry and barren sands. We turned in towards the river at noon, and gave our horses two hours for food and rest. I had no other thermometer than the one attached to the barometer, which stood at 890, the height of the column in the barometer being 26.235 at meridian. The sky was clear, with a high wind from the south. At 2 we continued our journey; the wind had moderated, and it became almost unendurably hot, and our animals suffered severely. In the course of the afternoon, the wind rose suddenly, and blew hard from the southwest, with thunder and lightning, and squalls of rain; these were down against us with violence by the wind; and, halting, we turned our backs to the storm until it blew over. Antelope were tolerably frequent, with a large gray hare; but the former were shy, and the latter hardly worth the delay of stopping to shoot them; so, as the evening drew near, we again had recourse to an old bull, and encamped at sunset on an island in the Platte.

We ate our meat with a good relish this evening, for we were all in fine health, and had ridden nearly all of a:ong summer's day, with a burning sun reflected from the sands. My companions slept rolled up in their blankets, and the Indians lay in the grass near the fire; but my sleeping place generally had an air of more pretension. Our rifles were tied together near the muzzle, the butts resting on the ground, and a knife laid on the rope, to cut away in case of an alarm. Over this, which made a kind of frame, was thrown a large India rubber cloth, which we used to cover our packs. This made a tent sufficiently large to receive about half of my bed, and was a place of shelter for my instruments; and as I was careful always to put this part against the wind, I could lie here with a sensation of satisfied enjoyment, and hear the wind blow, and the rain patter close to my head, and know that I should be at least half dry. Certainly I never slept more soundly. The barometer at sunset was 26.010, thermometer at 81°, and cloudy; but a gale from the west sprang up with the setting sun, and in a few minutes swept away every cloud from the sky. The evening was very fine, and I remained up to take astronomical observations, which made our position in latitude 400 51' 17", and longitude 103° 07' 00".

7th.—At our camp this morning, at six o'clock, the barometer was at 26.183, thermometer 69°, and clear, with a light wind from the southwest. The past night had been squally, with high winds, and occasionally a few drops of rain. Ota cooking did not occupy much time, and we left camp early. Nothing of interest occurred during the morning. The same dreary barrenness, except that a hard manly clay had replaced the sandy soil. Buffalo absolutely covered the plain, on both sides of the river, and whenever we ascended the hills scattered herds gave life to the view in every direction. A small drove of wild horses made their appearance on the low river bottoms, a mile or two to the left, and I sent off one of the Indians (who seemed very eager to catch one) on my led horse, a spirited and fleet animal. The savage maneuvered a little to get the wind of the horses, in which he succeeded—approaching within a hundred yards without being, discovered. The chase for a few minutes was interesting; My hunter easily overtook and passed the hindmost of the wild drove, which the Indian did not attempt to lasso; all his efforts being directed tc capture the leader. But the strength of the horse, weakened by the insufficient nourishment of grass, failed in a race, and all the drove escaped. We halted at noon on the bank of the river, the barometer at that time being 26.192, and the thermometer 1030, with a light air from the south and clear weather.

In the course of the afternoon, dust rising among the hills, at a particular place, attracted our attention; and, riding up, we found a band of eighteen or twenty buffalo bulls engaged , in a desperate fight. Though butting and goring were bestowed liberally, and without distinction, yet their efforts were evidently directed against one—a huge, gaunt old bull, very lean, while his adversaries were all fat and in good order. He appeared very weak, and had already received some wounds; and, while we were looking on, was several times knocked down and badly hurt, and a very few moments would have put an end to him. Of course, we took the side of the weaker party, and attacked the herd; but they were so blind with rage, that they fought on, utterly regardless of our presence although on foot and on horseback we were firing, in open view, within twenty yards of them. But this did not last long. In a very few seconds, we created a commotion among them. One or two, which were knocked over by the balls, jumped up and ran off into the hills; and they began to retreat slowly along a broad ravine to the river, fighting furiously as they went. By the time they had reached the bottom, we had pretty well dispersed them, and the old bull hobbled off to lie down somewhere. One of his enemies remained on the ground where we had first fired upon them, and we stopped there for a short time to cut from him some meat for our supper. We had neglected to secure our horses, thinking it an unnecessary precaution in their fatigued condition; but our mule took it into his head to start, and away he went, followed at full speed by the packhorse, with all the baggage and instruments on his back. They were recovered and brought back, after a chase of a mile. Fortunately, every thing was well secured, so that nothing, not even the barometer, was in the least injured.

The sun was getting low, and some narrow lines of timber, four or five miles distant, promised us a pleasant camp, where, with plenty of wood for fire, and comfortable shelter, and rich grass for our animals, we should find clear cool springs, instead of 'the warm water of the Platte. On our arrival, we found the bed of a stream fifty to one hundred feet wide sunk some thirty feet below the level of the prairie, with perpendicular banks, bordered by a fringe of green cottonwood, but not a drop of water. There were several small forks to the stream, all in the same condition. With the exception of the Platte bottom, the country seemed to be of a clay formation, dry, and perfectly devoid of any moisture, and baked hard by the sun. Turning off towards the river, we reached the bank in about a mile, and were delighted to find an old tree, with thick foliage and spreading branches, where we encamped. At sunset, the barometer was at 25.950, thermometer 81°, with a strong wind from S. 20° E., and the sky partially covered with heavy masses of cloud, which settled a little towards the horizon by ten o'clock, leaving it sufficiently clear for astronomical observations, which placed us in latitude 40o 33' 26", and longitude 103° 30' 37".

8th.—The morning was very pleasant. The breeze was fresh from S. 50° E., with few clouds; the barometer at six o'clock standing at 25.970, and the thermometer at 70°. Since leasing the forks our route had passed over a country alternately clay and sand, each presenting the same naked waste. On leaving camp this morning, we struck again a sandy region, in which the vegetation appeared somewhat more vigorous than that which we had observed for the last few days; and on the opposite side of the river were some tolerably large groves of timber.

Journeying along, we came suddenly upon a place where the ground was covered with horses' tracks, which had been made since the rain, and indicated the immediate presence of Indians in our neighborhood. The buffalo, too, which the day before had been so numerous, were nowhere in sight—another sure indication that there were people near. Riding on, we discovered the carcass of a buffalo recently killed—perhaps the day before. We scanned the horizon carefully with the glass, but no living object was to be seen. For the next mile or two, the ground was dotted with buffalo carcasses, which showed that the Indians had made a surround here, and were in considerable force. We went on quickly and cautiously, keeping the river bottom, and carefully avoiding the hills; but we met with no interruption, and began to grow careless again. We had already lost one of our horses, and here Basil's mule showed symptoms of giving out, and finally refused to advance, being what the Canadians call reste. He therefore dismounted, and drove her along before him; but this was a very slow way of traveling. We had inadvertently got about half a mile in advance, but our Cheyennes, who were generally a mile or two in the rear, remained with him. There were some dark looking objects among the hills, about two miles to the left, here low and undulating, which we had seen for a little time, and supposed to be buffalo coming in to water; but, happening to look behind, Maxwell saw the Cheyennes whipping up furiously, and another glance at the dark objects showed them at once to be Indians coming up at speed.

Had we been well mounted and disencumbered of instruments, we might have set them at defiance; but as it was, we were fairly caught. It was too late to rejoin our friends, and we endeavored to gain a clump of timber about half a mile ahead; but the instruments and tired state of our 'horses did not allow us to go faster than a steady canter, and they were gaining on us fast. At first, they did not appear to be more than fifteen or twenty in number, but group after group darted into view at the top of the hills, until all the little eminences seemed in motion; and, in a few minutes from the time the3 were first discovered, two or three hundred, naked to the breechcloth, were sweeping across the prairie. In a few hundred yards we discovered that the timber we were endeavoring to make was on the opposite side of the river; and before we wild reach the bank, down came the Indians upon us.

I am inclined to think that in a few seconds more the leading man, and perhaps some of his companions, would have rolled in the dust; for we had jerked the covers from our guns, and our fingers were on the triggers. Men in such cases generally act from instinct, and a charge from three hundred naked savages is a circumstance not well calculated to promote a cool exercise of judgment. Just as he was about to fire, Maxwell recognised the leading Indian, and shouted to him in the Indian language, "You're a fool, G— damn you—don't you know me?" The sound of his own language seemed to shock the savage; and, swerving his horse a little, he passed us like an arrow. He wheeled, as I rode out towards him, and gave me his hand, striking his' breast and exclaiming "Arapaho!" They proved to be a village of that nation, among whom Maxwell had resided as a trader a year or two previously, and recognised him accordingly. We were soon in the midst of the band, answering as well as we could a multitude of questions; of which the very first was, of what tribe were our Indian companions who were coming in the rear? They seemed disappointed to know that they were Cheyennes, for they had folly anticipated a grand dance around a Pawnee scalp that night.

The chief showed us his village at a grove on the river six miles ahead, and pointed out a band of buffalo on the other side of the Platte, immediately opposite us, which he said they were going to surround. They had seen the band early it 'he morning from their village, and had been making a large circuit, to avoid giving them the wind, when they discovered us. In a few minutes the women came galloping up, astride on their horses, and naked from their knees down and the hips up. They followed the men, to assist in cutting up and carrying off the meat.

The wind was blowing directly across the river, and the chief requested us to halt where we were for awhile, in order to avoid raising the herd. We therefore unsaddled our horses, and sat down on the bank to view the scene; and our new acquaintances rode a few hundred yards lower down, and began crossing the river. Scores of wild looking dogs followed, looking like troops of wolves, and having, in fact, but very little of the dog in their composition. Some of them remained with us, and I checked one of the men, whom I found aiming at one, which he was about to kill for a wolf. The day had become very hot. The air was clear, with a very slight breeze; and now, at 12 o'clock, while the barometer stood at 25.920, the attached thermometer was at 108°. Our Cheyennes had learned that with the Arapaho village *ere about twenty lodges of their own, including their own families , they therefore immediately commenced making their toilette. After bathing in the river, they invested themselves in some handsome calico shirts, which I afterwards learned they had stolen from my own men, and spent some time in arranging their hair and painting themselves with some vermilion I had them. While they were engaged in this satisfactory manner, one of their half wild horses, to which the crowd of prancing animals which had just passed had recalled the freedom of her existence among the wild droves on the prairie, suddenly dashed into the hills at the top of her speed. She was their packhorse, and had on her back all the worldly wealth of our poor Cheyennes, all their accoutrements, and all the little articles which they had picked up among us, with some few presents I had given them. The loss which they seemed to regret most were their spears and shields, and, some tobacco which they had received from me. However, they bore it all with the philosophy of an Indian, and laughingly continued their toilette. They appeared, however, to be a little mortified at the thought of returning to the village in such a sorry plight. "Our people will laugh at us," said one of them, "returning to the village on foot, instead of driving back a drove of Pawnee horses." He demanded to know if I loved my sorrel hunter very much; to which I replied, he was the object of my most intense affection. Far from being able to give, I was myself in want of horses; and any suggestion of parting with the few I had valuable, was met with a peremptory refusal,. In the meantime, the slaughter was about to commence on the other side. So soon as they reached it, the Indians separated into two bodies. One party proceeded line, while the other went up the river; and instantly as they had given the wind to the herd, the chase commenced. The buffalo started for the hills, but were intercepted and driven back towards the river, broken and running in every direction The clouds of dust soon covered the whole scene, preventing us from having any but an occasional view. It had a very singular ,appearance to us at a distance, especially when looking with the glass. We were too far to hear the report of the guns, or any sound; and at every instant, through the clouds of dust, which the sun made luminous, we could see for a moment two or three buffalo dashing along, and close behind them an Indian with his long spear, or other weapon, and instantly again they disappeared. The apparent silence, and the dimly seen figures flitting by with such rapidity, gave it a kind of dreamy effect, and seemed more like a picture than a scene of real life. It had been a large herd when the cerne commenced, probably three or four hundred in number; but, though I watched them closely, I did not see one emerge from the fatal cloud where the work of destruction was going on. After remaining here about an hour, we resumed our journey in the direction of the village.

Gradually, as we rode on, Indian after Indian came dropping along, laden with meat; and by the time we had neared the lodges, the backward road was covered with the returning horsemen. It was a pleasant contrast with the desert road we had been traveling. Several had joined company with us, an one of the chiefs invited us to his lodge. The village consisted of about one hundred and twenty-five lodges, of which twenty were Cheyennes; the latter pitched a little apart from the Arapahoes. They were disposed in a scattering manner on both sides of a broad, irregular street, about one hundred and fifty feet wide, and running along the river. As we rode along, I remarked near some of the lodges a kind of tripod frame, formed of three slender poles of birch, scraped very clean, to which were affixed the shield and spear, with some other weapons of u chief. All were seruptilously clean, the spearhead was burnished bright, and the shield white and stainless. It reminded me of the days of feudal chivalry; and when, as I rode by, I yielded to the passing impulse, and touched one of the spotless shields with the muzzle of my gun, I almost expected a grim warrior to start from the lodge and resent my challenge. The master of the lodge spread out a robe for me to sit upon, and the squaws set before us a large wooden dish of buffalo meat. He had lit his pipe in the meal while, and when it bad been passed around, we commenced our dinner while he continued to smoke. Gradually, however, five or six other chiefs came in, and took their seats in silence When we had finished, our host asked a number of questions relative to the object of our journey, of which I. made no concealment; telling him simply that I had made a visit to see the country, preparatory to the establishment of military posts on the way to the mountains. Although this was information of the highest interest to them, and by no means calculated to please them, it excited no expression of surprise, and in no way altered the grave courtesy of their demeanor. The others listened and smoked. I remarked, that in taking the pipe for the first time, each had turned the stem upward, with a rapid glance, as in offering to the Great Spirit, before he put it in his mouth. A storm had been gathering for the past hour, and some pattering drops in the lodge warned us that we had some miles to our camp. An Indian had given Maxwell a bundle of dried meat, which was very acceptable, as we had nothing; and, springing upon our horses, we rode off at dusk in the face of a cold shower and driving wind. We found our companions under some densely foliaged old trees, about three miles up the river. Under one of them lay the trunk of a large cottonwood, to leeward of which the men had kindled a fire, and we sat here and roasted our mesa in tolerable shelter. Nearly opposite was the mouth of one of the most considerable affluents of the South fork, la Fourche aux Castors, (Beaver fork,) heading off in the ridge to the southeast.

9th.—This morning we caught the first faint glimpse of the Rocky mountains, about sixty miles distant. Though a tolerably bright day, there was a slight mist, and we were just able to discern the, snowy summit of "Long's wait," les dein milks" of the Canadians,) showing like a cloud near the horizon. I found it easily distinguishable, there being a perceptible difference in its appearance from the white clouds that were floating about the sky. I was pleased to find that among the traders the name of " Long's peak" had been adopted and become familiar in the country. In the ravines near this place, a light brown sandstone made its first appearance. About 8, we discerned several persons on horseback a mile or two ahead, on the opposite side of the river. They turned in towards the river, and we rode down to meet them. We found them to be two white men, and a mulatto named Jim Beckwith, who had left St. Louis when a boy, and gone to live with the Crow Indians. He had distinguished himself among them by some acts of daring bravery, and had risen to the rank of chief, but had now, for some years, left them. They were in search of a band of horses that had gone off from a camp some miles above, in charge of Mr. Chabonard. Two of them continued down the river, in search of the horses, and the American turned back with us, and we rode on towards the camp. About eight miles from our sleeping place, we reached Bijou's fork, an affluent of the right bank. Where we crossed it, a short distance from the Platte, it has a sandy bed about four hundred yards broad; the water in various small streams, a few inches deep. Seven miles further brought us to the camp of some four or five whites, (New Englanders, I believe,) who had accompanied Captain Wyeth to the Columbia river, and were independent trappers. All had their squaws with them, and I was really surprised at the number of little fat, buffalo-fed boys that were tumbling about the camp, all apparently of the same age, about three or four years old. They were encamped on a rich bottom, covered with a profusion of rich grass, and had a large number of fine-looking horses and mules; We rested with them a few minutes, and in about two Miles arrived at Chabonard's camp, on an island in the Platte On the heights above, we met the first Spaniard I had seen in the country. Mr. Chabonard was in the service of Bent and St. Vrain's company, and had left their fort some forty or' fifty miles above, in the spring, with boats laden with the fur, of the last year's trade. He had met the same fortune as the voyageurs on the North fork; and, finding it impossible tc proceed, had taken up his summer's residence on this island, which he had named St. Helena. The river hills appeared to ne composed entirely of sand, and the Platte had lost the muddy character of its waters, and here was tolerably clear. From the mouth of the South fork, I had found it occasionally broken up by small islands; and at the time of our journey, which was at a season of the year when the waters were at a favorable stage, it was not navigable for any thing drawing six inches water. The current was very swift—the bed of the stream a coarse gravel. From the place at which we had encountered the Arapahoes, the Platte had been tolerably well fringed with timber, and the island here had a fine grove of very large cottonwoods, under whose broad shade the tents were pitched. There was a large drove of horses in the opposite prairie bottom; smoke was rising from the scattered fires, and the encampment had quite a patriarchal air. Mr. C. received us hospitably. One of the people was sent to gather mint, with the aid of which he concocted very good julep; and some boiled buffalo tongue, and coffee with the luxury of sugar, were soon set before us.. The people in his employ were generally Spaniards, and among them I saw a young Spanish woman from Taos, whom I found to be Beckwith's wife.

10th.—We parted with our hospitable host after breakfast the next morning, and reached St. Vrain's fort, about fortyfive miles from St. Helena, late in the evening. This post is situated on the South fork of the Platte, immediately under the mountains, about seventeen miles east of Long's peak. It is on the right bank, on the verge of the upland prairie, about forty feet above the river, of 'which the immediate valley is about six hundred yards wide. The stream is divided into various branches by small islands, among which it runs with a swift current. The bed of the river is sand and gravel, the water very clear, and here may be called a mountain stream. This region appears to be entirely free from the limestones and marls which give to the Lower Platte its yellow and dirty color.

The Black hills lie between the stream and the mountains, whose snowy peaks glitter a few miles beyond. At the fort we found Mr. St. Vrain, who received us with much kindness and hospitality. Maxwell had spent the last two or three years between this post and the village of Taos; and here he was at home, and among his friends. Spaniards frequently came over in search of employment; and several came in shortly after our arrival. They usually obtain about six dollars a month, generally paid to them in goods. They are very useful in a camp, in taking care of horses and mules; and I en gaged one, who proved to be an' active, laborious man, and was of very considerable" service to me. The elevation of the Platte here is five thousand four hundred feet above the sea. The neighboring mountains did not appear to enter far the region of perpetual snow, which was generally confined to the northern side of the peaks. On the southern, I remarked very little. Here it appeared, so far as I could judge in the distance, to descend but a few hundred feet below the summits.

I regretted that time did not permit me to visit them; but the proper object of my survey lay among the mountains farther north; and I looked forward to an exploration of their snowy recesses with great pleasure. The piney region of the mountains to the south was enveloped in smoke, and I was informed had been on fire for several months. Pike's peak is said to be visible from this place, about one hundred miles to the southward; but the smoky state of the atmosphere prevented my seeing it. The weather continued overcast during my stay here, so that I failed in determining the latitude, but obtained good observations for the time on the mornings of the 11th and 12th. An assumed latitude of 40° 22' 30" from the evening position of the 12th, enabled me to obtain for a tolerably correct longitude, 105° 12' 12".

12th.—The kindness of Mr. St. Vrain enabled me to obtain a couple of horses al d three good mules; and, with a further addition to our party of the Spaniard whom I had hired, and two others, who were going to obtain service at Laramie's fork, we resumed our journey at ten, on the morning of the 12th, we had been able to procure nothing at the post in the way of provision. An expected supply from Taos had not yet arrived, and a few pounds of coffee was all that could be spared to us. In addition to this we had dried meat enough for the first day; on the next, we expected to find buffalo. From this post, according to the estimate of the country, the fort at the mouth of Laramie's fork, which was our next point of destination, was nearly due north, distant about one hundred and twenty-five miles.

For a short distance our road lay down the valley of the Platte, which resembled a garden in the splendor of fields of varied flowers, which filled the air with fragrance. The only timber I noticed consisted of poplar, birch, cottonwood, and willow. In something less than three miles we crossed Thompson's creek, one of the affluents to the left bank of the South fork—a fine stream about sixty-five feet wide, and three feet deep. Journeying on, the low dark line of the Black hills lying between us and the mountains to the left, in about ten miles from the fort, we reached Cache a la Poudre, where we halted to noon. This is a very beautiful mountain stream, about one hundred feet wide, flowing with a full swift current over a rocky bed. We halted under the shade of some cotton woods, with which the stream is wooded scatteringly. In the upper part of its course, it runs amid the wildest mountain scenery, and, breaking through the Black hills, falls into the Platte about ten miles below this place. In the course of our late journey, I had managed to become the possessor of a very untractable mule—a perfect vixen— and her I had turned over `o my Spaniard. It occupied us about half an hour today to get the saddle upon her; but, once on her back,, Jose could not be dismounted, realizing the accounts given of Mexican horses and horsemanship, and we continued our route in the afternoon.

At evening, we encamped on Crow creek, having traveled about twenty-eight miles. None of the party were well acquainted with the country, and I had great difficulty in ascertaining what were the names of the streams we crossed between the North and 'South forks of the Platte. This I supposed to water stands in pools, having no continuous course. A fine grained sandstone made its appearance in the banks. The observations of the night placed us in latitude 40° 42', longitude 104° 57' 49". The barometer at sunset was 25.231; attached thermometer at 660. Sky clear, except in the east, with a light wind from the north.

13th.—There being no wood here, we used last night the bois de vache, which is very plentiful. At our camp this morning, the barometer was at 25.235; the attached thermometer 600. A few clouds were moving through a deep blue sky, with a light wind from the west. After a ride of twelve miles, in a northerly direction, over a plain covered with innumerable quantities of cacti, we reached a small creek in which there was water, and where several herds of buffalo were scattered about among the ravines, which always afford good pasturage. We seem now to be passing along the base of a plateau of the Black hills, in which the formation consists of marls, some of them white and laminated; the country to the left rising suddenly, and falling off gradually and uniformly to the right. In five or six miles of a northeasterly course, we struck a high ridge, broken into conical peaks, on whose summits large boulders were gathered in heaps. The magnetic direction of the ridge is northwest and southeast, the glittering white of its precipitous sides making it visible for many miles to the south. It is composed of a soft earthy limestone and marls, resembling that hereafter described in the neighborhood of the Chimney rock, on the North fork of the Platte, easily worked by the winds and rains, and sometimes moulded into very fantastic shapes. At the foot of the northern slope was the bed of a creek, some forty feet wide, coming, by frequent falls, from the bench above. It was shut in by high, perpendicular banks, in which were strata of white laminated marl. Its bed was perfectly dry, and the leading feature of the whole region is one of remarkable aridity, and perfect freedom from moisture. In about six miles we crossed the bed of another dry creek; and, continuing our ride over a high level prairie, a little before sundown we came suddenly upon beautiful creek which revived us with a feeling of delighted surprise by the pleasant contrast of the deep verdure of its banks with the parched desert we had passed. We had suffered much today, both men and horses, for want of water; having met with it but once in our uninterrupted march of forty miles; and an exclusive meal diet creates much thirst.

"Les bestias tienen mucha hombre," said the young Spaniard, inquiringly: "y genie tambien," said I, "amiago, we'll cam here." A stream of good and clear water ran winding abo through the little valley, and a herd of buffalo were quiet, feeding a little distance below. It was quite a hunter's paradise; and while some ran down towards the band to kill one for supper, others collected bois de vache for a fire, there being no wood; 'and I amused myself with hunting for plants among the grass.

It will be seen, by occasional remarks on the geological formation, that the constituents or the soil in these regions are good, and every day served to strengthen the impression in my mind, confirmed by subsequent observation, that the barren appearance of the country is due almost entirely to the extreme dryness of the climate. Along our route, the country had seemed to increase constantly in elevation. According to the Indication of the barometer, we were at our encampment 5,440 feet above the sea.

The evening was very clear, with a fresh breeze from the south, 500 east. The barometer at sunset was 24.862, the thermometer attached showing 68°. I supposed this to be a fork of Lodge Pole creek, so far as I could determine from our uncertain means of information. Astronomical observations gave for the camp a longitude of 104° 39' 37", and latitude 41° 08' 31".

14th.—The wind continued fresh from the same quarter in the morning; the day being clear, with the exception of a few clouds in the horizon. At our camp, at six o'clock, the height of the barometer was 24.830, the attached thermometer 61°. Our course this morning was directly north by compass, the variation being 15° or 16° easterly. A ride of four miles brought us to Lodge Pole creek, which we had seen at the mouth of the South fork; crossing on the way two dry streams, in eights en miles from our encampment of the past night, we reached a high bleak ridge, composed entirely of the same earthy limestone and marl previously described. I had never seen any thing which impressed so strongly on my mind a feeling of desolation. The valley, through which ran the waters of Horse creek, lay in view to the north, but too far to have any influence on the immediate view. On the peak of the ridge where I was standing, some seven hundred feet above the river, the wind was high and bleak; the barren and arid country seemed as if it had been swept by fires, and in every direction the same dull ash colored hue, derived from the formation, met the eye. On the summits were some stunted pines, many of them dead, all wearing the same ashen hue of desolation. We left the place with pleasure; and, after we had descended several hundred feet, halted in one of the ravines, which, at the distance of every mile or two, cut the flanks of the ridge with little rushing streams, wearing something of a mountain character. We had already begun to exchange the comparatively barren lands for those of a more fertile character. Though the sandstone formed the broken banks of the creek, yet they were covered with a thin grass; and the fifty or sixty feet which formed the bottom land of the little stream were clothed with very luxuriant grass, among which I remarked willow and cherry, (cerasus vir ginzana,) and a quantity of gooseberry and currant bushes occupied the greater part.

The creek was three or four feet broad, and about six inches deep, with a swift current of clear water, and tolerably cool We had struck it too low down to find the cold water, which we should have enjoyed nearer to its sources. At two, P. M., the barometer was at 25.050, and the attached thermometer 1040. A day of hot sunshine, with clouds, and moderate breeze from the south. Continuing down the stream, in about four miles we reached its mouth, at one of the main branches of Horse creek. Looking back upon the ridge, whose direct dot appeared to be a little to the north of east, we saw it seamed at frequent intervals with the dark lines of wooded streams, affluents of the river that flowed so far as we could

Bee along its base. We crossed, in the space of twelve miles from our noon halt, three or four forks of Horse creek, and encamped at sunset on the most easterly.

The fork on which we encamped appeared to have followed an easterly direction up to this place; but here it makes a very sudden bend to the north, passing' between two ranges of precipitous hills, called, as I was informed, Goshen's hole. There is somewhere in or near this locality a place so called, but I am not certain that it was the place of our encampment. Looking back upon the spot, at the distance of a few miles to the northward, the hills appear to shut in the prairie, through which runs the creek, with a semicircular sweep, which might very naturally be called a hole in the hills. The geological composition of the ridge is the same which constitutes the rock of the Courthouse and Chimney, on the North fork, which appeared to me a continuation of this ridge. The winds and rains work this formation into a variety of singular forms. The pass into Goshen's hole is about two miles wide, and the hill on the western side imitates, in an extraordinary manner, a massive fortified place, with a remarkable fulness of detail The rock is marl and earthy limestone, white, without the least appearance of vegetation, and much resembles masonry at a little distance; and here it sweeps around a level area two or three hundred yards in diameter, and in the form of a half moon, terminating on either extremity in enormous bastions. Along the whole line of the parapets appear domes and slender minarets, forty or fifty feet high, giving it every appearance of an old fortified town. On the waters of White river, where this formation exists in great extent, it presents appearances which excite the admiration of the solitary voyageur, and form a frequent theme of their conversation when speaking of the wonders of the country. Sometimes it offers the perfectly illusive appearance of a large city, with numerous streets and magnificent buildings, among which the Canadians never fail 'a see their cabaret—and sometimes it takes the form of a solitary house, with many large chambers, into which they drive their horses at night, and sleep in these native defences perfectly secure from any attack of prowling savages. Before reaching our camp at Goshen s hole, in crossing the immense detritus at the foot of the Castle rock, we were involved amidst winding passages cut by the waters of the hill; and where, with a breadth scarcely large enough for the passage of a horse, the walls rise thirty and forty feet perpendicularly. This formation supplies the discoloration of the Platte. At sunset, the height of the mercurial column was 25.500, the attached thermometer 80°, and wind moderate from S. 38° E. Clouds covered the sky with the rise of the moon, but I succeeded in obtaining the usual astronomical observations, which placed us in latitude 41° 40' 13", and longitude 104° 24' 36".

15th.—At six this morning, the barometer was at 25.515 the thermometer 720; the day was fine, with some clouds looking dark on the south, with a fresh breeze from the same quarter. We found that in our journey across the country we had kept too much to the eastward. This morning, accordingly, we traveled by compass some 15 or 20 to the west of north, and struck the Platte some thirteen miles below Fort Laramie. The day was extremely hot, and among the hills the wind seemed to have just issued from an oven.— Our horses were much distressed, as we had traveled hard; and it was with some difficulty that they were all brought to the Platte, which we reached at one o'clock. In riding in towards 'he river, we found the trail of our carts, which appeared to nave passed a day, or two since.

After having allowed our animals two hours for food and repose, we resumed our journey, and towards the close of the day came in sight of Laramie's fork. Issuing from the rivet hills, we came first in view of Fort Platte, a post belonging to Messrs. Sybille, Adams & Co., situated immediately in the point of land at the junction of Laramie with the Platte. Like the post we had visited on the South fork, it was built of earth, and still unfinished, being enclosed with walls (or rather houses) on three of the sides, and open on the fourth to the river. A few hundred yards brought us in view of the post of the American Fur Company, called Fort John or Laramie. This was a large post having more the air of military construction than the fort at the mouth of the river. It is on the left bank, on a rising ground some twenty-five feet above the water; and its lofty walls, whitewashed and picketed, with the large bastions at the angles, gave if quite an imposing appearance in the uncertain light of evening. A cluster of lodges, which the language told us belonged to Sioux Indians, was pitched under the walls; and, with the fine background of the Black hills and the prominent peak of Laramie mountain, strongly drawn in the clear light of the western sky, where the sun had already set, the whole formed at the moment a strikingly beautiful picture. From the company at St. Louis I had letters for Mr. Boudeau, the gentleman in charge of the post, by whom I was received with great hospitality and an efficient kindness, which was invaluable to me during my stay in the country. I found our people encamped on the bank, a short distance above the fort. All were well and, in the enjoyment of a bountiful supper, which coffee and bread made luxurious to us, we soon forgot the fatigues of the last ten days.

16th.—I, found that, during my absence, the situation of affairs had undergone some change; and the usual quiet and somewhat monotonous regularity of the camp had given place to excitement and alarm. The circumstances which occasioned this change will be found narrated in the following extract from the journal of Mr.

Preuss, which commences with the day of our separation on the South fork of the Platte:

"6th.—We crossed the plateau or highland between the two forks in about six hours. I let my horse go as slow as he liked, to indemnify us both for the previous hardship; and about noon we reached the North fork. There was no sign that our party had passed; we rode, therefore, to some pine trees, unsaddled the horses, and stretched our limbs on the grass, awaiting the arrival of our company. After remaining here two hours, my companion became impatient, mounted his horse again, and rode off down the river to see if he could discover our people. I felt so marode yet, that it was a horrible idea to me to bestride that saddle again; so I lay still. I knew they could not come any other way, and that my companion, one of the best men of the company, would not abandon me The sun went down—he did not come. Uneasy I did not fed but very hungry. I had no provisions, but I could make a fire; and as I espied two doves in a tree, I tried to kill one. But it needs a better marksman than myself to kill a little bird with a rifle. I made a fire, however, lighted my pipe—this true friend of mine in every emergency—lay down, and let my thoughts wander to the far east. It was not many minutes after when I heard the tramp of a horse, and my faithful companion was by my side. He had found the party, who had been delayed by making their cache, about seven miles below. To the good supper which he brought with him I did ample justice. He had forgotten salt, and I tried the soldier's substitute in time of war, and used gunpowder; but it answered badly—bitter enough, but no flavor of kitchen salt.. I slept well; and was only disturbed by two owls, which were attracted by the fire, and took their place in the tree under which, we slept. Their music seemed as disagreeable to my companion as to myself; he fired his rifle twice, and then they let us alone.

"7th.—At about 10 o'clock, the party arrived; and we continued our journey through a country which offered but little to interest the traveler. The soil was much more sandy than in the valley below the confluence of the forks, and the face of the country no longer presented the refreshing green which had hitherto characterized it.

The rich grass was now found only in dispersed spots, on low grounds, and on the bottom land of the streams. A long drought, joined to extreme heat, had so parched up the upper prairies, that they were in many places bald, or covered only with a thin growth of yellow and poor grass. The nature of the soil renders it extremely susceptible to the vicissitudes of the climate. Between the forks, and from their junction to the Black hills, the formation consists of marl and a soft earthy limestone, with granitic sand stone. Such a formation cannot give rise to a sterile soil; and, on our return in September, when the country had been watered by frequent rains, the valley of the Platte looked like a garden; so rich was the verdure of the grasses, and so luxuriant the bloom of abundant flowers. The wild sage begins to make its appearance, and timber is so scarce that we generally made our fires of the Bois de vache. With the exception of now and then an isolated tree or two, standing like a light house on the river bank, there is none to be seen.

"8th.—Our road today was a solitary one. No game made its appearance—not even a buffalo or a stray antelope; and nothing occurred to break the monotony until about 5 o'clock, when the caravan made a sudden halt. There was a galloping in of scouts and horsemen from every side—a hurrying to and fro in noisy confusion; rifles were taken from their covers; bullet pouches examined: in short, there was the cry of 4 Indians, heard again. I had become so much accustomed to these alarms, that they now made but little impression on me; and before I had time to become excited, the newcomers were ascertained to be whites. It was a large party of traders and trappers, conducted by Mr. Bridger, a man well known in the history of the country. As the sun was low, and there was a fine grass patch not far ahead, they turned back and encamped for the night with us. Mr. Bridger was invited to supper; and, after the tablecloth was removed, we listened with eager interest to an account of their adventures. What they had met, we would be likely to encounter; the chances which had befallen them, would probably happen to us; and we looked upon their life as a picture of our own. He informed us that the condition of the country had become exceedingly dangerous. The Sioux, who had been badly disposed, had broken out into open hostility, and in the preceding autumn his party had encountered them in a severe engagement, in which a number of lies had been lost on both sides. United with the Cheyenne and Gros Ventre Indians, they were scouring the upper country in war parties of great force, and were at this time in the neighborhood of the Red Buttes, a famous landmark, which was directly in our path. They had declared war, upon every living thing that should be found westward of that point , though the main object was to attack a large camp of whites and Snake Indians, who had a rendezvous in the Sweet Water valley. Availing hims If of his intimate knowledge of the country, he had reached Laramie by an unusual route through the Black hills, and avoided coming into contact with any of the scattered parties. This gentleman offered his services to accompany us as far as the head of the Sweet Water; but the absence of our leader, which was deeply regretted by us all, rendered it impossible for us to enter upon such arrangements In a camp consisting of men whose lives had been spent it this country, I expected to find every one prepared for occurrences of this nature; but, to my great surprise, I found, of the contrary, that this news had thrown them all into the greatest consternation; and, on every side, I heard only one exclamation, '11 n'y aura pas de vie pour nous.' All the night, scattered groups were assembled around the fires, smoking their pipes, and listening with the greatest eagerness to exaggerated details of Indian hostilities; and in the morning I found the camp dispirited, and agitated by a variety of conflicting opinions. A majority of the people were strongly disposed to return; but Clement Lambert, with some five or six others professed their determination to follow Mr. Fremont to the uttermost limit of his journey. The others yielded to their remonstrances, and somewhat ashamed of their cowardice, con eluded to advance at least as far as Laramie fork, eastward of which they were aware no danger was to be apprehended. Notwithstanding the confusion and excitement, we were very early on the road, as the days were extremely hot, and we were anxious to profit by the freshness of the morning. The soft manly formation, over which we were now journeying, frequently offers to the traveler views of remarkable and picturesque beauty. To several of these localities, where the winds and the rain have worked the bluffs into curious shapes, the voyageurs have given names according to some fancied resemblance. One of these, called the Courthouse, we passed about six miles from our encampment of last night, and towards noon came in sight of the celebrated Chimney rock. It looks, at this distance of about thirty miles, like what it is called—the long chimney of a steam factory establishment, or a shot tower in Baltimore. Nothing occurred to interrupt the quiet of the day, and we encamped on the river, after a march a twenty-four miles. Buffalo had become very scarce, and but one cow had been killed, of which the meat had been cut into thin slices, and hung around the carts to dry.

"10th.—We continued along the same fine plainly beaten road, which the smooth surface of the country afforded us, for a distance of six hundred and thirty miles, from the frontiers of Missouri to the Laramie fork. In the course of the day we met some whites, who were following along in the train of Mr. Bridger; and, after a day's journey of twenty-four miles, encamped about sunset at the Chimney rock. It consists of marl and earthy limestone, and the weather is rapidly diminishing its height, which is not more than two hundred feet above the river. Travelers who visited it some years since, placed its height at upwards of 500 feet.

"11th.—The valley of the North fork is of a variable breadth, from one to four, and sometimes six miles. Fifteen miles from the Chimney rock we leached one of those places where the river strikes the bluffs, and forces the road to make a considerable circuit over the uplands, This presented an escarpment on the river of about nine hundred yards in length, and is familiarly known as Scott's bluffs. We had made a journey of thirty miles before we again struck the river, at a place where some scanty grass afforded an insufficient pasturage to our animals. About twenty miles from the Chimney rock we had found a very beautiful spring of excellent and cold water; but it was in such a deep ravine, and so small, that the animals could not profit by it, and we therefore halted only a few minutes, and found a' resting place ten miles further on. The plain between Scott's bluffs and Chimney rock was almost entirely covered with driftwood, consisting principally of cedar, which, we were informed, had been supplied from the Black hills, in a flood five or six years since.

"12th.—Nine miles from our encampment of yesterday we crossed Horse creek, a shallow stream of clear water, about seventy yards wide, falling into the Platte on the light bank. It was lightly timbered, and great plentities of driftwood were piled up on the banks, appearing to be supplied by the creek from above. After a journey of twenty-six miles, we encamped on a rich bottom, which afforded fine grass to our animals Buffalo have entirely disappeared, and we live now upon the dried meat, which is exceedingly poor food. The marl and earthy limestone, which constituted the formation for several days past, had changed, during the day, into a compact white or grayish white limestone, sometimes containing hornstone; and at the place of our encampment this evening, some strata in the river hills cropped out to the height of thirty or forty feet, consisting of fine-grained granitic sandstone; one of the strata closely resembling gneiss.

"13th.—Today, about four o'clock, we reached Fort Laramie, where we were cordially received. We pitched our camp a little above the fort, on the bank of the Laramie river, in which the pure and clear water of the mountain stream looked refreshingly cool, and made a pleasant contrast to the muddy, yellow waters of the Platte."

I walked up to visit our friends at the fort, which is a quadangular structure, built of clay, after the fashion of the Mexicans, who are generally employed in building them. The walls are about fifteen feet high, surmounted with a wooden palisade, and term a portion of ranges of houses, which entirely surround a yard of about one hundred and thirty feet square. Every apartment has its door and window,—all, of course, opening on the inside. There are two entrances, opposite each other, and midway the wall, one of which is a large and public entrance; the other smaller and more private—a sort of postern gap. Over the great entrance is a square tower with loopholes, and, like the rest of the work, built of earth. At two of the angles, and diagonally opposite each other, are large square bastions, so arranged as to sweep the four faces of the walls.

This post belongs to the American Fur Company, and, at the time of our visit, was in charge of Mr. Boudeau: Two of the company's clerks, Messrs. Galpin and Kellogg, were with him, and he had in the fort about sixteen men. As usual, these had found wives among the Indian squaws; and, with the usual accompaniment of children, the place had quite a populous appearance. It is hardly necessary to say, that the object of the establishment is trade with the neighboring tribes, who, in the course of the year, generally make two or three visits to the fort. In addition to this, traders, with a small outfit, are constantly kept amongst them. The articles of trade consist, on the one side, almost entirely of buffalo robes; and, on the other, of blankets, calicoes, guns, powder and lead, with such cheap ornaments as glass beads, looking glasses, rings, vermilion for painting, tobacco, and principally, and in spite of the prohibition, of spirits, brought into the, country in the form of alcohol, and diluted with water before sold. While mentioning this fact, it is but justice to the American Fur Company to state, that, throughout the country, I have always found them strenuously opposed to the introduction of spirituous liquors. But in the present state of things, when the country is supplied with alcohol—when a keg of it will purchase from an Indian every thing he possesses—his furs, his lodge, his horses, and even his wife and children—and when any vagabond who has money enough to purchase a mule can go into a village and trade against them successfully, without withdrawing entirely from the trade, it is impossible for them to discontinue its use. In their opposition to this practice, the company is sustained, not only by their obligation to the laws of the country and the welfare of the Indians, but clearly, also, on grounds of policy; for, with heavy and expensive outfits, they contend at manifestly great disadvantage against the numerous independent and unlicensed traders, who enter the country from various avenues, from the United States and from Mexico, having no other stock in trade than some kegs of liquor, which they sell at the modest price of thirty-six dollars per gallon. The difference between the regular trader and the coureur des bois, (as the French call the Itinerant or peddling traders,) with respect to the sale of spirits, is here, as it always has been, fixed and permanent, and growing out of the nature of their trade. The regular trader looks ahead, and has an interest in the preservation of the Indians, and in the regular pursuit of their business, and the preservation of their arms, horses, and every thing necessary to their future and permanent success in hunting: the coureur des bois has nc permanent interest, and gets what he can, and for what he can, from every Indian he meets, even at the risk of disabling him from doing any thing more at hunting.

The fort had a very cool and clean appearance. The great entrance, in which I found the gentlemen assembled, and which was floored, and about fifteen feet long, made a pleasant, shaded seat, through which the breeze swept constantly; for this country Le famous for high winds. In the course of the conversation, I learned the following particulars, which will explain the condition of the country. For several years the Cheyennes and Sioux had gradually become more and more hostile to the whites, and in the latter part of August, 1841, had had a rather severe engagement with a part) of sixty men, under the command of Mr. Frapp of St. Louis. The Indians lost eight or ten warriors, and the whites had their leader and four men killed. This fight took place on the waters of Snake river; and it was this party, on their return under Mr. Bridger, which had spread so much alarm among my people. In the course of the spring, two other small parties had been cut off by the Sioux—one on their return from the Crow nation, and the other among the Black hills. The emigrants to Oregon and Mr. Bridger's party met here, a few days before our arrival. Divisions and misunderstandings had grown up among them; they were already somewhat disheartened by the fatigue of their long and wearisome Journey, and the feet of their cattle had become so much worn as to be scarcely able to travel. In this situation, they were not likely to find encouragement in the hostile attitude of the Indians, and the new and unexpected difficulties which sprang up before them. They were told that the country was entirely swept of grass, and that few or no buffalo were to be found on their line of route; and, with their weakened animals, it would be impossible for them to transport their heavy wagons over the mountains. Under these circumstances, they disposed of their wagons and cattle at the forts; selling them at the prices they had paid in the State's, and taking in exchange coffee and sugar at one dollar a pound, and miserable worn-out horses, which died before they reached the mountains. Mr. Boudeau informed me that he had purchased thirty, and the lower fort eighty head of fine cattle, some of them of the Durham breed. Mr. Fitzpatrick whose name and high reputation are familiar to all who interest themselves in the history of this country, had reached Laramie in company with Mr. Bridger; and the emigrants were fortunate enough to obtain his services to guide them as far as the British post of Fort Hall, about two hundred and fifty miles beyond the South Pass of the mountains. They had started for this post on the 4th of July, and immediately after their departure, a war party of three hundred and fifty braves set out upon their trail. As their principal chief or partisan had lost some relations in the recent fight, and had sworn to kill the first whites on his path, it was supposed that their intention was to attack the party, should a favorable opportunity offer; or, if they were foiled in their principal object by the vigilance of Mr. Fitzpatrick, content themselves with stealing horses and cutting off stragglers. These had been gone but a few days previous to our arrival.

The effect of the engagement with Mr. Frapp had been greatly to irritate the hostile spirit of the savages; and immediately subsequent to that event, the Gross Ventre Indians had united with the Oglallahs and Cheyennes, and taken the field in great force—so far as I could ascertain, to the amount of eight hundred lodges. Their object was to make an attack on a camp of Snake and Crow Indians, and a body of about one hundred whites, who had made a rendezvous somewhere in the Green river valley, or on the Sweet Water. After spending some time in buffalo hunting in the neighborhood of the Medicine Bow mountain, they were to cross over to the Green river waters, and return to Laramie by way of the South Pass and the Sweet Water valley. According to the calculation of the Indians, Mr. Boudeau informed me they were somewhere near the head of the Sweet Water. I subsequently learned that the party led by Mr. Fitzpatrick were overtaken by their pursuers near Rock Independence, in the valley of the Sweet Water; but his skill and resolution saved them from surprise; and, small as his force was, they did not venture to attack him continuing up the valley, they came suddenly upon the large village. From these they met with a doubtful reception. Long residence and familiar acquaintance had given to Mr. Fitzpatrick great personal influence among them, and a portion of them were disposed to let him pass quietly; but by far the greater number were inclined to hostile measures; and the, chiefs spent the whole of one night, during which they kept the little party in the midst of them, in council, debating the question of attacking them the next day; but the influence of " the Broken Hand," as they called Mr. Fitzpatrick, (one of his hands having „been shattered by the bursting of a gun,) at length prevailed, and obtained, for them an unmolested passage; but they sternly assured him that this path was no longer open, and that any party of the whites which should hereafter be found upon it would meet with certain destruction. From all that I have been able to learn, I have no doubt that the emigrants owe their lives to Mr. Fitzpatrick.

Thus it would appear that the country was swarming with scattered war parties; and when I heard, during the day, the, various contradictory and exaggerated rumors which were incessantly repeated to them, I was not surprised that so much alarm prevailed among my men. Carson, one of the best and most experienced mountaineers, fully supported the opinion given by Bridger of the dangerous state of the country, and openly expressed his conviction that we could not escape without some sharp encounters with the Indians. In addition to this, he made his will; and among the circumstances which were constantly occurring to increase their alarm, this was the most unfortunate; and I found that a number of my party had become so much intimidated, that they had requested to be discharged at this place. I dined today at Fort Platte, which has been mentioned as situated at the junction of Laramie river with the Nebraska. Here I heard a confirmation of the statements given above. The party of warriors, which had started a few days since on the trail of the emigrants, was expected hack in fourteen days, to join the village with which their families and the old men had remained. The arrival of the latter was hourly expected; and some Indians have just come in who had left them on the Laramie fork, about twenty miles above. Mr. Bissonette, one of the traders belonging to Fort Platte, urged the propriety of taking with me an interpreter and two or three old men of the village; in which case, he thought there would be little or no hazard in encountering any of the war parties. The principal danger was in being attacked before they should know who we were.

They had a confused idea of the numbers and power of our people, and dreaded to bring upon themselves the military force of the United States. This gentleman, who spoke the language fluently, offered his services to accompany me so far as the Red Buttes. He was desirous to join the large party on its return, for purposes of trade, and it would suit his views, as well as my own, to go with us to the Buttes; beyond which point it would be impossible to prevail on a Sioux to venture, on account of their fear of the Crows. From Fort Laramie to the Red Buttes, by the ordinary road, is one hundred and thirty-five miles; and, though only on the threshold of danger, it seemed better to secure the services of an interpreter for the partial distance, than to have none at all.

So far as frequent interruption from the Indians would allow, we occupied ourselves in making some astronomical calculations, and bringing the general map to this stage of our journey; but the tent was generally occupied by a succession of our ceremonious visitors. Some came for presents, and others for information of our object in coming to the country; now and then, one would dart up to the tent on horseback, jerk off his trappings, and stand silently at the door, holding his horse by the halter, signifying his desire to trade. Occasionally a savage would stalk in with an invitation to a feast of honor, a Jog feast, and deliberately sit down and wait quietly until I was ready to accompany him. I went to one; the women and children were sitting outside the lodge, and we took our seats on buffalo robes spread around. The dog was in a large pot over the fire, in the middle of the lodge, and immediately on our arrival was dished up in large wooden bowls, one of which was handed to each. The flesh appeared very glutinous, with something of the flavor and appearance of mutton. Feeling something move behind me, I looked round, and found that I had taken my seat among a litter of fat young puppies. Had I been nice in such matters, the prejudices of civilization might have interfered with my tranquillity; but, fortunately, I am not of delicate nerves, and continued quietly to empty my platter.

The weather was cloudy at evening, with a moderate south wind, and the thermometer at six o'clock 85o. I was disappointed in my hope of obtaining an observation of an occultation, which took place about midnight. The moon brought with her heavy banks of clouds, through which she scarcely made her appearance during the night.

The morning of the 18th was cloudy and calm, the thermometer at six o'clock at 64o. About nine, with a moderate wine from the west, a storm of rain came on, accompanied by sharp thunder and lightning, which lasted about an hour. During the day the expected village arrived, consisting principally of old men, women, and children. They had a considerable number of horses, and large troops of dogs. Their lodges were pitched near the fort, and our camp was constantly crowded with Indians of all sizes, from morning until night, at which time some of the soldiers generally came to drive them all off to the village. My tent was the only place which they respected. Here only came the chiefs and men of distinction, and generally one of them remained to drive away the women and children. The numerous strange instruments, applied to still stranger uses, excited awe and admiration among them; and those which I used in talking with the sun and stars they looked upon with especial reverence, as mysterious things of.4 great medicine."

Of the three barometers which I had brought with me thus far successfully, I found that two were out of order, and spent the greater part of the 19th in repairing them—an operation of no small difficulty in the midst of the incessant interruptions to which I was subjected. We had the misfortune to break here a large _thermometer, graduated to show fifths of a degree, which I used to ascertain the temperature of boiling water, and with which I had promised myself some interesting experiments in the mountains. We had but one remaining, on which the graduation extended sufficiently high; and this was too small for exact observations. During our stay here, the man had been engaged in making numerous repairs, arranging packsaddles, and otherwise preparing for the chance of a rough road and mountain travel. All things of this nature being ready, I gathered them around me in the evening, and told them that " I had determined to proceed the next day. They were all well armed. I had engaged the services of Mr. Bissonette as interpreter, and had taken, in the circumstances, every possible means to ensure our safety. In the rumors we had heard, I believed there was much exaggeration; that they were men accustomed to this kind of life and to the country; and that these were the dangers of everyday occurrence, aid to be expected in the ordinary course of their service. They had heard of the unsettled condition of the country before leaving St. Louis, and therefore could not make it a reason for breaking their engagements. Still, I was unwilling to take with me, on a service of some certain danger, men on whom I could not rely; and I had understood that there were among them some who were disposed to cowardice and anxious to return; they had but to come forward at once, and state their desire, and they would be discharged, with the amount due to them for the time they had served." To their honor be it said, there was but one among them who had the face to come forward and avail himself of the permission. I asked him some few questions, in order to expose him to the ridicule of the men, and let him go. The day after our departure, he engaged himself to one of the forts, and set off with a party to the Upper Missouri. I did not think that the situation of the country justified me in _taking our young companions, Messrs. Brant and Benton, along with us. In case of misfortune, it would have been thought, at the least, an act of great imprudence; and therefore, though reluctantly, ' determined to leave them. Randolph had been the life of the camp, and the "petit garcon" was much regretted by the trim, to whom his buoyant, spirits had afforded great merryment. They all, however, agreed in the propriety of leaving aim at the fort, because, as they said, he might cost the lives of some of the men in a fight with the Indians.

21st.—A portion of our baggage, with our field notes and observations, and several instruments, were left at the fort. One of the gentlemen, Mr. Galpin, took charge of a barometer which he engaged to observe during my absence; and I in trusted to Randolph, by way of occupation, the regular winding up of two of my chronometers, which were among the instruments left. Our observations showed that the chronometer which I retained for the continuation of our voyage had preserved its rate in a most satisfactory manner. As deduced from it, the longitude of Fort Laramie is 7h 01' 21", and from lunar distance 7h 01'.29"; giving for the adopted longitude 104° 47' 43". Comparing the barometrical observations made during our stay here, with those of Dr. G. Engleman at St Louis, we find for the elevation of the fort above the Gulf of Mexico 4,470 feet. The winter climate here is remarkably mild for the latitude; but rainy weather is frequent, and the place is celebrated for winds, of which the prevailing one is the west. An east wind in summer, and a south wind in winter, are said to be always accompanied with rain.

We were ready to depart; the tents were struck, the mules geared up, and our horses saddled, and we walked up to the fort to take the stirrup cup with our friends in an excellent homebrewed preparation. While thus pleasantly engaged, seated in one of the little cool chambers, at the door of which a man had been stationed to prevent all intrusion from the Indians, a number of chiefs, several of them powerful, fine-looking men, forced their way into the room in spite of all opposition. Handing me the following letter, they took their seats in silence:—

"FORT PLATTE, Juillet 21, 1842.

"MR. FREMONT:—Les chefs s'etant assembles presentement me disent de voue avertir de ne point vous mettre en route, avant que le parti de jeunes gene, qui est eo dehors, aoient de retour. De plus, ils me disent qu'ils soot treecertain gulls feront feu a la premiere rencontre. 116 doivent etre de retour dans rept a huit jours. Excusez si je vous fais ces observations, maim it me semble qu'il est mop devoir de vous avertir do danger. Mame le plus, les chefs scut lesoporteurs de ce billet, qui vow defendent de partis avant le retour dee guerriers.

"Je suis votre °beimserviteur,

"JOSEPH BISSONETTE,

"Par L. B. CHARTRAIN.

"Les noms de quelques chefs.—Le Chapeau de Loutre, le Cassels de

Caches, la Nuit Noir la Queue de Bœuf."

[Translation.]

"FORT PLATTE, Jury 21, 1842. "MR. Fimmosix:—The chiefs having assembled in council, have just told me to warn you not to set out before the party of young men which is now out shall have returned. Furthermore, they tell me that they are very sure they will fire upon you as soon as they meet you. They are expected back in seven or eight days. Excuse me for making these observations, but it seems my duty to warn you of danger. Moreover, the chiefs who prohibit your setting out before the return of the warriors are the bearers of this note "I am your obedient servant,

"JOSEPH BISSONETTE,

"By L. B. CHARTRAIN.

"Names of some of the chiefs.—The Otter Hat, the Breaker of Arrows, the Black Night, the Bull's Tail."

After reading this, I mentioned its purport to my companions; and, seeing that all were fully possessed of its contents, one of the Indians rose up, and, having first shaken hands with me, spoke as follows:

"You have come among us at a bad time. Some of our people have been killed, and our young men, who are gone to the mountains, are eager to avenge the blood of their relations, which has been shed by the whites. Our young men are bad, and, if they meet you, they will believe that you are carrying goods and ammunition to their enemies, and will fire upon you. You have told us that this will make war. We know that our great father has many soldiers and big guns, and we are anxious to have our lives. We love the whites, and are desirous of peace. Thinking of all these things, we have determined to keep you here until our warriors return. We are glad to see you among us. Our father is rich, and we expected that you would have brought presents to us— horses, guns.

9 and blankets. But we are glad to see you. We look upon your coming as the light which goes before the sun; for you will tell our great father that you have seen us, and that we are naked and poor, and have nothing to eat; and he will send us all these things." He was followed by others to the same effect.

The observations of the savage appeared reasonable; but I was aware that they had in view only the present object of detaining me, and were unwilling I should go further into the country. In reply, I asked them, through the interpretator of Mr. Boudeau, to select two or three of their number to accompany us until we should meet their people—they should spread their robes in my tent, and eat at my table, and on their return I would give them presents in reward of their services. They declined, saying, that there were no young men left in the village, and that they were too old to travel so many days on horseback, and preferred now to smoke their pipes in the lodge, and let the warriors go on the warpath. Besides, they had no power over the young men, and were afraid to interfere with them. In my turn I addressed them.

"You say that you love the whites; why have you killed so many already this spring? You say that you love the whites, and are full of many expressions of friendship to us; but you are not willing to undergo the fatigue of a few days' ride to save our lives. We do not believe what you have said, and will not listen to you. Whatever a chief among us tells his soldiers to do, is done. We are the soldiers of that great chief, your father. He has told us to come here and see this country, and all the Indians, his children. Why should we not go? Before we came, we heard that you had killed his people, and ceased to be his children; but we came among you peaceably, holding out our hands. Now we find that the stories we heard are not lies, and that you are no longer, his friends and children. We have thrown away our bodies, and will not turn back. When you told us that your young men would kill us, you did not know that our hearts were strong and you did not see the rifles which my young men carry it their 'hands. We are few, and you are many, and may kill us all; but there will be much crying in your villages, for many of your young men will stay behind, and forget to return with your warriors from the mountains. Do you think that our great chief will let his soldiers die, and forget to cover their graves? Before he snows melt again, his warriors will sweep away your villages as the fire does the prairie in the autumn. See! I have pulled down my white houses, and my people are ready: when the sun is ten paces higher, we shall go on the march. If you have any thing to tell us, you will say it soon."

I broke up the conference, as I could do nothing with these people; and, being resolved to proceed, nothing was to be gained by delay. Accompanied by Our hospitable friends, we returned to the camp. We had mounted our horses, and our parting salutations had been exchanged, when one of the chiefs (the Bull's Tail) arrived to tell me that they had determines to send a young man with us; and if I would point out the place of our evening camp, he should join us there. " The young man is poor,' said he; " he has no horse, and expects you to give him one," I described to him the place where I intended to encamp, and, shaking hands, in a few minutes we were among the hills, and this last habitation of whites shut out from our view.

The road led over an interesting plateau between the North fork of the Platte on the right, and Laramie river on the left. At the distance of ten miles from the fort, we entered the sandy bed of a creek, a kind of defile, shaded by precipitous rocks, down which we wound our way for several hundred yards, to a place where, on the left bank, a very large spring gushes with considerable noise and force out of the limestone rock. It is called the " Warm Spring," and furnishes to the hitherto dry bed of the creek a considerable rivulet. On the opposite side, a little below the spring, is a lofty limestone escarpment, partially shaded by a grove of large trees, whose green foliage, in contrast with the whiteness of the rock, renders this a picturesque locality. The rock is fossiliferous, and, so far as I was able to determine the character of the fossils, belongs to the carboniferous limestone of the Missouri river, and is probably the western limit of that formation. Beyond this point I met with as fossils of any description.

I was desirous to visit the Platte near the point where it leaves the Black hills, and therefore followed this stream, for two or three miles, to its mouth, where I encamped on a spot which afforded good grass and prele (equisetum) for our animals. Our tents having 'been found too thin to protect ourselves and the instruments from the rains, which in this ele7ated country are attended with cold and unpleasant weather, I had procured from the Indians at Laramie a tolerably large lodge, about eighteen feet in diameter, and twenty feet in height. Such a lodge, when properly pitched, is, from its conical form, almost perfectly secure against the violent winds which are frequent in this region, and, with a fire in the centre, is a dry and warm shelter in bad weather. By raising the lower part, so as to permit the breeze to pass freely, it is converted into a pleasant summer residence, with the extraordinary advantage of being entirely free from musquitoes, one of which I never saw in an Indian lodge. While we were engaged very unskilfully in erecting this, the interpreter, Mr. Bissonette, arrived, accompanied by the Indian and his wife. She laughed at our awkwardness, and offered her assistance, which we were frequently afterwards obliged to avail our selves, before the men acquired sufficient expertness to pitch it without difficulty. From this place we had a fine view of the gorge where the Platte issues from the. Black hills, changing its character abruptly from a mountain stream into a river of the plains: immediately around us the valley of the stream was, tolerably open; and at the distance of a few miles, where the river had cut its way through the hills, was the narrow cleft, on one side of which a lofty precipice of bright red rock rose vertically above the low hills which lay between us.

22d.—In the morning, while breakfast was being prepared, I visited this place with my favorite man, Basil Lajeuriesse., Entering so far as there was footing for the mules, we dismounted,, and, tying our animals, continued our way on foot. Like the whole country, the scenery of the, river had under gone an entire change, and was in this place the most beautiful have ever seen. The breadth of the stream, generally near that of its valley, was from two to three hundred feet, with a swift current, occasionally broken by rapids, and the water perfectly clear. On either side rose the red precipices, and sometimes overhanging, two and four hundred feet in height, crowned with green summits, on which were scattered a few pines.

At the foot of the rocks was the usual detritus, formed of masses fallen from above. Among the pines that grew here, and on the occasional banks, were the cherry, (cerasus virgzniana,) currants, and grains de boeuf; (shepherdia argentea.) Viewed In the sunshine of a pleasant morning, the scenery was of a most striking and romantic beauty, which arose from the picturesque disposition of the objects, and the vivid contrast of colors. I thought with much pleasure of our approaching descent in the canoe through such interesting places; and, in the expectation of being able at that time to give to them a full examination, did not now dwell so much as might have been desirable upon the geological formations along the line of the river, where they are developed with great clearness. The upper portion, of the red strata consists of very compact clay, in which are occasionally seen imbedded large pebbles. Below was a stratum of compact red sandstone, changing a little above the river into a very hard silicious limestone. There is a small but handsome open prairie immediately below this place, on the left bank of the river, which would be a good locality for a military post. There are some open groves of cottonwood on the Platte. The small stream which comes in at this place is well timbered with pine, and good building rock: is abundant.

If it is in contemplation to keep open the communication with Oregon territory, a show of military force in this country is absolutely necessary; and a combination of advantages renders the neighborhood of Fort Laramie the most suitable place, on the line of the Platte, for the establishment of a military post. It is connected with the mouth of the Platte and the Upper Missouri by excellent roads, which are in frequent use, and would not in any way interfere with the range of the buffalo, on which the neighboring Indians mainly depend for support. It would render any posts on the Lower Platte unnecessary; the ordinary communication between it and the Missouri being sufficient to control the intermediate Indians. It would operate effectually to prevent any such coalitions as are now formed among the Gros Ventres, Sioux, Cheyennes, and other Indians, and would keep the Oregon road through the valley of the tweet Water and the South Pass of the mountains constantly open. It lies at the foot of a broken and mountainous region, along which, by the establishment of small posts in the neighborhood of St. Vrain's fort, on the South fork of the Platte, and Bent's fort, on the Arkansas, a line of communication would be formed, by good wagon roads, with our southern military posts, which would entirely command the mountain passes, hold some of the most troublesome tribes in check, and protect and facilitate our intercourse with the neighboring Spanish settlements. The valleys of the rivers on which they would be situated are fertile; the country, which supports immense herds of buffalo, is admirably adapted to grazing; and herds of cattle might be maintained by the posts, or obtained from the Spanish country, which already supplies a portion of their provisions to the trading posts mentioned above.

Just as we were leaving the camp this morning, our Indian came up, and stated his intention of not proceeding any further until he had seen the horse which I intended to give him. I felt strongly tempted to drive him out of the camp; but his presence appeared to give confidence to my men, and the interpreter thought it absolutely necessary. I was therefore obliged to do what he requested, and pointed out the animal, with which he seemed satisfied, and we continued our journey. I had imagined that Mr. Bissonette's long residence had made hip acquainted with the country; and, according to his advice, proceeded directly forward, without attempting to gain the usual road. He afterwards informed me that he had rarely ever lost sight of the fort; but the effect of the mistake was to involve us for a day or two among the hills, where, although we lost no time, we encountered an exceedingly rough road.

To the south, along our line of march today, the main chain of the Black or Laramie hills rises precipitously. Time lid not permit me to visit them; but, from comparative information, the ridge is composed of the coarse sandstone or conglomerate hereafter described. It appears to enter the region of clouds, which are arrested in their course, and lie in masses along the summits. An inverted cone of black cloud (cumulus) rested during all the: forenoon on the lofty peak Laramie mountain, which I estimated to be about two thousand feet above the fort, or six thousand five hundred above he sea. We halted to noon on the Fourche Amere, so called, from being timbered principally with the hard amere, (a species of poplar,) with which the valley of the little stream is tolerably well wooded, and which, with large expansive summits, grows to the height of sixty or seventy feet.

The bed of the creek is sand and gravel, the water dispersed over the broad bed in several shallow streams. We found here, on the right bank, in the shade of the trees, a fine spring of very cold water. It will be remarked that I do not mention, in this portion of the journey, the temperature of the air, and, springs, &c.—an omission which will be explained in due course of the narrative. In my search for plants, I was well rewarded at this place.

With the change in the geological formation on leaving Fort Laramie, the whole face of the country has entirely altered its appearance. Eastward of that meridian, the principal objects which strike the eye of a traveler are the absence of timber, and the immense expanse of prairie, covered with the verdure of rich grasses, and highly adapted for pasturage. Wherever they are not disturbed by the vicinity of man, large herds of buffalo give animation to this country. Westward of Laramie river, the region is sandy, and apparently sterile; and the place of the grass is usurped by the artemisia and other odoriferous plants, to whose growth the sandy soil and dry air of this elevated region seem highly favorable.

One of the prominent characteristics in the face of the country is the extraordinary abundance of the artemisias. They grow everywhere—on the hills, and over the river bottoms, in tough, twisted, wiry clumps; and, wherever the beaten track was left, they rendered the progress of the carts rough and slow. As the country increased in elevation on our advance to the west, they increased in size; and the whole air is strongly impregnated and saturated with the odor of camphor and spirits of turpentine which belongs to this plant. This climate has been found very favorable to, the restoration of health, particularly in cases of consumption; and possibly the respiration of air so highly impregnated with aromatic plants may have some influence.

Our dried meat had given out, and we began to be in want of food; but one of the hunters killed an antelope this evening, which afforded some relief, although it did not go far among so many hungry men. At eight o'clock at night, after a march of twenty-seven miles, we reached our proposed encampment on the FeràCheval, or Horseshoe creek. Here we found good grass, with a great quantity of prele, which furnished good food for our tired animals. This creek is well timbered, principally with Hard amere, and, with the exception of Deer creek, which we had not yet reached, is the largest affluent of the right bank between Laramie and the mouth of the Sweet Water.

23d.—The present year had been one of unparalleled drought, and throughout the country the water had been almost dried up. By availing themselves of the annual rise, the traders had invariably succeeded in carrying their furs to the Missouri; but this season, as has already been mentioned, on both forks of the Platte they had entirely failed. The greater number of the springs, and many of the streams, which made halting places for the voyageurs, had been dried up. Everywhere the soil looked parched and burnt, the scanty yellow grass crisped under the foot, and even the hardest plants were destroyed by want of moisture. I think it necessary to mention this fact, because the rapid evaporation in such an elevated region, nearly five thousand feet above the sea, almost wholly unprotected by timber, should be attributed much of the sterile appearance of the country, in the destruction of vegetation, and the numerous saline efflorescences which covered the ground. Such I afterwards found to be the case.

I was informed that the roving villages of Indians and travelers had never met with difficulty in finding abundance of grass for their horses; and now it was after great search that we were able to find a scanty patch of grass sufficient to keep them from sinking; and in the course of a day or two they began to suffer very much. We found none today at noon; and, in the course of our search on the Platte, came to a grove of cottonwood, where some Indian village had recently encamped. Boughs of the cottonwood yet green covered the ground, which the Indians had cut down to feed their horses upon. It is only in the winter that recourse is had to this means of sustaining them; and their resort to it at this time was a striking evidence of the state of the country. We followed their example, and turned our horses into a grove of young poplars. This began to present itself as a very serious evil, for on our animals depended altogether the further prosecution of our journey.

Shortly after we had left this place, the scouts came galloping in with the alarm of Indians. We turned in immediately towards the river, which here had a steep, high bank, where we formed with the carts a very close barricade, resting on the river, within which the animals were strongly hobbled and picketed. The guns were discharged and reloaded, and men thrown forward under cover of the bank, in the direction by which the Indians were expected. Our interpreter, who, with the Indian, had gone to meet them, came in, in about ten minutes, accompanied by two Sioux. They looked sulky, and we could obtain from them only some confused information. We learned that they belonged to the party which had been on the trail of the emigrants, whom they had overtaken at Rock Independence, on the Sweet Water. Here the party had disagreed, and came nigh fighting among themselves. One portion were desirous of attacking the whites, but the others were opposed to it; and finally they had broken up into small bands, and dispersed over the country. The greatest portion of them had gone over into the territory of the Crows, and intended to return by way of the Wind River valley, in the hope of being able to fall upon some small parties of Crow Indians. The remainder were returning down the Platte, in scattered parties of ten and twenty; and those whom we had encountered belonged to those who had advocated an attack on the emigrants. Several of the men suggested shooting them on the spot; but I promptly discountenanced any such proceeding. They further informed me that buffalo were very scarce, and little or no grass to be found. There had been no rain, and innumerable quantities of grasshoppers had destroyed the grass. The insects had been so numerous since leaving Fort Laramie, that the ground seemed alive with them; and in walking, a little moving cloud preceded our footsteps. This was bad news. No grass, no buffalo—food for neither horse nor man. I gave them some plugs of tobacco, and they went off, apparently well satisfied to be clear of us; for my men did not look upon them very lovingly, and they glanced suspiciously at our warlike preparations, and the little ring of rifles which surrounded them. They were evidently in a bad humor, and shot one of their horses when they had left us a short distance.

We continued our match, and after a journey of about twenty-one miles, encamped on the Platte. During the day, I had occasionally remarked among the hills the psoralea eseulenta, the bread root of the Indians. The Sioux use this root very extensively, and I have frequently met with it among them, cut into thin slices and dried. In the course of the evening we were visited by six Indians, who told us that a large party was encamped a few miles above. Astronomical observations placed us in longitude 104° 59' 59", and latitude 42° 29' 25".

We made the next day twenty-two miles, and encamped on the right bank of the Platte, where a handsome meadow afforded tolerably good grass. There were the remains of an old fort here, thrown up in some sudden emergency, and on the opposite side was a picturesque bluff of ferruginous sandstone. There was a handsome grove a little above, and scattered groups of tree bordered the river. Buffalo made their appearance this afternoon, and the hunters came in, shortly after we had encamped, with three fine cows. The night was fine and observations gave for the latitude of the camp, 42° 47' 40"

25th.—We made but thirteen miles this day, and encamped about noon in a pleasant grove on the right bank. Low scaffolds were erected, upon which the meat was laid, cut up into thin strips, and small fires kindled below. Our object was to profit by the vicinity of the buffalo, to lay in a stock of provisions for ten or fifteen days. In the course of the afternoon the hunters brought in five or six cows, and all hands were kept busily employed in preparing the meat, to the drying of which the guard attended during the night. Our people had recovered their gayety, and the busy figures around the blazing fires gave a picturesque air to the camp. A very serious accident occurred this morning, in the breaking of one of the barometers. These had been the object of my constant solicitude, and, as I had intended them principally for mountain service, I had used them as seldom as possible, taking them always down at night, and on the occurrence of storms, in order to lessen the chances of being broken. I was reduced to one, a standard barometer of Troughton's construction. This I determined to preserve, if possible. The latitude is 42° 51' 35", and by a mean of the results from chronometer and lunar distances, the adopted longitude of this camp is 105o 50 45".

26th.—Early this morning we were again in motion. We had a stock of provisions for fifteen days carefully stored away in the carts, and this I resolved should only be encroached upon when our rifles should fail to procure us present support. I determined to reach the mountains, if it were in any way possible. In the mean time, buffalo' were plenty. In six miles from our encampment (which, by way of distinction, we Alan call Dried Meat caw) we crossed a handsome stream, called La Fourche Boistg. It is well timbered, and, among the flowers in bloom on its banks, I remarked several asters.

Five miles further, we made our noon halt on the banks of the Platte, in the shade of some cottonwoods. There were here, as generally now along the river, thickets of hippophce, the grains de boeuf of the country. They were of two kinds—one bearing a red berry, (the shepherdia argentea of Nuttall;) the other a yellow berry, of which the Tartars are said to make a kind of rob.

By a meridian observation, the latitude of the place was 42o 50' 08". It was my daily practice to take observations of the sun's meridian altitude; and why they are not given, will appear in the sequel. Eight miles further we reached the mouth of Deer creek, where we encamped. Here was abundance of rich grass, and our animals were compensated for past privations. This stream was at this time twenty feet broad, and well timbered with cottonwood of an uncommon size. It is the largest tributary of the Platte, between the mouth of the Sweet Water and the Laramie. Our astronomical observations gave for the mouth of the stream a longitude of 106° 08' 24", and latitude 42° 52' 24".

27th.—Nothing worthy of mention occurred on this day; we traveled later than usual, having spent some time searching for grass, crossing and recrossing the river before we could find a sufficient quantity for our animals. Towards dusk we encamped among some artemisia bushes, two and three feet in height, where some scattered patches of short tough grass afforded a scanty supply. In crossing, we had occasion to observe that the river was frequently too deep to be forded, though we always succeeded in finding a place where the water did not enter the carts. The stream continued very clear, with two or three hundred feet breadth of water, and the sandy bed and banks were frequently covered with large round pebbles. We had traveled this day twenty-seven miles. The main chain of the Black hills was here only about seven miles to the south, on the right bank of the river, rising abruptly to the height of eight and twelve hundred feet. Patches of green grass in the ravines on the steep sides marked the presence of springs, and the summits were clad with pines.

28th.—In two miles from our encampment, we reached the, place where the regular road crosses the Platte. There was two hundred feet breadth of water at this time In the bed, which has a variable width of eight to fifteen hundred feet. The channels were generally three feet deep, and there were large angular rocks on the bottom, which IDE de the ford in some places a little difficult. Even at its low stages, this river cannot be crossed at random, and this has always been used as the best ford. The low stage of the water the 'Resent year had made it fordable in almost any part of its course, where access could be had to its bed.

For the satisfaction of travelers, I will endeavor to give some description of the nature of the road from Laramie to this point. The nature of the soil may be inferred from its geological formation. The limestone at the eastern limit of this section is succeeded by limestone without fossils, a great variety of sandstone, consisting principally of red sandstone and fine conglomerates. The red sandstone is argillaceous, with compact white gypsum or alabaster, very beautiful. The other sandstones are gray, yellow, and ferruginous, sometimes very coarse. The apparent sterility of the country must therefore be sought for in other causes than the nature of the soil. The face of the country cannot with propriety be called hilly. It is a succession of long ridges made by the numerous streams which come down from the neighboring mountain range. The ridges have an undulating surface, with some such appearance as the ocean presents in an ordinary breeze.

The road which is now generally followed through this re gion is therefore a very good one, without any difficult ascents to overcome. The principal obstructions are near the river, where the transient waters of heavy rains have made deep ravines with steep banks, which render frequent circuits necessary. It will be remembered that wagons pass this road only once of twice a year, which is by no means sufficient to break down the stubborn roots of the innumerable artemisia bushes. A partial absence of these is often the only indication of the track; and the roughness produced by their roots in many places gives the road the character of one newly opened in a wooded country. This is usually considered the worst part of the road east of the mountains; and, as it passes through an open prairie region, may be much improved, so as to avoid the greater part of the inequalities it now presents.

From the mouth of the Kansas to the Green River valley, west of the mountains, there is no such thing as a mountain road on the line of communication.

We continued our way, and four miles beyond the ford Indians were discovered again; and I halted while a party were sent forward to ascertain who they were. In a short time they returned, accompanied by a number of Indians of the OgWish band of Sioux. From them we received some interesting in formation. They had formed part of the great village, which they informed us had broken up, and was on its way home. The greater part of the village, including the Arapahoes, Cheyennes, and Oglallahs, had crossed the Platte eight or ten miles below the mouth of the Sweet Water, and were now behind the mountains to the south of us, intending to regain the Platte by way of Deer creek. They had taken this unusual route in search of grass and game. They gave us a very discouraging picture of the country. The great drought, and the plague of grasshoppers, had swept it so that scarce a blade of grass was to be seen, and there was not a buffalo to be found in the whole region. Their people, they further said, had been nearly starved to death, and we would find their road marked by lodges; which they had thrown away in order to move more rapidly, and by the carcasses of the horses which they had eaten, or which had perished by starvation. Such was the prospect before us.

When he had finished the interpretation of these things, Mr. Bissonette immediately rode up to me, and urgently advised that I should entirely aba on the further prosecution of my exploration. "Le meilleur avis que je pourrais vow donner e'est de virer de suite." 'The best advice I can give you, is to turn back at once." It was his own intention to return, as we had now reached the point to which he had engaged to attend me. In reply, I called up my men, and communicated to them fully the information I had just received. I then ex. Dressed to them my fixed determination to proceed to the end of the enterprise on which I had been sent; but as the situation of the country gave me some reason to apprehend that it might be attended with an unfortunate result to some of us, I would leave it optional with them to continue with me or to return.

Among them were some five or six who I knew would remain. We had still ten days' provisions; and should no game ne found, when this stock was expended, we had our horses and mules, which we could eat when other means of subsistence failed. But not a man flinched from the undertaking. "We'll eat the mules," said Basil Lajeurxesse; and thereupon we shook hands with our interpreter and his Indians, and parted. With them I sent back one of my men, Durres, whom the effects of an old wound in the leg rendered incapable or continuing the journey on foot, and his horse seemed on the point of giving out. Having resolved to disencumber ourselves immediately of every thing not absolutely necessary to our future _operations, I turned directly in towards the river, and encamped on the left bank, a little above the place where our council had been held, and where a thick grove of willows offered a suitable spot for the object I had in view.

The carts having been discharged, the covers and wheels were taken off, and, with the frames, carried into some low places, among the willows, and concealed in the dense foliage in_ such a manner that the glitter of the ironwork might not attract the observation of some straggling Indian. In the sand, which had been blown up into waves among the willows, a large hole was then dug, ten feet square and six feet deep. In the mean time, all our effects had been spread out upon the ground, and whatever was designed to be carried along with us separated and laid aside, and the remaining part carried to the hole and carefully covered up. As much as possible, all traces of our proceedings were obliterated, and it wanted but a rain to render our cache safe beyond discovery. All the men were now set at work to arrange the packsaddles and make up the packs.

The day was very warm; and calm, and the sky entirely clear, except where, as usual along the summits of the mountainous ridge opposite, the clouds had congregated in masses. Our lodge had been planted, and, on account of the heat, the groundpins had been taken out, and the lower part slightly raised. Near to it was standing the barometer, which swung in a tripod frame; and within the lodge, where a small fire had been built, Mr. Preuss was occupied in observing the temperature of boiling water. At this instant, and without any warning until it was within fifty yards, a violent gust of wind dashed down the lodge, burying under it Mr. Preuss and about a dozen men, who had attempted to keep it from being carried away. I succeeded in saving the barometer, which the lodge was carrying off with itself, but the thermometer was broken. We had no others of a high graduation, none of those which remained going higher than 135° Fahrenheit. Our astronomical observations gave to this place, which we named Cache camp, a longitude of 106° 38' 26", latitude 42° 50' 53".

29th.—All our arrangements having been completed, we left the, encampment at 7 o'clock this morning. In this vicinity the ordinary road leaves the Platte, and crosses over to the Sweet Water river, which it strikes near Rock Independence. Instead of following this road, I had determined to keep the immediate valley of the Platte so far as the mouth of the Sweet Water, in the expectation of finding better grass. To this I was further prompted by the nature of my instructions. To Mr. Carson was assigned the office of guide, as we had now reached a part of the country with which, or a great part of which, long residence had made him familiar. In a few miles we reached the Red Buttes, a famous landmark in this country, whose geological composition is red sandstone, limestone., and calcareous sandstone and puddingstone.

The river here cuts its way through a ridge; on the eastern side of it are the lofty escarpments of red argillaceous sandstone, which are called the Red Buttes. In this passage the stream is not much compressed or pent up, there being a bank of considerable though variable breadth on either side. Immediately on entering, we discovered a band of buffalo. The hunters failed to kill any of them; the leading hunter being thrown into a ravine, which occasioned some delay, and in the mean time the herd clambered up the steep face of the ridge. It is sometimes wonderful to see these apparently clumsy animals make their way up and down the most broken precipices. We halted to noon before we had cleared this passage at a spot twelve miles distant from Cache camp, where we found an abundance of grass. So far, the account of the, Indians was found to be false. On the banks were willow and cherry trees. The cherries were not yet ripe, but in the thickets were numerous fresh tracks of the grizzly bear, which are very fond of this fruit. The soil here is red, the competition being derived from the red sandstone. Abo& seven miles brought us through the ridge, in which the course of the river is north and south. Here the valley opens out broadly, and high walls of the red formation present themselves among the hills to the east. We crossed here a pretty little creek, an affluent of the right bank. It is well timbered with cotton wood in this vicinity, and the absinthe has lost its shrub-like character, and small trees six and eight feet in height, and sometimes eight inches in diameter. Two or three miles above this creek we made our encampment, having traveled today twenty-five miles. Our animals fared well here, as there is an abundance of grass. The river bed is made up of pebbles, and in the bank, at the level of the water, is a conglomerate of coarse pebbles, about the size of ostrich eggs, and which I remarked in the banks of the Laramie fork. It is overlaid by a soil of mixed clay and sand, six feet thick. By astronomical observations, our position is in longitude 1060 54 32", and latitude 420 38'.

30th.—After traveling about twelve miles this morning, we reached a place where the Indian village had crossed the river. Here were the poles of discarded lodges and skeletons of horses lying about. Mr. Carson, who had never been higher up than this point on the river, which has the character of being exceedingly rugged, and walled in by precipices above, thought it advisable to encamp near this place, where we were certain of obtaining grass.; and tomorrow make our crossing among the rugged hills to the Sweet Water river. Accordingly' we turned back and descended the river to an island near by, which was about twenty acres in size, covered with a luxuriant growth of grass. The formation here I found highly interesting. Immediately at this island the river is again shut up hi the rugged hills, which come down to it from the main ridge in a succession of spurs three or four hundred feet high and alternated with green level prairillons or meadows, bordered on the river banks with thickets of willow, and having many plants to interest the traveler. The island lies between two of these ridges, three or four hundred yards apart, of which that on the right bank is composed entirely of red argillaceous sandstone, with thin layers of fibrous gypsum. On the left bank, the ridge is composed entirely of silicious puddingstone, the pebbles in the numerous strata increasing in size from the top to the bottom, where they are as large as a man's head. So far as I was able to determine, these strata incline to the northeast, with a dip of about 15°. This puddingstone, or conglomerate formation, I was enabled to trace through an extended range of country, from a few miles cast of the meridian of Fort Laramieto where I found it superposed on the granite of the Rocky mountains, in longitude 1090 00'. From its appearance, the main chain of the Laramie mountain is composed of this rock; and in a number of places I found isolated hills, which served to mark a former level which had been probably swept away.

These conglomerates are very friable, and easily decomposed; and I am inclined to think this formation is the source from which was derived the great deposite of sand and gravel which forms the surface rock of the prairie country west of the Mississippi.

Crossing the ridge of red sandstone, and traversing the little prairie which lies to the southward of it, we made in the afternoon an excursion to a place which we called the Hot Spring Gate. This place has much the appearance of a gate, by which the Platte passes through a ridge composed of a white and calcareous sandstone. The length of the passage is about four hundred yards, with a smooth green prairie on either side. Through this place, the stream flows with a quiet current, unbroken by any rapid, and is about seventy yards wide between the walls, which rise perpendicularly from the water. To that on the right bank, which is the lower, the barometer gave a height of three hundred and sixty feet. This place will be more particularly described hereafter, as we passed through it on our return

We saw here numerous herds of mountain sheep, ana frequently heard the volley of rattling stones which accompanied their rapid descent down the steep hills. This was the first place at which we had killed any of these animals; and, in consequence of this circumstance, and of the abundance of these sheep or goats, (for they are called by each name,) we gave our encampment the name of Goat Island. Their flesh is much esteemed by the hunters, and has very much the flavor of Allegheny mountain sheep. I have frequently seen the horns of this animal three feet long and seventeen inches in circumference at the base, weighing eleven pounds. But two or three of these were killed by our party at this place, and of these the horns were small. The use of these horns seems to be to protect the animal's head in pitching down precipices to avoid pursuing wolves—their only safety being in places where they cannot be followed. The bones are very strong and solid, the marrow occupying but a very small portion of the bone in the leg, about the thickness of a rye straw. The hair is short, resembling the winter color of our common deer, which it nearly approaches in size and appearance. Except in the horns, it has no resemblance whatever to the goat. The longitude of this place, resulting from chronometer and lunar distances, and an occultation of Arietis, is 107o 13' 29", and the latitude 42° 33' 27". One of our horses, which had given out, we left to receive strength on the island, intending to take her, perhaps, on our return.

31st.—This morning we left the course of the Platte, to cross over to the Sweet Water. Our way, for a few miles, lay up the sandy bed of a dry creek, in which I found several interesting plants. Leaving this, we wended our way to the summit of the hills, of which the peaks are here eight hundred feet above the Platte, bare and rocky. A long and gradual slope led from these hills to the Sweet Water, which we reached in fifteen miles from Goat Island. I made a,, early encampment here, in order to give the hunters an opportunity to procure a supply from several bands of buffalo, which made their appearance in the valley near by. The stream is about sixty feet wide, and at this time twelve to eighteen inches nee", with a very moderate current.

The adjoining prairies are sandy, but the immediate rivet bottom is a good soil, which afforded an abundance of soft green grass to our horses, and where I found a variety of interesting plants, which made their appearance for the first time. A rain tonight made it unpleasantly cold; and there was no tree here, to enable us to pitch our single tent, the poles of which had been left at our Cache camp. We had, therefore, no shelter except what was to be found under cover of the absinthe bushes, which grew in many thick patches one or two and sometimes three feet high.

AUGUST. 1st.—The hunters went ahead this morning, as buffalo appeared tolerably abundant, and I was desirous to secure a small stock of provisions; and we moved about seven miles up the valley, and encamped one mile below Rock Independence. This is an isolated granite rock, about six hundred and fifty yards long, and forty in height. Except in a depression of the summit, where a little soil supports a scanty growth of shrubs, with a solitary dwarf pine, it is entirely bare. Everywhere within six or eight feet of the ground, where the surface is sufficiently smooth, and in some places sixty or eighty feet above, the rock is inscribed with the names of travelers. Many a name famous in the history of this country, and some well known to science, are to be found mixed among those of the traders and travelers for pleasure and curiosity,, and of missionaries among the savages. Some of these have been washed away by the rain, but the greater number are still very legible. The position of this rock is in longitude 107056', latitude 42° 29' 36". We remained at our camp of August 1st until noon of the next Clay, occupied in drying meat.

By observation, the longitude of the place is 107° 25' 23", latitude 120 29' 56".

2d.—Five miles above Rock Independence we came to a place called the Devil's Gate, where the Sweet Water cuts through the point of a granite ridge. The length of the pas sage is about three hundred yards, and the width thirty-five yards. The walls of rock are vertical, and about four hundred feet in height; and the stream in the gate is almost entirely choked up by masses which have fallen from above. In the wall, on the right bank, is a dike of traprock, cutting through a fine-grained gray granite. Near the point of this ridge crop out some strata of the valley formation, consisting of a grayish micaceous sandstone, and fine-grained conglomerate, and marl. We encamped eight miles above the Devil's Gate. There was no timber of any kind on the river, but good fires were made of drift wood, aided by the bois de vache.

We had tonight no shelter from the rain, which commenced with squalls of wind about sunset. The country here is exceedingly picturesque. On either side of the valley, which is five miles broad, the mountains rise to the height of twelve and fifteen hundred or two thousand feet. On the south side, the range appears to be timbered, and tonight is luminous with fires—probably the work of the Indians, who have just passed through the valley. On the north, broken and granite masses rise abruptly from the green sward of the river, terminating in a line of broken summits. Except in the, crevices of the rocks and here and there on a ledge or bench of the mountain, where a few hardy pines have clustered together, these are perfectly bare and destitute of vegetation.

Among these masses, where there are sometimes isolated hills and ridges, green valleys open in upon the river, which sweeps the base of these mountains for thirty-six miles. Everywhere its deep verdure and profusion of beautiful flowers is in pleasing contrast with the sterile grandeur of the rock and the barrenness of the sandy plain, which, from the right bank of the river, sweeps up to the mountain range that forms its southern boundary. The great evaporation on the sandy soil of this elevated plain, and the saline efflorescences which whiten the ground, and shine like lakes reflecting in the sun, make a soil wholly unfit for cultivation.

3d.—We were early on the road the next morning, trail el i ng along the upper part of the valley, which is overgrown with artemisia. Scattered about on the plain are occasional small isolated hills. One of these which I have examined, about fifty feet high, consisted of white clay and marl, in nearly horizontal strata. Several bands of buffalo made their appearance today, with herds of antelope;. and a grizzly bear —the only one we encountered during the journey—was seen scrambling up among the rocks. As we passed over a slight rise near the river, we caught the first view of the Wind River mountains, appearing, at this distance of about seventy miles, to be a low and dark mountainous ridge. The view dissipated in a moment the pictures which had been created in our minds, by many descriptions of travelers, who have compared these mountains to the Alps in Switzerland, and speak of the glittering peaks which rise in icy majesty amidst the eternal glaciers nine or ten thousand feet into the region of eternal snows. The nakedness of the river was relieved by groves of willows, where we encamped at night, after a march of twenty-six miles; and numerous bright colored flowers had made the river bottom look gay as a garden. We found here a horse, which had been abandoned by the Indians, because his hoofs had been so much worn that he was unable to travel; and during the night a dog came into the camp.

4th.—Our camp was at the foot of the granite mountains, which we climbed this morning to take some barometrical heights; and here among the rocks was seen the first magpie. On our return, we saw one at the mouth of the Platte river. We left here one of our horses, which was unable to proceed farther. A few miles from the encampment we left the river, which makes a bend to the south, and traversing an undulating country, consisting of a grayish micaceous sandstone and fine-grained conglomerates, struck it again, and encamped after a journey of twenty-five miles. Astronomical observations placed us in latitude 42° 32' 30", and longitude 108° 30/ 13".

5th.—The morning was dark, with a driving rain, and disagreeably cold. We continued our route as usual; but the weather became so bad, that we were glad to avail ourselves of the shelter offered by a small island, about ten miles above our last encampment, which was covered with a dense growth of willows. There was fine grass for our animals, and the timber afforded us comfortable protection and good fires. In the afternoon, the sun broke through the clouds for a short time, and the barometer at 5 PM. was 23'713, the thermometer 600, with the wind strong from the northwest. We availed ourselves of the fine weather to make excursions in the neighborhood. The river, at this place, is bordered by hills of the valley formation. They are of moderate height; one of the highest peaks on the right bank being, according to the barometer, one hundred and eighty feet above the river. On the left bank they are higher. They consist of a fine white clayey sandstone, a white calcareous sandstone, and coarse sandstone or puddingstone.

6th.—It continued steadily raining all day; but, notwithstanding, we left our encampment in the afternoon. Our animals had been much refreshed by their repose, and an abundance of rich, soft grass, which had been much improved by the rains. In about three miles, we reached the entrance of a kanyon, where the Sweet Water issues upon the more open valley we had passed over. Immediately at the entrance, and superimposed directly upon the granite, are strata of compact calcareous sandstone and chert, alternating with fine white and reddish white, and fine gray and red sandstones. These strata dip to the eastward at an angle of about 180, and form the western limit of the sandstone and limestone formations on the line of our route. Here we entered among the primitive rocks. The usual road passes to the right of this place; but we wound, or rather scrambled, our way up the narrow valley for several hours. Wildness and disorder were the, character of this scenery. The river had been swollen by the late rains, and came rushing through with an impetuous current, three or four feet deep, and generally twenty yards broad. The valley was sometimes the breadth of the stream, and sometimes opened into little green meadows, sixty yards wide, with open groves of aspen. The stream was bordered throughout with aspen, beech, acid willow; and tall pines grew on the sides and summits of the crags. On both sides the granite rocks rose precipitously to the height of three hundred and five hundred feet, terminating in jagged and broken pointed peaks; and fragments of fallen rock lay piled up at the foot of the precipices. Gneiss, mica slate, and a white granite, were among the varieties I noticed. Here were many old traces of beaver on the stream; remnants of dams, near which were lying trees, which they had cut down, one and two feet in diameter The hills entirely shut up the river at the end of about five miles, and we turned up a ravine that led to a high prairie, which seemed to be the general level of the country. Hence, to the summit of the ridge, there is a regular and very gradual rise. Blocks of granite were piled up at the heads of the ravines, and small bare knolls of mica slate and milky quartz protruded at frequent intervals on the prairie, which was whitened in occasional spots with small salt lakes, where the water had evaporated, and left the bed covered with a shining incrustation of salt. The evening was very cold, a northwest wind driving a fine rain in our faces; and at nightfall we descended to a little stream, on which we encamped, about two miles from the Sweet Water. Here had recently been a very large camp of the Snake and Crow Indians; and some large poles lying about afforded the means of pitching a tent, and making other places of shelter. Our fires tonight were made principally of the dry branches of the artemisia which covered the slopes. It burns quickly, and with a clear, oily flame, and makes a hot fire. The hills here are composed of hard, compact mica slate, with veins of quartz.

7th.—We left our encampment with the rising sun. As we rose from the bed of the creek, the snow line of the mountains stretched gradually before us, the white peaks glittering in the sun. They had been hidden in the dark weather of the last few days, and it had been snowing on them, while it rained in the plains. We crossed a ridge, and again struck the Sweet Water—here a beautiful, swift stream, with a more open valley,, timbered with beech and cottonwood. It now began to lose itself in the many small forks which make its head; and we continued up the main stream until near noon, when we left it a few miles, to make our noon halt on a small creek 'among the hills, from which the stream issues by a small opening.

Within was a beautiful grassy spot, covered with an open grove of large beech trees, among which I found several plants that I had not previously seen.

The, afternoon was cloudy, with squalls of rain; but the weather became, fine at sunset, when we again encamped on the Sweet

Water, within a friw miles of the SOUTH PASS. The country over which we have passed today consists principally of the compact mica slate, which crops out on all ridges, making the uplands very gray and slaty. In the escarpments which border the creeks, it is wan alternating with a light-colored granite, at an inclination of 45'; the beds varying in thickness from two or three feet to six or eight hundred. At a distance, the granite frequently has the appearance of irregular lumps of clay, hardened by exposure. A variety of asters may now be numbered among the characteristic plants, and the artemisia continues in full glory; but cacti have become rare, and mosses begin to dispute the hills with them. The evening was damp and unpleasant—the thermometer, at ten o'clock, being at 36°, and the grass wet with a heavy dew. Our astronomical observations placed this encampment in longitude 109° 21' 32", and latitude 42° 27' 15".

Early in the morning we resumed our journey, the weather still cloudy with occasional rain. Our general course was west, as I had determined to cross the dividing ridge by a bridlepath among the country more immediately at the foot of the mountains, and return by the wagon road, two and a half miles to the south of the point where the trail crosses.

About six miles from our encampment brought us to the summit. The ascent had been so gradual, that, with all the intimate knowledge possessed by Carson, who had made the country his home for seventeen years, we were obliged to watch very closely to find the place at which we had reached the culminating point. This was between two low hills, rising on either hand fifty or sixty feet. When I looked back at them from the foot of the immediate slope on the western plain, their summits appeared to be about one hundred and twenty feet above. From the impression on my mind at this time, and subsequently on our return, I should compare the elevation which we surmounted immediately at the Pass, to the ascent of the Capitol hill from the avenue, at Washington. It is difficult for me to fix positively the breadth of this Pass. From the broken ground where it commences, at the foot of the Wind River chain, the view to the southeast is over a Champaign country, broken, at the distance of nineteen miles, by the Table rock; which, with the other isolated hills in its vicinity, seem to stand on a comparative plain. This I judged to be its termination, the ridge recovering its rugged character with the Table rock. It will be seen that it in no manner resembles Ole places to which the term is commonly applied—nothing of the gorge like character and winding ascents of the Allegheny passes in America; nothing of the Great St. Bernard and Simplon passes in Europe. Approaching it from the mouth of the Sweet Water, a sandy plain, one hundred and twenty miles long, conducts, by a gradual and regular ascent, to the summit, about seven thousand feet above the sea; and the traveler, without being reminded of any change by toilsome ascents, suddenly finds himself on the waters which flow to the Pacific ocean. By the route we had traveled, the distance from Fort Laramie is three hundred and twenty miles, or nine hundred and fifty from the mouth of the Kansas.

Continuing our march, we reached, in eight miles from the Pass, the Little Sandy, one of the tributaries of the Colorado, or Green river of the Gulf of California. The weather had grown fine during the morning, and we remained here the rest of the day, to dry our baggage and take some astronomical observations. The stream was about forty feet wide, and two or three deep, with clear water and a full swift current, over a sandy bed. It was timbered with a growth of low bushy and dense willows, among which were little verdant spots, which gave our animals fine grass, and where I found a number of interesting plants. Among the neighboring hills I notices fragments of granite containing magnetic iron. Longitude of the camp was 109° 37' 59". and latitude 420 27' 24"

9th.—We made our noon halt on Big Sandy, another tributary of Green river. The face of the country traversed was of a brown sand of granite materials, the detritus of the neighboring mountain.

Strata of the milky quartz cropped out, and blocks of granite were scattered about, containing magnetic iron. On Sandy creek the formation was of particolored sand, exhibited in escarpments fifty to eighty feet high. Ir the afternoon we had a severe storm of hail, and encamped at sunset on the first New Fork. Within the space of a few miles, the Wind mountains supply a number of tributaries to Green river, which are called the New Forks. Near our camp were two remarkable isolated hills, one of them sufficiently large to merit the name of mountain. They are called the Two Buttes, and will serve to identify the place of our encampment, which the observations of the evening placed in longitude 109° 58' 11", and latitude 42° 42' 46". On the right bank of the stream, opposite to the large hill, the strata which are displayed consist of decomposing granite, which supplies the brown sand of which the face of the country is composed to a considerable depth.

10th.—The air at sunrise is clear and pure, and the morning extremely cold, but beautiful. A lofty snowy peak of the mountain is glittering in the first rays of the sun, which have not yet reached us. The long mountain wall to the east, rising two thousand feet abruptly from the plain, behind which we see the peaks, is still dark, and cuts clear against the glowing sky. A fog, just risen from the river, lies along the base of the mountain. A little before sunrise, the thermometer was at 350, and at sunrise 330. Water froze last, night, and fires are very comfortable. The scenery becomes hourly more interesting and grand, and the view here is truly magnificent; but, indeed, it needs something to repay the long prairie journey of a thousand miles. The sun has shot above the wall, and makes a magical change. The whole valley is glowing and bright, and all the mountain peaks are gleaming like silver. Though these snow mountains are not the Alps, they have their own character of grandeur and magnificence, and doubtless will find pens and pencils to do them justice. In the scene before us, we feel how much wood improves a view. The pines on the mountain seemed to give it much additional beauty. I was agreeably disappointed in the character of the streams on this side of the ridge. Instead of the creeks, which description had led me to expect, I find bold, broad streams, with three or four feet water, and a rapid current. The fork on which we are encamped is upwards of a hundred feet wide, timbered with groves or thickets of the low willow. 'We were now approaching the loftiest part of the Wind River chain; and I left the valley a few miles from our encampment, intending to penetrate the mountains as far as possible with the whole party. We were soon involved in very broken ground, among long ridges covered with fragments of granite. Winding our way up a long ravine, we came unexpectedly in view of a most beautiful lake, set like a gem in the mountains. The sheet of water lay transversely across the direction we had been pursuing; and, descending the steep, rocky ridge, where it was necessary to lead our horses, we followed its banks to the southern extremity. Here a view of the utmost magnificence and grandeur burst upon our eyes. With nothing between us and their feet to lessen the effect of the whole height, a grand bed of snowcapped mountains rose before us, pile upon pile, glowing in the bright light of an August day. Immediately below them lay the lake, between two ridges, covered with dark pines, which swept down from the main chain to the spot where we stood. Here, where the lake glittered in the open sunlight, its banks of yellow sand and the light foliage of aspen groves contrasted well with the gloomy pines. "Never before," said Mr. Preuss, "in this country or in Europe, have I seen such grand, magnificent rocks." I was so much pleased with the beauty of the place, that I determined to make the main camp here, where our animals would find good pasturage, and explore the mountains with a small party of men. Proceeding a little further, we came suddenly upon the outlet of the lake, where it found its way through a narrow passage between low hills. Dark pines which overhung the stream, and masses of rock, where the water foamed along, gave it much romantic beauty. Where we crossed, which was immediately at the outlet, it is two hundred and fifty fee! wide, and so deep that with difficulty we were able to ford it. Its bed was an accumulation of rocks, boulders, and broad slabs, and large angular fragments, among which the animals fell repeatedly.

The current was very swift, and the water cold, and of a crystal purity. In crossing this stream, I met with a great misfortune in having my barometer broken. It was the only one. A great part of the interest of the journey for me was in the exploration of these mountains, of which so much had been said that was doubtful and contradictory; and now their snowy peaks rose majestically before me, and the only means of giving them authentically to science, the object of my anxious solicitude by night and day, was destroyed. We had brought this barometer in safety a thousand miles, and broke it almost among the snow of the mountains. The loss was felt by the whole camp—all had seen my anxiety, and aided me in preserving it. The height of these mountains, considered by many hunters and traders the highest in the whole range, lad been a theme of constant discussion among them; and all had looked forward with pleasure to the moment when the instrument, which they believed to be as true as the sun, should stand upon the summits, and decide their disputes. Their grief was only inferior to my own.

The lake is about three miles long, and of very irregular width, and apparently great depth, and is the headwater of the third New Fork, a tributary to Green river, the Colorado of the west. In the narrative I have called it Mountain lake. I encamped on the north side, about three hundred and fifty yards from the outlet. This was the most western point at which I obtained astronomical observations, by which this place, called Bernier's encampment, is made in 1100 08' 03" West longitude from Greenwich, and latitude 43° 49' 49". The mountain peaks, as laid down, were fixed by bearings from this and other astronomical points. We had no other compass than the small ones used in sketching the country; but from an azimuth, ,in which one of them was used, the variation of the compass is 18° east. The correction made in our fieldwork by the astronomical observations indicates that this is a very correct observation.

As soon as the camp was formed, I set about endeavoring tc repair my barometer. As I have already said, this was a standard cistern barometer, of Troughton's construction. The glass cistern had been broken about midway; but as the instrument had been kept in a proper position, no air had found its way into the tube, the end of which had always remained covered. I had with me a number of vials of tolerably thick glass, some of which were of the same diameter as the cistern, and I spent the day in slowly working on these, endeavoring to cut them of the requisite length; but, as my instrument was a very rough file, I invariably broke them. A groove was cut in one of the trees, where the barometer was placed during the night, to be out of the way of any possible danger, and in the morning I commenced again. Among the powderhorns in the camp, I found one which was very transparent, so that its contents could be almost as plainly seen as through glass. This I boiled and stretched on a piece of wood to the requisite diameter, and scraped it very thin, in order to increase to the utmost its transparency. I then secured it firmly in its place on the instrument, with strong glue made from a buffalo, and filled it with mercury, properly heated. A piece of skin, which had covered one of the vials, furnished a good pocket, which was well secured with strong thread and glue, and there, the brass cover was screwed to its place. The instrument was left some time to dry; and when I reversed it, a few hours after, I had the satisfaction to find it in perfect order; its indications being about the same as on the other side or the lake before it had been broken. Our success in this little incident diffused pleasure throughout the camp; and we immediately set about our preparations for ascending the mountains.

As will be seen on reference to a map, on this short mountain chain are the headwaters of four great rivers on the continent, namely: the Colorado, Columbia, Missouri, and Platte rivers. It had been my design, after ascending the mountains, to continue our route on the western side of the range, and crossing through a pass at the northwestern end of the chain, about thirty miles from our present camp, return along the eastern slope, across the heads of the Yellowstone river, and join on the line to our station of August 7, immediately at the foot of the ridge. In this way, I should be enabled to include the whole chain, and its numerous waters, in my survey; but various considerations induced me, very reluctantly, to abandon this plan.

I was desirous to keep strictly within the scope of my instructions, and it would have required ten or fifteen additional 'days for the accomplishment of this object; our animals had become very much worn out with the length of the journey; game was very scarce; and, though it does not appear in the course of the narrative, (as I have avoided dwelling upon tri. Ring incidents not connected with the objects of the expedition,) the spirits of the men had been much exhausted by the hardships and privations to which they had been, subjected. Our provisions had well-nigh all disappeared. Bread had been long out of the question; and of all our stock, we had remaining two or three pounds of coffee, and a small quantity of macaroni, which had been husbanded with great care for the mountain expedition we were about to undertake. Our daily meal consisted of dry buffalo meat, cooked in tallow; and, as we had not dried this with Indian skill, part of it was spoiled; and what remained of good, was as hard as wood, having much the take and appearance of so many pieces of bark. Even of this, our stock was rapidly diminishing in a camp which was capable of consuming two buffaloes in every twenty-four hours. These animals had entirely disappeared; and it was not probable that we should fall in with them again until we returned to the Sweet Water.

Our arrangements for the ascent were rapidly completed. We were in a hostile country, which rendered the greatest vigilance and circumspection necessary. The pass at the north end of the mountain was greatly infested by Blackfeet and immediately opposite was one of their forts, on the edge of a little thicket, two or three hundred feet from our encampment. We were posted in a grove of beech, on the margin of the lake, and a few hundred feet long, with a narrow prairillon on she inner side, bordered by the rocky ridge. In the upper end of this grove we cleared a circular space about forty feet in diameter, and, with the felled timber, and interwoven branches, surrounded it with a breastwork five feet in height. A. gap was left for a gate oil the inner side, by which the animals were to be driven in and secured, while the men slept around the little work. It was half hidden by the foliage, and garrisoned by twelve resolute men, would have set at defiance any band of savages which might chance to discover them it the interval of our absence. Fifteen of the best mules, with fourteen men, were selected for the mountain party. Our pro visions consisted of dried meat for two days, with our little stock of coffee and some macaroni. In addition to the barometer and thermometer, I took with me a sextant and spy glass, and we had of course our compasses. In charge of the camp I left Bernier, one of my most trustworthy men, who possessed the most determined courage.

12th.—Early in the morning we left the camp, fifteen in number, well armed, of course, and mounted on our best mules. A packanimal carried our provisions, with a coffeepot and kettle, and three or four tin cups. Every man had a blanket strapped over his saddle, to serve for his bed, and the_ instruments were carried by turns on their backs. We entered directly on rough and rocky ground; and, just after crossing the ridge, had the good fortune to shoot an antelope. We heard the roar; and had a glimpse of a waterfall as we rode along, and, crossing in our way two fine streams, tributary to the Colorado, in about two hours' ride we reached the top of the first row or range of the mountains. Here, again, a view of the most romantic beauty met our eyes. It seemed as if; from the vast expanse Of uninteresting prairie we had passed over, Nature had collected all her beauties together in one chosen place. We were overlooking a deep valley, which was entirely occupied by three lakes, and from the brink to the surrounding ridges rose precipitously five hundred and a thousand feet, covered with the dark green of the balsam pine, relieved on the border of the lake with the light foliage of the aspen. They all communicated with each other, and the green of the waters, common to mountain lakes of great depth, showed that it would be impossible to cross them. The surprise manifested by our guides when these impassable obstacles suddenly barred our progress, proved that they were among the hidden treasures of the place, unknown even to the wandering trappers of the region. Descending the hill, we proceeded to make our way along the margin to the southern extremity. A narrow strip of angular fragments of rock sometimes afforded a rough pathway for our mules, but generally we rode along the shelving side, occasionally scrambling up, at a considerable risk of tumbling back into the lake.

The slope was frequently 60°; the pines grew densely together, and the ground was covered with the branches and trunks of trees. The air was fragrant with the odor of the pines; and I realized this delightful morning the pleasure of breathing that mountain air which makes a constant theme of the hunter's praise, and which now made us feel as if we had all been drinking some exhilarating gas. The depths of this unexplored forest were a place to delight the heart of a botanist. There was a rich undergrowth of plants, and numerous gay colored flowers in brilliant bloom. We reached the outlet at length, where some freshly barked willows that lay in the water showed that beaver had been recently at work. There were some small brown squirrels jumping about in the pines, and a couple of large mallard ducks swimming about in the stream.

The hills on this southern end were low, and the lake looked like a mimic sea, as the waves broke on the sandy beach in the force of a strong breeze. There was a pretty open spot, with fine grass for our mules; and we made our noon halt on the beach, under the shade of some large hemlocks. We resumed our journey after a halt of about an hour, making our way up the ridge on the western side of, the lake. In search of smoother ground, we rode a little inland; and, passing through groves of aspen, soon found ourselves again among the pines. Emerging from these, we struck the summit of the ridge above the upper end of the lake.

We had reached a very elevated point, and in thy, valley below, and among the hills, were a number of lakes of different levels; some two or three hundred feet above others, with which they communicated by foaming torrents. Even to our great height the roar of the cataracts came up, and we could see them leaping down in lines of snowy foam. From this scene of busy waters, we turned abruptly into the stillness of a forest, where we rode among the open bolls of the pines, over a lawn of verdant grass, having strikingly the air of cultivated grounds. This led us, after a time, among masses of rock, which had no vegetable earth but in hollows and crevices, though still the pine forest continued. Towards evening we reached a defile, or rather a hole in the mountains, entirely shut in by dark pine covered rocks.

A small stream, with scarcely perceptible current, flowed through a level bottom of perhaps eighty yards width, where the grass was saturated with water. Into this the mules were turned, and were neither hobbled nor picketed during the night, as the fine pasturage took away all temptation to stray; and we made our bivouac L. the pines. The surrounding masses were all of granite. While supper was being prepared, I set out on an excursion in the neighborhood, accompanied by one of m) men. We wandered about among the crags and ravines until dark, richly repaid for our walk by a fine collection of plants, many of them in full bloom. Ascending a peak to find the place of our camp, we saw that the little, defile in which we lay, communicated with the long green valley of some stream, which, here locked up in the mountains, far away to the south, found its way in a dense forest to the plains.

Looking along its upward course, it seemed to conduct, by a smooth gradual slope, directly towards the peak, which, from long consultation as we approached the mountain, we had decided to be the highest of the range. Pleased with the discovery of so fine a road for the next day, we hastened down to the camp, where we arrived just in time for supper. Our table service was rather scant; and we held the meat in our hands, and clean rocks made good plates, on which we spread our macaroni. Among all the strange places on which we had occasion to encamp during our long journey, none have left so vivid an impression on my mind as the camp of this evening. The disorder of the masses which surrounded us—the little hole through which we saw the stars over head—the dark pines where we slept—and the rocks lit up with the glow of our fires, made a night picture of very wild beauty.

13th.—The morning was bright and pleasant, just cool enough to make exercise agreeable, and we soon entered the defile I had seen the preceding day. It was smoothly carpeted with soft grass, and scattered over with groups of flowers, of which yellow was the predominant color. Sometimes we were forced, by an occasional difficult pass, to pick our way on a narrow ledge along the side of the defile, and the mules were frequently on their knees; but these obstructions were rare, and we journeyed on in the sweet morning air, delighted at our good fortune in having found such a beautiful entrance to the mountains. This road continued for about three trifles, when we suddenly reached its termination in one of the grand views which, at every turn, meet the traveler in this magnificent region. Here the defile up which we had traveled opened out into a small lawn, where, in a little lake, the stream had its source.

There were some fine asters in bloom, but all the flowering plants appeared to seek the shelter of the rocks, and to be of lower growth than below, as if they loved the warmth of the soil, and kept out of the way of the winds. Immediately at our feet, a precipitous descent led to a confusion of defiles, and before us rose the mountains, as we have represented them in the annexed view. It is not by the splendor of far-off views, which have lent such a glory to the Alps, that these impress the mind; but by a gigantic disorder of enormous masses, and a savage sublimity of naked rock, in wonderful contrast with innumerable green spots of a rich floral beauty, shut up in their stern recesses. Their wildness seems well suited tc the character of the people who inhabit the country.

1 determined to leave our animals here, and make the rest of our way on foot. The peak appeared so near that there was no doubt of our returning before night; and a few men were left in ,charge of the mules, with our provisions and blankets. We took with us nothing but our arms and instruments, and, as the day had become warm, the greater part left our coats. Having made an early dinner, we started again. We were soon involved in the most ragged precipices, nearing the central chain very slowly, and rising but little. The first ridge hid a succession of others; and when, with great fatigue and difficulty, we had climbed up five hundred feet, it was but to make an equal descent on the other side; all these intervening places were filled with small deep lakes, which met the eye in every direction, descending from one level to another, sometimes under bridges formed by huge fragments of granite, beneath which was heard the roar of the water. These constantly obstructed our path, forcing us to make long detours; frequently obliged to retrace our steps, and frequently falling among the rocks. Maxwell was precipitated towards the face of a precipice, and saved himself from going over by throwing himself flat on the ground. We clambered on, always expecting, with every ridge that we crossed, to reach the foot of the peaks, and always disappointed, until about four o'clock, when,

pretty well worn out, we reached the shore of a little lake, in which was a rocky island. We remained here a short time to rest, and continued on around the lake, which had in some places a beach of white sand, and in others was bound with rocks, over which the way was difficult and dangerous, as the water from innumerable springs made them very slippery.

By the time we had reached the further side of the lake, we found ourselves all exceedingly fatigued, and, much to the satisfaction of the whole party, we encamped. The spot we had chosen was a broad flat rock, in some measure protected from the winds by the surrounding crags, and the trunks of fallen pines afforded us bright fires. Near by was a foaming torrent, which tumbled into the little lake about one hundred and fifty feet below us, and which, by way of distinction, we have called Island lake. We had reached the upper limit 3f the piney region; as, above this point, no tree was to be seen, and patches of snow lay everywhere around us, on die cold sides of the rocks. The flora of the region we had traversed since leaving our mules was extremely rich, and, among the characteristic plants, the scarlet flowers of the dodecatheon dentatunz everywhere met the eye, in great abundance. A small green ravine, on the edge of which we were encamped, was filled with a profusion of alpine plants, in brilliant bloom. From barometrical observations, made during our three days' sojourn at this place, its elevation above the Gulf of Mexico is 10,000 feet. During the day, we had seen no sign of animal life; but among the rocks here, we heard what was supposed to be the bleat of a young goat, which we searched for with hungry activity, and found to proceed from a small animal of a gray color, with short ears and no tail—probably the Siberian squirrel. We saw a considerable number of them, and, with the exception of a small bird like a sparrow, it is the only inhabitant of this elevated part of the mountains. On our return, we saw, below this lake, large flocks of the mountain goat. We had nothing, to eat tonight. Lajeunesse, with several others, took their guns, and sallied out in search of a goat; but returned unsuccessful. At sunset, the barometer stood at 20.522; the attached thermometer 50°. Here we had the misfortune to break our thermometer, having now only that attached to the barometer. I was taken ill shortly after we had encamped, and continued so until late in the night with violent headache and vomiting. This was probably caused by the excessive fatigue I had undergone, and want of food, and perhaps, also, in some measure, by, the rarity of the air. The night was cold, as a violent gale from the north had sprung up at sunset, which entirely blew away the heat of the tires: The cold, and our granite beds, had not been favorable to sleep, and we were glad to see the face of the sun in the morning. Not being delayed by any preparation for breakfast, we set out immediately.

On every side, as we advanced, was heard the roar of waters, and of a torrent, which we followed up a short distance, until 't expanded into a lake about one mile in length. On the northern side 3f the lake was a bank of ice, or rather of snow covered with a crust of ice. Carson had been our guide into the mountains, and, agreeably to his advice, we left this little valley, and took to the ridges again, which we found extremely broken, and where we were again involved among precipices. Here were icefields; among which we were all dispersed, seeking each the best path to ascend the peak. Mr. Preuss attempted to walk along the upper edge of one of these fields, which sloped away at an angle of about twenty degrees; but his feet slipped from under him, and he went plunging down the plain. A few hundred feet below, at the bottom, were some fragments of sharp rock, on which he landed; and, though he turned a couple of somersets, fortunately received no injury beyond a few bruises. Two of the men, Clement Lambert and Descoteaux, had been taken ill, and lay down on the rocks, a short distance below; and at this point I was attacked with headache and giddiness, accompanied by vomiting, as on the day before. Finding myself unable to proceed, I sent the barometer over to Mr. Preuss, who was in a gap two or three hundred yards distant, desiring him to reach the peak if possible, and take an observation there. He found himself unable to proceed further in that direction, and took an observation, where the barometer stood at 19'401; attached thermometer 500, in the gap. Carson, who had gone over to him, succeeded in reaching one of the snowy summits of the main ridge, whence he saw the peak towards which all our efforts had been directed, towering eight or ten hundred feet into the air above him. In the mean time, finding myself grow rather worse than better, and doubtful how far my strength would carry me, I sent Basil Lajeunesse, with four men, back to the place where the mules had been left.

We were now better acquainted with the 'topography of the country, and I directed him to bring back with him, if it were in any way possible, four or five mules, with provisions and blankets. With me were Maxwell and Ayer; and after we had remained nearly an hour on the rock, it became so unpleasantly cold, though the day was bright, that we set out on Sur return to the camp, at which we all arrived safely, straggling in one after the other. I continued ill during the afternoon, but became better towards sundown, when my recovery was completed by the appearance of Basil and four men, all mounted,. The men who had gone with him had been too much fatigued to return, and were relieved by those in charge of the horses; but in his powers of endurance Basil resembled more a mountain goat than a man. They brought blankets and provisions, and we enjoyed well our dried meat and a cup of good coffee. We rolled ourselves up in our blankets, and, with our feet turned to a blazing fire, slept, soundly until morning.

15th.—It had been supposed, that we had finished with the mountains; and the evening before it had been arranged that Carson should set out at daylight, and return to breakfast at the Camp of the Mules, taking with him all but four or five men, who were to stay with me and bring back the mules and instruments. Accordingly, at the break of day they set out. With Mr. Preuss and myself remained Basil Lajeunesse, Clement Lambert, Janisse, and Descoteaux. When we had secured strength for the day by a hearty breakfast, we covered what remained, which was enough for one meal, with rocks, in order that it might be safe from any marauding bird, and, saddling our mules, turned our faces once more towards the peaks. This time we determined to proceed quietly and cautiously, deliberately resolved to accomplish our object if it were within the compass of human means. We were of opinion that a long defile which lay to the left of yesterday's route would lead us to the foot of the main peak. Our mules had been refreshed by the fine grass in the little ravine at the Island camp, and we intended to ride up the defile as far as possible, in order to husband our strength for the main ascent. Though this was a fine passage, still it was a defile of the most rugged mountains known, and we had many a rough and steep slippery place to cross before reaching the end. In this place the sun rarely shone; snow lay along the border of the small stream which flowed through it, and occasional icy passages made the footing of the mules very insecure, and the rocks and ground were moist with the trickling waters in this spring mighty rivers. We soon had the satisfaction to find ourselves riding aloe the huge wall which forms the central summits of the chain. There at last it rose by our sides, a nearly perpendicular wall of granite, terminating 2,000 to 3,000 feet above our heads in a serrated line of broken, jagged cones. We rode on until we came almost immediately below the main peak, which I denominated the Snow peak, as it exhibited more snow to the eye than any of the neighboring summits. Here were three small lakes of a green color, each, perhaps, of a thousand yards in diameter, and apparently very deep. These lay in a kind of chasm; and, according to the barometer, we had attained but a few hundred feet above the Island lake. The barometer here stood at 20.450, attached thermometer 700.

We managed to get our mules up to a little bench about a hundred feet above the lake, where there was a patch of good grass, and turned them loose to graze. During our rough ride to this place, they had exhibited a wonderful surefootedness. Parts of the defile were filled with angular, sharp fragments of rock, three or four and eight or ten feet cube; and among these they had worked their way, leaping from one narrow point to another, rarely making a false step, and giving us no occasion to dismount. Having divested ourselves of every unnecessary encumbrance, we commenced the ascent. This time, like experienced travelers, we did not press ourselves, but climbed leisurely, sitting down so soon as we found breath beginning to fail. At intervals we reached places where a number of springs gushed from the rocks, and about 1800 feet above the lakes came to the snow line. From this point our progress was uninterrupted climbing. Hitherto I had worn a pair of thick moccasins, with soles of parjleche, but here I put on a light, thin pair, which I had brought for the purpose, as now the use of our toes became necessary to a further advance. I availed myself of a sort of comb of the mountain, which stood against the wall like a buttress, and which the wind and the solar radiation, joined to the steepness of the smooth rock, had kept almost entirely free from snow. Up this I made my way rapidly. Our cautious method of advancing at the outset had spared my strength; and, with the exception of slight disposition to headache, I felt no remains of yesterday's illness. In a few minutes we reached a point where the buttress was overhanging, and there was no other way of surmounting the difficulty than by passing around one side of it, which was the face of a vertical precipice of several hundred feet.

Putting hands and feet in the crevices between the blocks, I succeeded in getting over it, and, when I reached the top, found my companions in a small valley below. Descending to them, we continued climbing, and in a short time reached the crest. I sprang upon the summit, and another step would have precipitated me into an immense snowfield five hundred feet below. To the edge of this field was a sheer icy precipice; and then, with a gradual fall, the field sloped off for about a mile, until it struck the foot of another lower ridge. I stood on a narrow crest, about three feet in width, with an inclination of about 20° N. 51° E. As soon as I had gratified the first feelings of curiosity, I descended, and each man ascended in his turn; for I would only allow one at a time to mount the unstable and precarious slab, which it seemed a breath would hurl into the abyss below. We mounted the barometer in the snow of the summit, and fixing a ramrod in a crevice, unfurled the national flag to wave in the breeze where never flag waved before. During our morning's ascent, we had met no sign of animal life, except the small sparrow like bird already mentioned. A stillness the most profound and a terrible solitude forced themselves constantly on the mind as the great features of the place. Here, on the summit, where the stillness was absolute, unbroken by any sound, and solitude complete, we thought ourselves beyond the region of animated life; but while we were sitting on the rock, a solitary bee (bromus, the bumblebee) came winging his flight from the eastern valley, and lit on the knee of one of the men.

It was a strange place, the Icy rock and the highest peak of the Rocky mountains, for a lover of warm sunshine and flowers; and we pleased ourselves with the idea that he was the first of his species to cross the mountain barrier—a solitary pioneer to foretell the advance of civilization. I believe that a moment's thought would have made us let him continue his way unharmed; but we carried out the law of this country, where all animated nature seems at war; and, seizing him immediately, put him in at least a fit place—in the leaves of a large book, among the flowers we had collected on our way. The barometer stood at 18.293, the attached thermometer at 440; giving for the elevation of this summit 13,570 feet above the Gulf of Mexico, which may be called the highest flight of the bee. It is certainly the highest known flight of that insect. From the description given by Mackenzie of the mountains where he crossed them, with that of a French officer still farther to the north, and Colonel Long's measurements to the south, joined to the opinion of the oldest traders of the country, it is presumed that this is the highest peak of the Rocky mountains. The day was sunny and bright, but a slight shining mist hung over the lower plains, which interfered with our view of the surrounding country. On one side we overlooked innumerable lakes and streams, the spring of the Colorado of the Gulf of California; and on the other was the Wind River valley, where were the heads of the Yellowstone branch of the. Missouri; far to the north, we could just discover the snowy heads of the Trois Teton, where were the sources of the Missouri and Columbia rivers; and at the southern extremity of the ridge, the peaks were plainly visible, among which were some of the springs of the Nebraska or Platte river. Around us, the whole scene had one main, striking feature, which was that of terrible convulsion. Parallel to its length, the ridge was split into chasms and fissures; between which rose the thin lofty walls, terminated with slender minarets and columns. According to the barometer, the little crest of the wall on which we stood was three thousand five hundred and seventy feet above that place, and two thousand seven hundred and eighty above the little lakes at the bottom, immediately at our feet. Our camp at the Two Hills (an astronomical station) bore south 3° east, which, with a bearing afterwards obtained from a fixed position, enabled us to locate the peak. The bearing of the Trois Tans was north 500 west, and the direction of the central ridge of the Wind River mountains south 390 east. The summit rock was gneiss, succeeded by sienitic gneiss. Sienite and feldspar succeeded in our descent to the snow line, where we found a feldspathic granite. I had remarked that the noise produced by the explosion of our pistols had the usual degree of loudness, but was not in the least prolonged, expiring almost instantaneously.

Having now made what observations our means afforded, we proceeded to descend. We had accomplished an object of laudable ambition, and beyond the strict order of our instructions. We had climbed the loftiest peak of the Rocky mountains, and looked down upon the snow a thousand feet below; and, standing where never human foot had stood before, felt the exultation of first explorers. It was about two o'clock when we left the summit, and when we reached the bottom, the sun had already sunk behind the wall, and the day was drawing to a close. It would have been pleasant to have lingered here and on the summit longer; but we hurried away as rapidly as the ground would permit, for it was an object to regain our party as soon as possible, not knowing what accident the next hour might bring forth.

We reached our deposite of provisions at nightfall. Here was not the inn which awaits the tired traveler on his return from Mont Blanc, or the orange groves of South America, with their refreshing juices and soft fragrant air; but we found our little cache of dried meat and coffee undisturbed. Though the moon was bright, the road was full of precipices, and the fatigue of the day had been great. We therefore abandoned the idea of rejoining our friends, and lay down on the rock, and, in spite of the cold, slept soundly.

16th.—We left our encampment with the daylight. We saw on our way large flocks of the mountain goat looking down on us from the cliffs. At the crack of the rifle, they would bound off among the rocks, and in a few minutes make their appearance on some lofty peak, some hundred or a thousand feet above. It is needless to attempt any further description of the country; the portion over which we traveled this morning was rough as imagination could picture it, and to us seemed equally beautiful. A concourse of lakes and rushing waters—mountains of rocks naked and destitute of vegetable earth—dells and ravines of the most exquisite beauty, all kept green and fresh by the great moisture in the air, and sown with brilliant flowers, and everywhere thrown around all the glory of most magnificent scenes,—these constitute the features of the place, and impress themselves vividly on the mind of the traveler. It was not until 11 o'clock that we reached the place where our animals had been left, when we first attempted the mountains on foot. Near one of the still burning fires we found a piece of meat, which our friends had thrown away; and which furnished us a mouthful—a very scanty breakfast. We continued directly on, and reached our camp on the mountain lake at dusk. We found all well. Nothing had occurred to interrupt the quiet since our departure, and the fine grass and good cool water had done much to reestablish our animals. All heard with great delight the order to turn our faces homeward; and towards sundown of the 17th, we encamped again at the Two Buttes.

In the course of this afternoon's march, the barometer was broken past remedy. I regretted it, as I was desirous to compare it again with Dr. Engleman's barometers at St. Louis, to which mine were referred; but it had done its part well, and my objects were mainly fulfilled.

19th.—We left our camp on Little Sandy river about seven in the morning, and traversed the same sandy, undulating country. The air was filled with the turpentine scent of the various artelftisias, which are now in bloom, and, numerous as they are, give much gayety to the landscape of the plains. At ten o'clock, we stood exactly on the divide in the pass, where the wagonroad crosses; and, descending immediately upon the Sweet Water, halted to take a meridian observation of the sun. The latitude was 42° 24' 32".

In the course of the afternoon we saw buffalo again, and at our evening halt on the Sweet Water the roasted ribs again made their appearance around the fires; and with them, good humor, and laughter and song, were restored to the camp

Our coffee had been expended, but we now made a kind of tea from the roots of the wild cherry tree.

23d.—Yesterday evening we reached our encampment at Rock Independence, where I took some astronomical observations. Here, not unmindful of the custom of early travelers and explorers in our country, I engraved on this rock of the Far West a symbol of the Christian faith. Among the thickly inscribed names, I made oh the hard granite the impression of a large cross, which I covered with a black preparation of India rubber, well calculated to resist the influence of wind and rain. It stands amidst the names of many who have long since found their way to the grave, and for whom the huge rock is a giant gravestone.

One George Weymouth was sent out to Maine by the Earl of Southampton, Lord Arundel, and others; and in the narrative of their discoveries, he says: " The next day we ascended in our pinnace that part of the river which lies more to the westward, carrying with us a cross—a thing never omitted by any Christian traveler—which we erected at the ultimate end of our route." This was in the year 1605; ana in 1842 I obeyed the feeling of early travelers, and left the impression of the cross deeply engraved on the vast rock one thousand miles beyond the Mississippi, to which discoverers have given the national name of Rock Independence.

In obedience to my instructions to survey the river Platte, if possible, I had determined to make an attempt at this place. The India rubber boat was filled with air, placed in the water, and loaded with what was necessary for our operations; and I embarked with Mr. Preuss and a party of men. When we had dragged our boat a mile or two over the sands, I abandoned the impossible undertaking; and waited for the arrival of the party, when we packed up J u r boat and equipage, and at nine o'clock were again moving along on our land journey. We continued along the valley on the right bank of the Sweet Water, where the formation, as already described, consists of a grayish micaceous sandstone, and fine-grained conglomerate, and marl. We passed over a ridge which borders or constitutes the river hills of the Platte, consisting of huge blocks sixty or eighty feet cube, of decomposing granite. The comen which united them was probably of easier decomposition, and has disappeared and left them isolate, and separated by small spaces.

Numerous horns of the mountaingoat, were lying among the rocks; and in the ravines were cedars, whose trunks were of extraordinary size. From this ridge we descended to a small open plain, at the mouth of the Sweet Water, which rushed with a rapid current into the Platte, here flowing along in a broad and apparently deep stream, which seemed, from its turbid appearance, to be considerably swollen. I obtained here some astronomical observations, and the afternoon was spent in getting our boat ready for navigation the next day.

24th.—We started before sunrise, intending to breakfast at Goat island I had directed the land party, in charge of Bernier, to proceed to this place, where they were to remain, should they find no note to apprize them of our having passed. In the event of receiving this information, they were to continue their route, passing by certain places which had been designated. Mr. Preuss accompanied me, and with us were five of my best men, viz.: C. Lambert, Basil Lajeunesse, Honore Ayot, Benoist, and Descoteaux. Here appeared no scarcity of water, and we took on board, with various instruments and baggage, provisions for ten or twelve days. We paddled down the river rapidly, for our little craft was light as a duck on the water; and the sun had been some time risen, when we heard before us a hollow roar, which we supposed to be that of a fall, of which we had heard a vague rumor, but whose exact locality no one had been able to describe to us. We were approaching a ridge, through which the river passes by a place called "canon," (pronounced kanyon,)—a Spanish word, signifying a piece of artillery, the barrel of a gun, or any kind of tube; and which, in this country, has been adopted to describe the passage of a river between perpendicular rocks of great height, which frequently approach each other so closely overhead as to form a kind of tunnel over the stream, which foams along below, half choked up by fallen fragments. Between the mouth of the Sweet Water and Goat island, there is probably a fall of three hundred feet, and that was principally made in the canons before us; as, without them, the water was comparatively smooth. As we neared the ridge, the river made a sudden turn, and swept squarely down against one of the walls of the canon, with great velocity, and so steep a descent that i+ had, to the eye, the appearance of an inclined plane. When we launched into this, the men jumped overboard, to check the velocity of the boat; but were soon in water up to their necks, and our boat ran on. But we succeeded in bringing her to a small point of rocks on the right, at the mouth of the canon. Here was a kind of elevated sandbeach, not many yards square, backed by the rocks; and around the point the rivet swept at a right angle. Trunks of trees deposited on jutting points, twenty or thirty feet above, and other marks, showed that the water here frequently rose to a considerable height. The, ridge was of the same decomposing granite already mentioned, and the water had worked the surface, in many places, Into a wavy surface of ridges and holes. We ascended the rocks to reconnoitre the ground, and from the summit the passage appeared to be a continued cataract, foaming over many obstructions, and broken by a number of small falls. We saw nowhere a fall answering to that which had been described to us as having twenty or twenty-five feet; but stilt concluded this to be the place in question, as, in the season of floods, the rush of the river against the wall would produce a great rise; and the waters, reflected squarely off, would descend through the passage in a sheet of foam, having every appearance of a large fall. Eighteen years previous to this time, as I have subsequently learned from himself, Mr. Fitzpatrick, somewhere above on this river, had embarked with a valuable cargo of beaver. Unacquainted with the stream, which he believed would conduct him safely to the Missouri, he came unexpectedly into this canon, where he was wrecked, with the total loss of his furs. It would have been a work of great time and labor to pack our baggage across the ridge, and I determined to run the canon. We all again embarked, and at first attempted to check the way of the boat; but the water swept through with so much violence that we narrowly escaped being swamped, and were obliged to let' her go in the full force of the current, and trust to the skill of the boatmen: The dangerous places in this canon were where huge rocks had fallen from above, arid hemmed in the already narrow pass of the river to an open space of three or four and five feet. These obstructions raised the water considerably above, which was sometimes precipitated over in a fall; and at other places, where this dam was too high, rushed through the contracted opening with tremendous violence. Had our boat been made of wood, in passing the narrows she would have been staved; but her elasticity preserved her unhurt from every shock, and she seemed fairly to leap over the falls.

In this way we passed three cataracts in succession, where perhaps 100 feet of smooth water intervened; and, finally with a shout of pleasure at our success, issued from our tunnel into the open day beyond. We were so delighted with that performance of our boat, and so confident in her powers, that we would not have hesitated to leap a fall of ten feet with her. We put to shore for breakfast at some willows on the right bank, immediately below the mouth of the canon; for it was now eight o'clock, and we had been working since daylight, and were all wet, fatigued, and hungry. While the men were preparing breakfast, I went out to reconnoitre. The view was very limited. The course of the river was smooth, so far as j could see; on both sides were broken hills; and but a mile or two below was another high ridge. The rock at the month of the canon was still the decomposing granite, with great quantities of mica, which made a very glittering sand.

We reembarked at nine o'clock, and in about twenty minutes reached the next canon. Landing on a rocky shore at its commencement, we ascended the ridge to reconnoitre. Portage was out of the question. So far as we could see, the jagged rocks pointed out the course of the canon, on a winding line of seven or eight miles. It was simply a narrow, dark chasm in the rock; and here the perpendicular faces were much higher than in the previous pass, being at this end two to three hundred, and further down, as we afterwards ascertained, five hundred feet it vertical height. Our previous success had made us bold, and we determined again o run the canon. Every thing was secured as firmly as possible; and having divested ourselves of the greater part of our clothing, we pushed into the stream. To save our chronometer from accident, Mr. Preuss took it, and attempted to proceed along the shore on the masses of rock, which in places were piled up on either side; but, after he had walked about five minutes, every thing like shore disappeared, and the vertical wall came squarely down into the water. He therefore waited until we came up. An ugly pass lay before us. We had made fast to the stern of the boat a strong rope about fifty feet long; and three of the men clambered along among the rocks, and with this rope let her slowly through the pass. In several places high rocks lay scattered about in the channel; and in the narrows it required all our strength and skill to avoid staving the boat on the sharp points. In one of these, the boat proved a little too broad, and stuck fast for an instant, while the water flew over us; fortunately, it was but for an instant, as our united strength forced her immediately through. The water swept overboard only a sextant and a pair of saddle bags. I caught the sextant as it passed by me; but the saddlebags became the prey of the whirlpools. We reached the place where Mr. Preuss was standing, took him on board, and, with the aid of the boat, put the men with the rope on the succeeding pile of rocks. We found this passage much worse than the previous one, and our position was rather a bad one. To go back was impossible; before us, the cataract was a sheet of foam; and shut up in the chasm by the rocks, which, in some places, seemed almost to meet overhead, the roar of the water was deafening. We pushed off again; but, after making a little distance, the force of the current became too great for the men on shore, and two of them let go the rope. Lajeunesse, the third man, hung on, and was jerked headforemost into the river from a rock about twelve feet high; and down the boat shot like an arrow, Basil following us in the rapid current, and exerting all his strength to keep in mid channel—his head only seen occasionally like a black spot in the white foam , How far we went, I do not exactly know; but we succeeded in turning the boat into an eddy below "'Cre Dieu," said Basil Lajeunesse, as he arrived immediate ly after us, "Je crois Bien que j'ai nage un demi mile." He had owed his life to his skill as a swimmer, and I determined to take him and the two others on board, and trust to skill and fortune to reach the other end in safety. We placed ourselves on our knees with the short paddles in our hands, the most skilful boatman being at the bow; and again we commenced our rapid descent. We cleared rock after rock, and shot past fall after fall, our little boat seeming to play with the cataract We became flushed with success, and familiar with the danger; and, yielding to the excitement of the occasion, broke forth into a Canadian boatsong. Singing, or rather shouting, we dashed along, and were, I believe, in the midst of the chorus, whet the boat struck a concealed rock immediately at the foot of a fall, which whirled her over in an instant. Three of my men could not swim, and my first feeling was to assist them, and save some of our effects; but a sharp concussion or two convinced me that I had not yet saved myself. A few strokes brought me into an eddy, and I landed on a pile of rocks on the left side. Looking around, I saw that Mr. Preuss had gained the shore on the same side, about twenty yards below; and a little climbing and swimming soon brought him to my side. On the opposite side, against the wall, lay the boat bot om up; and Lambert was in the act of saving Descoteaux, whom he had grasped by the hair, and who could not swim; "Lade pas," said he, as I afterwards learned, "Riche pas, cher frere." " Crains pas," was the reply: "je m'en vain mourir avant que de to lticher." Such was the reply of courage and generosity in this danger. For a hundred yards below the current was covered with floating books and boxes, bales and blankets, and scattered articles of clothing; and so ' strong and boiling was thb stream, that even our heavy instruments, which were all in cases, kept on the surface, and the sextant, circle, and the long black box of the telescope, were in view at once. For a moment, I felt somewhat disheartened. All our books—almost every record of the journey—out journals and registers of astronomical and barometrical observations—had been lost in a moment. But it was no time to indulge in regrets; and I immediately set about endeavoring to save something from the wreck. Making ourselves understood as well as possible by signs, (for nothing could be heard in the roar of the waters,) we commenced our operations. Of every thing on board, the only article that had been saved was my double-barreled gun, which Descoteaux had caught and clung to with drowning tenacity. The men continued down the river on the left bank. Mr. Preuss and myself descended on the side we were on; and Lajeunesse, with a paddle in his hand, jumped on the boat alone, and continued down the canon. She was now light, and cleared every bad place with much less difficulty. In a short time he was joined by Lambert, and the search was continued for about a mile and a half, which was as far as the boat could proceed in the pass.

Here the walls were about five hundred feet high, and the fragments of rocks from above had choked the river into a hollow pass, but one or two feet above the surface. Through this and the interstices of the rock, the water found its way. Favored beyond our expectations, all of our registers had been recovered, with the exception of one of my journals, which contained the notes and incidents of travel, and topographical descriptions, a number of scattered astronomical observations, principally meridian altitudes of the sun, and our barometrical register west of Laramie. Fortunately, our other journals contained duplicates of the most important barometrical observations which had been taken in the mountains. These, with a few scattered notes, were all that had been preserved of our meteorological observations. In addition to these, we saved the circle; and these, with a few blankets, constituted every thing that had been rescued from the waters.

The day was running rapidly away, and it was necessary to reach Goat island, whither the party had preceded us, before night. In this uncertain country, the traveler is so much in the power of chance, that we became somewhat uneasy in regard to them. Should any thing have occurred, in the brief interval of our separation, to prevent our rejoining them, our situation would be rather a desperate one. We had not a morsel of provisions—our arms and ammunition were gone—and we were entirely at the mercy of any straggling party of savages, and not a little in danger of starvation. We therefore set out at once in two parties, Mr. Preuss and myself on the left, and the men on the opposite side of the river. Climbing out of the canon, we found ourselves in a very broken country where we were not yet able to recognise any locality. In the course of our descent through the canon, the rocks, which at the upper end was of the decomposing granite, changed into a varied sandstone formation. The hills and points of the ridges were covered with fragments of a yellow sandstone, of which the strata were sometimes displayed in the broken ravines which interrupted our course, and made our walk extremely fatiguing. At one point of the canon the red argillaceous sand stone rose in a wall of five hundred feet, surmounted by a stratum of white sandstone; and in an opposite ravine a canyon of red sandstone rose, in form like a steeple, about one hundred and fifty feet high: The scenery was extremely picturesque, and notwithstanding our forlorn condition, we were frequently obliged to stop and admire it. Our progress was not very rapid. We had emerged from the water half naked, and, on arriving at the top of the precipice, I found myself with only one moccasin. The fragments of rock made walking painful, and I was frequently obliged to stop and pull out the thorns of the cactus, here the prevailing plant, and with which a few minutes' walk covered the bottoms of my feet. From this ridge the river emerged into a smiling prairie, and, descending to the bank for water, we were joined by Benoist. The rest of the party were out of sight, having taken a more inland route. We crossed the river repeatedly—sometimes able to ford it, and sometimes swimming—climbed over the ridges of two more canons, and toward evening reached the cut, which we here named the Hot Spring gate. On our previous visit in July, we had not entered this pass, reserving it for our descent in the boat; and when we entered it this evening, Mr. Preuss was a few hundred feet in advance. Heated with the long march, he came suddenly upon a fine bold spring gushing from the rock, about ten feet above the river. Eager to enjoy the crystal water, he threw himself down for: a hasty draught, and took a mouthful of water almost boiling hot. He said nothing to Benoist, who laid himself down to drink; but the steam from the water arrested his eagerness, and he escaped the hot draught. We had no thermometer to ascertain the temperature, but I could hold my hand in the water just long enough to count two seconds. There are eight or ten of these springs discharging themselves by streams large enough to be called runs. A loud hollow noise was heard from the rock, which I supposed to be produced by the fall of water. The strata immediately where they issue is a fine white and calcareous sandstone, covered with an incrustation of common salt. Leaving this Thermopylae of the wet, in a short walk we reached the red ridge which has been described as lying just above Goat island. Ascending this, we found some fresh tracks and a button, which showed that the other men had already arrived. A shout from the man who first reached the top of the ridge, responded to horn below, informed us that our friends were all on the island; and we, were soon among them. We found some pieces of buffalo standing around the fire for us, and managed to get some dry clothes among the people. A sudden storm of rain drove us into the best shelter we could find, where we slept soundly, after one of the most fatiguing days I have ever experienced.

25th.—Early this morning Lajeunesse was sent to the wreck for the articles which had been saved, and about noon we left the island. The mare which we had left here in July had much improved` in condition, and she served us well again for some time, but was finally abandoned at a subsequent part of the journey. At 10 in the morning of the 26th we reached Cache camp, where we found every thing undisturbed. We disinterred our deposite, arranged our carts which had been left here on the way out; and, traveling a few miles in the afternoon, encamped for the night at the ford of the Platte.

27th.—At midday we halted at the place where we had taken dinner on the 27th of July. The country which, when we passed up, looked as if the hard winter frosts had passed over it, had now assumed a new face, so much of vernal fresh ness had been given to it by the rains. The Platte was exceedingly low—a mere line of water among the sandbars. We reached Laramie 'fort on the last day of August, after an absence of fortytwo days, and had the pleasure to find our friends all well. The fortieth day had been fixed for our return; and the quick eyes of the Indians, who were on the lookout for us, discovered our flag as we wound among the hills. The fort saluted us with repeated discharges of its single piece, which we returned with scattered volleys of our small arms, and felt the joy of a home reception in getting back to this remote station, which seemed so far off as we went out.

SEPTEMBER.

On the morning of the 3d September we bade adieu to out kind friends at the fort, and continued our homeward journey down the Platte, which was glorious with the autumnal splendor of innumerable flowers in full and brilliant bloom. On the warm sands, among the helianthz, one of the characteristic plants, we saw great numbers of rattlesnakes, of which five or six were killed in the morning's ride. We occupied ourselves in improving our previous survey of the river and, as the weather was fine, astronomical observations were generally made at night and at noon.

We halted for a short time on the afternoon of the 5th with a village of Sioux Indians, some of whose chiefs we had met at Laramie. The water in the Platte was exceedingly low; in many places, the large expanse of sands, with some occasional stunted tree on its banks, gave it the air of the sea coast; the bed of the river being merely a succession of sandbars, among which the channel was divided into rivulets of a few inches deep. We crossed and recrossed with our carts repeatedly and at our pleasure; and, whenever an obstruction barred our way in the shape of precipitous bluffs that came down upon the river, we turned directly into it, and made our way along the sandy bed, with no other inconvenience than the frequent quicksands, which greatly fatigued our animals. Disinterring on the way the cache which had been made by our party when they ascended the river, we reached without accident, on the evening of the 12th of September, our old encampment of the 2d of July, at the junction of the forks. Our cache of the barrel of oak was found undisturbed, and proved a seasonable addition to our stock of provisions. At this place I had determined to make another attempt to descend the Platte by water, and accordingly spent two days in the construction of a bull boat. Men were sent out on the evening of our arrival, the necessary number of bulls killed, and their skins brought to the camp. Four of the best of them were strongly sewed together with buffalo sinew, and stretched over a basket frame of willow. The seams were then covered with ashes and tallow, and the boat left exposed to the sun for the greater part of one day, which was sufficient to dry and contract the skin, and make the whole work solid and strong. It had a rounded bow, was eight feet long and five broad, and drew with four men about four inches water. On the morning of the 15th we embarked in our hide boat, Mr. Preuss and myself, with two men. We dragged her over the sands for three or four miles, and then left her on a bar, and abandoned entirely all further attempts to navigate this river. The names given by the Indians are always remarkably appropriate; and certainly none was ever more so than that which they have given to this stream—"The Nebraska, or Shallow river." Walking steadily the remainder of the day, a little before dark we overtook our people at their remaining camp, about twenty-one miles below the junction. The next morning we crossed the Platte, and continued our way down the river bottom on the left bank, where we found an excellent, plainly beaten road.

On the 18th we reached Grand Island, which is fifty-two miles long, with an average breadth of one mile and three quarters. It has on it some small eminences, and is sufficiently elevated to be secure from the annual floods of the river. A has been already remarked, it is well timbered, with an excellent soil, and recommends itself to notice as the best point for a military position on the Lower Platte.

On the 22d we arrived at the village of the Grand Pawnees, on the right bank of the river, about thirty miles above the mouth of the Loup fork. They were gathering in their corn, and we obtained from them a very welcome supply of vegetables.

The morning of the 24th we reached the Loup fork of the Platte. At the place where we forded it, this stream was four hundred and thirty yards broad, with a swift current of clear water; in this respect, differing from the Platte, which has a yellow muddy color, derived from the limestone and marl formation, of which we have previously spoken. The ford was difficult, as the water was so deep that it came into the body of the carts, and we reached the opposite bank after repeated attempts, ascending and descending the bed of the river, in order to avail ourselves of the bars. We encamped on the left bank of the fork, in the point of land at its junction with the Platte. During the two days that we remained here for astronomical observations, the bad weather permitted us to obtain but one good observation for the latitude—a meridian altitude of the sun, which gave for the latitude of the mouth of the Loup fork, 41° 22' 11".

Five or six days previously, I had sent forward C. Lambert, with two men, to Bellevue, with directions to ask from Mr. P. Sarpy, the gentleman in charge of the American Company's establishment at that place, the aid of his carpenters in constructing a boat, in which I proposed to descend the Missouri. On the afternoon of the 27th we met one of the men, who had been dispatched by Mr. Sarpy with a welcome supply of provisions and a very kind note, which gave us the very gratifying intelligence that our boat was in rapid progress.

On the evening of the 30th we encamped In an almost impenetrable undergrowth on the left bank of the Platte, in the point of land at its confluence with the Missouri 315 miles, according to our reckoning, from the junction of the forks, and 520 from Fort Laramie. From the junction we had found the bed of the Platte occupied with numerous islands, many of them very large, and all well timbered; possessing, as well as the bottom lands of the river, a very excellent soil. With the exception of some scattered groves on the banks, the bottoms are generally without timber. A portion of these consist of low grounds, covered with a profusion of fine grasses, and are probably inundated in the spring; the remaining part is high river prairie, entirely beyond the influence of the floods. The breadth of the river is usually three porters of a mile, except where it is enlarged by islands. That portion of its course which is occupied by Grand island has an average breadth, from shore to shore, of two and a half miles.

OCTOBER.

1st. I rose this morning long before daylight, and heard with a feeling of pleasure the tinkling of cowbells at the settlements on the opposite side of the Missouri. Early in the day we reached Mr. Sarpy's residence; and, in the security and comfort of his hospitable mansion, felt the pleasure of being within the pale of civilization. We found our boat on the stocks; a few days sufficed to complete her; and, in the afternoon of the 4th, we embarked on the Missouri. All our equipage—horses, carts, and the materiel of the camp—had been sold at public auction at Bellevue. The strength of my party enabled me to man the rout with ten oars, relieved every hour; and we descended rapidly. Early on the morning of the 10th, we halted to make some astronomical observations at the mouth of the Kansas, exactly four months since we had left the tradingpost of Mr. Cyprian Chouteau, on the same river, ten miles above. On our descent to this place, we had employed ourselves in surveying and sketching the Missouri, making astronomical observations regularly at night and at midday, whenever the weather permitted. These operations on the river were continued until our arrival at the city of St Louis, Missouri, on the 17th. At St. Louis, the sale of out remaining effects was made; and, leaving that city by steamboat on the 18th, I had the honor to report to you at the city of Washington on the 29th of October.

Very respectfully, sir,

Your obedient servant,

J. C. FREMONT

An accident among some rough ground in the neighborhood of the Kansas river, strained the balance of this chronometer, (No. 7,810,) and rendered it useless during the remainder of the campaign. From the 9th of June to the 24th of August, inclusively, the longitudes depend upon the Brockbank pocket chronometer; the rate of which, on leaving St. Louis, was fourteen seconds. The rate obtained by observations at Fort Laramie, 14".05, has been used in calculation.

From the 24th of August until the termination of the journey, No. 4,632 (of which the rate was 35".79) was used for the same purposes. The rate of this watch was irregular, and I place little confidence in the few longitudes which depend upon it, though, so far as we have any means of judging, they appear tolerably correct.

OREGON AND NORTH CALIFORNIA

TO COLONEL J.J. ABERT,
CHIEF OF THE CORPS OF TOPOGRAPHICAL ENGINEERS

SIR:—In pursuance of your instructions, to connect the reconnoisance of 1842, which I had the honor to conduct, with the surveys of Commander Wilkes on the coast of the Pacific ocean, so as to give a connected survey of the interior of our continent, I proceeded to the Great West early in the spring of 1843, and arrived, on the 17th of May, at the little town of Kansas, on the Missouri frontier, near tie junction of the Kansas river with the Missouri river, where I was detained near two weeks in completing the necessary preparations for the extended explorations which my instructions contemplated.

My party consisted principally of Creole and Canadian French, and Americans, amounting in all to thirty-nine men; among whom you will recognise several of those who were with me in my first expedition, and who have been favorably brought to your notice in a former report. Mr. Thomas Fitzpatrick, whom many years of hardship and exposure, in the western territories, had rendered familiar with a portion of the country it was designed to explore, had been selected as out guide; and Mr. Charles Preuss, who had been my assistant in a previous journey, was again associated with me in the same capacity, on the present expedition. Agreeably to your directions, Mr. Theodore Talbot, of Washington city, had been attached to the party, with a view to advisement in his profession; and at St. Louis I had been joined by Mr. Frederick Dwight, a gentleman of Springfield, Massachusetts, who availed himself of our overland journey to visit the Sandwich Islands and China, by way of Fort Vancouver.

The men engaged for the service were: Alexis Ayot, Francis Badeau, Oliver Beaulieu, Baptiste Bernier, John A. Camp, John G. Campbell, Manuel Chapman, Ransom Clark, Philibert Courteau, Michel Crelis, William Creuss, Clinton Deforest, Baptiste Derosier, Basil Lajeunesse, Francois Lajeunesse, Henry Lee, Louis Menard,

Louis Montreuil, Samuel Neal, Alexis Pera, Francois Pera, James Power, Raphael Prone, Oscar Sarpy, Baptiste Tabeau, Charles Taplin, Baptiste Tesson, Auguste Vasquez, Joseph Verrot, Patrick White, Tiery Wright, Louis Zindel, and Jacob Dodson, a free young colored man of Washington city, who volunteered to accompany the expedition, and performed his duty manfully throughout the voyage. Two Delaware Indian.—a fine-looking old man and his son—were engaged to accompany the expedition es hunters, through the kindness of Major Cummins, the excellent Indian agent. L. Maxwell, who had accompanied the expedition as one of the hunters in 1842, being on his way tc Taos, in New Mexico, also joined us at this place.

The party was generally armed with Hall's carbines, which with a brass twelve pound howitzer, had been furnished to me from the United States arsenal at St. Louis, agreeably to the orders of Colonel S. W. Kearney, commanding the third min, ary division. Three men were especially detailed for the management of this piece, under the charge of Louis Zindel, a native of Germany, who had been nineteen years a noncommissioned officer of artillery in the Prussian army, and regularly instructed in the duties of his profession. The camp equipage and provisions were transported in twelve carts, drawn each by two mules; and a light covered wagon, mounted on good springs, had been provided for the safer carriage of instruments. These were:

One refracting telescope, by Frauenhofer.

One reflecting circle, by Gambev.

Two sextants, by Troughton.

One pocket chronometer, No. 837, by Goffe, Falmouth.

One pocket chronometer, No. 739, by Brockbank.

One syphon barometer, by Bunten, Paris.

One cistern barometer, by Frye and Shaw, New York.

Six thermometers, and a number of small compasses.

To make the exploration as useful as possible, I determined, In conformity to your general instructions, to vary the route to the

Rocky mountains from that followed in 1842. The route was then up the valley of the Great Platte river to the South Pass, in north latitude 420; the route now determined on was up the valley of the Kansas river, and to the head of the Arkansas river, and to some pass in the mountains, if any could be found, at the sources of that river.

By making this deviation from the former route, the problem of a new road to Oregon and California, in a climate more genial, might be solved; and a better knowledge obtained of an important river, and the country it drained, while the great object of the expedition would find its point of commencement at the termination of the former, which was at that great gate in the ridge of the Rocky mountains called the South Pass, and on the lofty peak of the mountain which overlooks it, deemed the highest peak in the ridge, and from the opposite side of which four great rivers take their rise, and flow to the Pacific or the Mississippi.

Various obstacles delayed our departure until the morning of the 29th, when we commenced our long voyage; and at the close of a day, rendered disagreeably cold by incessant rain, encamped about foul miles beyond the frontier, on the verge of the great prairies.

Resuming our journey on the 31st, after the delay of a day to complete our equipment and furnish ourselves with some of the comforts of civilized life, we encamped in the evening at Elm Glove, in company with several emigrant wagons, constituting a party which was proceeding to Upper California, under the direction of Mr. J. B. Childs, of Missouri. The wagons were variously freighted with goods, furniture, and farming utensils, containing among other things an entire set of machinery for a mill which Mr. Childs designed erecting on the waters of the Sacramento river, emptying into the bay of San Francisco.

We were joined here by Mr. Wm. Gilpin of Mo., who, in tending this year to visit the settlements in Oregon, had been invited to accompany us, and proved a useful and agreeable addition to the party.

JUNE

From Elm Grove, our route until the third of June was nearly the same as that described to you in 1842. Trains of wagons were almost constantly in sight; giving to the road a populous and animated appearance, although the greater portion of the emigrants were collected at the crossing, or already on their march beyond the Kansas river. Leaving at the ford the usual emigrant n ad to the mountains, we continued our route along the southe n side of the Kansas, where we found the country much more broken than on the northern side of the river, and where our progress was much delayed by the numerous small streams, which obliged us to make frequent bridges. On the morning of the 4th we crossed a handsome stream, called by the Indians Otter creek about 130 feet wide, where a flat stratum of limestone, which forms the bed, made an excellent ford. We met here a small party of Kansas and Delaware Indians, the latter returning from a hunting and trapping expedition on the upper waters of the river; and on the heights above were five or six Kansas women, engaged in digging prairie potatoes, (psoralea eseulenici.) On the afternoon of the 6th, whilst busily engaged in crossing a wooded stream, we were thrown into a little confusion by the sudden arrival of Maxwell, who entered the camp at full speed at the head of a war party of Osage Indians, with gay red blankets; and heads shaved to the scalp lock. They had run him a distance of about nine miles, from a creek on which we had encamped the day previous, and to which he had returned search of a runaway horse belonging to Mr. Dwight, which had taken the homeward road, carrying with him saddle, bridle, and holster pistols. The Osages were probably ignorant of our strength, and, when they charged into the camp, drove off a number of our best horses; but we were fortunately well mounted, and, after a hard chase of seven or eight miles, succeeded in recovering them all. This accident, which occasioned delay and trouble, and threatened danger and loss, and broke down some good horses at the start, and actually endangered the expedition, was a first fruit of having gentlemen in company—very estimable, to be sure, but who are not trained to the care and vigilance and self dependence which such an expedition required, and who are not subject to the orders which enforce attention and exertion. We arrived on the 8th at the mouth of the Smokyhill fork, which is the principal southern branch of the Kansas; forming here, by its junction with the Republican, or northern branch, the main Kansas river. Neither stream was fordable, and the necessity of making a raft, together with bad weather, detained us her, until the morning of the 11th; when we resumed our journey along the Republican fork. By our observations, the junction of the streams is in lat. 39° 30' 38", long. 96° 24' 36", and at an elevation of 926 feet above the Gulf of Mexico. For several days we continued to travel along the Republican, through a country beautifully watered with numerous streams, and handsomely timbered; and rarely an incident occurred to vary the monotonous resemblance which one day on the prairies here bears to another, and which scarcely require a particular description. Now and then, we caught a glimpse of a small herd of elk; and occasionally a band of antelopes, whose curiosity sometimes brought them within rifle range, would circle round us and then scour off into the prairies. As we advanced on our road, these became more frequent; but as we journeyed on the line usually followed by the trapping and hunting parties of the Kansas and Delaware Indians, game of every kind continued very shy and wild. The bottoms which form the immediate valley of the main river, were generally about three miles wide; having a rich soil of black vegetable mould, and, for a prairie country, well interspersed with wood. The country was everywhere covered with a considerable variety of grasses, occasionally poor and thin, but far more frequently luxuriant and rich. We had been gradually and regularly ascending in our progress westward, and on the evening of the 14th, when we encamped on a little creek in the valley of the Republican, 265 miles by our traveling road from the mouth of the Kansas, we were at an elevation of 1,520 feet. That part of the river where we were now encamped is called by the Indians the Big Timber. Hitherto our route had been laborious and extremely slow, the unusually wet spring and constant rain having so saturated the whole country that it was necessary to bridge every watercourse, and, for days together, our usual march averaged only five or six miles. Finding that at such a rate of travel it would be impossible to comply with your instructions, I determined at this place to divide the party, and, leaving Mr. Fitzpatrick with twentyfive men in charge of the provisions and heavier baggage of the camp, to proceed myself in advance, with a light party of fifteen men, taking with me the howitzer and the light wagon which carried the instruments.

Accordingly, on the morning of the 16th, the parties sepa rated; and, bearing a little out from the river, with a view of heading some of the numerous affluents, after a few hours' travel over somewhat broken ground, we entered upon an extensive and high level prairie, on which we encamped towards evening at a little stream, where a single dry cottonwood afforded the necessary fuel for preparing supper. Among a variety of grasses which today made their first appearance, I noticed bunchgrass, (festuca,) and buffalograss, (sesleria dactyloides.) Amorpha canescens (lead plant) continued the characteristic plant of the country, and a narrowleaved lathyrus occurred during the morning, in beautiful patches. Sida cocanea occurred frequently, with a psoralea near psoralea floribunda, and a number of plants not hitherto met, just verging into bloom. The water on which we had encamped belonged to Solomon's fork of the Smoky hill river, along whose tributaries we continued to travel for several days.

The country afforded us an excellent road, the route being generally over high and very level prairies; and we met with no other delay than being frequently obliged to bridge one of the numerous streams, which were well timbered with ash, elm, cottonwood, and a very large oak—the latter being occasionally five and six feet in diameter, with a spreading summit. Sida coccinea is very frequent in vermilion colored patches on the high and low prairie; and I remarked that it has a very pleasant perfume.

The wild sensitive plant (schrankia angustata) occurs frequently, generally on the dry prairies, in valleys of streams, and frequently on the broken prairie bank. I remark that the leaflets close instantly to a very light touch. Amorpha, with the same psoralea, and a dwarf species of lupinus, are the characteristic plants.

On the 19th, in the afternoon, we crossed the Pawnee road to the Arkansas, and traveling a few miles onward, the monotony of the prairies was suddenly dispelled by the appearance of five or six buffalo bulls, forming a vanguard of immense herds, among which we were traveling a few days afterwards. Prairie dogs were seen for the first time during the day; and we had the good fortune to obtain an antelope for supper. Our elevation had now increased to 1,900 feet. Sida coccinea was the characteristic on the creek bottoms, and buffalo grass is becoming abundant on the higher parts of the ridges.

21st.—During the forenoon we, traveled up a branch of the creek on which we had encamped, in a broken country, where, however, the dividing ridges always afforded a good road. Plants were few; and with the short sward of the buffalograss, which now prevailed everywhere, giving to the prairies a smooth and mossy appearance, were mingled frequent patches of a beautiful red grass, (aristida pallens,) which had made its appearance only within the last few days.

We halted to noon at a solitary cottonwood in a hollow, near which was killed the first buffalo, a large old bull.

Antelope appeared in bands during the day. Crossing here to the affluents of thee Republican, we encamped on a fork, about Imy feet wide and one foot deep, flowing with a swift current over a sandy bed, and well wooded with ashleaved maple, (negundo fraxinillium,) elm, cottonwood, and a few white oaks. We were visited in the evening by a very violent storm, accompanied by wind, lightning, and thunder; a cold rain falling in torrents. According to the barometer, our elevation was 2,130 feet above the gulf.

At noon, on the 23d, we descended into the valley of a principal fork of the Republican, a beautiful stream with a dense border of wood, consisting principally of varieties of ash, forty feet wide and four deep. It was musical with the notes of many birds, which, from the vast expanse of silent prairie around, seemed all to have collected here. We continued during the afternoon our route along the river, which was populous with prairie dogs, (the bottoms being entirely occupied with their villages,) and late in the evening encamped on its banks. The prevailing timber is a bluefoliaged ash, cfrax inus, near F. Americana,) and ashleaved maple. With them were fraxinus Americana, cottonwood, and longleaved willow We gave to this stream the name of Prairie Dog river. Elevation 2,350 feet. Our road on the 25th lay over high smooth ridges, 3,100 feet above the sea; buffalo in great numbers absolutely covering the face of the country. At evening we encamped within a few miles of the main Republican, on a tittle creek, where the air was fragrant with the perfume of artemisia filifolia, which we here saw for the first time, and which was now in bloom. Shortly after leaving our encampment on the 26th, we found suddenly that the nature of the country had entirely changed. Bare sandhills everywhere surrounded us in the undulating ground along which we were moving, and the plants peculiar to a sandy soil made their appearance in abundance. A few miles further we entered the valley of a large stream, afterwards known to be the Republican fork of the Kansas, whose shallow waters, with a depth of only a few inches, were spread out over a bed of yellowish white sand 600 yards wide. With the exception of one or two distant and detached groves, no timber of any kind was to be seen; and the features of the country assumed a desert character, with which the broad river, struggling for existence among the quicksands along the treeless banks, was strikingly in keeping. On the opposite side, the broken ridges assumed almost a mountainous appearance; and fording the stream, we continued on our course among these ridges, and encamped late in the evening at a little pond of very bad water, from which we drove away a herd of buffalo that were standing it and about it. Our encampment this evening was 3,500 feet above the sea. We traveled now for several days through a broken and dry sandy 'region, about 4,000 feet above the sea, where there were no running streams; and some anxiety was constantly felt on account of the uncertainty of water, which was only to be found in small lakes that occurred occasionally among the hills. The discovery of these always brought pleasure to the camp, as around them were generally green flats, which afforded abundant pasturage for our animals; and here we usually collected herds of the buffalo, which now were scattered over all the country in countless numbers.

The soil of bare and hot sands supported a varied and exuberant growth of plants, which were much farther advanced than we had previously found them, and whose showy bloom somewhat relieved the appearance of general sterility. Crossing the summit of an elevated and continuous range of rolling hills, on the afternoon of the 30th of June, we found ourselves overlooking a broad and misty valley, where, about ten miles distant, and 1,000 feet below us, the South fork of the Platte was rolling magnificently along, swollen with the waters of the melting snows. It was in strong and refreshing contrast with the parched country from which we had just issued; and when, at night, the broad expanse of water grew indistinct, it almost seemed that we had pitched our tents on the shore of the sea.

JULY.

Traveling along up the valley of the river, here 4,000 feet above the sea, in the afternoon of July 1, we caught a far and uncertain view of a faint blue mass in the west, as the sun sank behind it; and from our camp in the morning, at the In° ith of Bijou, Long's peak and the neighboring mountains stood out into the sky, grand and luminously white, covered to their bases with glittering snow.

On the evening of the 3d, as we were journeying along the partially overflowed bottoms of the Platte, where our passage stirred up swarms of musquitoes, we came unexpectedly on an Indian, who was perched upon a bluff, curiously watching the movements of our caravan. He belonged to a village of Oglallah Sioux, who had lost all their animals in the severity of the preceding winter, and were now on their way up the Bijou fork to beg horses from the Arapahoes, who were hunting buffalo at the head of that river. Several came into our camp at noon; and, as they were hungry, as usual, they were provided with buffalo meat, of which the hunters had brought in an abundant supply.

About noon, on the 4th of July, we arrived at the fort, where Mr. St. Vrain received us with his customary kindness, and invited us to join him in a feast which had been prepared in honor of the day.

Our animals were very much worn out, and our stock of provisions entirely exhausted, when we arrived at the fort; but I was disappointed in my hope of obtaining relief, as I found it in a very impoverished condition; and we were able to procure only a little unbolted Mexican flour, and some salt, with a few pounds of powder and lead.

As regarded' provisions, it did not much matter in a country where rarely the day passed without seeing some kind of game, and where it was frequently abundant. It was a rare thing tc tie down hungry, and w had already learned to think bread a luxury; but we could not proceed without animals, and our own were not capable of prosecuting the journey beyond the mountains without relief.

I had been informed that a large number of mules had recently arrived at Taos, from Upper California; and as our friend, Mr. Maxwell, was about to continue his journey to that place, where a portion of his family resided, I engaged him to purchase for me ten or twelve mules, with the understanding that he should pack them with provisions and other necessaries and meet me at the mouth of the Fontainequibouit, on the Arkansas river, to which point I would be led in the course of the survey.

Agreeably, to his own request, and in the conviction that his habits of life and education had not qualified him to endure the hard life of a voyageur, I discharged here one, of my party, Mr. Oscar Sarpy, having furnished him with arms and means of transportation to Fort Laramie, where he would be in the line of caravans returning to the States.

At daybreak, on the 6th of July, Maxwell was on his way to Taos; and a few hours after we also had recommenced our journey up the Platte, which was continuously timbered with cottonwood and willow, on a generally sandy soil. Passing on the way the remains of two abandoned forts, (one of which, however, was still in good condition,) we reached, in ten miles, Fort Lancaster, the trading establishment of Mr. Lupton.

His post was beginning to assume the appearance of a comfortable farm: stock, hogs, and cattle, were ranging about on the prairie—there were different kinds of poultry; and there was a wreck of a promising garden, in which a considerable variety of vegetables had been in a flourishing condition; but it had been almost entirely ruined by the recent high waters. I remained to spend with him an agreeable hour, and set off in a cold storm of rain, which was accompanied with violent thunder and lightning. We encamped immediately on the river, sixteen miles from St. Vrain's. Several Arapahoes, on their way to the village which was encamped a few miles above us, passed by the camp in the course of the afternoon. Night set in stormy and cold, with heavy and continuous rain, which lasted until morning.

7th.—We made this morning an early start, continuing to travel up the Platte; and in a few miles frequent bands of horses and mules, scattered for several miles round about, indicated our approach to the Arapaho village, which we found encamped in a beautiful bottom, and consisting of about one hundred and sixty lodges. It appeared extremely populous with a great number of children—a circumstance watch indicated a regular supply of the means of subsistence chiefs, who were gathered together at the farther end if the village, received us (as probably strangers are always received o whom they desire to show respect or regard) by throwing heir arms around our necks and embracing us.

It required some skill in horsemanship to keep the saddle during the performance of this ceremony, as our American horses exhibited for them the same fear they have for a bear,, or any other wild animal. Having very few goods with me, I was only able to make them a meager present, accounting for the poverty of the gift by explaining that my goods had been left with the wagons in charge of Mr. Fitzpatrick, who was well known to them 'as the White Head, or the Broken Hand.

I saw here, as I had remarked in an Arapaho village the preceding year, near the lodges of the chiefs, tall tripods of win poles supporting their spears and shields, which showed it to be a regular custom.

Though disappointed in obtaining the presents which had been evidently expected, they behaved very courteously; and, after a little conversation, I left them, and, continuing on up the river, halted to noon on the bluff, as the bottoms are almost inundated; continuing in the afternoon our route along the mountains, which were dark, misty, and shrouded—threatening a storm; the snow peaks sometimes glittering through the clouds beyond the first ridge.

We surprised a grizzly bear sauntering along the river, which, raising himself upon his hind legs, took a deliberate survey of us, that did not appear very satisfactory to him, and he scrambled into the river and swam to the opposite side. We halted for the night a little above Cherry creel(; the evening cloudy, with many musquitoes. Some indifferent observations placed the camp in lat. 39° 43' 53", and chronometric long. 1050 24' 34".

&h.—We continued today to travel up the Platte: the morning pleasant, with a prospect of fairer weather. During the forenoon our way lay over a more broken country, with a gravelly and sandy surface; although the immediate bottom of the river was a good soil, of a dark and sandy mould, resting upon a stratum of large pebbles, or rolled stones, as at Laramie fork. On our right, and apparently very near, but probably 8 or 10 miles distant, and two or three thousand feet above us, ran the first range of the mountains, like a dark corniced line, in clear contrast with the great snowy chain which, immediately beyond, rose glittering five thousand feet above them. We caught this morning a view of Pike's peak; but it appeared for a moment only, as clouds rose early over the mountains, and shrouded them in mist and rain all the day. In the first range were visible, as at the Red Buttes on the North fork, very lofty escarpments of red rock. While traveling through this region, I remarked that always in the morning the lofty peaks were visible and bright, but very soon small white clouds began to settle around them—brewing thicker and thicker as the day advanced, until the afternoon, when the thunder began to roll; and invariably at evening we had more or less of a thunder storm. At 11 o'clock, and 21 miles from St Vrain's fort, we reached a point in this southern fork of the Platte, where the stream is divided into three forks; two of these (one of them being much the largest) issuing directly from the mountains on the west, and forming, with the easternmost branch, a river of the plains. The elevation of this point is about 5,500 feet above the sea; this river falling 2,800 feet in a distance of 316 miles, to its junction with the North fork of the Platte. In this estimate, the elevation of the junction is assumed as given by our barometrical observations in 1842. On the easternmost branch, up which we took our way, we first came among the pines growing on the top of a very high bank, and where we halted on it to noon; quaking asp (populus tremuloides) was mixed with the cottonwood, and there were excellent grass and rushes for the animals.

During the morning there occurred many beautiful flowers, which we had not hitherto met. Among them, the common blue flowering flax made its first appearance; and a tall and handsome species of gilia, with slender scarlet flowers, which appeared yesterday for the firs' time, was very frequent today.

We had found very little game since leaving the fort, awl provisions began to get unpleasantly scant, as we had had no meat for several days; but towards sundown, when we had already made up our minds to sleep another night without supper, Lajeunesse had the good fortune to kill a fine deer, which he found feeding in a hollow near by; and as the rain began to fall, threatening an unpleasant night, we hurried to secure a comfortable camp in the timber.

Tonight the camp fires, girdled with appalas of fine venison, looked cheerful in spite of the stormy weather.

9th.—On account of the low state of our provisions and the scarcity of game, I determined to vary our route, and proceed several camps to the eastward, in the hope of falling in with the buffalo. This route along the dividing grounds between the South fork of the Platte and the Arkansas, would also afford some additional geographical information. This morning, therefore, we turned to the eastward, along the upper waters of the stream on which we had encamped, entering a country of picturesque and varied scenery; broken into rocky hills of singular shapes; little valleys, with pure crystal water, here leaping swiftly along, and there losing itself in the sands; green spots of luxuriant grass, flowers of all colors, and timber of different kinds—every thing to give it a varied beauty, except game. To one of these remarkably shaped hills, having on the summit a circular flat rock two or three hundred yards in circumference, some one gave the name of Poundcake, which it has been permitted to retain, as our hungry people seemed to think it a very agreeable comparison. In the afternoon a buffalo bull was killed, and we encamped on a small stream, near the road which runs from St. Vrain's fort to the Arkansas.

10th.—Snow fell heavily on the mountains during the night, and Pike's peak this morning is luminous and grand, covered from the summit, as low down as we can see, with glittering white. Leaving the encampment at 6 o'clock, we continued our easterly course over a rolling country, near to the high ridges, which are generally rough and rocky, with a coarse conglomerate displayed in masses, and covered with pines The rock is very friable and it is undoubtedly from its do composition that the prairies derive their sandy and gravelly formation. In six miles we crossed a headwater of the Kioway river, on which we found a strong fort and coral that had been built in the spring, and halted to noon on the principal branch of the river. During the morning our route led over a dark and vegetable mould, mixed with sand and gravel, the characteristic plant being esparcette, (onobrychis sativa,) a species of clover which is much used in certain Parts of Germany for pasturage of stock—principally hogs. It is sown on rocky waste ground, which would otherwise be useless, arid grows very luxuriantly, requiring only a renewal of the seed about once in fifteen years. Its abundance here greatly adds to the pastoral value of this region. A species of antennaria in flower was very common along the line of road, and the creeks were timbered with willow and pine. We encamped on Bijou's fork, the water of which, unlike the clear streams we had previously crossed, is of a whitish color, and the soil of the bottom a very hard, tough clay. There was a prairie dog village on the bottom, and, in the endeavor to unearth one of the little animals, we labored ineffectually in the tough clay until dark. After descending, with a slight inclination, until it had gone the depth of two feet, the hole suddenly turned at a sharp angle in another direction for one more foot in depth, when it again turned, taking an ascending direction to the next nearest hole. I have no doubt that all their little habitations communicate with each other. The greater part of the people were sick today, and I was inclined to attribute their indisposition to the meat of the bull which had been killed the previous day.

11th.—There were no indications of buffalo having been recently in the neighborhood; and, unwilling to travel farther eastward, I turned this morning to the southward, up the valley of Bijou. Esparcette occurred universally, and among the plants on the river I noticed, for the first time during this journey, a few small bushes of the absinthe of the voyageurs, which is commonly used for firewood, (artemzsia tridentata.) Yesterday and today the road has been ornamented with the showy bloom of a beautiful lupinus, a characteristic in many parts of the mountain region, on which were generally great numbers of an insect with very bright colors, (litta vesicatoria.)

As we were riding quietly along, eagerly searching every hollow in search of gene, we discovered, at a little distance in the prairie, a large grizzly bear, so busily engaged in digging roots that he did not perceive us until we were galloping down a little hill fifty yards from him, when he charged upon us with such sudden energy that several of us came near losing out saddles. Being wounded, he commenced retreating to a rocky piny ridge near by, from which we were not able to cut him off, and we entered the timber with him. The way was very much blocked up with fallen timber; and we kept up a running fight for some time, animated by the bear charging among the horses. He did not fall until after he had received six rifle balls. He was miserably poor, and added nothing to our stock of provisions.

We followed the stream to its head in a broken ridge, which, according to the barometer, was about 7,500 feet above the sea. This is a piny elevation, into which the prairies are gathered, and from which the waters flow, in almost every direction, to the Arkansas, Platte, and Kansas rivers; the latter stream having here its remotest sources. Although somewhat rocky and broken, and covered with pines, in comparison with the neighboring mountains, it scarcely forms an interruption to the great prairie plains which sweep up to their bases.

We had an excellent view of Pike's peak from this camp, at the distance of forty miles. This mountain barrier presents itself to travelers on the plains, which sweep almost directly to its bases—an immense and comparatively smooth and grassy prairie, in very strong contrast with the black masses of timber, and the glittering snow above them. With occasional exceptions, comparatively so very small as not to require mention, these prairies are everywhere covered with a close and vigorous growth of a great variety of grasses, among which the most abundant is the buffalo grass, (sesleria dactyloides.) Between the Platte and Arkansas rivers, that part of this region which forms the basin drained by the waters of the Kansas, with which our operations made us more particularly acquainted, is based upon a formation of calcareous rocks. The soil of all this country is excellent, admirably adapted to agricultural purposes, and would support a large agricultural and pastoral population. A glance at the map, along our several lines of travel, will show you that this plain is watered by many streams. Throughout the western half of the plain, these are shallow, with sandy beds, becoming deeper as they reach the richer lands approaching the Missouri river; they generally have bottom lands, bordered by bluffs varying from fifty to five hundred feet in height. In all this region the timber is entirely confined to the streams. In the eastern half, where the soil is a deep, rich, vegetable mould, retentive of rain and moisture, it is of vigorous growth, and of many different kinds; _and throughout the western half it consists entirely of various species of cottonwood, which deserves to be called the tree of the desert—growing in sandy soils, where no other tree will grow—pointing out the existence of water, and furnishing to the travler fuel, and food for his animals. Add to this that the westun border of the plain is occupied by the Sioux, Arapaho, and Cheyenne nations, with the Pawnees and other half civilized tribes in its eastern limits, for whom the intermediate country is a war ground, and you will have a tolerably correct idea of the appearance and condition of the country. Descending a somewhat precipitous and rocky hillside among the pines, which rarely appear elsewhere than on the ridge, we encamped at its foot, where there were several springs, which you will find laid down upon the map as one of the extreme sources of the Smoky Hill fork of the Kansas. From this place the view extended over the Arkansas valley, and the Spanish peaks in the south beyond. As the greater part of the men continued sick, I encamped here for the day, and ascertained conclusively, from experiments on myself, that their illness was caused by the meat of the buffalo bull.

On the summit of the ridge, near the camp, were several rock built forts, which in front were very difficult of approach, and in the rear were protected by a precipice entirely beyond the reach of a rifleball. The evening was tolerably clear, with a temperature at sunset of 63o. Elevation of the camp seven thousand and three hundred feet.

Turning the next day to the southwest, we reached, in the course of the morning, the wagonroad to the settlements on the Arkansas river, and encamped in the afternoon on the Fontainequibouit (or Boiling Spring) river, where it was fifty feet wide, with a swift current. I afterwards found that the spring and river owe their names to the bubbling of the effervescing gas in the former, and not to the temperature of the water, which is cold. During the morning a tall species of gilia, with a slender white flower, was characteristic; and, in the latter part of the day, another variety of esparcette, (wild clover,) having the flower white, was equally so. We had a fine sunset of golden brown; and, in the evening, a very bright moon, with the near mountains, made a beautiful scene. Thermometer, at sunset, was 69o, and our elevation above the sea 5,800 feet.

13th.—The morning was clear, with a northwesterly breeze, and the thermometer at sunrise at 46. There were no clouds along the mountains, and the morning sun showed very clearly their rugged character.

We resumed our journey very early down the river, following an extremely good lodgetrail, which issues by the head of this stream from the bayou Salade, a high mountain valley behind Pike's peak. The soil along the road was sandy and gravelly, and the river well timbered. We halted to noon under the shade of some fine large cottonwoods, our animals luxuriating on rushes, (equisetum hyemale,) which, along this river, were remarkably abundant. A variety of cactus made its appearance, and among several strange plants were numerous and beautiful clusters of a plant resembling mirabilis jalapa, with a handsome convolvulus I had not hitherto seen, (calystegia.) In the afternoon we passed near the encampment of a hunter named Maurice, who had been out into the plains in pursuit of buffalo calves, a number of which I saw among some domestic cattle near his lodge. Shortly afterwards, a party of mountaineers galloped up to us—fine-looking and hardy men, dressed in skins, and mounted on good fat horses; among them were several Connecticut men, a portion of Wyeth's party, whom I had seen the year before, and others were men from the western state.

Continuing down the river, we encamped at noon on the 14th, at its mouth, on the Arkansas river. A short distance above our encampment, on the left bank of the Arkansas, is a pueblo, (as the Mexicans call their civilized Indian villages,) where a number of mountaineers, who had married Spanish women in the valley of Taos, had collected together and occupied themselves in farming, carrying on at the same time a desultory Indian trade. They were principally Americans, and treated us with all the rude hospitality their situation admitted; but as all commercial intercourse with New Mexico was now interrupted, in consequence of Mexican decrees to that effect, there was nothing to be had in the way of provisions. They had, however, a fine stock of cattle, and furnished as an abundance of excellent milk. I learned here that Maxwell, in company with two other men, had started for Taos on the morning of the 9th, but that he would probably fall into the hands of the Utah Indians, commonly called the Spanish Yutes. As Maxwell had no knowledge of their being in the vicinity when he crossed the Arkansas, his chance of escape was very doubtful; but I did not entertain much apprehension for his life, having great confidence in his prudence and courage. I was further informed that there had been a popular tumult among the pueblos, or civilized Indians, residing near Taos, against the "foreigners" of that place, in which they had plundered their houses and ill-treated their families. Among those whose property had been destroyed, was Mr. Beaubien, father-in-law of Maxwell, from whom I had expected to obtain supplies, and who had been obliged to make his escape to Santa Fe.

By this position of affairs, our expectation of obtaining supplies from Taos was cut off. I had here the satisfaction to meet our good buffalo hunter of 1842, Christopher Carson, whose services I considered myself fortunate to secure again and as a reinforcement of mules was absolutely necessary, I dispatched him immediately, with an account of our necessities, to Mr. Charles Bent, whose principal post is on the Arkansas river, about seventy-five miles below Fontainequibouit. He was directed to proceed from that post by the nearest route across the country, and meet me, with what animals he should be able to obtain, at St. Vrain's fort. I also admitted into the party Charles Towns, a native of St. Louis, a serviceable man, with many of the qualities of a good voyageur. According to our observations, the latitude of the mouth of the river is 38° 15' 23", its longitude 104° 58' 30", and its elevation above the sea 4,880 feet.

On the morning of the 16th, the time for Maxwell's arrival having expired, we resumed our journey, leaving for him a note, in which it was stated that I would wait for him at St. Vrain's fort, until the morning of the 26th, in the event that he should succeed in his commission. Our direction was up the Boiling Spring river, it being my intention to visit the celebrated springs from which the river takes its name, and which are on its upper waters, at the foot of Pike's peak. Our animals fared well while we were on this stream, there being everywhere a great abundance of prele. Ipomea leptcrphylla in bloom, was a characteristic plant along the river, general; in large bunches, with two to five flowers on each. Beautiful clusters of the plant resembling mirabilis Jalapa were numerous, and glycyrrhiza lepidota was a characteristic of the bet toms. Currants nearly ripe were abundant, and among tilt shrubs which covered the bottom was a very luxuriant growth of chenopodiaceous shrubs, four to six feet high. On the afternoon of the 17th we entered among the broken ridges at the foot of the mountains, where the river made several forks. Leaving the camp to follow slowly, I rode ahead in the afternoon in search of the springs. In the mean time, the clouds, which had been gathered all the afternoon over the mountains, began to roll down their sides; and a storm so violent bursa upon me, that it appeared I had entered the storehouse of the thunderstorms. I continued, however, to ride along up the river until about sunset, and was beginning to be doubtful of finding the springs before the next day, when I came suddenly upon a large smooth rock, about twenty yards in diameter, where the water from several springs was bubbling and boiling up in the midst of a white incrustation, with which it had covered a portion of the rock. As this did not correspond with the description given me by the hunters, I did not stop to taste the water, but dismounting, walked a little way up the river, and, passing through a narrow thicket of shrubbery bordering the stream stepped directly upon a huge white rock, at the foot of which the river, already become a torrent, foamed along, broken by a small fall. A deer which had been drinking at the spring was startled by my approach, and, springing across the river, bounded off up the mountain. In the upper part of the rock, which had apparently been formed by deposition, was a beautiful white basin, overhung by currant bushes, in which the cold clear water bubbled up, kept in constant motion by the escaping gas, and overflowing the rock, which it had almost entirely covered with a smooth crust of glistening white. I had all day refrained from drinking, reserving myself for the spring; and as I could not well be more wet than the rain had already made me, I lay down by the side of the basin, and drank heartily of the delightful water. The spring is situated immediately at the foot of lofty mountains, beautifully timbered, which sweep closely round, shutting up the little valley in a kind of cove. As it was beginning to grow dark, I rode quickly down the river, on which I found the camp a few miles below.

The morning of the 18th was beautiful and clear; and, all the people being anxious to drink of these famous waters, we encamped immediately at the springs, and spent there a very pleasant day. On the opposite side of the river is another locality of springs, which are entirely of the same nature. The water has a very agreeable taste, which Mr. Preuss found very much to resemble that of the famous Selter springs in the grand duchy of Nassau, a country famous for wine and mineral waters; and it is almost entirely of the same character, though still more agreeable than that of the famous Bear springs, near Bear river of the Great Salt lake. The following is an analysis of an incrustation with which the water had covered a piece of wood lying on the rock:

At eleven o'clock, when the temperature of the air was 73°, that of the water in this was 60.5°; and that of the upper spring, which issued from the flat rock, more exposed to the sun, was 69o. At sunset, when the temperature of the air was 66°, that of the lower springs was 58°, and that of the upper 61°.

19th.—A beautiful and clear morning, with a slight breeze from the northwest; the temperature of the air at sunrise being 57.5°. At this time the temperature of the lower spring was 57.8o, springs was 58°, and that of the upper 543o.

The trees in the neighborhood were birch, willow, pine, and an oak resembling quercus alba. In the shrubbery along the river are currant bushes, (ribes,) of which the fruit has a singular piny flavor; and on the mountain side, in a red gravelly soil, is a remarkable coniferous tree, (perhaps an abies,) having the leaves singularly long, broad and scattered, with bushes of spircea aricefolia. By our observations, this place is 6,350 feet above the sea, in latitude 38° 52' 10", and longitude 105° 22' 45".

Resuming our journey on this morning, we descended the river, in order to reach the mouth of the eastern fork, which I proposed to ascend. The left bank of the river here is very much broken. There is a handsome little bottom on the right, and both banks are exceedingly picturesque—strata of red rock, in nearly perpendicular walls, crossing the valley from north to south. About three miles below the springs, on the right bank of the Fiver, is a nearly perpendicular limestone rock, presenting a uniformly unbroken surface, twenty to forty feet high, containing very great numbers of a large univalve shell, which appears to belong to the genus inoceramus.

In contact with this, to the westward, was another stratum of limestone, containing fossil shells of a different character; and still higher up on the stream were parallel strata, consisting of a compact somewhat crystalline limestone, and argillaceous bituminous limestone in thin layers. During the morning, we traveled up the eastern fork of the Fontainequibrmit river, our road being roughened by frequent deep gullies timbered with pine, and halted to noon on a small branch of the stream, timbered principally with the narrow leaved cottonwood, (populus angustifolia,) called by the Canadians Hard amere. On a hill near by, were two remarkable columns of a grayish-white conglomerate rock, one of which was about twenty feet high, and two feet in diameter. They are surmounted, by slabs of a dark ferruginous conglomerate, forming black caps, and adding very much to their columnar effect at a distance. This rock is very destructible by the action of the weather, and the hill, of which they formerly constituted a part, is entirely abraded.

A shaft of the guncarriage was broken in the afternoon; and we made an early halt, the stream being from twelve to twenty feet wide, with clear water. As usual, the clouds had gathered to a storm over the mountains, and we had a showery evening. At sunset, the thermometer stood at 62o, and our elevation above the sea was 6,530 feet.

20th.—This morning (as we' generally found the mornings under these mountains) was very clear and beautiful, and the air cool and pleasant, with the thermometer at 44°. We continued our march up the stream, along a green sloping bottom, between pine hills on the one hand, and the main Black hills on the other, towards the ridge which separates the waters of the Platte from those of the Arkansas. As we approached the diving ridge, the whole valley was radiant with flowers; blue, yellow, pink, white, scarlet, and purple, vie with each other in splendor. Esparcette was one of the highly characteristic plants, and a brightlooking flower (gaillardia aristata) was very frequent; but the most abundant plant along our road to day, was geranium maculagum, which is the characteristic plant on this portion of the diving grounds. Crossing to the waters of the Platte, fields of blue flax added to the magnificence of this mountain garden; this was occasionally four feet in height, which was a luxuriance of growth that I rarely saw this al most universal plant attain throughout the journey. Continuing down a branch of the Platte, among high and very steep timbered hills covered with fragments of rock, towards evening we issued from the piny region, and made a late encampment near Poundcake rock, on that fork of the river which we had ascended on the 8th of July. Our animals enjoyed the abundant rushes this evening, as the flies were so bad among the pines that they had been much harassed. A deer was killed here this evening; and again the evening was overcast, and a collection of brilliant red clouds in the west was followed by the customary squall of rain.

Achillea millefolium (milfoil) was among the characteristic plants of the river bottoms today. This was one of the most common plants during the whole of our journey, occurring in almost every variety of situation. I noticed it on the lowlands of the rivers, near the coast of the Pacific, and near to the snow among the mountains of the Sierra Nevada.

During this excursion, we had surveyed to its head one of the two principal branches of the upper Arkansas, 75 miles in length, and entirely completed our survey of the South fork of the Platte, to the extreme sources of that portion of the river which belongs to the plains, and heads in the broken hills of the Arkansas dividing ridge, at the foot of the mountains. That portion of its waters which were collected among these mountains, it was hoped to explore on our homeward voyage. '

Reaching St. Vrain's fort on the morning of the 23d, we found Mr. Fitzpatrick and his party in good order and excellent health, and my true and reliable 'friend, Kit Carson, who had brought with him ten good mules, with the necessary packsaddles. Mr. Fitzpatrick, who had often endured every extremity of want during the course of his mountain life, and knew well the value of provisions in this country, had watched over our stock with jealous vigilance, and there was an abundance of flour, rice, sugar, and coffee, in the camp; and again we fared luxuriously. Meat was, however, very scarce; and two very small pigs, which we obtained at the fort, did not go far among forty men. Mr. Fitzpatrick had been here a week, during which time his men had been occupied in refitting the camp; and the repose had been very beneficial to his animals, which were now in tolerably good condition.

I had been able to obtain no certain information in regard o the character of the passes in this portion of the Rocky Mountain range, which had always been represented as impracticable for carriages, but the exploration of which was incidentally contemplated by my instructions, with the view of finding some convenient point of passage for the road of emigration, which would enable it to reach, on a more direct line, the usual ford of the Great Colorado—a place considered as determined by the nature of the country beyond that river. It is singular, that immediately at the foot of the mountains, I could find no one sufficiently acquainted with them to guide us to the plains at their western base; but the race of trappers, who formerly lived in their recesses, has almost entirely disappeared— dwindled to a few scattered individuals—some one or two of whom are regularly killed in the course of each year by the Indians. You will remember, that in the previous year I brought with me to their village near this post, and hospitably treated on the way, several Cheyenne Indians, whom I met on the Lower Platte. Shortly after their arrival here, these were out with a party of Indians, (themselves the principal men,) which discovered a few trappers in the neighboring mountains, whom they immediately murdered, although one of them had been nearly thirty years in the country, and was perfectly well known, as he had grown gray among them.

Through this portion of the mountains, also, are the customary roads of the war parties going out against the Utah and Shoshonee Indians; and occasionally parties from the Crow nation make their way down to the southward along this chain, in the expectation of surprising some straggling lodges of their enemies. Shortly before our arrival, one of their parties had attacked an Arapaho village in the vicinity which they had found unexpectedly strong.; and their assault was turned into a rapid flight and a hot pursuit, in which they had been compelled to abandon the animals they had rode and escape on their warhorses.

Into this uncertain and dangerous region, small parties of three or four trappers, who now could collect together, rarely ventured; and consequently it was seldom visited and little known. Having determined to try the passage by a pass through a spur of the mountains made by the CaehedlaPoudre river, which rises in the high bed of mountains around Long's peak, I thought it advisable to avoid any encumbrance which would occasion detention, and accordingly again separated the party into two divisions—one of which, under the command of Mr. Fitzpatrick, was directed to cross the plains to the mouth of Laramie river, and, continuing thence its route along the usual emigrant road, meet me at Fort Hall, a post belonging to the Hudson Bay Company, and situated on Snake river, as it is commonly called in the Oregon Territory, although better known to us as Lewis's fork of the Columbia. The latter name is there restricted to one of the upper forks of the river.

Our Delaware Indians having determined to return to their homes, it became necessary to provide this party with a good hunter; and I accordingly engaged in that capacity Alexander Godey, a young man about 25 years of age, who had been in this country six or seven years, all of which time had been actively employed in hunting for the support of the posts, of in solitary trading expeditions among the Indians. In courage and professional skill he was a formidable rival to Carson, and constantly afterwards was among the best and most efficient of the party, and in difficult situations was of incalculable value. Hiram Powers, one of the men belonging to Mr. Fitzpatrick's party, was discharged at this place.

A French engage, at Lupton's fort, had been shot in the back on the 4th of July, and died during our absence to the Arkansas. The wife of the murdered man, an Indian woman of the Snake nation, desirous, like Naomi of old, to return to her people, requested and obtained permission to travel with my party to the neighborhood of Bear river, where she expected to meet with some of their villages. Happier than the Jewish widow, she carried with her two children, pretty little half breeds, who added much to the liveliness of the camp. Their baggage was carried on five or six packhorses; and I gave her a small tent, for which I no longer had any use, as I had procured a lodge at the fort.

For my own party I selected the following men, a number of Whom old associations had rendered agreeable to me:

Charles Preuss, Christopher Carson, Basil Lajeunesse, Fran Bois Badeau, J. B. Bernier, Louis Menard, Raphael Proue. Jacob Dodson, Louis Zindel, Henry Lee, J. B. Derosier, Francois Lajeunesse, and Auguste Vasquez.

By observation, the latitude of the post is 40o 16' 33", and its longitude 105o 12' 23", depending, with all the other longitudes along this portion of the line, upon a subsequent occultation of September 13, 1843, to which they are referred by the chronometer. Its distance from Kansas landing, by the road we traveled, (which, it will be remembered, was very winding along the lower Kansas river,) was 750 miles. The rate of the chronometer, determined by observations at this place for the interval of our absence, during this month, was 33.72", which you will hereafter see did not sensibly change during the ensuing month, and remained nearly constant during the remainder of our journey across the continent. This was the rate used in referring to St. Vrain's fort, the longitude between that place and the mouth of the Fontaznequibouit.

Our various barometrical observations, which are better worthy of confidence than the isolated determination of 1842, give, for the elevation of the fort above the sea, 4,930 feet The barometer here used was also a better one, and less liable to derangement.

At the end of two days, which was allowed for necessary repose, all the arrangements had been completed, and on the afternoon of the 26th we resumed our respective routes. Some little trouble was experienced in crossing the Platte, the waters of which were kept up by rains and melting snow; and having traveled only about four miles, we encamped in the evening on Thompson's creek, where we were very much disturbed by musquitoes.

The following days we continued our march westward over compelative plains, and, fording the Cachea laPoudre on the morning of the 28th, entered the Black hilly, and nooned on this stream in the mountains beyond them. Passing over a fine large bottom in the afternoon, we reached a place where the river was shut up in the hills; and, ascending a ravine, made a laborious and very difficult passage around by a gap, striking the river again about dusk. A little labor, however, and remove this difficulty, and render the road to this point a very excellent one. The evening closed in dark with rain, and the mountains looked gloomy.

29th.—Leaving our encampment about seven in the morning, we traveled until three in the afternoon along the river, which, for the distance of about six miles, runs directly through a spur of the main mountains.

We were compelled by the nature of the ground to cross the river eight or nine times, at difficult, deep, and rocky fords, the stream running with great force, swollen by the rains—a true mountain torrent, only forty or fifty feet wide. It was a mountain valley of the narrowest kind—almost a chasm—and the scenery very wild and beautiful. Towering mountains rose round about; their sides sometimes dark with forests of pine, and sometimes with lofty precipices, washed by the river; while below, as if they indemnified themselves in luxuriance for the scanty space, the green river bottom was covered with a wilderness of flowers, their tall spikes some times rising above our heads as we rode among them. A profusion of blossoms on a white flowering vine, (clematis lasianthi,) which was abundant along the river, contrasted handsomely with the green foliage of the trees. The mountains appeared to be composed of a greenish-gray and red granite, which in some places appeared to be in a state of decomposition, making a red soil.

The stream was wooded with cottonwood, boxelder, and cherry, with currant and serviceberry bushes. After a some what laborious day during which it had rained incessantly, we encamped near the end of the pass at the mouth of a small creek, in sight of the great Laramie plains. It continued to rain heavily, and at evening the mountains were hid in mists; but there was no lack of wood, and the large fires we made to dry our clothes were very comfortable; and at night the hunters came in with a fine deer. Rough and difficult as we found the pass today, an excellent road may be made with a little labor. Elevation of the camp 5,540 feet, and distance from St. Vrain's fort 56 miles.

30th.—The day was bright again; the thermometer at sun rise 52°; and leaving our encampment at eight o'clock, in about half a mile we crossed the Cacheala Poudre river for the last time; and, entering a smoother country, we traveled along a kind of vallon, bounded on the right by red buttes and precipices, while to the left a high rolling country extended to a range of the Black hills, beyond which the great mountains around Long's peak.

By the great quantity of snow visible among them, it had probably snowed heavily there the previous day, while it had rained on us in the valley.

We halted at noon on a small branch ,in the afternoon traveled over a high country, gradually ,;coming towards a range of buttes, or high hills covered pines, which forms the dividing ridge between the waters we Lad left and those of Laramie river:

Late in the evening we encamped at a spring of cold water, near the summit of the ridge, having increased our elevation to 7.520 feet. During the day we had traveled 24 miles. By some indifferent observations, our latitude is 410 02' 19". A species of hedeome was characteristic along the whole day's route.

Emerging from the mountains, we entered a region of bright, fair weather. In my experience in this country, I was forcibly impressed with the different character of the climate on opposite sides of the Rocky Mountain range. The vast prairie plain on the east is like the ocean; the rain and clouds from the constantly evaporating snow of the maintains rushing down into the heated air of the plains, on which you will have occasion to remark the frequent storms of rain we encountered during our journey.

31st.—The morning was clear; temperature 480. A rolling road, among piny and grassy hills, brought us this morning into a large trail where an Indian village had recently passed. The weather was pleasant and cool; we were disturbed by neither musquitoes nor flies; and the country was certainly extremely beautiful. The slopes and broad ravines were absolutely covered with fields of flowers of the most exquisitely beautiful colors. Among those which had not hitherto made their appearance, and which here were characteristic, was a new delphinium, of a green and lustrous metallic blue color, mingled with compact fields of several bright-colored varieties of astragalus, which were crowded together in splendid profusion. This trail conducted us, through a remark able defile, to a little timbered, creek, up which we wound our way, passing by a singular and massive wall of dark red granite. The formation of the country is a red feldspathic granite, overlaying a decomposing mass of the same rock, forming the soil of all this region, which everywhere is red and gravelly, and appears to be of a great floral fertility.

As we emerged on a small tributary of the Laramie river, coming in sight of its principal stream, the flora became perfectly magnificent; and we congratulated ourselves, as we rode along our pleasant road, that we had substituted this for the uninteresting country between Laramie hills and the Sweet Water valley. We had no meat for supper last night or breakfast this mottling, and were glad to see Carson come in at noon with a good antelope.

A meridian observation of the sun placed us in latitude 41o 04' 06". In the evening we encamped on the Laramie river, which is here very thinly timbered with scattered groups of cottonwood at considerable intervals. From our camp, we are able to distinguish the gorges, in which are the sources of Cachea la.Poudre and Laramie rivers; and the Medicine flow mountain, towards the point of which we are directing our course this afternoon, has been in sight the greater part of the day. By observation the latitude was 41o 15' 02", and longitude 106° 16, 54". The same beautiful flora continued till about four in the afternoon, when it suddenly disappeared, with the red soil, which became sandy, and of a whitish gray color,

The evening was tolerably clear; temperature at sunset 64o, The day's journey was 30 miles.

AUGUST. 1at.—The morning was calm and clear, with sunrise temperature at 42o. We traveled today over a plain, or open rolling country, at the foot of the Medicine Bow mountain; the soil in the morning being sandy, with fragments of rock abundant, and in the afternoon, when we approached closer to the mountain, so stony that we made but little way. The beautiful plants of yesterday reappeared occasionally; flax in bloom occurred during the morning, and esparcette in luxuriant abundance was a characteristic of the stony ground in the afternoon. The camp was roused into a little excitement by a chase after a buffalo bull, and an encounter with a war party of Sioux and Cheyenne Indians about 30 strong.

Hares and antelope were seen during the day, and one of the latter was killed. The Laramie peak was in sight this afternoon. The evening was clear, with scattered clouds; temperature 62o. The day's journey was 26 miles.

2d.—Temperature at sunrise 52o, and scenery and weather made our road today delightful. The neighboring mountain is thickly studded with pines, intermingled with the brighter, foliage of aspens, and occasional spots like lawns between the patches of snow among the pines, and here and there on the heights. Our route below lay over a comparative plain, covered with the same brilliant vegetation, and the day was clear and pleasantly cool. During the morning, we crossed many streams, clear and rocky, and broad grassy valleys, of a strong black soil, washed down from the mountains, and producing excellent pasturage. These were timbered with the red willow and long-leaved cottonwood, mingled with aspen, as we approached the mountain more nearly towards noon. Esparaegis was a characteristic, and flax occurred frequently in bloom. We halted at noon on the most western fork of Laramie river—a handsome stream about sixty feet wide and two feet deep, with clear water and a swift current, over a bed composed entirely of boulders or rollstones: There was a large open bottom here, on which were many lodge pales lying about: and in the edge of the surrounding timber were three strong forts, that appeared to have been recently occupied. At this place I became first acquainted with the yampah, (anethum graveolens,) which I found our Snake woman engaged in digging in the low timbered bottom of the creek. Among the Indians along the Rocky Mountains, and more particularly among the Shoshonee or Snake Indians, in whose territory it is very abundant, this is considered the best among the roots used for food. To us it was an interesting plant—a little link between the savage and civilized life. Here, among the Indians, its root is a common article of food, which they take pleasure in offering to strangers; while with us, in a considerable portion of America and Europe, the seeds are used to flavor soup. It grows more abundantly, and in greater luxuriance, on one of the neighboring tributaries of the Colorado, than in any other part of this region; and on that stream, to which the Snakes are accustomed to resort every year to procure a supply of their favorite plant, they have bestowed the name of Yampah river. Among the trappers it is generally Known as Little Snake river; but in this and other instances, where it illustrated the history of the people inhabiting the country, I have preferred to retain on the map the aboriginal name. By a meridional observation, the latitude is 41o 45'59".

In the afternoon we took our way directly across the spurs from the point of the mountain, where we had several ridges to cross; and, although the road was not rendered bad by the nature of the ground, it was made extremely rough by the stiff tough bushes of artemisia tridentata,* in this country commonly called sage.

This shrub now began to make its appearance in compact fields; and we were about to quit tor a long time this country of excellent pasturage and brilliant flowers. Ten or twelve buffalo bulls were seen during the afternoon; and we were surprised by the appearance of a large red ox. We gathered around him as if he had been an old acquaintance, with all our domestic feelings as much awakened as if we had come in sight of an old farmhouse. He had probably made his escape from some party of emigrants on Green river; and, with a vivid remembrance of some old green field, he was pursuing the straightest course for the frontier that the country admitted. We carried him along with us as a prize; and, wasn't was found in the morning that he had wandered off, I would not let him be pursued, for I would rather have gone through a starving time of three entire days, than let him be killed after he had successfully run the gauntlet so far among the Indians. I have been told by Mr. Bent's people of an ox born and raised at St. Vrain's fort, which made his escape from them at Elm grove, near the frontier, having come in that year with the wagons. They were on their way out, and saw occasionally places where he had eaten and laid down to rest; but did not see him for about 700 miles, when they overtook him on the road, traveling along to the fort, having unaccountably escaped Indians and every other mischance.

We encamped at evening on the principal fork of Medicine Bow river, near to an isolated mountain palled the Medicine Butte, which appeared to be about 1,800 feet above the plain, from which it rises abruptly, and was still white, nearly to its base, with a great quantity of snow. The streams were timbered with the longleaved cottonwood and red willow; and during the afternoon a species of onion was very abundant obtained here an immersion of the first satellite of Jupiter, which, corresponding very nearly with the chronometer, placed us in longitude 106° 47' 25". The latitude, by observation, was 41° 37'16"; elevation above the sea, 7,800 feet, and distance from St. V rain's fort, 147 miles.

3d.—There was a white frost last night, the morning is clear and cool. We were early on the road, having breakfasted before sunrise, and in a few miles' travel entered the pass of the Medicine Butte, through which led a broad trail, which had been recently traveled by a very large party immediately in the pass, the road was broken by ravines, and we were obliged to clear a way through groves of aspens, which generally made their appearance when we reached elevated regions. According to the barometer, this was 8,300 feet; and while we were detained in opening a road, I obtained a meridional observation of the sun, which gave 41° 35' 48" for the latitude of the pass. The Medicine Butte is isolated by a small tributary of the North fork of the Platte, but the mountains approach each other very nearly; the stream running at their feet. On the south they are smooth, with occasional streaks of pine; but the butte itself is ragged, with escarpments of red feldspathic granite, and dark with pines; the snow reaching from the summit t within a few hundred feet of the trail. The granite here was more compact and durable than that in the formation which we had passed through a few days before to the eastward of Laramie. Continuing our way over a plain on the west side of the pass, where the road was terribly rough with artemisia, we made our evening encampment on the creek, where it took a northern direction, unfavorably to the course we were pursuing. Bands of buffalo were discovered as we came down upon the plain; and Carson brought into the camp a cow which had the fat on the fleece two inches thick. But in this country of rich pasturage and abundant game, it is rare that a hunter chances upon a finer animal. Our voyage had already been long, but this was the first good buffalo meat we had obtained. We traveled today 26 miles.

4th.—The morning was clear and calm; and, leaving the creek, we traveled towards the North fork of the Platte, over a plain which was rendered rough and broken by ravines. With the exception of some thin grasses, the sandy soil here was occupied almost exclusively by artemisia, with its usual turpentine odor. We had expected to meet with some difficulty in crossing the river, but happened to strike it where there was a very excellent f3rd, and halted to noon on the left bank, two hundred miles from St. Vrain's fort. The hunters brought in pack animals loaded with fine meat. According to our imperfect knowledge of the country, there should have been a small affluent to this steam a few miles higher up; and in the afternoon we continued our way among the river hills, in the expectation of encamping upon it in the evening. The ground proved to be so exceedingly difficult, broken up into hills, terminating in escarpments and broad ravines, five hundred or six hundred feet deep, with sides so precipitous that we could scarcely find a place to descend, that, towards sunset, I turned directly in towards the river, and, after nightfall, entered a sort of ravine. We were obliged to feel our way, and clear a road in the darkness; the surface being much broken, and the progress of the carriages being greatly obstructed by the artemisia, which had a luxuriant growth of four to six feet in height. We had scrambled along this gulley for several hours, during which we had knocked off the carriage lamps, broken a thermometer and several small articles, when, fearing to lose something of more importance, I halted for the night at ten o'clock Our animals were turned down towards the river, that they might pick up what little grass they could find; and after a little search, some water was found in a small ravine, and improved by digging. We lighted up the ravine with fires of artemisia, and about midnight sat down to a supper which we were hungry enough to find delightful—although the buffalo meat was crusted with sand, and the coffee was bitter with the wormwood taste of the artemisia leaves.

A successful day's hunt had kept our hunters occupied until late, and they slept out, but rejoined us at daybreak, when, finding ourselves only about a mile from the river, we followed the ravine down, and camped in a cottonwood grove on a beautiful grassy bottom, where our animals indemnified themselves for the scanty fare of the past night. It was quite a pretty and pleasant place; a narrow strip of prairie, about five hundred yards long, terminated at the ravine where we entered by high precipitous hills closing in upon the river, and at the upper end by a ridge of low rolling hills.

In the precipitous bluffs were displayed succession of strata containing fossil vegetable remains, and several beds of coal. In some of the beds the coal did not appear to be perfectly mineralized, and in some of the seams it was compact, and remarkably lustrous. In these latter places, there were also thin layers of a very fine white salts, in powder. As we had a large supply of meat in the camp, which it was necessary to dry, and the surrounding country appeared to be well stocked with buffalo, which it was probable, after a day or two, we would not see again unt41 our return to the Mississippi waters, I determined to make here a provision of dried meat, which would be necessary for our subsistence in the region we were about entering, which was said to be nearly destitute of game, Scaffolds were accordingly soon erected, fires made, and the meat cut into thin slices to be dried; and all were busily occupied, when the camp was thrown into a sudden tumult, by a charge from about seventy mounted Indians, over the low hills at the upper end of the little bottom. Fortunately, the guard, who was between them and our animals, had caught a glimpse of an Indian's head, as he raised himself in his stirrups to look over the hill, a moment before he made the charge, and succeeded in turning the band into the camp, as the Indians charged into the bottom with the usual yell. Before they reached us, the grove on the verge of the little bottom was occupied by our people, and the Indians brought to a sudden halt, which they made in time to save themselves from a howitzer shot, which would undoubtedly have been very effective in such a compact body; and further proceedings were interrupted by their signs for peace. They proved to be a war party of Arapaho and Cheyenne Indians, and informed us that they had charged upon the camp under the belief that we were hostile Indians, and had discovered their mistake only at the moment of the attack—an excuse which policy required us to receive as true, though under the full conviction that the display of our little howitzer, and our favorable position in the grove, certainly saved our horses, and probably ourselves, from their marauding intentions. They had been on a war party, and had been defeated, and were consequently in the state of mind which aggravates their innate thirst for plunder and blood. Their excuse, however, was taken in good part, and the usual evidences of friendship inter changed. The pipe went round, provisions were spread, and the tobacco and goods furnished the customary presents, which they look for even from traders, and much more from government authorities.

They were returning from an expedition against the Shoshonee Indians, one of whose villages they had surprised, at Bridger's fort, on Ham's fork of Green river, (in the absence of the men, who were engaged in an antelope surround,) and succeeded in carrying off their horses, and taking several scalps. News of the attack reached the Snakes immediately, who pursued and overtook them, and recovered their horses; and, in the running fight which ensued, the Arapahoes had lost several men killed, and a number wounded, who were coming on more slowly with a party in the rear. Nearly all the horses they had brought off were the property of the whites at the fort.. After remaining until nearly sunset, they took their departure; and the excitement which their arrival had afforded subsided into our usual quiet, a little enlivened by the vigilance rendered necessary by the neighborhood of our uncertain visitors. At noon the thermometer was at 75°, at sunset 700, and the evening clear. Elevation above the sea 6,820 feet; latitude 41° 36' 00"; longitude 107° 22' 27".

6th.—At sunrise the thermometer was 46°, the morning being clear and calm. We traveled today over an extremely rugged country, barren and uninteresting—nothing to be seen but artemisia bushes; and, in the evening, found a grassy spot among the hills, kept green by several springs, where we encamped late. Within a few hundred yards was a very pretty little stream of clear cool water, whose green banks looked refreshing among the dry, rocky hills. The hunters brought in a fat mountain sheep, (ovis montana.)

Our road the next day was through a continued and dense field of artemisia, which now entirely covered the country it such a luxuriant growth that it was difficult and laborious for a man on foot to force his way through, and nearly impracticable for our light carriages. The region through which we were traveling was a high plateau, constituting the dividing ridge between the waters of the Atlantic and Pacific oceans, a extending to a considerable distance southward, from the neighborhood of the Table rock, at the southern side of the South Pass. Though broken up into rugged and rocky hills of a dry and barren nature, it has nothing of a mountainous character the small streams which occasionally occur belonging neither to Platte nor the Colorado, but losing themselves either in the sand or in small lakes. From an eminence, in the afternoon, a mountainous range became visible in the north, in which were recognised some rocky peaks belonging to the range of the Sweet Water valley; and, determining to abandon any further attempt to struggle through this almost impracticable country, we turned our course directly north, towar's a pass in the valley of the Sweet Water river. A shaft of the gun carriage was broken during the afternoon, causing a considerable delay; and it was late in an unpleasant evening before we succeeded in finding a very poor encampment, where there was a little water in a deep trench of a creek, and some scanty grass among the shrubs. All the game here consisted of a few straggling buffalo bulls, and during the day there had been but very little grass, except in some green spots where it had collected around springs or shallow lakes. "Within fifty miles of the Sweet Water, the country changed into a vast saline plain, in many places extremely level, occasionally resembling the flat sandy beds of shallow lakes. Here the vegetation consisted of a shrubby growth, among which were several varieties of chenopodiaceous plants; but the characteristic shrub was Fremontia vermlcularis, with smaller saline shrubs growing with singular luxuriance, and in many places holding exclusive possession of the ground.

On the evening of the 8th we encamped on one of these freshwater lakes, which the traveler considers himself fortunate to find; and the next day, in latitude, by observation, 420 20' 06", halted to noon immediately at the foot of the southern side of the range which walls in the Sweet Water valley, on the head of a small tributary to that river.

Continuing in the afternoon our course down the stream which here cuts directly through the ridge, forming a very practicable pass, we covered the valley; and, after a march of about nine miles, encamped on our familiar river, endeared to us by the acquaintance of the previous expedition—the night having already closed in with a cold rainstorm. Our camp was about twenty miles above the Devil's gate, which we had been able to see in coming down the plain; and, in the course of the night, the clouds broke away around Jupiter for a shun time, during which we obtained an emersion of the first satellite, the result of which agreed very nearly with the chronometer, giving for the mean longitude 1070 50' 07"; elevation above the sea 6,040 feet; and distance from St. Vrain's fort, by the road we had just traveled, 315 miles.

Here passes the road to Oregon; and the broad smooth highway, where the numerous heavy wagons of the emigrants had entirely beaten and crushed the artemisia, was a happy exchange to our poor animals, for the sharp rocks and tough shrubs among which they had been toiling so long; and we moved up the valley rapidly and pleasantly. With very little deviation from our route of the preceding year, we continued up the valley; and on the evening of the 12th encamped on the Sweet Water, at a point where the road turns off to cross to the plains of Green river. The increased coolness of, the weather indicated that we had attained a greater elevation, which the barometer here placed at 7,220 feet; and during the night water froze in the lodge.

The morning of the 13th was clear and cold, there being a whitefrost, and the thermometer, a little before sunrise, standing at 26.50. Leaving this encampment, (our last on the waters which flow towards the rising sun,) we took our way along the upland, towards the dividing ridge which separates the Atlantic from the Pacific waters, and crossed it by a road some miles further south than the one we had followed on our return in 1842. We crossed very near the Table mountain, at the southern extremity of the. South Pass, which is near twenty miles in width, and already traversed by several difference roads. Selecting, as well as I could, in the scarcely disguisable ascent, what might be considered the dividing ridge in this remarkable depression in the mountain, I took a barometrical observation, which gave 7,490 feet for the elevation above the Gulf of Mexico. You will remember that, in my report of 1842, I estimated the elevation of this pass at about 7,000 feet; a correct observation with a good barometer enables me to give it with more precision. Its importance, as the great gate through which commerce and traveling may hereafter pass between the valley of the Mississippi and the North Pacific, justifies a precise notice of its locality and distance from leading points, in addition to this statement of its elevation. As stated in the report of 1842, its latitude, at the point where we crossed, is 42° 24' 32"; its longitude 109° 26' 00"; its distance from the mouth of the Kansas, by the common traveling route, 962 miles; from the mouth of the Great Platte, along the valley of that river, according to our survey of 1842, 882 miles; and its distance from St. Louis about 400 miles more by the Kansas, and about 700 by the Great Platte route; these additions being steamboat conveyance in both instances. From this pass to the mouth of the Oregon is about 1,400 miles by the common traveling route; se that under a general point of view, tit may be assumed to be about halfway between the Mississippi and the Pacific ocean, on the common traveling route. Following a hollow of slight and easy descent, in which was very soon formed a little tributary to the Gulf of California, (for the waters which flow west from the South Pass go to this gulf,) we made our usual halt four miles from the pass, in latitude, by observation, 420 19' 53". Entering here the valley of Green river—the great Colorado of the West—and inclining very much to the southward along the streams which form the Sandy river, the road led for several days over dry and level uninteresting plains; to which a low scrubby growth of artemisia gave a uniform dull grayish color; and on the evening of the 15th we encamped in the Mexican territory, on the left bank of Green river, 69 miles from the South Pass, in longitude 110° 05' 05", and latitude 41° 53' 54", distant 1,031 miles from the mouth of the Kansas. This is the emigrant road to Oregon, which bears much to the southward, to avoid the mountains about the western heads of Green river—the Rio Verde of the Spaniards

16th.—Crossing the river, here about 400 feet wide, very good ford, we continued to descend for seven or eight miles on a pleasant road along the right bank of the stream, of which the islands and shores are handsomely timbered with cottonwood. The refreshing appearance of the broad river, with its timbered shores and green wooded islands, in contrast to its dry and sandy plains, probably obtained for it the name of Green river, which was bestowed on it by the Spaniards who first came into this country to trade some 25 years ago. It was then familiarly known as the Seedskedeeagie, or Prairie Hen (tetrao urophasianus) river; a name which it received from the Crows, to whom its upper waters belong, and on which this bird is still very abundant. By the Shoshonee and Utah Indians, to whom belongs, for a considerable distance below, the country where we were now traveling, it was called the Bitter Root river, from a great abundance in its valley of a plant which affords them one of their favorite roots. Lower down, from Brown's hole to the southward, the river runs through lofty chasms, walled in by precipices of red rock and even among the wilder tribes which inhabit that portion of its course, I have heard it called by Indian refugees from the California settlements the Rio Colorado. We halted to noon at the upper end of a large bottom, near some old houses, which had been a trading post, in lat. 41° 46' 54" At this place the elevation of the river above the sea is 6,230 feet. That of Lewis's fork of the Columbia at Fort Hall is, according to our subsequent observations, 4,500 feet. The descent of each stream is rapid, but that of the Colorado is but little known, and that little derived from vague report. Three hundred miles of its lower part, as it approaches the Gulf of California, is reported to be smooth and tranquil; but its upper part is manifestly broken into many falls and rapids. From many descriptions of trappers, it is probable that in its foaming course among its lofty precipices it presents many scenes of wild grandeur; and though offering many temptations, and often discussed, no trappers have been found bold enough to undertake a voyage which has so certain a prospect of a fatal termination The Indians have strange stories of beautiful valleys abounding with beaver, shut up among inaccessible walls of rock in the lower course of the river; and to which the neighboring Indians, in their occasional wars with the Spaniards and among themselves, drive their herds of cattle and flocks of sheep, leaving them to pasture in perfect security.

The road here leaves the river, which bends considerably to the east; and in the afternoon we resumed our westerly course, passing over a somewhat high and broken country; and about sunset, after a day's travel of 26 miles, reached Black's fork of the Green river—a shallow stream, with a somewhat sluggish current, about 120 feet wide, timbered principally with willow, and here and there an occasional large tree. At three in the morning I obtained an observation of an emersion of the first satellite of Jupiter, with other observations. The heavy wagons have so completely pulverized the soil, that clouds of fine light dust are raised by the slightest wind, making the road sometimes very disagreeable.

17th.—Leaving our encampment at six in the morning, we traveled along the bottom, which is about two miles wide, bordered by low hills, in which the strata contained handsome and very distinct vegetable fossils. In a gully a short distance farther up the river, and underlying these, was exposed a stratum of an impure or argillaceous limestone. Crossing on the way. Black's fork, where it is one foot deep and forty wide, with clear water and a pebbly bed, in nine miles we reached Ham's fork, a tributary to the former stream, having now about sixty feet breadth, and a few inches depth of water. It is wooded with thickets of red willow, and in the bottom is a tolerably strong growth of grass. The road here makes a Traverse of twelve miles across a bend of the river. Passing in the way some remarkable hills, two or three hundred feet high, with frequent and nearly vertical escarpments of a green stone, consisting of an argillaceous carbonate of lime, alternating with strata of an iron-brown limestone, and worked into picturesque forms by wind and at two in the afternoon we reached the river again, having made today 21 miles. Since crossing the great dividing ridge of the Rocky mountains, plants have been very few in variety, the country being covered principally with artemisia.

18th.—We passed on the road, tins morning, the grave of one of the emigrants, being the second we had seen since falling into their trail; and halted to noon on the river, a short distance above.

The Shoshonee woman took leave of us here, expecting to find some of her relations at Bridger's fort, which is only a mile or two distant, on a fork of this stream. In the evening we encamped on a salt creek, about fifteen feet wide, having today traveled 32 miles.

I obtained an emersion of the first satellite under favorable circumstances, the night being still and clear.

One of our mules died here, and in this portion of our journey we lost six or seven of our animals. The grass which the country had lately afforded was very poor and insufficient; and animals which have been accustomed to grain become soon weak and unable to labor, when reduced to no other nourishment than grass. The American horses (as those are usually called which are brought to this country from the States) are not of any serviceable value until after they have remained a winter in the country, and become accustomed to live entirely on grass.

19th. Desirous to avoid every delay not absolutely necessary, I sent on Carson in advance to Fort Hall this morning, to make arrangements for a small supply of provisions. A few miles from our encampment, the road entered a high ridge, which the trappers called the " little mountain," connecting the Utah with the Wind river chain; and in one of the hills near which we passed I remarked strata of a conglomerate formation, fragments of which were scattered over the surface. We crossed a ridge of this conglomerate, the road passing near a grove of low cedar, and descending upon one of the heads of Ham's fork, called Muddy, where we made our midday halt in the river hills at this place, I discovered strata of fossiliferous rock, having an oolitic structure, which, in connection with the neighboring 5.sta, authorize us to believe that here, on the west side of the Rocky mountains, we find repeated the modern formations of Great Britain and Europe, which have hitherto been wanting to complete the system of North American geology.

In the afternoon we continued our road, and searching among the hills a few miles up the stream, and on the same bank, I discovered, among the alternate beds of coal and clay, a stratum of white indurated clay, containing very clear and beautiful impressions of vegetable remains. This was the most interesting fossil locality I had met in the country, and I deeply regretted that time did not permit me to remain a day or two in the vicinity; but I could not anticipate the delays to which I might be exposed in the course of our journey—or, rather, I knew that they were many and inevitable; and after remaining here only about an hour, I hurried off, loaded with as many specimens as I could conveniently carry.

Coal made its appearance occasionally in the hills during the afternoon, and was displayed in rabbit burrows in a kind of gt p, through which we passed over some high hills, and we descended to make our encampment on the same stream, where we found but very poor grass. In the evening a fine cow, with her calf, which had strayed off from some emigrant party, a, found several miles from the road, and brought into camp; and as she gave an abundance of milk, we enjoyed tonight an excellent cup of coffee. We traveled today 28 miles, and, as has been usual since crossing the Green river, the road has been very dusty, and the weather smoky and oppressively hot. Artemisia was characteristic among the few plants.

20th.—We continued to travel up the creek by a very gradual ascent and a very excellent grassy road, passing on the way several small forks of the stream. The hills here are higher, presenting escarpments of party colored and apparently clay rocks, purple, dark red, and yellow, containing strata of sandstone and limestone with shells, with a bed of cemented pebbles, the whole overlaid by beds of limestone. The alternation of red and yellow gives a bright appearance to the hills, one of which was called by our people the Rainbow hill, and the character of the country became more agreeable, and traveling far more pleasant, as now we found timber ana very good grass. Gradually ascending, we reached the lower level of a bed of white limestone, lying upon a white clay, on the upper line of which the whole road is abundantly supplied with beautiful cool springs, gushing out a foot in breadth and several inches deep, directly from the hillside.

At noon we halted at the last main fork of the creek, at an elevation of 7,200 feet, and in latitude, by observation, 410.39' 45"; and in the afternoon continued on the same excellent road, up the left or northern fork of the stream, towards its head, in a pass which the barometer placed at 8,230 feet above the sea. This is a connecting ridge between the Utah or Bear River mountains and the Wind River chain of the Rocky mountains, separating the waters of the Gulf of California on the east, and those on the west belonging more directly to the Pacific, from a vast interior basin whose rivers are collected into numerous lakes having no outlet to the ocean. From the summit of this pass, the highest which the road crosses between the Mississippi and the Western ocean, our view was over a very mountainous region, whose rugged appearance was greatly increased by the smoky weather, through which the broken ridges were dark and dimly seen. The ascent to the summit of the gap was occasionally steeper than the national road in the Alleghanies; and the descent, by way of a spur on the western side, is rather precipitous, but the pass, may still be called a good one. Some thickets of the willow in the hollows below deceived us into the expectation of finding a camp at our usual hour at the foot of the mountain; but we found them without water and continued down a ravine, and encamped about dark at a place where the springs began again to make their appearance, but where our animals fared badly; the stock of the emigrants having razed the grass as completely as if we were again in the midst of the buffalo.

21st.—An hour's travel this morning brought us into the fertile and picturesque valley of Bear river, the principal tributary to the Great Salt lake. The stream is here two hundred feet wide, fringed with willows and occasional groups of hawthorns. We were now entering a region which, for us, possessed a strange and extraordinary interest. We were upon the waters of the famous lake which forms a salient point among the remarkable geographical features of the country, and around which the vague and superstitious accounts of the trappers had thrown a delightful obscurity, which we anticipated pleasure in dispelling, but which, in the mean time, left a crowded field for the exercise of our imagination.

In our occasional conversations with the few old hunters who had visited the region, it had been a subject of frequent speculation; and the wonders which they related were not the less agreeable because they were highly exaggerated and impossible.

Hitherto this lake had been seen only by trappers who were wandering through the country in search of new beaver streams, caring very little for geography; its islands had never been visited; and none were to be found who had entirely made the circuit of its shores; and no instrumental observations or geographical survey, of any description, had ever been made any where in the neighboring region. It was generally supposed that it had no visible outlet; but among the trappers, including those in my own camp, were many who believed that somewhere on its surface was a terrible whirlpool, through which its waters found their way to the ocean by some subterranean communication. All these things had made a frequent subject of discussion in our desultory conversations around the fires at night; and my own mind had become tolerably well filled with their indefinite pictures, and insensibly colored with their romantic descriptions, which, in the pleasure of excitement, I was well disposed to believe, and half expected to realize.

Where we descended into this beautiful valley, it is three to four miles in breadth, perfectly level, and bounded by mountainous ridges, one above another, rising suddenly from the plain.

We continued our road down the river, and at night and camped with a family of emigrants—two men, women, and several children—who appeared to be bringing up the rear of me great caravan. I was struck with the fine appearance of their cattle, some six or eight yoke of oxen, which really looked as well as if they had been all the summer at work on some good farm. It was strange to see one small family traveling along through such a country, so remote from civilization

Some nine years since, such a security might have been a fatal one, but since their disastrous defeats in the country a little north, the

Blackfeet have ceased to visit these waters. Indians, however, are very uncertain in their localities; and the friendly feelings, also, of those now inhabiting it may be changed.

According to barometrical observation at noon, the elevation of the valley was 6,400 feet above the sea; and our encampment at night in latitude 42o 03' 47", and longitude 111o 10' 53", by observation—the day's journey having been 26 miles. This encampment was therefore within the territorial limit of the United States; our traveling, from the time we entered the valley of the Green river, on the 15th of August, having been south of the 42d degree of north latitude, and consequently on Mexican territory; and this is the route all the emigrants now travel to Oregon.

The temperature at sunset was 65o; and at evening there was a distant thunderstorm, with a light breeze from the north.

Antelope and elk were seen during the day on the opposite prairie; and there were ducks and geese in the river.

The next morning, in about three miles from our encampment, we reached Smith's fork, a stream of clear water, about

50 feet in breadth. It is timbered with cottonwood, willow, and aspen, and makes a beautiful debouchement through a pass about 600 yards wide, between remarkable mountain hills, rising abruptly on either side, and forming gigantic columns to the gate by which it enters Bear River valley. The bottoms, which below Smith's fork had been two miles wide, narrowed as we advanced to a gap 500 yards wide, and during the greater part of the day we had a winding route, the river making very sharp and sudden bends, the mountains steep and rocky, and the valley occasionally so narrow as only to leave space for a passage through.

We made our halt at noon in a fertile bottom, where the common blue flax was growing abundantly, a few miles below the mouth of Thomas's fork, one of the larger tributaries of the river.

Crossing, in the afternoon, the point of a narrow spur, we descended into a beautiful bottom,, formed by a lateral valley, which presented a picture of home beauty that went directly to our hearts.

The edge of the wood, for several miles along the river, was dotted with the white covers of emigrant wagons, collected in groups at different camps, where the smoke was rising lazily from the fires, around which the women were occupied in preparing the evening meal, and the children playing in the grass; and herds of cattle, grazing about in the bottom, had an air of quiet security, and civilized comfort, that made a are sight for the traveler in such a remote wilderness.

In common with all the emigration, they had been reposing for several days in this delightful valley, in order to recruit their animals on its luxuriant pasturage after their long journey, and prepare them for the hard travel along the comparatively sterile banks of the Upper Columbia. At the lower end of this extensive bottom, the river passes through an open canon, where there were high vertical rocks to the water's edge, and the road here turns up a broad valley to the right. It was already near sunset; but, hoping to reach the river again before night, we continued our march along the valley, finding the road tolerably good, until we arrived at a point where it crosses the ridge by an ascent of a mile in length, which was so very steep and difficult for the gun and carriage, that we did not reach the summit until dark.

It was absolutely necessary to descend into the valley for water and grass; and we were obliged to grope our way in the darkness down a very steep, bad mountain, reaching tie river at about ten o'clock. It was late before our animals were gathered into the camp, several of those which were very weak being necessarily left to pass the night on the ridge; and we sat down again to a midnight supper. The road, in the morning, presented an animated appearance. We found that, we had encamped near a large party of emigrants, and a few miles below, another party was already in motion. Here the valley had resumed its wile,' breadth, and the river swept off along toe mountains on the western side, the' road continuing directly on.

In about an hour's travel we met several Shoshonee Indians, who informed us that they belonged to a large village which had just come into the valley from the mountain to the westward, where they had been hunting antelope and gathering serviceberries. Glad at the opportunity of seeing one of their villages, and in the hope of purchasing from them a few horses, I turned immediately off into the plain towards their encampment, which was situated on a small stream near the river.

We had approached within something more than a mile of the village, when suddenly a single horseman emerged from it at full speed, followed by another and another in rapid succession; and then party after party poured into the plain, until, when the foremost rider reached us, all the whole intervening plain was occupied by a mass of horsemen, which came charg ing down upon us with guns and naked swords, lances, and bows and arrows— Indians entirely naked, and warriors fully dressed for war, with the long red streamers of their war bonnets reaching nearly to the ground, all mingled together in the bravery of savage warfare. They had been thrown into a sudden tumult by the appearance of our flag, which, among these people, is regarded as an emblem of hostility—it being usually borne by the Sioux and the neighboring mountain Indians, when they come here to war; and we had, accordingly been mistaken for a body of their enemies. A few words from the chief quieted the excitement; and the whole band, increasing every moment in number, escorted us to their encampment where the chief pointed out a place for us to encamp, near his own lodge, and we made known our purpose in visiting the village. In a very short time we purchased eight horses, for which we gave in exchange blankets, red and blue cloth, beads, knives, and tobacco, and the usual other articles of Indian traffic. We obtained from them also a considerable quantity of berries, of different kinds, among which serviceberries were the most abundant; and several kinds of roots and seeds, which we could eat with pleasure, as any kind of vegetable food was gratifying to us. I ate here, for the first time, the kooyah, tobaccoroot, (valerian edulis,)—the principal each of the Indians who inhabit the upper waters of the streams on the western side of the mountains. It has a very strong and remarkably peculiar taste and odor, which I can compare no other vegetable that I am acquainted with, and to some persons is extremely offensive. It was characteristically Mr. Preuss as the most horrid food he had ever put to mouth; and when, in the evening, one of the chiefs sent his, wife to me with a portion which she had prepared to regale us, the odor immediately drove him out of the edge and frequently afterwards he used to beg that when those wile liked it had taken what they desired, it might be sent away To others, however, the taste is rather an agreeable one; and was afterwards glad when it formed an addition to our scant meals. It is full of nutriment; and in its unprepared state it said by the Indians to have very strong poisonous qualities, of which it is deprived by a peculiar process, being baked in the ground for about two days.

The morning of the 24th was disagreeably cool, with at easterly wind, and very smoky weather. We made a late start from the village, and, regaining the road, (on which during all the day, were scattered the emigrant wagons,) we continued on down the valley of the river, bordered by high and mountainous hills, on which fires are seen at the summit. The soil appears generally good, although, with the grasses, many of the plants are dried up, probably on account of the great heat and want of rain. The common blue flax of cultivation, now almost entirely in seed—only a scattered flower here and there remaining—is the most characteristic plant of the Bear River valley. When we encamped at night, on the right bank of the river, it was growing as in a sown field. We had traveled during the day twentytwo miles, encamping in latitude (by observation) 420 36" 56", chronometric longitude 111° 42' 05".

In our neighborhood the mountains appeared extremely rugged, giving still greater value to this beautiful natural pass

25th.—This was a cloudless but smoky autumn morning with a cold wind from the southeast and a temperature of 45' at sunrise. In a few miles I noticed, where a little stream crossed the road, fragments of scoriated basalt scattered about—the first volcanic rock we had seen, and which now became a characteristic rock along our future road. In about six miles' travel from our encampment, we reached one of the points in our journey to which we had always looked forward with great nterest—the famous Beer springs. The place in which they are situated is a basin of mineral waters enclosed by the mountains, which sweep around a circular bend of Bear river, here at its most northern point, and which, from a northern, in the course of a few miles acquires a southern direction towards the GREAT SALT LAKE. A pretty little stream of clear water enters the upper part of the basin, from an open valley in the mountains, and, passing through the bottom, discharges into Bear river. Crossing this stream, we descended a mile below, and made our encampment in a grove of cedar immediately at the Beer springs, which, on account of the effervescing gas and acid taste, have received their name from the voyageurs and trappers of the country, who, in the midst of their rude and hard lives, are fond of finding some fancied resemblance to the luxuries they rarely have the fortune to enjoy.

Although somewhat disappointed in the expectations which various descriptions had led me to form of unusual beauty of situation and scenery, I found it altogether a place of very great interest; and a traveler for the first time in a volcanic region remains in a constant excitement, and at every step is arrested by something remarkable and new. There is a confusion of interesting objects gathered together in a small space. Around the place of encampment the Beer springs were numerous; but, as far as we could ascertain, were confined entirely to that locality in the bottom. In the bed of the river, in front, for a space of several hundred yards, they were very abundant; the effervescing gas rising up and agitating the water in countless bubbling columns. In the vicinity round about were numerous springs of an entirely different and equally marked mineral character. In a rather picturesque spot, about 1,300 yards below our encampment, and immediately on the river bank, is the most remarkable spring of the place in an opening on the rock, a white column of scattered water is thrown up, in form like a jetd'eau, to a variable height of about three feet, and, though it is maintained in a constant supply, its greatest height is only attained at regular intervals, according to the action of the force below. It is accompanied by a subterranean noise, which, together with the motion of the water, makes very much the impression of a steamboat in motion; and, without knowing that it had been already previously so called, we gave to it the name of the Steamboat spring. The rock through which it is forced is slightly raised in a convex manner, and gathered at the opening into an unmouthed form, and is evidently formed by continued deposition from the water, and colored bright red by oxide of iron. An analysis of this deposited rock, which I subjoin, will give you some idea of the properties of the water, which, with the exception of the Beer springs, is the mineral water of the place.* It is a hot spring, and the water has a pungent and disagreeable metallic taste, leaving a burning effect on the tongue. Within perhaps two yards 'of the jetd'eau is a small hole of about an inch in diameter, through which, at regular intervals, escapes a blast of hot air, with a light wreath of smoke, accompanied by a regular noise. This hole had been noticed by Dr. Wislizenus, a gentleman who had several years since passed by this place, and who remarked, with very nice observation, that smelling the gas which issued from the orifice produced a sensation of giddiness and nausea. Mr. Preuss and myself repeated the observation, and were so well satisfied with its correctness, that we did not find it pleasant to continue the experiment, as the sensation of giddiness which it produced was certainly strong and decided. A huge emigrant wagon, with a large and diversified family had overtaken us and halted to noon at our encampment; and., while we were sitting at the spring, a band of boys and girls, with two or three young men, came up, one of whom I asked to stoop down and smell the gas, desirous to satisfy myself further of its effects. But his natural caution had been awakened by the singular and suspicious features of the place and he declined my proposal decidedly, and with a few indistinct remarks about the devil, whom he seemed to consider the genius loci. The ceaseless motion and the play of the fountain, the red rock and the green trees near, make this a picturesque spot.

A short distance above the spring, and near the foot of the same spur, is a very remarkable, yellow colored rock, soft and friable, consisting principally of carbonate of lime and oxide of iron, of regular structure, which is probably a fossil coral. The rocky bank along the shore between the Steamboat spring and our encampment, along which is dispersed the water from the hills, is composed entirely of strata of a calcareous tufg, with the remains of moss and reedlike grasses, which ie probably the formation of springs. The Beer or Soda springs, which have given name to this locality, are agreeable, but less highly flavored than the Boiling springs at the foot of Pike's peak, which are of the same character. They are very numerous, and half hidden by tufts of grass, which we amused ourselves in removing and searching about for more highly impregnated springs. They are some of them deep, and of various sizes—sometimes several yards in diameter, and kept in constant motion by the columns of escaping gas. [analysis omitted]

The carbonic acid, originally contained in the water, had mainly escaped before it was subjected to analysis; and it was not, therefore, taken into consideration.

In the afternoon I wandered about among the cedars, which occupy the greater part of the bottom towards the mountains. The soil here has a dry and calcined appearance; in some places, the open grounds are covered with saline efflorescences, and there are a number of regularly shaped and very remarkable hills, which are formed of a succession of convex strata that have been deposited by the waters of extinct springs, the orifices of which are found on their summits, some of them having the form of funnel shaped cones. Others of these remarkably shaped hills are of a red colored earth, entirely bare, and composed principally' of carbonate of lime, with oxide of iron, formed in the same manner. Walking near one of them, on the summit of which the springs were dry, my attention was attracted by an underground noise, around which I circled repeatedly until I found the spot from beneath which it came; and, removing the red earth, discovered a hidden spring, which was boiling up from below, with the same disagreeable metallic taste as the Steamboat spring. Continuing up the bottom, and crossing the little stream which has been already mentioned, I visited several remarkable red and white hills, which had attracted my attention from the road in the morning. These are immediately upon the stream, and, like those already mentioned, are formed by the deposition of successive strata from the springs. On their summits, the orifices through which the waters had been discharged were so large, that they resembled miniature craters, being some of them several feet in diameter, circular, and regularly formed as if by art. At a former time, when these dried-up fountains were all in motion, they must have made a beautiful display on a grand scale; and nearly all this basin appears to me to have been formed under their action, and should be called the place of fountains. At the foot of one of these hills, or rather on its side near the base, are several of these small limestone Columns, about one foot in diameter at the base, and tapering upwards to a height of three or four feet; and on the summit the water is boiling up and bubbling over, constantly adding to the height of the little obelisks. In some, the water only boils up, no longer overflowing, and has here the same taste as at the Steamboat spring. The observer will remark a gradual subsidence in the water, which formerly supplied the fountains; as on all the summits of the hills the Springs are now dry, and are found only low down upon their sides, or on the surrounding plain.

A little higher up the creek its banks are formed by strata of very heavy and hard scoriaceous basalt, having a bright metallic lustre when broken. The mountains overlooking the plain are of an entirely different geological character. Continuing on, I walked to the summit of one of them, where the principal rock was a granular quartz. Descending the mountains, and returning towards the camp along the base of the ridge which skirts the plain, I found, at the foot of a mountain spur, and issuing from a compact rock of a dark blue color, a great number of springs having the same pungent and disagreeably metallic taste already mentioned, the water of which was collected into a very remarkable basin, whose singularity, perhaps, made it appear to me very beautiful. It is large—perhaps fifty yards in circumference; and in it the water is contained, at an elevation of several feet above the surrounding ground, by a wall of calcareous tufa, composed principally of the remains of mosses, three or four, and sometimes ten feet high. The water within is very clear and pure, and three or four feet deep, where it could be measured, near the wall; at a considerably low level, is another pond or basin of very clear water, and apparently of considerable depth, from the bottom of which the gas was escaping in bubbling columns at many places. This water was collected into a small stream, which, in a few hundred yards, sank under ground, reappearing among the rocks between the two great springs near the river, which it entered by a little fall.

Late in the afternoon I set out on my return to the camp, and, crossing in the way a large field of salt that was several inches deep, found on my arrival that our emigrant friends, who had been encamped in company with us, had resumed their journey, and the road had again assumed its solitary character. The temperature of the largest of the Beer springs at our encampment was 65o at sunset, that of the air being 62.5o. Our barometric observation gave 5,840 feet for the elevation above the gulf, being about 500 feet lower than the Boiling springs, which are of a similar nature, at the foot of Pike's peak. The astronomical observations gave for our latitude 42° 39' 57", and 111o 46' 00" for the longitude. The night was very still and cloudless, and I sat up for an observation of the first satellite of Jupiter, the emersion of which took place about midnight; but fell asleep at the telescope, awaking just a few minutes after the appearance of the star.

The morning of the 26th was calm, and the sky without clouds, but smoky, and the temperature at sunrise 28.5o. At the same time, the temperature of the large Beer spring, where we were encamped, was 56o; that of the Steamboat, spring 87°, and that of the steamhole, near it, 81.5o. In the course of the morning, the last wagons of the emigration passed by, and we were again left in our place, in the rear.

Remaining in camp until nearly 11 o'clock, we traveled a short distance down the river, and halted to noon on the bank, at a point where the road quits the valley of Bear river, and, crossing a ridge which divides the Great basin from the Pacific waters, reaches Fort Hall, by way of the Portneuf river, in a distance of probably fifty miles, of two and a half days' journey for wagons. An examination of the great lake which is the outlet of this river, and the principal feature of geographical interest in the basin, was one of the main objects contemplated in the general plan of our survey, and I accordingly determined at this place to leave the road, and, after having completed a reconnoissance of the lake, regain it subsequently at Fort Hall. But our little stock of provisions had again become extremely low; we bad only dried meat sufficient fin one meal, and our supply of flour and other comforts was entirely exhausted. I therefore immediately dispatched one of the party, Henry Lee, with a note to Carson, at Fort Hall, directing him to load a packhorse with whatever could be obtained there in the way of provisions, and endeavor to overtake me on the river. In the mean time, we had picked up along the road two tolerably well grown calves, which would have become food for wolves, and which had probably been left by some of the earlier emigrants, none of those we had met having made any claim to them; and on these I mainly relied for support during our circuit to the lake.

In sweeping around the point of the mountain which runs down into the bend, the river here passes between perpendicular walls of basalt, which always fix the attention, from the regular form in which it occurs, and its perfect distinctness from the surrounding rocks among which it had been placed. The mountain, which is rugged and steep, and, by our measurement, 1,400 feet above the river directly opposite the place of our halt, is called the Sheeprock—probably because a flock of the mountain sheep (ovis montana) had been seen on the craggy point.

As we were about resuming our march in the afternoon, I was attracted by the singular appearance of an isolated hill with a concave summit, in the plain, about two miles from the river, and turned off towards it, while the camp proceeded on its way southward in search of the lake. I found the thin and stony soil of the plain entirely underlaid by the basalt which forms the river walls; and when I reached the neighborhood of the hill, the surface of the plain was rent into frequent fissures and chasms of the same scoriated volcanic rock, from 40 to 60 feet deep, but which there was not sufficient light to penetrate entirely, and which I had not time to descend. Arrived at the summit of the hill, I found that it terminated in a very perfect crater, of an oval, or nearly circular form, 360 paces in circumference, and 60 feet at the greatest depth. The walls, which were perfectly vertical, and disposed like masonry in a very regular manner, were composed of a brown colored scoriaceous lava, similar to the light scoriaceous lava of Mt. Etna, Vesuvius, and other volcanoes. The faces of the walls were reddened and glazed by the fire, in which they had been melted, and which had left them contorted and twisted by its violent action.

Our route during the afternoon was a little rough, being (in the direction we had taken) over a volcanic plain, where oqr progress was sometimes obstructed by fissures, and black beds composed of fragments of the rock. On both sides, the moi l'. tains appeared very broken, but tolerably well timbered.

Crossing a point of ridge which makes in to the river, we fell upon it again before sunset, and encamped on the right bank, opposite to the encampment of three lodges of Snake Indians. They visited us during the evening, and we obtained from them a small quantity of roots of different kinds, in exchange for goods. Among them was a sweet root of very pleasant flavor, having somewhat the taste of preserved quince. My endeavors to become acquainted with the plants which furnish to the Indians a portion of their support, were only gradually successful, and after long and persevering attention; and even after obtaining, I did not succeed in preserving them until they could be satisfactorily determined. In this portion, of the journey, I found this particular root cut up into small pieces, that it was only to be identified by its taste, when the bulb was met with in perfect form among the Indians lower down on the Columbia, among whom it is the highly celebrated kamas. It was long afterwards, on our return through Upper California, that I found the plant itself in bloom, which I supposed to furnish the kamas root, (camassia esculenta.) The root diet had a rather mournful effect at the commencement, and one of the calves was killed this evening for food. The animals fared well on rushes.

:7th.—The morning was cloudy, with appearance of rain, and the thermometer at sunrise at 290. Making t n unusually early start, we crossed the liver at a good ford; and, following for about three hours a trail which led along the bottom, we entered a labyrinth of hills below the main ridge, and halted to noon in the ravine of a pretty little stream, timbered with cottonwood of a large size, ashleaved maple, with cherry and other shrubby trees. The hazy weather, which had prevented any very extended views since entering the Green River valley, began now to disappear. There was a slight rain in the earlier part of the day, and at noon, when the thermometer had risen to 79.50, we had a b t sun, with blue ay and scattered cumuli. According to the barometer, out halt here among the hills was at an elevation of 5,320 feet. Crossing a dividing ridge m the afternoon, we followed down another little Bear River tributary, to the point where it emerged on an open green flat among the hills, timbered with groves, and borlered with cane thickets, but without water. A pretty little rivulet coming out of the hillside, and overhung by tall flowering plants of a species I had not hitherto seen, furnished us with a good campingplace. The evening was cloudy the temperature at sunset 69°, and the elevation 5,140 feet. Among the plants occurring along the road during the day, cpinettes des prairies (grinaelia squarraso) was in considerable abundance, and is among the very few plants remaining in bloom—the whole country having now an autumnal appearance, in the crisp and yellow plants, and driedup grasses Many cranes were seen during the day, with a few antelope, very shy and wild.

28th.—During the night we had a thunderstorm, With moderate rain, which has made the air this morning very clear, the thermometer being at 550. Leaving our encampment at the Cane spring, and quitting the trail on which we had been traveling, and which would probably have afforded us a good road to the lake, we crossed some very deep ravines, and, in about an hour's traveling, again reached the river. We were now in a valley five or six miles wide, between mountain ranges, which, about thirty miles below, appeared to close up and terminate the valley, leaving for the river only a very narrow pass, or canon, behind which we imagined we would find the broad waters of the lake. We made the usual halt at the mouth of a small clear stream, having a slightly mineral taste, (perhaps of salt,) 4,760 feet above the gulf. In the afternoonwe climbed a very steep sandy hill; and after a slow a winding day's march of 27 miles, encamped at a slough on ti river. There were great quantities of geese and ducks, of which only a few were shot; the Indians having probably made them very wild. The men employed themselves in fishing, but caught nothing. A skunk, (mephitis Americana,; which was killed in the afternoon, made a supper for one of the messes. The river is bordered occasionally with fields o cane, which we regarded as an indication of our approach c a lakecountry. We had frequent showers of rain during e night, with thunder.

29th.—The thermometer at sunrise was 54o, with air from the NW., and dark rainy clouds moving on the horizon; rain squalls and bright sunshine by intervals. I rode ahead with Basil to explore the country, and, continuing about three miles along the river, turned directly off on a trail running towards three marked gaps in the bordering range, where the mountains appeared cut through their bases, towards which the river plain rose gradually. Putting our horses into a gallop on some fresh tracks which showed very plainly in the wet path, we came suddenly upon a small party of Shoshonee Indians, who had fallen into the trail from the north. We could only communicate by signs; but they made us understand that the road through the chain was a very excellent one, leading into a broad valley which ran to the southward. We halted to noon at what may be called the gate of the pass; on either side of which were huge mountains of rock, between which stole a little pure water stream, with a margin just sufficiently large for our passage. From the river, the plain had gradually risen to an altitude of 5,500 feet, and, by meridian observation, the latitude of the entrance was 42°.

In the interval of our usual halt, several of us wandered along up the stream to examine the pass more at leisure. Within the gate, the rocks receded a little back, leaving a very narrow, but most beautiful valley, through which the little stream wound its way, hidden by the different kinds of trees and shrubs—aspen, maple, willow, cherry, and elder; a fine verdure of smooth short grass spread over the remaining space to the bare sides of the rocky walls. These were of a blue limestone, which constitutes the mountain here; and opening directly on the grassy bottom were several curious caves, which appeared to be inhabited by rootdiggers. On one side was gathered a heap of leaves for a bed, and they were dry, open, and pleasant. On the roofs of the caves I remarked bituminous exudations from the rock.

The trail was an excellent one for packhorses; but as it sometimes crossed a shelving point, to avoid the shrubbery we were obliged in several places to open a road for the carriage through the wood. A squaw on horseback, accompanied by five or six dogs, entered the pass in the afternoon; but was too much terrified at finding herself in such unexpected company to make any pause for conversation, and hurried off at a good pace—being, of course, no further disturbed than by an accelerating shout. She was well and showily dressed, and was probably going to a village encamped somewhere near, and evidently did not belong to the tribe of rootdiggers. We now had entered a country inhabited by these people; and as in the course of the voyage we shall frequently meet with them in various stages of existence, it will be well to inform you that, scattered over the great region west of the Rocky mountains, and south of the Great Snake river, are numerous Indians whose subsistence is almost solely derived from roots and seeds, and such small animals as chance and great good fortune sometimes bring within their reach. They are miserably poor, armed only with bows and arrows, or clubs; and, as the country they inhabit is almost destitute of game, they have no means of obtaining better arms. In the northern part of the region just mentioned, they live generally in solitary families; and farther to the south they are gathered together in villages. Those who live together in villages, strengthened by association, are in exclusive possession of the more genial and richer parts of the country; while the others are driven to the ruder mountains, and to the more inhospitable parts of the country. But by simply observing, in accompanying us along our road, you will become better acquainted with these people than we could make you in any other than a very long description, and you will find them worthy of your interest.

Roots, seeds, and grass, every vegetable that affords any nourishment, and every living animal thing, insect or worm, they eat. Nearly approaching to the lower animal creation, their sole employment is to obtain food; and they, are constantly occupied in struggling to support existence.

The most remarkable feature of the pass is the Standing rock, which has fallen from the cliffs above, and standing perpendicularly near the middle of the valley, presents itself like a watchtower in the pass. It will give you a tolerably correct idea of the character of the scenery in this country, there generally the mountains rise abruptly up from comparatively unbroken plains and level valleys; but it will entirely fail in representing the picturesque beauty of this delightful place, where a green valley, full of foliage and a hundred yards wide, contrasts with naked crags that spire up into a blue line of pinnacles 3,000 feet _above, sometimes crested with cedar and pine, and sometimes ragged and bare.

The detention that we met with in opening the road, and perhaps a willingness to linger on the way, made the after noon's travel short; and about two miles from the entrance, we passed through another gate, and encamped on the stream at the junction of a little fork from the southward, around which the mountains stooped more gently down, forming a small open cove.

As it was still early in the afternoon, Basil and myself in one direction, and Mr. Preuss in another, set out to explore the country, and ascended different neighboring peaks, in the hope of seeing some indications of the lake; but though our elevation afforded magnificent views, the eye ranging over a large extent of Bear river, with the broad and fertile Cache valley in the direction of our search, was only to be seen a bed of apparently impracticable mountains. Among these, the trail we had been following turned sharply to the northward, and it began to be doubtful if it would not lead us away from the object of our destination; but I nevertheless determined to keep it, in the belief that it would eventually bring us right. A squall of rain drove us out of the mountain, and it was late when we reached the camp. The evening closed in with frequent showers of rain, with some lightning and thunder.

30th.—We had constant thunder storms during the night, but in the morning the clouds were sinking to the horizon, and the air was clear and cold, with the thermometer at sunrise at 39°. Elevation by barometer 5,580 feet. We were in motion early, continuing up the little stream without encountering any ascent where a horse would not easily gallop; and, crossing a slight dividing ground at the summit, descended upon a small stream, along which continued the same excellent road. In riding through the pass, numerous cranes were seen and prairie hens, or grouse, (bonasia umbellua,) which lately had been rare, were very abundant.

This little affluent brought us to a larger stream, down which we traveled through a more open bottom, on a level road, where heavilyladen wagons could pass without obstacle. The hills on the right grew lower, and, on entering a more open country, we discovered a Shoshonee village; and being desirous to obtain information, and purchase from them some roots and berries, we halted on the river, which was lightly wooded with cherry, willow, maple, serviceberry, and aspen. A meridian observation of the sun, which I obtained here, gave 42o 14' 22" for our latitude, and the barometer indicated a height of 5,170 feet. A number of Indians came immediately over to visit us, and several men were sent to the village with goods, tobacco, knives, cloth, vermilion, and the usual trinkets, to exchange for provisions. But they had no game of any kind; and it was difficult to obtain any roots from them, as they were miserably poor, and had but little to spare from their winter stock of provisions. Several of the Indians drew aside their blankets, showing me their lean and bony figures; and I would not any longer tempt them with a display of our merchandise to part with their wretched subsistence, when they gave as a reason that it would expose them to temporary starvation. A great portion of the region inhabited by this nation, formerly abounded in game—the buffalo ranging about in herds, as we had found them on the eastern waters, and the plains dotted with scattered bands of antelope; but so rapidly have they disappeared within a few years, that now, as we journeyed along, en occasional buffalo skull and a few wild antelope were all that remained of the abundance which had covered the country with animal life.

The extraordinary rapidity with which the buffalo is disappearing from our territories will not appear surprising when we remember the great scale on which their destruction is yearly carried on. With inconsiderable exceptions, the business of the American tradingposts is carried on in their skins; every year the Indian villages make new lodges, for which the skin of the buffalo furnishes the material; and in that portion of the country where they are still found, the Indians derive their entire support from them, and slaughter them with a thoughtless and ah)minable extravagance. Like the Indians themselves, they have, been a characteristic of the Great West; and as, like them, they are visibly diminishing, it will be interesting to throw a glance backward through the last twenty years, and give some account of their former distribution through the country, and the limit of their western range.

The information is derived principally from Mr. Fitzpatrick, supported by my own personal knowledge and acquaintance with the country. Our knowledge does not go farther back than the spring of 1824, at which time the buffalo were spread in immense numbers over the Green River and Bear River valleys, and through all the country lying between the Colorado, or Green river of the Gulf of California, and Lewis's fork of the Columbia river; the meridian of Fort Hall then formmg the western limit of their range. The buffalo then remained for many years in that country, and frequently moved down the valley of the Columbia, on both sides of the river as far as the Fishing falls. Below this point they never descended in any numbers. About the year 1834 or 1835 they began to diminish very rapidly, and continued to decrease until 1838 or 1840, when, with the country we have just described, they entirely abandoned all the waters of the Pacific north of Levis's fork of the Columbia. At that time, the Flathead Indians were in the habit of finding their buffalo on the heads of Salmon river, and other streams of the Columbia; but now they never meet with them farther west than the three forks of the Missouri,: or the plains of the Yellowstone river.

In the course of our journey it will be remarked that the buffalo have not so entirely abandoned the waters of the Pacific the RockyMountain region south of the Sweet Water, as in the country north of the Great Pass. This partial distribution can only be accounted for in the great pastoral beauty of let country, which bears marks of having been one of their favorite haunts, and by the fact that the white hunters have more frequented the northern than the southern region—it be ing north of the South Pass that the hunters, trappers, and traders, have had their rendezvous for many years past; and from that section also the greater portion of the beaver and rich furs were taken, although always the most dangerous as well as the most profitable hunting ground.

In that region lying between the Green or Colorado river and the headwaters of the Rio del Norte, over the Yampah, liaoyah, White, and Grand rivers—all of which are the waters of the Colorado—the buffalo never extended so far to the westward as they did on the waters of the Columbia; and only in one or two instances have they been known to descend as far west as the mouth of White river. In traveling through the country west of the Rocky mountains, observation readily led me to the impression that the buffalo had, for the first time, crossed that range to the waters of the Pacific only a few years prior to the period we are considering; and in this opinion I am sustained by Mr. Fitzpatrick, and the older trappers in that country. In the region west of the Rocky mountains, we never meet with any of the ancient vestiges which, throughout all the r:ountry lying upon their eastern waters, are found in the great highways, continuous for hundreds of miles, always several inches, and sometimes several feet in depth, which the buffalo have made in crossing from one river to another, or in traversing the mountain ranges. The Snake Indians, more particularly those low down upon Lewis's fork, have always been very grateful to the American trappers, for the great kindness (as they frequently expressed it) which they did to them, in driving the buffalo so low down the Columbia river.

The extraordinary abundance of the buffalo on the east side „of the Rocky mountains, and their extraordinary diminution, will be made clearly evident from the following statement: At any time between the years 1824 and 1836, a traveler might start from any given point south or north in the Rocky Mountain range, journeying by the most direct route to the Missouri river; and, during the whole distance, his road would always be among large bands of buffalo, which would never r,e out of his view until he arrived almost within sight of Inc abodes of civilization.

At this time, the buffalo occupy but a very limited space, principally along the eastern base of the Rocky mountains; sometimes extending at their southern extremity to a considerable distance into the plains between the Platte and Arkansas rivers, and along the eastern frontier of New Mexico as far south as Texas.

The following statement, which I owe to the kindness of Mr Sanford, a partner in the American Fur Company, will further illustrate this subject, by extensive knowledge acquired during several years of travel through the region inhabited by the buffalo:

" In the northwest, the Hudson's Bay Company purchase from the Indians but a very small number—their only market being Canada, to which the cost of transportation nearly equals the produce of the furs; and it is only within a very recent period that they have received buffalo robes in trade; and out of the great number of buffalo annually killed throughout the extensive region inhabited by the Camanches and other kindred tribes, no robes whatever are furnished for trade. During only four months of the year, (from November until March,) the skins are good for dressing; those obtained in the remaining eight months are valueless to traders; and the hides of bulls are never taken off or dressed as robes at any season. Probably not more than one third of the skins are taken from the animals killed, even when they are in good season, the labor of preparing and dressing the robes being very great; end it is seldom that a lodge trades more than twenty skins in a year. It is during the summer months and in the early part of autumn, that the greatest number of buffalo are killed, and yet at this time a skin is never taken for the purpose of trade."

From these data, which are certainly limited, and decidedly within bounds, the reader is left to draw his own inference of he immense number annually killed.

In 1842, I found the Sioux Indians of the Upper Platte demontes, as their French traders expressed it, with the failure of the buffalo; and in the following year, large villages from the Upper Missouri came over to the mountains at the heads of the Platte, in search of them. The rapidly progressive failure of their principal, and almost their only means of subsistence, has created great alarm among them; and at this time there are only two modes presented to them, by which they see a good prospect for escaping starvation: one of these is to rob the settlements along the frontier of the States; and the other is to form a league between the various tribes of the Sioux nation, the Cheyennes, and Arapahoes, and make war against the Crow nation, in order to take from them their country, which is now the best buffalo country in the west. This plan they now have in consideration; and it would probably be a war of extermination, as the Crows have long been advised of this state of affairs, and say that they are perfectly prepared. These are the best warriors in the Rocky mountains, and are now allied with the Snake Indians; and it is probable that their combination would extend itself to the Utahs, who have long been engaged in war against the Sioux. It is in this section of country that my observation formerly led me to recommend the establishment of a military post.

The farther course of our narrative will give fuller and more detailed information of the present disposition of the buffalo in the country we visited.

Among the roots we obtained here, I could distinguish only five or six different kinds; and the supply of the Indians whom we met consisted principally of yampah, (anethum graveolens,) tobaccoroot, (valeriana,) and a large root of a species of thistle, (circium Virginianum,) which now is occasionally abun dant, and is a very agreeably flavored vegetable.

We had been detained so long at the village, that in the afternoon we made only five miles, and encamped on the same river after a day's journey of 19 miles. The Indians informed us that we should reach the big salt water after having slept twice and traveling in a south direction. The stream had here entered nearly a level plain or valley, of good soil, eight or ten miles broad, to which no termination was to be seen, and lying between ranges of mountains which, on the right, were grassy and smooth, unbroken by rock, and lower than on the left, where they were rocky and bald, increasing in height to the southward. On the creek were fringes of young willows, older trees being rarely found on the plains, where the Indians burn the surface to produce better grass, Several magpies (pica Hudsopica) were seen on the creek this afternoon; and a rattlesnake was killed here, the first which had been seen since leaving the eastern plains. Our camp tonight had such a hungry appearance that

I suffered the little cow to be killed, and divided the roots and berries among the people. A number of Indians from the village encamped near.

The weather the next morning was clear, the thermometer at sunrise at 44.50; and, continuing down the valley, in about five miles we followed the little creek of our encampment to its junction with a larger stream, called Roseaux, or Reed river. Immediately opposite, on the right, the range was gathered into its highest peak, sloping gradually low, and running off to a point apparently some forty or fifty miles below. Between this (now become the valley stream) and the foot of the mountains, we journeyed along a handsome sloping level, which frequent springs from the hills made occasionally miry, and halted to noon at a swampy spring, where there were good grass and abundant rushes. Here the river was forty feet wide, with a considerable current, and the valley a mile and a half in breadth; the soil being generally good, of a dark color, and apparently well adapted to cultivation. The day had become bright and pleasant, with Cie thermometer at 710. By observation, our latitude was 41° 59' 31", and the elevation above the sea 4,670 feet. On our left, this afternoon, the range at long intervals formed itself into peaks, appearing to terminate about forty miles below, in a rocky cape beyond which several others were faintly visible; and we were disappointed when, at every little rise, we did not see the lake. Towards evening, our way was somewhat obstructed by fields of artemisia, which began to make their appearance here, and we encamped on the Roseaux, the water of which had acquired a decidedly salt taste, nearly opposite to a canon gap in the mountains, through which the Bear river enters this valley. As we encamped, the night set in dark and cold, with heavy rain, and the artemisia, which was our only wood, was so wet that it would not 'hum. A poor, nearly starved dog, with a wound in his side from a ball, came to the camp, and remained with us until the winter, when he met a very unexpected fate.

SEPTEMBER.

1st.—The morning was squally and cold; the sky scattered over with clouds; and the night had been so uncomfortable, that we were not on the road until eight o'clock. Traveling between Roseaux and Bear rivers, we continued to descend the valley, which gradually expanded, as we advanced, into a level plain, of good soil, about 25 miles in breath, between mountains 3,000 and 42000 feet high, rising suddenly to the clouds, which all day rested upon the peaks. These gleamed out in the occasional sunlight, mantled with the snow which had fallen upon them, while it rained on us in the valley below, of which the elevation here was 4,500 feet above the sea. The country before us plainly indicated that we were approaching the lake, though, as the ground we were traveling afforded no elevated point, nothing of it as yet could be seen; and at a great distance ahead were several isolated mountains resembling islands, which they were afterwards found to be. On this upper plain the grass was everywhere dead; and among the shrubs with which it was almost exclusively occupied, (artemisia being the most abundant,) frequently occurred handsome clusters of several species of dieteria in bloom. Purshia denials was among the frequent shrubs. Descending to the bottoms of Bear river, we found good grass for the animals, and encamped about 300 yards above the mouth of Ro5eaux, which here makes its junction, without communicating any of its salty taste to the main stream, of which the water remain, perfectly pure. On the river are only willow thickets, (salin lonefolia,) and in the bottoms the abundant plants are canes, soldiago, and helianthi, and along the banks of Roseaux are fields of malva rotundifolia. At sunset the thermometer was at 54.50, and the evening clear and calm; but I deferred making any use of it until one o'clock in the morning, when endeavored to obtain an emersion of the first satellite; but if was lost in a bank of clouds, which also rendered our usual observations indifferent.

Among the useful things which formed a portion of ow equipage, was an Indiarubber boat, 18 feet long, made somewhat in the form of a bark canoe of the northern lakes. The sides were formed 'by two airtight cylinders, eighteen inches in diameter, connected with others forming the bow and stern To lessen the danger from accidents to the boat, these were divided into four different compartments, and the interior space was sufficiently large to contain five or six persons, and a considerable weight of baggage.

The Roseaux being too deep to be forded, our boat was filled with air, and in about one how all the equipage of the camp, carriage and gun included, ferried across. Thinking that perhaps in the course of the day we might reach the outlet of the lake, I got into the boat wit/Basil Lajeunesse, and paddled down Bear river, intending a night to rejoin the party, which in the mean time proceeded on its way. The river was from sixty to one hundred yards broad, and the water so deep, that even on the comparatively shallow points we could not reach the bottom with 15 feet. On either side were alternately low boroms and willow points, with an occasional high prairie; and for five or six hours we allowed slowly the winding course of the river, which crept along with a sluggish current among frequent detours several miles around, sometimes running for a considerable distance directly up the valley. As we were stealing quietly down the stream, trying in vain to get a shot at a strange large bird that was numerous among the willows, but very shy, we came unexpectedly upon several families of RootDiggers, who were encamped among the rushes on the shore, and appeared very busy about several weirs or nets which had been rudely made of canes and rushes for the purpose of catching fish. They were very much startled at our appearance, but we soon established an acquaintance; and finding that they had some roots, I promised to send some men with goods to trade with them. They had the usual very large heads, remarkable among the Digger tribe, with matted hair, and were almost entirely naked: looking very poor and miserable, as if their lives had been spent in the rushes where they were, beyond which they seemed to have very little knowledge of any thing. From the words we could comprehend, their language was that of the. Snake Indians.

Our boat moved so heavily, that we had made very little progress; and, finding that it would be impossible to overtake the camp, as soon as we were sufficiently far below the Indians, we put to the shore near a high prairie bank, hauled up the boat, and cached our effects in the willows. Ascending the bank, we found that our desultory labor had brought us only a few miles in a direct line; and, going out into the prairie, after a search we found the trail of the camp, which was nowhere in sight, but had followed the general course of the river in a large circular sweep which it makes at this place. The sun was about three hours high when we found the trail; and as our people bad passed early in the day, we had the prospect of a vigorous walk before us. Immediately where we landed, the high arable plain on which we had been traveling, for several days past, terminated in extensive low flats, very generally occupied by salt marshes, or beds of shallow lazes, whence the water had in most places evaporated, leaving their hard surface incrusted with a shining white residue, and absolutely covered with very small live shells. As we advanced, the whole country around us assumed this appearance; ana there was no other vegetation than the shrubby chenopodiaceous arid other apparently saline plants, which were confined to the rising grounds. Here and there, on the river bank, which was raised like a levee above the flats through which it ran, was a narrow border of grass and short blackburnt willows; the stream being very deep and sluggish, and sometimes six hundred to eight hundred feet wide. After a rapid walk of about fifteen miles, we caught sight of the campfires among clumps of willows, just as the sun had sunk behind the mountains on the west side of the valley, filling the clear sky with a golden yellow. These last rays, to us so precious, could not have revealed a more welcome sight. To the traveler and the hunter, a campfire in the lonely wilderness is always cheering; and to ourselves, in our present situation, after a hard march in a region of novelty, approaching the debauches of a river, in a lake of almost fabulous reputation, it was doubly so. A plentiful supper of aquatic birds, and the interest of the scene, soon dissipated fatigue; and I obtained during the night emersions of the second, third, and fourth satellites of Jupiter, with observations for time and latitude.

V.—The morning was clear, with a light air from the north, and he thermometer at sunrise at 45.50. At three in the morning, Basil was sent back with several men and horses for the boat, which, in a direct course across the flats, was not ten miles distant; and in the mean time there was a pretty spot of grass here for the animals. The ground was so low that we could not get high enough to see across the river, on account of the willows; but we were evidently in the vicinity of the lake, and the waterfowl made this, morning a noise like thunder. A pelican (pelecanus onocrotalus) was killed as he passed by, and many geese and ducks flew over the camp. On the dry salt marsh here is scarce any other plant than salicornia herbacea.

In the afternoon the men returned with the boat, bringing with them a small quantity of roots and some meat, which the Indians had told them was bear meat.

Descending the river for about three miles, in the afternoon we found a bar to any further traveling in that direction—the stream being spread out in several branches, and covering the low grounds with water, where the miry nature of the bottom did not permit any further advance. We were evidently on the border of the lake, although the rushes and canes which covered the marshes prevented any view; and we accordingly encamped at the little delta which forms the mouth of Beat river—a long arm of the lake stretching up to the north, between us and the opposite mountains. The river was bordered with a fringe of willows and canes, among which were interspersed a few plants; and scattered about on the marsh was a species of uniola, closely allied to U. spicata of our seacoast. The whole morass was animated with multitudes of waterfowl, which appeared to be very wild—rising for the space of a mile round about at the sound of a gun, with a noise like distant thunder. Several of the people waded out into the marshes, and we had tonight a delicious supper of ducks, geese, and plover.

Although the moon was bright, the night was otherwise favorable; and I obtained this evening an emersion of the first satellite, with the usual observations. A mean result, depending on various observations made during our stay in the neighborhood, places the mouth of the river in longitude 1120 19' 30" west from Greenwich; latitude 41° 30' 22"; and, according to the barometer, in elevation 4,200 feet above the Gulf of Mexico. The night was clears with considerable dew, which I had remarked every night since the first of September.. The next morning, while we were preparing to start, Carson rode into the camp with flour and a few other articles of light provision, sufficient for two or three days—a scanty but very acceptable supply. Mr. Fitzpatrick had not yet arrived, and provisions were very scarce, and difficult to be had at Fort Hall, which had been entirely exhausted by the necessities of the emigrants. He brought me also a letter from Mr. Dwight, who, in company with several emigrants, had reached that place in advance of Mr. Fitzpatrick, and was about continuing its journey to Vancouver.

Returning about five miles up the river we were occupied until nearly sunset in crossing to the left bank—the stream which in the last five or six miles of its course is very much narrower than above, being very deep immediately at the banks; and we had great difficulty in getting our animals over. The people with the baggage were easily crossed in the boat, and we encamped on the left bank where we crossed the river. At sunset the thermometer was at 75o, and there was some rain during the night, with a thunderstorm at a distance.

5th.—Before us was evidently the bed of the lake, being a great salt marsh, perfectly level and bare, whitened in places by saline efllorescences, with here and there a pool of water, and having the appearance of a very level seashore at low tide. Immediately along the river was a very narrow strip of vegetation, consisting of willows, helianthi, roses, flowering vines, and grass; bordered on the verge of the great marsh by a fringe of singular plants, which appear to be a shrubby salicornia, or a genus allied to it.

About 12 miles to the southward was one of those isolated mountains; now appearing to be a kind of peninsula; and towards this we accordingly directed our course, as it probably afforded a good view of the lake; but the deepening mud as we advanced forced us to return towards the river, and gain the higher ground at the foot of the eastern mountains. Here we halted for a few minutes at noon, on a beautiful little stream of pure and remarkably clear water, with a bed of rock in situ, on which was an abundant waterplant with a white blossom. There was good grass in the bottoms; and, amidst a rather luxuriant growth, its banks were bordered with a large showy plant, (eupatorium purpureum,) which I here saw for the first time. We named the stream Clear creek.

We continued our way along the mountain, having found here a broad plainlybeaten trail, over what was apparently the shore of the lake in the spring; the ground being high and firm, ana the soil excellent, and covered with vegetation, among which a leguminous plant (glycyrrhiza lepidota) was a characteristic plant. The ridge here rises abruptly to the height of about 4,000 feet, its face being very prominently marked with a massive stratum of rosecolored granular quartz, which is evidently an altered sedimentary rock, the lines of deposition being very distinct. It is rocky and steep—divided into several mountains—and the rain in the valley appears tc be always snow on their summits at this season. Near a remarkably rocky point of the mountain, at a large spring of pure water, were several hackberrytrees, (celtis,) probably a new species, the berries still green; and a short distance farther, thickets of sumach, (Aug.)

On the plain here I noticed blackbirds and grouse. In about seven miles from Clear creek, the trail brought us to a place at the foot of the mountain where there issued, with considerable force, 10 or 12 hot springs, highly impregnated with salt. In one of these the thermometer stood at 136o, and in another at 132.5o, and the water, which was spread in pools over the low ground, was colored red.

An analysis of the red earthy matter deposited in the bed of the stream from the springs, gives the following result:

At this place the trail we had been following turned to the left, apparently with a view of entering a gorge in the mountain, from which issued the principal fork of a large and comparatively well-timbered stream, called Weber's fork. We accordingly turned off towards the lake, and encamped on this river, which was 100 to 150 feet wide, with high banks; and very clear pure water, without the slightest indication of salt.

6th.—Leaving the encampment early, we again directed our course for the peninsular butte across a low shrubby plain, crossing in the way a sloughlike creek with miry banks, and wooded with thickets of thorn, (cratcegus,) which were loaded with berries. This time we reached the butte without any difficulty, and, ascending to the summit, immediately at our feet beheld the object of our anxious search—the waters of the Inland Sea, stretching in still and solitary grandeur far beyond the limit of our vision. It was one of the great points of the exploration; and as we looked eagerly over the lake in the first emotions of excited pleasure, I am doubtful if the followers of Balboa felt more enthusiasm when, from the heights of the Andes, they saw for the first time the great Western ocean. It was certainly a magnificent object, and a noble terminus m this part of our expedition; and to travelers so long shut up among mountain ranges, a sudden view over the expanse of silent waters had in it something sublime. Several large islands raised their high rocky heads out of the waves; but whether or not they were timbered, was still left to our imagination, as the distance was too great to determine if the dark hues upon them were woodland or naked rock. During the day the clouds had been gathering black over the mountains to the westward, and, while we were looking, a storm burst down with sudden fury upon the lake, and entirely hid the inlands from our view. So far as we could see, along the shores there was not a solitary tree, and but little appearance of grass; and on Weber's fork, a few miles below our last encampment, the timber was gathered into groves, and then disappeared entirely. As this appeared to be the nearest point to the lake, where a suitable camp could be found; we directed our course to one of the groves, where we found a handsome encampment, with good grass and an abundance of rushes, (equisetum hyemale.) At sunset the thermometer was at 55°; the evening clear and calm, with some cumuli.

7th.—The morning was calm and clear, with a temperature at sunrise of 39.5°. The day was spent in active preparation for our intended voyage on the lake. On the edge of the stream a favorable spot was selected in a grove, and, felling the timber, we made a strong coral, or horse pen, for the animals, and a little fort for, the people who were to 'remain. We were now probably in the country of the Utah Indians, though none reside on the lake. The Indiarubber boat was repaired with prepared cloth and gum, and filled with air, in readiness for the next day.

The provisions which Carson brought with him being now exhausted, and our stock reduced, to a small quantity of roots, I determined to retain with me only a sufficient number of men for the execution of our design; and accordingly seven were sent back to Fort Hall, under the guidance of Francois Lajeunesse, who, having been for many years a trapper in the country, was considered an experienced mountaineer. Though they were provided with good horses, and the road was a remarkably plain one of only four days' journey for a horseman, they became bewildered, (as we afterwards learned,) and, losing their way, wandered about the country in parties of one or two, reaching the fort about a week afterwards. Some straggled in of themselves, and the others were brought in by Indians who had picked them up on Snake river, about sixty miles below the fort, traveling along the, emigrant road in full march for the Lower Columbia. The leader of this adventurous party was Francois.

Hourly barometrical observations were made during the day, and, after the departure of the party for Fort Hall, we occupied ourselves in continuing our little preparations, and in becoming acquainted with the country in the vicinity. The bottoms along the river were timbered with several kinds of willow, hawthorn, and fine cottonwood trees (populu,s canaden84) with remarkably large leaves, and sixty feet in height by measurement.

We formed now but a small family. With Mr. Preuss arra myself, Carson, Bernier, and Basil Lajeunesse, had been selected for the boat expedition—the first attempted on this interior sea; and Badeau, with Derosier, and Jacob, (the colored man,) were to be left in charge of the camp. We were favored with most delightful weather. Tonight there was a brilliant sunset of golden orange and green, which left the western sky clear and beautifully pure; but clouds in the east made me lose an occultation. The summer frogs were singing around us, and the evening was very pleasant, with a temperature of 60o—a night of a more southern autumn. For our supper we had yampah, the most agreeably flavored of fine roots, seasoned by a small fat duck, which had come in the way of Jacob's rifle. Around our fire tonight were many speculations on what tomorrow would bring forth, and in our busy conjectures we fancied that we should find every one of the large islands a tangled wilderness of trees and shrubbery, teeming with game of every description that the neighboring region afforded, and which the foot of a white man or Indian had never violated. Frequently, during the day, clouds had rested on the summits of their lofty mountains, and we believed that we should find clear streams and springs of fresh water; and we indulged in anticipations of She luxurious repasts with which we were to indemnify ourselves for past privations. Neither, in our discussions, were the whirlpool and other mysterious dangers forgotten, which Indian and hunters' stories attributed to this unexplored lake. The men had found that, instead of being strongly sewed, (like that of the preceding year, which had so triumphantly rode the canons of the upper Great Platte,) our present boat was only pasted together in a very insecure manner, the maker having been allowed so little time in the construction, that he was obliged to crowd the labor of two months into several days. The insecurity of the boat was sensibly felt by us; and, mingled with the enthusiasm and excitement that we all felt at the prospect of an undertaking which had never before been accomplished, was a certain impression of danger, sufficient to give a serious character to our conversation. The momentary view which had been had of the lake the day before, its great extent and rugged islands, dimly seen amidst the dark waters in the obscurity of the sudden storm, were calculated to heighten the idea of undefined danger with which the lake was generally associated.

8th.—A calm, clear day, with a sunrise temperature of 41°. In view of our present enterprise, a part of the equipment of the boat had been made to consist in three airtight bags, about 'three feet long, and capable each of containing five gallons. These had been find with water the night before, and were now placed in the boss, with our blankets and instruments, consisting of a sextant, telescope, spyglass, thermometer, and barometer.

We left the camp at sunrise, and had a very pleasant voyage down the river, in which there was generally eight or ten feet of water, deepening as we neared the mouth in the latter part of the day. In the course of the morning we discovered that two of the cylinders leaked so much as to require one man constantly at the bellows, to keep them sufficiently full of air to support the boat. Although we had made a very early start, we loitered so Much on the way—stopping every now and then, and floating silently along, to get a shot at a goose or duck—that it was late in the day when we reached the outlet. The river here divided into several branches, filled with fluvials, and so very shallow that it was with difficulty we could get the boat along, being obliged to get out and wade. We encamped on a low point among rushes and young willows, where was a quantity of driftwood, which served for our fires. The evening was mild and clear; we made a pleasant bed of young willows; and geese and ducks enough had been killed for an abundant supper at night, and for breakfast the next morning. The stillness of the night was enlivened by millions of waterfowl. Lat. (by observation) 41° 11' 26"; and long. 112° 11' 30".

9th.—The day was clear and calm; the thermometer at sunrise at 49°. As is usual with the trappers on the eve of any enterprise, our people had made dreams, and theirs happened to be a bad one—one which always preceded evil—and consequently they looked very gloomy this morning; but we hurried through our breakfast, in order to made an early start, and have all the day before us for our adventure. The channel in a short distance became so shallow that our navigation was at an end, being merely a sheet of soft Mud, with a few inches of water, and sometimes none at all, forming the lowwater shore of the lake. All this place was absolutely covered with flocks of screaming plover. We took off our clothes, and, getting overboard, commenced dragging the boat—making, by this operation, a very curious trail, and a very disagreeable smell in stirring up the mud, as we sank above the knee as every step. The water here was still fresh, with only an in sipid and disagreeable taste, probably derived from the bed of fetid mud. After proceeding in this way about a mile, we came to a small black ridge on the bottom, beyond which the water became suddenly salt, beginning gradually to deepen, and the bottom was sandy and firm. It was a remarkable division, separating the fresh waters of the rivers from the brut) water of the lake, which was entirely saturated with common salt. Pushing our little vessel across the narrow boundary, we sprang on board, and at length were afloat on the waters Jf the unknown sea.

We did not steer for the mountainous islands, but directed our course towards a lower one, which it had been decided we should first visit, the summit of which was formed like the crater at the upper end of Bear River valley. So long as we could touch the bottom with our paddles, we were very gay; gradually, as the water deepened, we became more still in our frail batteau of gumcloth distended with air, and with pasted seams. Although the day was very calm, there was a considerable swell on the lake; and there were white patches of foam on the surface, which were slowly moving to the southward, indicating the set of a current in that direction, and recalling the recollection of the whirlpool stories. The water continued to deepen as we advanced—the lake becoming almost transparently clear, of an extremely beautiful bright green color; and the spray, which was thrown into the boat and over our clothes, was directly converted into a crust of common salt, which covered also our hands and arms. "Captain," said Carson, who for some time had been looking suspiciously at some whitening appearances outside the nearest islands, what are those yonder?—won't you just take a look with the glass?" We ceased paddling for a moment, and found them to be the caps of the waves that were beginning to break under the force of a strong breeze that was coming up the lake.

The form of the boat seemed to be an admirable one, and it code on the waves like a waterbird; but, at the same time, it was extremely slow in its progress. When we were a little more than half way across the reach, two of the divisions between the cylinders gave way, and it required the constant use of the bellows to keep in a sufficient quantity or air. For long time we scarcely seemed to approach our island, but gradually we worked across the rougher sea of the open channel, into the smoother water under the lee of the island, and began to discover that what we took for a long row of pelicans, ranged on the beach, were only low cliffs whitened with salt by the spray of the waves; and about noon we reached the shore, the transparency of the water enabling us to see the bottom at a considerable depth.

It was a handsome broad beach where we landed, behind which the hill, into which the island was gathered, rose somewhat abruptly; and a point of rock at one end enclosed it in a sheltering way; and as there was an abundance of driftwood along the shore, it offered us a pleasant encampment. We did not suffer our frail boat to touch the sharp rocks, but, getting overboard, discharged the baggage, and, lifting it gently out of the water, carried it to the upper part of the beach, which was composed of very small fragments of rock.

Among the successive banks of the beach, formed by the action of the waves, our attention, as we approached the island, had been attracted by one 10 to 20 feet in breadth, of a dark-brown color. Being more closely examined, this was found to be composed, to the depth of seven or eight and twelve inches, entirely of the larva of insects, or, in common language, of the skins of worms, about the size of a grain of oats, which had been washed up by the waters of the lake.

Alluding to this subject some months afterwards, when traveling through a more southern portion of this region, in company with Mr. Joseph Walker, an old hunter, I was informed by him, that, wandering with a party of men in a mountain country east of the great California range, he surprised a party of several Indian families encamped near a small salt lake, who abandoned their lodges at his approach, leaving every thing behind them. Being in a starving condition, they were delighted to find in the abandoned lodges a number of skin and pounded. On this they made a hearty supper, and were gathering around an abundant breakfast the next morning, when Mr. Walker discovered that it was with these, or a similar worm, that the bags had been filled. The stomachs of the stout trappers, were not proof against their prejudices, and the repulsive food was suddenly rejected. Mr. Walker had further opportunities of 'seeing these worms used as an article of food; and I am inclined to think they are the same as those we saw, 'and appear to be a product of the salt lakes. It may be well to recall to your mind that Mr. Walker was associated with Capt. Bonneville in his expedition to the Rocky mountains, and has since that time remained in the country, generally residing in some one of the Snake villages, when not engaged in one of his numerous trapping expeditions, in which he is celebrated as one of the best and bravest leaders who have ever been in t: e country.

The cliffs and masses of rock along the shore were whitened by an incrustation of salt where the waves dashed up against them; arid the evaporating water, which had been left in holes and hollows on the surface of the rocks, was covered with a crust of salt about one eighth of an inch in thickness. It appeared strange that, in the midst of this grand reservoir, one of our greatest wants lately had been salt. Exposed to be more perfectly dried in the sun, this became very white and fine, having the usual flavor of very excellent common salt, without any foreign taste; but only a little was collected for present use, as there was in it a number of small black insects.

Carrying with us the barometer and other instruments, in the afternoon we ascended to the highest point of the island—a hare, rocky peak, eight hundred feet above the lake. Standing on the summit, we enjoyed an extended view of the lake, enclosed in a basin of rugged mountains, which sometimes left marshy flats and extensive bottoms between them and the shore, and in other places came directly down into the water with bold and precipitous bluffs. Following with our glasses the irregular shores, we searched for some indications of a communication with other bodies of water, or the entrance of other rivers; but the distance was so great that we could make out nothing with certainty. To the southward, several peninsular mountains, 3,000 or 4,000 feet high, entered the lake, appearing, so far as the distance and our position enabled us to determine, to be connected by flats and low ridges with the mountains in the rear. These are probably the islands usually indicated an maps of this region as entirely detached from the shore "the season of our operations was when the waters were at their lowest stage. At the season of high waters in the spring, it, is probable that the marshes and low grounds are overflowed, and the surface of the lake considerably greater. In several places the view was of unlimited extent—here and there a rocky islet appearing above the waters, at a great distance; and beyond, every thing was vague and undefined. As we looked over the vast expanse of water spread out beneath us, and strained our eyes along the silent shores over which hung so much doubt and uncertainty, and which were so full of interest to us, I could hardly repress the almost irresistible desire to continue our explorations; but the lengthening snow on the mountains was a plain indication of the advancing season, and our frail linen boat appeared so insecure that I was unwilling to trust our lives to the uncertainties of the lake. I therefore unwillingly resolved to terminate our survey here, and remain satisfied for the present with what we had been able to add to the unknown geography of the region. We felt pleasure, also, in remembering that we were the first who, in the traditional annals of the country, had visited the islands and broken, with the cheerful sound of human, voices, the long, solitude of the place. From the point where we were standing, the ground fell off on every side to the water, giving us a perfect view of the island, which is twelve or thirteen miles in circumference, being simply a rocky hill, on which there is neither water nor trees of any kind; although the Fremontia vermicularis, which was in great abundance, might easily be taken for timber at a distance. The plant seemed here to delight in a congenial air, growing in extraordinary luxuriance seven to eight feet high, and was very abundant on the upper parts of the island, where it was almost the only plant This is eminently a saline shrub; its leaves have a salt taste; and it luxuriates in saline soils, where it is usually a characteristic It is widely diffused over all this country. A chenopodiaceous shrub, which is a new species of osioNs, (o. rigida, Torr and Frem.,) was equally characteristic of the lower parts of the island. These two are the strikiplants on the island, and belong to a class of plants which form a prominent feature in the vegetation of this country. On the lower parts of the island, also, a prickly pear of very large size was frequent. On the shore, near the water, was a woolly species of phaca; and a new species of umbelliferous plant (leptoicemia) was scattered about in very considerable abundance. These constituted all the vegetation that now appeared upon the island.

I accidentally left on the summit the_ brass cover to the object end of my spyglass: and as it will probably remain there undisturbed by Indians, it will furnish matter of speculation to some future traveler.

In our excursions about the island, we did not meet with any kind of animal; a magpie, and another larger bird, probably attracted by the smoke of our fire, paid us a visit from the shore, and were the only living things seen during our stay. The rock constituting the cliffs along the shore, where we were encamped, is a talcous rock, or steatite, with brown spar.

At sunset, the temperature was 70°. We had arrived just in time to obtain a meridian altitude of the sun, and other observations were obtained this evening; which placed our camp in latitude 41° 10' 42", and longitude 112° 21' 05" from Greenwich. From a discussion of the barometrical observations made during our stay on the shores of the lake, we have adopted 4,200 feet for its elevation above the Gulf of Mexico. In the first disappointment we felt from the dissipation of our dream of the fertile islands, I called this Disappointment island.

Out of the driftwood, we made ourselves pleasant little lodges, open to the water; and, after having kindled large fires to excite the wonder of any straggling savage on the lake shores, lay down, for the first time in a long journey, in perfect security; no one thinking about his arms. The evening was extremely bright and pleasant; but the wind rose during the night, and the waves began to break heavily on the shore making our island tremble. I had not expected in our inland journey to hear the roar of an ocean surf; and the strangeness of our situation, and the excitement we felt in the associated interest of the place, made this one of the most interesting nights I made during our long expedition.

In the morning, the surf was breaking heavily on the shore, and we were up early. The lake was dark and agitated, and we hurried through our scanty breakfast, and embarked—having first filled one of the buckets with water from the lake, of which' it was intended to make salt. The sun had risen by the time we were ready to start; and it was blowing a strong gale of wind, almost directly off the shore, and raising a considerable sea, in which our boat strained very much. It roughened as we got away from the island, and it required all the efforts of the men to make any head against the wind and sea, the gale rising with the sun; and there was danger of being blown into one of the open reaches beyond the island. At the distance of half a mile from the beach, the depth of the water was 16 feet, with a clay bottom; but, as the working of the boat was very severe labor, and during the operation of sounding it was necessary to cease paddling, during which the boat lost considerable way, I was unwilling to discourage the men, and reluctantly gave up my intention of ascertaining the depth and the character of the bed. There was a general shout in the boat when we found ourselves in one fathom, and we soon after landed on a low point of mud, immediately under the butte of the peninsula, where we unloaded the boat, and carried the baggage about a quarter of a mile to firmer ground. We arrived just in time for meridian observation, and carried the barometer to the summit of the butte, which is 500 feet above the lake. Mr. Preuss set off on foot for the camp, which was about nine miles distant; Basil accompanying him, to bring back horses for the boat and baggage.

The rude looking shelter we raised on the shore, our scattered baggage and boat lying on the beach, made quite a picture; and we called this the Fisherman's camp. Lynosiria graveolena, and another new species of OBIONE, (o. confertifolikTorr. Prem.) were crowing on the low rounds, with interspersed spots of an unwholesome salt grass, on a saline clay soil, with a few other plants.

The horses arrived late in the afternoon, by which time the gale had increased to such a height that a man could scarcely stand before it; and we were obliged to pack our baggage hastily, as the rising water of the lake had already reached the point where we were halted. Looking back as we rode off, we found the place of recent encampment entirely covered. The low plain through which we rode to the camp was covered with a compact growth of shrubs of extraordinary size and luxuriance. The soil was sandy and saline; flat places, resembling the beds of ponds, that were bare of vegetation, and covered with a powdery white salt, being interspersed among the shrubs. Artemisia tridentata was very abundant, but the plants were principally saline; a large and vigorous chenopodiaceous shrub, five to eight feet high, being characteristic, with Fremontia vermicularis, and a shrubby plant which seems to be a new salicornia. We reached the camp in time to escape a thunderstorm which blackened the sky, and were received with a discharge of the howitzer by the people, who, having been unable to see any thing of us on the lake, had begun to feel some uneasiness.

11th.—Today we remained at this camp, in order to obtain some further observations, and to boil down the water which had been brought from the lake, for a supply of salt. Roughly evaporated over the fire, the five gallons of water yielded fourteen pints of very fine-grained and very white salt, of which the whole lake may be regarded as a saturated solution. A portion of the salt thus obtained has been subjected to analysis giving, in 100 parts, the following proportions:

Analysis of the salt.

Chloride of sodium, (common salt,). 97.80

Chloride of calcium, (HI

Chloride of magnesium, 0/4

Sulphate of soda, 0/3

Sulphate of lime, I.12

Glancing your eye along the map, you will see a small stream entering Utah lake, south of the Spanish fort, and the first waters of that lake which our road of 1844 crosses in coming up from the southward. When I was on this stream with Mr. Walker in that year, he informed me that on the upper part of the river are immense beds of rocksalt of very great thickness, which ne had frequently visited. Farther to the southward, the rivers which are affluent to the Colorado, such as the Rio Virgen, and Gila river, near their mouths, are impregnated with salt by the cliffs of rocksalt between which they pass. These mines occur in the same ridge in which, about 120 miles to the northward, and subsequently in their more immediate neighborhood, we discovered the fossils belonging to the oolitic period, and they are probably connected with that formation, and are the deposite from which the Great Lake obtains its salt. Had we remained longer, we should have found them in its bed, and in the mountains around its shores. By observation the latitude of this camp is 41° 15' 50", and longitude 112° 06' 43"

The observations made during our stay give for the rate of the chronometer 31.72", corresponding almost exactly with the rate obtained at St. Vrain's fort. Barometrical observations were made almost hourly during the day. This morning we breakfasted on yampah, and had only kamas for supper; but a cup of good coffee still distinguished us from our Digger acquaintances. The morning was clear and calm, with a temperature at sunrise of 320. We resumed our journey late in the day, returning by nearly the same route which we had traveled in coming to the lake; and, avoiding the passage of Hawthorn creek, struck the hills a little below the hot salt springs. The flat plain we had here passed over consisted alternately of tolerably good sandy soil and of saline plats. We encamped early on Clear creek, at the foot of the high ridge; one of the peaks of which we ascertained by measurement to be 4,210 feet above the lake, or about 8,400 feet above the sea. Behind these front peaks the ridge rises towards the Bear River mountains, which are probably as high as the Wind River chair This creek is here unusually well-timbered with a variety or trees. Among them were birch, (betula,) the larrow leaved poplar, (populus angusttfolia,) several kinds of willow, (solix,) hawthorn, (sratagus,) alder, (alnus vz idis,) and cerasus, with an oak allied to quercus alba, but yen distinct from that or any other species in the United States.

We had tonight a supper of sea gulls, which Carson killed near the lake. Although cool, the thermometer standing at 47°, musquitoes were sufficiently numerous to be troublesome this evening.

13th .Continuing up the river valley, we crossed several small streams; the mountains on the right appearing to consist of the blue limestone which we had observed in the same ridge to the northward, alternating here with a granular quartz already mentioned. One of these streams, which forms a smaller lake near the river, was broken up into several channels; and the irrigated bottom of fertile soil was covered with innumerable flowers, among which were purple fields of eurazor.N m purpureum, with helianthi, a handsome solidago, (S. canadensis,) and a variety of other plants in bloom. Continuing along the foot of the hills, in the afternoon we found rive or six hotsprings gushing out together, beneath a conglomerate, consisting principally of fragments of a grayishblue limestone, efflorescing a salt upon the surface. The temperature of these springs was 1340, and the rocks in the bed were colored with a red deposite, and there was common salt crystallized on the margin. There was also a white incrustation upon leaves and roots, consisting principally of carbonate of lime. There were rushes seen along the road this afternoon, and the soil under the hills was very black, and apparently very good; but at this time the grass is entirely dried up. We encamped on Bear river, immediately below a cutoff the canon by which the river enters this valley bearing north by compass. The night ,was mild, with a very clear sky; and I obtained a very excellent observation of an occultation of Tau. Arietis, with other observations. Both immersion and emersion of the star were observed; but, as our observations have shown, the phase at the bright limb generally gives incorrect longitudes, and we have adopted the result obtained from the emersier it the dark limb, without allowing any weight to the immersion. According to these observations, the longitude is 1120 05' 12", and the latitude 410 42' 43". All the longitudes on the line of our outward journey, between St. Vrain's fort and the Dalles of the Columbia, which were not directly determined by satellites, have been chronometrically referred to this place.

The people today were rather lowspirited, hunger making them very quiet and peaceable; and there was rarely an oath to be heard in the camp—not even a solitary enfant de garce. It was time for the men with an expected supply of provisions from Mr. Fitzpatrick to be in the neighborhood; and the gun was fired at evening, to give notice of our locality, but met with no response.

14th.—About four miles from this encampment, the trail led us down to the river, where we unexpectedly found an excellent ford—the stream being widened by an island, and not yet disengaged from the hills at the foot of the range. We encamped on a little creek where we had made a noon halt in descending the river. The night was very clear and pleasant, the sunset temperature being 670.

The people this evening looked so forlorn, that I gave them permission to kill a fat young horse which I had_ purchased with goods from the Snake Indians, and they were very soon restored to gayety and good humor. Mr. Preuss and myself could not yet overcome some remains of civilized prejudices, and preferred to starve a little longer; feeling as much saddened as if a crime had been committed.

The next day we continued up the valley, the soil being sometimes very black and good, occasionally gravelly, and occasionally a kind of naked salt plains. We found on the way this morning a small encampment of two families of Snake Indians, from whom we purchased a small quantity of kooyah. They had piles of seeds, of three different kinds, spread out upon pieces of buffalo robe; and the squaws had just gathered about a bushel of the root of a thistle, (czrcium Virginianum.) They were about the ordinary size of carrots, and, as I have previously mentioned, are sweet and web flavored, requiring only a long preparation. They had a band, of twelve or fifteen horses, and appeared to be growing in the sunshine with about as little labor as the plants they were eating.

Shortly afterwards we met an Indian on horseback who had killed an antelope, which we purchased of him for a little powder and some balls. We crossed the Roseaux, and encamped on the left bank; halting early for the pleasure of enjoying a wholesome and abundant supper, and were pleasantly engaged in protracting our unusual comfort, when Tabeau galloped into the camp with news that Mr. Fitzpatrick was encamped close by us, with a good supply of provisions—flour, rice, and dried meat, and even a little butter. Excitement tonight made us all wakeful; and after a breakfast before sunrise the next morning, we were again on the road, and, continuing up the valley, crossed some high points of hills, and halted to noon on the same stream, near several lodges of Snake Indians, from whom we purchased about a bushel of serviceberries, partially dried. By the gift of a knife, I prevailed upon a little boy to show me the kooyah plant, which proved to be valeriana edulis. The root which constitutes the kooyah, is large, of a very bright yellow color, with the characteristic odor, but not so fully developed as in the prepared substance. It loves the rich moist soil of river bottoms, which was the locality in which I always afterwards found it. It was now entirely out of bloom; according to my observation, flowering in the months of May and June. In the afternoon we entered a long ravine leading to a pass in the dividing ridge between the waters of Bear river and the Snake river, or Lewis's fork of the Columbia; our way being very much impeded, and almost entirely blocked up, by compact fields of luxuriant artemisia. Taking leave at this point of the waters of Bear river, and of the geographical basin which encloses the system of rivers and creeks which belong to the Great Salt Lake, and which so richly deserves a future detailed and ample exploration, I can say of it, in general terms, that the bottoms of this river, (Bear,) and of some of the creeks which saw, Ram a natural resting and recruiting station for travel ere, now, and in all time to come. The bottoms are extensive; water excellent; timber sufficient; the soil good, and well adapted to grains and grasses suited to such an elevated region. A military post, and a civilized settlement, would be of great value here; grass and salt so much abound. The lake will furnish exhaustless supplies of salt. All the mountains here are covered with a valuable nutritious grass, called bunchgrass, from the form in which it grows, which has a second growth in the fall. The beasts of the Indians were fat upon it; our own found it a good subsistence; and its quantity will sustain any amount of cattle, and make this truly a bucolic region.

We met here an Indian family on horseback, which had been out to gather serviceberries, and were returning loaded. This tree was scattered about on the hills; and the upper part of the pass was timbered with aspen, (populv,s trent.;) the common blue flowering flax occurring among the plants. The approach to the pass was very steep, and the summit about 6,300 feet above the sea—probably only an uncertain approximation, as at the time of observation it was blowing a violent gale of wind from the northwest, with cumuli scattered in masses over the sky, the day otherwise bright and clear. We descended, by a steep slope, into a broad open valley—good soil—from four to five miles wide, coming down immediately upon one of the headwaters of the Pannack river, which here loses itself in swampy ground. The appearance of the country here is not very interesting. On either side is a regular range of mountains of the usual character, with a little timber, tolerably rocky on the right, and higher and more smooth on the left, with still higher peaks looking out above the range. The valley afforded a good level road, but it was late when it brought us to water, and we encamped at dark. The northwest wind had blown up very cold weather, and the artemisia, which was our firewood tonight, did not happen to be very abundant. This plant loves a dry, sandy soil, and cannot grow in the good bottoms where it is rich and moist, but on every little eminence, where water does not rest long, it maintains absolute possession. Elevation above the sea about 5,100 feet

At night scattered fires glimmered along the mountains, pointing out camps of the Indians; and we contrasted the comparative security in which we traveled through this country, with the guarded vigilance we were compelled to exert among the Sioux and other Indians on the eastern side of the Rocky mountains.

At sunset the thermometer was at 50°, and at midnight at

30°.17th.—The morning sky was calm and clear, the temperature at daylight being 25°, and at sunrise 20°. There is throughout this country a remarkable difference between the morning and midday temperatures, which at this season was very generally 400 or 500, and occasionally greater; and frequently, after a very frosty morning, the heat in a few hours would render the thinnest clothing agreeable. About noon we reached the main fork. The Pannack river was before us, the valley being here 11 miles wide, fertile, and bordered by smooth hills, not over 500 feet high, partly covered with cedar; a high ridge, in which there is a prominent peak, rising behind those on the left. We continued to descend this stream, and found on it at night a warm and comfortable camp. Flax occurred so frequently during the day as to be almost a characteristic, and the soil appeared excellent. The evening was gusty, with a temperature at sunset of 590. I obtained, about midnight, an observation of an emersion of the first satellite, the night being calm and very clear, the stars remarkably bright, and the thermometer at 30°. Longitude, from mean of satellite and chronometer, 112° 29' 52", and latitude, by observation, 420 44' 40".

18th.—The day clear and calm, with a temperature of 25° at sunrise. After traveling seven or eight miles, we emerged on the plains of the Columbia, in sight of the famous " Three Buttes," a wellknown landmark in the country, distant about 45 miles. The French word butte, which so often occurs in this narrative, is retained from the familiar language of the country, and identifies the objects to which it refers. It is naturalized in the region of the Rocky mountains, and, even it desirable to render it in English, I know of no word which would be its precise equivalent. It is applied to the detached hills and ridges which rise rapidly, and reach too high to be called hills or ridges, and not high enough to be called mountains. Knob, as applied in the western states, is their descriptive term in English. Cerro is the Spanish term; but no translation, or periphrasis, would preserve the identity of these picturesque landmarks, familiar to the traveler, and often seen at a great distance. Covered as far as could be seen with artemisia, the dark and ugly appearance of this plain obtained for it the name of Sage Desert; and we were agreeably surprised, on reaching the Portneuf river, to see a beautiful green valley with scattered timber spread out beneath us, on which, about four miles distant, were glistening the white walls of the fort. The Portneuf runs along the upland plain nearly to its mouth, and an abrupt descent of perhaps two hundred feet brought us down immediately upon the stream, which at the ford is one hundred yards wide, and three feet deep, with clear water, a swift current, and gravelly bed; but a little higher up the breadth was only about thirty-five yards, with apparently deep water.

In the bottom I remarked a very great number of springs and sloughs, with remarkably clear water and gravel beds. At sunset we encamped with Mr. Talbot and oar friends, who came on to Fort Hall when we went to the lake, and whom we had the satisfaction to find all well, neither party having met with any mischance in the interval of our separation. They too, had had their share of fatigue and scanty provisions, as there had been very little game left on the trail of the populous emigration; and Mr. Fitzpatrick had rigidly husbanded our stock of flour and light provisions, in view of the approaching winter and the long journey before us.

19th.—This morning the sky was very dark and gloomy, and at daylight it began snowing thickly, and continued all day, with cold, disagreeable weather. At sunrise the temperature was 43o. I rode up to the fort, and purchased from Mr. Grant (the officer in charge of the post) several very indifferent horses, and five oxen, in very fine order, which were received at the camp with great satisfaction: and, one being killed at evening, the usual gayety and good humor were a once restored. Night came in stormy.

20th.—We had a night of snow and rain, an the thermometer at sunrise was at 34o; the morning was dark, with a steady rain, and there was still an inch of snow on the ground, with an abundance on the neighboring hills and mountains. The sudden change in the weather was hard for our animals, who trembled and shivered in the cold—sometimes taking refuge in the timber, and now and then coming out and raking the snow off the ground for a little grass, or eating the young willows.

21st.—Ice made tolerably thick during this night, and in the morning the weather cleared up very bright, with a tempera ture at sunrise of 29o; and I obtained a meridian observation for latitude et the fort, with observations for time. The sky was again covered in the afternoon, and the thermometer at sunset 48°.

22d.—The morning was cloudy and unpleasant, anu at sunrise a cold rain commenced, with a temperature of 41o.

The early approach of winter, and the difficulty of supporting a large party, determined me to send back a number of the men who had become satisfied that they were not fitted for the laborious service and frequent privation to which they were necessarily exposed, and which there was reason to believe would become more severe in the further extension of the voy age. I accordingly called them together, and, informing them of my intention to continue our journey during the ensuing winter, in the course of which they would probably be exposed to considerable hardship, succeeded in prevailing on a number of them to return voluntarily. These were: Charles de For rest, Henry Lee, J. Carnpbell, Wm. Creuss, A. Vasquez, A.

Pera, Patrick White, B. Tesson, M. Creely, Francois Lajeunesse, Basil Lajeunesse. Among these I regretted very much to lose Basil Lajeunesse, one of the best men in my party, who was obliged, by the condition of his family, to be at home in the coming winter. Our preparations having been completed in the interval of our stay here, both parties were ready this morning to resume their respective routes.

Except that there is a greater quantity of wood used in its construction, Fort Hall very much resembles the other trading posts which have already been described to you, and would be another excellent post of relief for the emigration. It is in the low rich bottom of a valley, apparently 20 miles long, formed by the confluence of Portneuf river with Lewis's fork of the Columbia, which it enters about nine miles below the fort, and narrowing gradually to the mouth of the Pannack river, where it has a breadth of only two or three miles. Allowing 50 miles for the road from the Beer springs of Bear river to Fort Hall, its distance along the traveled road from the town of Westport, on the frontier of Missouri, by way of Fort Laramie and the great South Pass, is 1,323 miles. Beyond this place, on the line of road along the barren valley of the Upper Columbia, there does not occur, for a distance of nearly 300 miles to the westward, a fertile spot of ground sufficiently large to produce the necessary quantity of grain, or pasturage enough to allow even a temporary repose to the emigrants. On their recent passage, they had been able to obtain, at very high prices and in insufficient quantity, only such assistance as could be afforded by a small and remote tradingpost—and that a foreign one—which, in the supply of its own wants, had necessarily drawn around it some of the resources of civilization, but which obtained nearly all its supplies from the distant depot of Vancouver, by a difficult water carriage of 250 miles up the Columbia river, and a land carriage by packhorses of 600 miles. An American military post, sufficiently strong to give to their road a perfect security against the Indian tribes, who are unsettled in locality and very uncertain in their disposition, and which, with the necessary facilities for the repair of their equipage, would be able to afford them relief in stock and grain from the produce of the post, would be of extraordinary value to the emigration. Such a post (and all others which may be established on the line to Oregon) would naturally form the nucleus of a settlement, at which supplies and repose would be obtained by the emigrant, or trading caravans, which may hereafter traverse these elevated, and in many places, desolate and inhospitable regions.

I subjoin an analysis of the soil in the river bottom nea Fort Hall, which will be of assistance in enabling you to Porn some correct idea of its general character in the neighboring country. I characterize it as good land, but the analysis will show its precise properties.

Analysis of the Soil.

Silicina   68.55

Alumina   7.45

Carbonate of lime   8.51

Carbonate of magnesia   5.09

Oxide of iron   140

Organic vegetable matter   4.74

Water and loss.   4.26

    100.00

Our observations place this post in longitude 1120 29' 54" latitude 430 01' 30", and the elevation above the sea, 4,500 feet.

Taking leave of the homeward party, we resumed our journey down the valley, the weather being very cold, and the rain coming in hard gusts, which the wind blew directly in our faces. We forded the Portneuf in a storm of rain, the water in the river being frequently up to the axles, and about 110 yards wide. After the gust, the weather improved a little, and we encamped about three miles below, at the mouth of the Pannack river, on Lewis's fork, which here has a breadth of about 120 yards. The temperature at sunset was 420; the sky partially covered with dark, rainy clouds.

23d.—The temperature at sunrise was 320; the morning dark, and snow falling steadily and thickly, with a light ail from the southward. Profited of being obliged to remain it camp, to take hourly barometrical observations from sunrise tc midnight. The wind at eleven o'clock set in from the northward in heavy gusts, and the snow changed into rain. In the afternoon, when the sky brightened, the rain had washed all the mow from the bottoms; but the neighboring mountains, from summit to foot, were luminously white—an inauspicious commencement of the autumn, of which this was the first day.

24th.—The thermometer at sunrise was 350, and a blue sky in the west promised a fine day. The river bottoms here are narrow and swampy, with frequent sloughs; and after crossing the Pannack, the road continued along the uplands, rendered very slippery by the soil of wet clay, and entirely covered with artemisia bushes, among which occur frequent fragments of obsidian. At noon we encamped in a grove of willows, at the upper end of a group of islands about half a mile above the American falls of SnaltO river. Among the willows here, were some bushes of Lewis and Clarke's currant, (litres aureum.) The river here enters between low mural banks, which consist of a fine vesicular traprock, the intermediate portions being compact and crystalline. Gradually becoming higher in its downward course, these banks of scoriated volcanic rock form, with occasional interruptions, its characteristic Feature along the whole line to the Dalles of the Lower Columbia, resembling a chasm which had been rent through the country, and which the river had afterwards taken for its bed. The immediate valley of the river is a high plain covered with black rocks and artemisias. In the south is a bordering range of mountains, which, although not very high, are broken and covered with snow and at a great distance to the north is seen the high, snowy line of the Salmon river mountains, in front of which stand out prominently in the plain the three isolated rugged looking mountains commonly known as the Three Buttes. Between the river and the distant Salmon river range, the plain is represented by Mr. Fitzpatrick as so entirely broken up and rent into chasms as to be impracticable for a man even on foot. In the sketch annexed, the point of view is low, but it conveys very well some idea of the open character of the country, with the buttes rising out above the general line. By measurement, the river above is 870 feet wide, immediately contracted at the fall in the form of a lock, by jutting piles of scoriaceous basalt, over which the foaming river must present a grand appearance at the time of high water. The evening was clear and pleasant, with dew; and at sunset the temperature was 540. By observation, the latitude is 420 47' 05", and the longitude 1120 40' 13". A few hundred yards below the falls, and on the left bank of the river, is an escarpment from which we obtained some specimens.

25th.—Thermometer at sunrise 470. The day came in clear, with a strong gale from the south, which commenced at eleven of the last night. The road today led along the rive,. which is full of rapids and small falls. Grass is very scanty; and along the rugged banks are scattered cedars, with an abundance of rocks and sage. We traveled fourteen miles and encamped in the afternoon near the river, on a rocky creek, the bed of which was entirely occupied with boulders of a very large size. For the last three or four miles the right bank of the river has a palisaded appearance. One of the oxen was killed here for food. The thermometer at evening was at 55°, the sky almost overcast, and the barometer indicated an elevation of 4,400 feet.

26th.—Rain during the night, and the temperature at sun rise 420. Traveling along the river, in about four miles we reached a picturesque stream, to which we gave the name or Fall creek. It is remarkable for the many falls which omit in a short distance; and its bed is composed of a calcareous tufa, or vegetable rock, composed principally of the remains of reeds and mosses, resembling that at the Basin spring, on Bear river.

The road along the river bluffs had been occasionally very bad; and imagining that some rough obstacles rendered such a detour necessary, we followed for several miles a plain wagonroad leading up this stream, until we reached a point whence it could be seen making directly towards a low place in the range on the south side of the valley, and we became immediately aware that we were on a trail formed by a party of wagons, in company with whom we had encamped at Elm grove, near the frontier of Missouri, and which you will remember were proceeding to Upper California under the direction of Mr. Jos. Chiles. At the time of their departure, no practicable passes were known in the southern Rocky mountains within the territory of the United States; and the probable apprehension of difficulty in attempting to pass near the settled frontier of New Mexico, together with the desert char meter of the unexplored region beyond, had induced them to take a more northern and circuitous route by way of the Sweet Water pass and Fort Hall. They had still between them and the valley of the Sacramento a great mass of mountains, forming the Sierra Nevada, here commonly known as the Great California mountain, and which were at this time ,considered as presenting an impracticable barrier to wheeled carriages. Various considerations had suggested to them a division of the party; and a greater portion of the camp, including the wagons, with the mail and other stores, were now proceeding under the guidance of Mr. Joseph Walker, who had engaged to conduct them, by a long sweep to the southward, around what is called the point of the mountain; and, crossing through a pass known only to himself, gain the banks of the Sacramento by the, valley of the San Joaquin. It was a long and a hazardous journey for a party in which there were women and children. Sixty days was the shortest period of time in which they could reach the point of the mountain, and their route lay through a country inhabited by wild and badly disposed Indians, and very poor in game; but the leader was a man possessing great and intimate knowledge of the Indians, with an extraordinary firmness and decision of character. In the mean time, Mr. Chiles had passed down the Columbia with a patty of ten or twelve men, with the intention of reaching the settlements on the Sacramento by a more direct course, which indefinite information from hunters had indicated in the direction of the headwaters of the Riviere aux Malheurs; and having obtained there a reinforcement of animals, and a supply of provisions, meet the wagons before they should have reached the point of the mountain, at a place which had been previously agreed upon. In the course of our narrative, we shall be able to give you some information of the fortunes which attended the movements of these adventurous travelers.

Having discovered our error, we immediately regained the line along the river, which the road quitted about noon, and encamped at five o'clock on the stream called Raft river, (Ri:dire aux Cajeux,) baying traveled only 13 miles. In the north, the Salmon River mountains are visible at a very far distance and on the left, the ridge in which Raft rive: heads is about 20 miles distant, rocky, and tolerably high. Thermometer at sunset 44°, with a partially clouded sky, and a sharp wind from the S.W.

27th.—It was now no longer possible, as in our previous journey, to travel regularly every day, and find ai any moment a convenient place for repose at noon or a camp at night , but the halting places were now generally fixed along the road, by the nature of the country, at places where, with water, there was a little scanty grass. Since leaving tie American falls, the road had frequently been very bad; the many short, steep ascents, exhausting the strength of our wornout animals, requiring always at such places the assistance of the men to get up each cart, one by one; and our progress with twelve or fourteen wheeled carriages, though light and made for the purpose, in such a rocky country, was extremely slow; and I again determined to gain time by a division of the camp. Accordingly, today, the parties again separated, constituted very much as before—Mr. Fitzpatrick remaining in charge of the heavier baggage.

The morning was calm and clear, with a white frost, and the temperature at sunrise 240.

Today the country had a very forbidding appearance; and, after traveling 20 miles over a slightly undulating plain, we encamped at a considerable spring, called Swamp creek, ris ing in low grounds near the point of a spur from the mountain. Returning with a small party in a starving condition from the westward 12 or 14 years since, Carson had met here three or four buffalo bulls, two of which were killed. They were among the pioneers which had made the experiment of colonizing in the valley of the Columbia, and which had failed, as heretofore stated. At sunset the thermometer was at 46°, and the evening was overcast, with a cool wind from the S. E., and tonight we had only sage for firewood. Mingled with the artemisia was a snubby and thorny chenopodiaceous plant.

28th.—Thermometer at sunrise 10°. The wind rose earl to a gale from the west, with a very cold driving rain; at 4 niter an uncomfortable day's ride of 25 miles, we were ea] when at evening we found a sheltered camp, where there was an abundance of wood, at some elevated rocky islands covered with cedar, near the commencement of another long canon of the riser. With the exception of a short detention at a deep little stream called Goose creek, and some occasional rocky places, we had to day a very good road; but the country has a barren appearance, sandy, and densely covered with the artemisias from the banks of the river to the foot of the mountains. Here I remarked, among the sage bushes green bunches of what is called the second growth of grass. The river today has had a smooth appearance, free from rapids, with a low sandy hillslope bordering the bottoms, in which there is a little good soil. Thermometer at sunset 45°, blowing a gale, and disagreeably cold.

29th.—The thermometer at sunrise 36°, with a bright sun, and appearance of finer weather. The road for several miles was extremely rocky, and consequently bad; but, entering after this a sandy country, it became very good, with no other interruption than the sage bushes, which covered the river plain as far as the eye could reach, and, with their uniform tint of dark gray, gave to the country a gloomy and sombre appearance. All the day the course of the river has been between walls of the black volcanic rock, a dark line of the escarpment on the opposite side pointing out its course, and sweeping along in foam at places where the mountains which border the valley present always on the left two ranges, the lower one a spur of the higher; and, on the opposite side, the Salmon River mountains are visible at a great distance. Having made 24 miles, we encamped about five o'clock on Rock creek—a stream having considerable water, a swift current, and wooded with willow.

30th.—Thermometer at sunrise 28°. In its progress towards the river, this creek soon enters a chasm of the volcanic rock, which in places along the wall presents a columnar appearance; and the road becomes extremely rocky whenever it passes near its banks. It is only about twenty feet wide where the road crosses it, with a deep pea and steep banks, covered with rocky fragments, with willows and a little grass on its narrow bottom The soil appears to be full of calcareous matter, with whit the rocks are incrusted. The fragments of rock which had been removed by the emigrants in making a road, where we ascended from the bed of this creek, were whitened with lime; and during the afternoon's march I remarked in the soil a considerably quantity of calcareous concretions. Towards evening the sages became more sparse, and the clear spaces were occupied by tufts of green grass. The river still continued its course through a trough, or open canon; and towards sunset we followed the trail of several wagons which had turned in towards make river, and encamped, as they had dope, on tin top of the escarpment. There was no grass here, the soil among the sage being entirely naked; but there is occasionally a little bottom along the river, which a short ravine of 2 cks, at rare intervals, leaves accessible; and by one of these we drove our animals down, and found some tolerably good grass bordering the water.

Immediately opposite to us, a subterranean river bursts out directly from the face of the escarpment, and falls in white foam to the river below. The main river is enclosed with mural precipices, which form its characteristic feature along a great portion of its course. A melancholy and strange looking country—one of fracture, and violence, and fire.

We had brought with us, when we separated from the camp, a large gaunt ox, in appearance very poor; but, being killed tonight, to the great joy of the people, he was found to be remarkably fat. As usual at such occurrences, the evening was devoted to gayety and feasting; abundant fare now mace an epoch among us; and in this laborious life, in such a country as this, our men had but little else to enjoy. The temperature at sunset was 650, with a clear sky and a very high wind. By the observation of the evening, the encampment was in longitude 1140 25' 04", and in latitude 420 38' 44",

OCTOBER.

1st.—The morning clear, with wind from the west, and the thermometer at 55°. We descended to the bottoms, taking with us the boat, for the purpose of visiting the fall in the opposite cliffs; and while it was being filled with air, we occupied ourselves in measuring the river, which is 1,786 feet in breadth, with banks 200 feet high. We were surprised, on our arrival at the opposite side, to find a beautiful basin of clear water, formed by the falling river, around which the rocks were whitened by some saline incrustation. Here the Indians had constructed wicker dams, although I was informed that the salmon do not ascend the river so far; and its character below would apparently render it impracticable.

The ascent of the steep hillside was rendered a little difficult by a dense growth of shrubs and fields of cane; and there were frequent hidden crevices among the rocks, where the water was heard rushing below; but we succeeded in reaching the main stream, which, issuing from between strata of the traprock in two principal branches, produced almost immediately a torrent, 22 feet wide, and white with foam. It is a picturesque spot of singular beauty, overshadowed by bushes, from under which the torrent glances, tumbling into the white basin below, where the clear water contrasted beautifully with the muddy stream of the river. Its outlet was covered with a rank growth of canes, and a variety of unusual plants, and nettles, (urtica canabina,) which, before they were noticed, had set our hands and arms on fire. The temperature of the spring was 58o, while that of the river was 51o. The perpendicular height of the place at which this stream issues is 45 feet above the river, and 162 feet below the summit of the precipice—making nearly 200 feet for the height of the wall. On the hillside here was obtained a specimen consisting principally of fragments of the shells of small crustacea, and which was probably formed by deposition from these springs, proceeding from some lake or river in the highlands above.

We resumed ou journey at noon, the day being hit and bright; and, atter a march of 17 miles, encamped, at sunset on the river, near several lodges of Snake Indians.

Our encampment was about one mile below the Fishing falls—a series of cataracts with very inclined planes, which are probably so named because they form a barrier to the ascent of the salmon; and the great fisheries, from which the inhabitants of this barren region almost entirely derive a subsistence, commence at this place. These appeared to be unusually gay savages, fond of loud laughter; and, in their apparent good nature and merry character, struck me as being entirely different from the Indians we had been accustomed to see.

From several who visited our camp in the evening, we purchased, in exchange for goods, dried salmon. At this season they are not very fat, but we were easily pleased. The Indians made us comprehend, that when the salmon came up the river in the spring, they are so abundant that they merely throw in their spears at random, certain of bringing out a fish.

These poor people are but slightly provided with winter clothing; there is but little game to furnish skins for the purpose; and of a little animal which seemed to be the most numerous, it required 20 skins to make a covering to the knees. But they are still a joyous, talkative race, who grow fat and become poor with the salmon, which at least never fail them—the dried being used in the absence of the fresh. We are encamped immediately on the river bank, and with the salmon jumping up out of the water, and Indians paddling about in boats made of rushes, or laughing around the fires, the camp tonight has quite a lively appearance.

The river at this place is more open than for some distance above, and, for the time, the black precipices have disappeared, and no calcareous matter is visible in the soil. The thermometer at sunset 740, clear and calm.

2d.—The sunrise temperature was 480; the weather clear and calm. Shortly after leaving the encampment, we crossed a stream of clear water, with a variable breadth of 10 to 25 yards, broken by rapids, and lightly wooded with willow, and having a little grass on its small bottomland. The barrenness of the country is in fine contrast today with the mingled beauty ana grandeur of the river, which is mote open than hitherto, with a constant succession of falls acid rapids. Over the edge of the black cliffs, and out from their faces, are falling numberless streams and springs; and all the line of the river is in motion with the play of the water. In about seven miles we reached the most beautiful and picturesque fall had seen on the river.

On the opposite side, the vertical fall is perhaps 18 feet high; and nearer, the sheet of foaming water is divided and broken into cataracts, where several little islands on the brink and in the river above, give it Much picturesque beauty, and make it one of those places the traveler turns again and again to fix in his memory. There were several lodges of Indians here, from whom we traded salmon. Below this place the river makes a remarkable bend; and the road, ascending the ridge, gave us a fine view of the river below, intersected at many places by numerous fish dams. In the north, about 50 miles distant, v ere some high snowy peaks of the Salmon River mountains; and in the northeast, the last peak of the range was visible at the distance of perhaps 100 miles or more. The river hills consist of very broken masses of sand, covered everywhere with the same interminable fields of sage, and oc., casionally the road is very heavy. We now frequently saw Indians, who were strung along the river at every little rapid where fish are to be caught, and the cry haggaz, haggai, (fish,) was constantly heard whenever we passed near their huts, or met them in the road. Very many of them were oddly and partially dressed in overcoat, shirt, waistcoat, or pantaloons, or whatever article of clothing they had been able to procure in trade from the emigrants; for we had now entirely quitted the country where hawks' bells, beads, and vermilion were the current coin, and found that here only useful articles, and chiefly clothing, were in great request. These, however, are eagerly sought after; and for a few trifling pieces of clothing, travelers may procure food sufficient to carry them to the Columbia.

We made a long stretch across the upper plain, and encamped on the bluff, where the grass was very green and good, the soil of the upper plains containing a considerable proportion of calcareous matter. This green freshness of the grass was very remarkable for the season of the year. Again we heard the roar of the fall in the river below, where the water in an unbroken volume goes over a descent of several fee.. The night is clear, and the weather continues very warm and pleasant, with a sunset temperature of 70°.

3d.—The morning was pleasant, with a temperature at sunrise of 420. The road was broken by ravines among the hills, and in one of these, which made the bed of a dry creek, I found a fragmentary stratum, or brecciated conglomerate, consisting of flinty slate pebbles, with fragments of limestone containing fossil shells.

On the left, the mountains are visible at the distance of 20 or 30 miles, appearing smooth and rather low; but at intervals higher peaks look out from beyond, and indicate that the main ridge, which we are leaving with the course of the river, and which forms the northern boundary of the Great Basin, still maintains its elevation. About two o'clock we arrived at the ford where the road crosses to the right bank of Snake river. An Indian was hired to conduct us through the ford, which proved impracticable for us, the water sweeping away , the howitzer and nearly drowning the mules, which we were obliged to extricate by cutting them out of the harness. The river here is expanded into a little bay, in which there are two islands, across which is the road of the ford; and the emigrants had passed by placing two of their heavy wagons abreast of each other, so as to oppose a considerable mass against the body of water. The Indians informed us that one of the men, in attempting to turn some cattle which had taken a wrong direction, was carried off by the current and drowned. Since their passage, the water had risen considerably; but, fortunately, we had a resource in a boat, which was filled with air and launched; and at seven o'clock we were safely encamped on the opposite bank, the animals swimming across, and the carriage, howitzer, and baggage of the camp, being carried over in the boat. At the place where we crossed, above the islands, the river had narrowed to a breadth of 1,04Q feet, by measurement, the greater portion of which was from six to eight feet deep. We were obliged to make our camp where we landed, among the Indian lodges, which are semicircular huts made of willow, thatched over with straw, and open to the sunny south. By observation, the latitude of our encampment on the right bank of the river was 42° 55' 58"; chronometric longitude 115° 04' 46", and the traveled distance from Fort Hall 208 miles.

4th.—Calm, pleasant day, with the thermometer at sunrise at 47°. Leaving the river at a considerable distance to the left, and following up the bed of a rocky creek, with occasional holes of water, in about six miles we ascended, by a long and rather steep hill, to a plain 600 feet above the river, over which we continued to travel during the day, having a broken ridge 2,000 or 3,000 feet high on the right. The plain terminates, where we ascended, in an escarpment of vesicular traprock, which supplies the fragments of the creek below. The sky clouded over with a strong wind from the northwest, with a few drops of rain and occasional sunlight, threatening a change.

Artemisia still covers the plain, but Purshza tridentata makes its appearance here on the hillsides and on bottoms of the creeks—quite a tree in size, larger than the artemisia. We crossed several hollows with a little water in them, and improved grass; and, turning off from the road in the afternoon in search of water, traveled about three miles up the bed of a willow creek, towards the mountain, and found a good encampment, with wood and grass, and little ponds of water in the bed of the creek; which must be of more importance at other seasons, as we found there several old fixtures for fishing. There were many holes on the creek prairie, which had been made by the Diggers in search of roots.

Wind increased to a violent galc from the N. W., with a temperature at sunset of 57°.

5th.—The morning was calm and clear, and at sunrise the thermometer was at 32°. The road bday was occasionally extremely rocky, with hard volcanic fragments, and our traveling yen' slow. In about nine miles the road brought us t) a group of smoking hot springs, with a temperature of 164°. There were a few helianhi in bloom, with some other low plants, and the place was green round about; the ground warm and the air pleasant, with a summer atmosphere that was very grateful in a day of high and cold, searching wind. The rocks were covered with a white and red incrustation; and the water has on the tongue the same unpleasant effect as that of the Basin spring on Bear river. They form several branches, and bubble up with force enough to raise the small pebbles several inches.

These springs are near the front of the ridge, (a dark and ragged-looking mountain) in which some of the nearer rocks „Jive a reddish appearance, and probably consist of a reddish-brown trap, fragments of which were scattered along the road after leaving the spring. The road was now about to cross the point of this mountain, which we judged to be a spur from the Salmon River range. We crossed a small creek, and encamped about sunset on a stream, which is probably Lake river. This is a small stream, some five or six feet broad, with a swift current, timbered principally with willows and some few cottonwoods. Along the banks were canes, rosebushes, and clematis, with Purshia tridentata and artemisias on the upper bottom. The sombre appearance of the country is somewhat relieved in coming unexpectedly from the dark rocks upon these green and wooded watercourses, sunk in chasms; and, in the spring, the contrasted effect must make them beautiful.

The thermometer at sunset 47o, and the night, threatening snow.

6th.—The morning warm, the thermometer 46o at sunrise, and sky entirely clouded. After traveling about three miles over an extremely rocky road, the volcanic fragments began to disappear; and, entering among the hills at the point of the mountain, we found ourselves suddenly in a granite country. Here, the character of the vegetation was, very much changed; the artemisia disappeared almost entirely, showing only at intervals towards the close of the day, and was replaced by Purshia tridentata, with flowering shrubs, and small fields of dieteria divaricata, which gave bloom and gayety to the hills. These were everywhere covered with a fresh and green short grass, like that of the early spring. This is the fall or second growth, the dried grass having been burnt off by the Indians; and wherever the fite has passed, the bright, green color is universal. The soil among the hills is altogether different from that of the river plain, being in many places black, in others sandy and gravelly, but of a firm and good character appearing to result from the decomposition of the granite rocks which is proceeding rapidly.

In quitting for a time the artemisia (sage) through which w had been so long voyaging, and the sombre appearance of which is so discouraging, I have to remark, that I have beer informed that in Mexico wheat is grown upon the ground whicl' produces this shrub; which, if true, relieves the soil from the character of sterility imputed to it. Be this as it may, there is no dispute about the grass, which is almost universal on the hills and mountains, and always nutritious, even in its dry state. We passed on the way masses of granite on the slope of the spur, which was very much weathered and abraded. This is a white feldspathic granite, with small scales of black mica; smoky quartz and garnets appear to constitute this portion of the mountain.

The road at noon reached a broken ridge, on which were scattered many boulders or blocks of granite; and, passing very small streams, where, with a little more than the usual timber, was sometimes gathered a little: wilderness of plants, we encamped on a small stream, after a march of 22 miles, in company with a few Indians. Temperature at sunset 51o; and the night was partially clear, with a few stars visible through drifting white clouds. The Indians made an unsuccessful attempt to steal a few horses from us—a thing of course with them, and to prevent which the traveler is on perpetual watch.

7th.—The day was bright, clear, pleasant, with a temperature of 45o; and we breakfasted at sunrise, the birds singing in the trees as merrily as if we were in the midst of summer. On the upper edge of the hills on the opposite side of the creek, the black volcanic rock appears; and ascending these, the road passed through a basin, around which the hills swept in such a manner as to give it the appearance of an old crater. Here were strata and broken beds of black scoriated rock, and hills composed of the same, on the summit of one of which there was an opening resembling a rent. We traveled today through a country resembling that of yesterday, where, although the surface was hilly, the road was good, being firm, and entirely free from rocks and artemisia. To our left, below, was the great sage plain; and on the right were the near mountains, which presented a smoothly broken character, or rather a surface waved into numberless hills. The road was occasionally enlivened by meeting Indians, and the day was extremely beautiful and pleasant; and we were pleased to be free from the sage, even for a day. When we had traveled about eight miles, we were nearly opposite to the highest position of the mountains on the left side of the Smoke River valley; and, continuing on a few miles beyond, we came suddenly in sight of the broad green line of the valley of the Riviere Boisee, (wooded river,) black near the gorge where it debouches into the plains, with high precipices of basalt, between walls of which it passes, on emerging from the mountains. Following with the eye its upward course, it appears to be shut in among lofty mountains, confining its valley in a very rugged country.

Descending the hills, after traveling a few miles along the plain, the road brought us down von the bottoms of the river, which is a beautiful, rapid stream, with clear mountain water; and, as the name indicatus, well wooded with some varieties of timber—among which 'are handsome cottonwoods. Such a stream had become quite a novelty in this country, and we were delighted this afternoon to make a pleasant camp under fine old trees again.. There were several Indian encampments scattered along the river; and a number of their inhabitants, in the course of the evening, came to the camp on horseback with dried and fresh fish, to trade. The evening was clear, and the temperature at sunset 57°.

At the time of the _first occupation of this region by parties engaged in the furtrade, a small party of men, under the command of — Reid, constituting all the garrison of a small fort on this river, were surprised and massacred by the, Indians; and to this event the stream owes its occasional name of Reid's river. On the 8th we traveled about 26 miles, the ridge on the right having scattered pines on the upper parts; and, continuing the next day our road along the river bottom, after a day's travel of 24 miles, we encamped in the, evening on the right bank of the river, a mile above the mouth, and early the next morning arrived at Fort Boise. This is a simple dwelling house on the right bank of Snake river, about a mile below the mouth of Riviere Boisee; and on our arrival we were received with an agreeable hospitality by Mr. Payette, an officer of the Hudson's Bay Company, in charge of the fort, all of whose garrison consisted in a Canadian engage.

Here the road recrosses the river, which is broad and deep; but, with our good boat, aided by two canoes, which were found at the place, the camp was very soon transferred to the left bank. Here we found ourselves again surrounded by the sage; artemisia tridentate, and the different shrubs which during our voyage had always made their appearance abundantly on saline soils, being here the prevailing and almost the only plants. Among them the surface was covered with the usual saline efilorescences, which here consist almost entirely of carbonate of soda, with a small portion of chloride of sodium. Mr. Payette had made but slight attempts at cultivation, his efforts being limited to raising a few vegetables, in which he succeed, tolerably well; the post being principally supported by salmon. He was very hospitable and kind to us, and we made a sensible impression upon all his comestibles; but our principal inroad was into the dairy, which was abundantly supplied, stock appearing to thrive extremely well; and we had an unusual luxury in a present of fresh butter, which was, however, by no means equal that of Fort Hall—probably from some accidental cause. During the day we remained here, there were considerable numbers of miserable, half naked Indians around the fort, who had arrived from the neighboring mountains. During the summer, the only subsistence of these people is derived from the salmon, of which they are not provident enough to lay up a sufficient store for the winter, during which many of them die from absolute starvation.

Many little accounts and scattered histories, together with an acquaintance which I gradually acquired of their modes of life, had left the aboriginal inhabitants of this vast region pictured in my mind as a race of people whose great and constant occupation was the means of procuring a subsistence; and though want of space and other reasons will prevent me from detailing the many incidents which made this familiar to me, this great feature among the characteristics of the country will gradually be forced upon your mind.

Pointing to the group of Indians who had just arrived from the mountains on the left side of the valley, and who were regarding our usual appliances of civilization with an air of bewildered curiosity, Mr. Payette informed me that, every year since his arrival at this post, he had unsuccessfully endeavored to induce these people to lay up a store of salmon for their winter provision. While the summer weather and the salmon lasted, they lived contentedly and happily, scattered along the different streams where fish are to be found; and as soon as the winter snows began to fall, little smokes would be seen rising among the mountains, where they would be found in miserable groups, starving out the winter; and sometimes, according to the general belief, reduced to the horror of cannibalism—the strong, of course, preying on the weak. Certain it is they are driven to any extremity for food, and eat every insect, and every creeping thing, however loathsome and repulsive. Snails, lizards, ants—all are devoured with the readiness and greediness of mere animals.

In common with all the other Indians we had 'encountered since reaching the Pacific waters, these people use the Shoshonee or Snake language, which you will have occasion to remark, in the course of the narrative, is the universal language over a very extensive region.

On the evening of the 10th, I obtained, with the usual observations, a very excellent emersion of the first satellite, agreeing very nearly with the chronometer. From these observations, the longitude of the fort is 116° 47' 00", latitude 43° 49 22", and elevation above the sea 2,100 feet.

Sitting by the fire on the river bank, and waiting for the immersion of the satellite, which did not take place until after midnight, we heard the monotonous song of the Indians, with which they accompany a certain game of which they are very fond. Of the poetry we could not judge, but the music was miserable.

11th.—The morning was clear, with a light breeze from the east, and a temperature at sunrise of 330. A part of a bullock purchased at the fort, together with the boat, to assist him in crossing, was left here for Mr. Fitzpatrick, and at 11 o'clock we resumed our journey; and directly leaving the river, and crossing the artemisia plain, in several ascents we reached the foot of a ridge, where the road entered a dry sandy up which it continued to the head; and, crossing a dividing ridge, entered a similar one. We met here two poor emigrants, (Irishmen,) who_ had lost their horses two days since— probably stolen by the Indians; and were returning to the fort, in hopes to hear something of them there. They had recently had nothing to eat; and I halted to unpack an animal, and gave them meat for their dinner. In this hollow, the artemisia is partially displaced on the hillsides by grass; and descending it — miles, about sunset we reached the Bitnere aux Malheure, (the unfortunate or unlucky river,)—a considerable stream, with an average breadth of 50 feet, and, at this time, 18 inches' depth of water.

The bottom lands were generally one and a half mile broad, covered principally with long grass; and we had difficulty to find sufficient good grass for the camp. With the exception of a bad place of a few hundred yards long, which occurred in rounding a point of hill to reach the ford of the river, the road during the day had been very good.

12th.—The morning was clear and calm, and the thermometer at sunrise 23o. My attention was attracted by a smoke on the right side of the river, a little below the ford, where I found, on the low banks near the water, a considerable number of hot springs, in which the temperature of the water was 193o. The ground, which was too hot for the naked foot, was covered above and below the springs with an incrustation of common salt, very white and good, and fine-grained.

Leading for five miles up a broad dry branch of the Malheurs river, the road entered a sandy hollow, where the surface was rendered firm by the admixture of other rock; being good and level until arriving near the head of the ravine, where it became a little rocky, and we met with a number of sharp ascents over an undulating surface. Crossing here a dividing ridge, it becomes an excellent road of gradual descent down a very marked hollow; in which, after ten miles, willows began to appear in the dry bed of a head of the Riviere aux Bouleaux, (Birch river;) and descending seven miles, we found, at its junction with another branch, a little water, not very good or abundant, but sufficient, in case of necessity, for a camp. Crossing Birch river, we continued for about four miles across a point of hill; the country on the left being entirely mountainous, with no level spot to be seen; whence we descended to Snake river—here a fine-looking stream, with a large body)f water and a smooth current; although we hear the roar, and see below us the commencement of rapids, where it enters among the hills. It forms here a deep bay, with a low sand island in the midst; and its course among the mountains is agreeably exchanged for the black volcanic rock. The weather during the day had been very bright and extremely hot; but, as usual, so soon as the sun went down, it was necessary to put on overcoats.

I obtained this evening an observation of an emersion of the first satellite, and our observations of the evening place this encampment in latitude 44° 17' 36", and longitude 116° 56' 45", which is the mean of the results from the satellite and chronometer. The elevation above the sea is 1,880 feet. At this encampment, the grass is scanty and poor.

13th.—The morning was bright, with the temperature at sunrise 280. The horses had strayed off during the night, probably in search of grass; and, after a considerable delay, we had succeeded in finding all but two, when, about nine o'clock, we heard the sound of an Indian song and drum approaching; and shortly after, three Cayuse Indians appeared in sight, bringing with them the two animals. They belonged to a party which had been on a buffalo hunt in the neighborhood of the Rocky mountains, and were hurrying home in advance. We presented them with some tobacco and other things, with which they appeared well satisfied, and, moderating their pace, traveled in company with us.

We were now about to leave the valley of the great southern branch of the Columbia river, to which the absence of timber, and the scarcity of water, give the appearance of a desert, to enter a mountainous region, where the soil is good, and in which the face of the country is covered with nutritious grasses and dense forest—land embracing many varieties of trees peculiar to the country, and on which the timber exhibits a luxumance of growth unknown to the eastern part of the continent and to Europe. This mountainous region connects itself in the southward and westward with the elevated country belonging to the Cascade or California range; and, as will be remarked in the course of the narrative, forms the eastern limit of the fertile and timbered lands along the desert and mountainous region included within the Great Basin—a term which I apply to the intermediate region between the Rocky mountains and the next range, containing many lakes, with their own system of rivers and creeks, (of which the Great Salt is the principal,) and which have no connection with the ocean, or the great rivers which flow into it. This Great Basin is yet to be adequately explored. And here, en quitting the banks of a sterile river, to enter on arable mountains, the remark may be made, that, on this western slope of our continent, the usual order or distribution of good and bad soil is often reversed; the river and creek bottoms being often sterile, and darkened with the gloomy and barren artemisia; while the mountain is often fertile, and covered with rich grass, pleasant to the eye, and good for flocks and herds.

Leaving entirely the Snake river, which is said henceforth to pursue its way through canons, amidst rocky and impracticable mountains, where there is no possibility of traveling with animals, we ascended a long and steep hill; and crossing he dividing ridge, came down into the valley of Burnt river, which here looks like a hole among the hills. The average breadth of the stream here is thirty feet; it is well fringed with the usual small timber; and the soil in the bottoms is good, with better grass than we had lately been accustomed to see.

We now traveled through a very mountainous country; the stream running rather in a ravine than a valley, and the road is decidedly bad and dangerous for single wagons, frequently crossing the stream where the water is sometimes deep; and all the day the animals were fatigued in climbing up and descending a succession of steep ascents, to avoid the precipitous hillsides; and the common trail, which leads along the mountainside at places where the river strikes the base, is sonic times bad even for a horseman. The mountains along this day's journey were composed, near the river, of a slaty calcareous rock in a metamorphic condition. It appears originally to have been a slaty sedimentary limestone, but it; present condition indicates that it has been altered, and haft become partially crystalline—probably from the proximity of canic rocks. But though traveling was slow and fatiguing to the animals, we were delighted with the appearance of the country, which was green and refreshing after our tedious journey down the parched valley of Snake river. The mountains were covered with good bunchgrass, (festuca;) the water of the streams was cold and pure; their bottoms were handsomely wooded with various kinds of trees; and huge and lofty picturesque precipices where the river cut through the mountain.

We found in the evening some good grass and rushes; and encamped among large timber, principally birch, which had been recently burnt, and blackened, and almost destroyed by fire. The night was calm and tolerably clear, with the thermometer at sunset at 590. Our journey today was 'about twenty miles.

14th.—The day was clear and calm, with a temperature at sunrise of 46°. After traveling about three miles up the valley, we found the river shut up by precipices in a kind of canon, and the road makes a circuit over the mountains. In the afternoon we reached the river again, by another little ravine; and, after traveling along it for a few miles, left it enclosed among rude mountains; and, ascending a smaller branch, encamped on it about five o'clock, very much elevated above the valley. The view was everywhere limited by mountains, on which were no longer seen the black and barren rocks, but a fertile soil, with excellent grass, and partly well covered with pine. I have never seen a wagonroad equally bad in the same space, as this of yesterday and today. I noticed where one wagon had been overturned twice, in a very short distance; and it was surprising to me that those wagons which were in the rear, and could not have had much assistance, got through at all. Still, there is no mud; and the road has one advantage, in being perfectly firm. The day had been warm and very pleasant, and the night was perfectly clear.

15th.—The thermometer at daylight was 42°, and at sunrise 40°; clouds, which were scattered over all the sky, disappeared with the rising sun. The trail did not much improve until we had crossed the dividing ground between the Brill& (Burnt) and Powder rivers. The rock displayed on the mountains, as we approached the summit, was a compact trap, decomposed on the exposed surfaces, and apparently an altered argillaceous sandstone, containing small crystalline nodules of anolcime, apparently filling cavities originally existing. From the summit here, the whole horizon shows high mountains; AG high plain or level is to be seen; and on the left, from south around by the west to north, the mountains are black with pines; while, through the remaining space to the eastward they are bald, with the exception of some scattered pines

You will remark that we are now entering a region where all the elevated parts are covered with dense and heavy forests.

From the dividing grounds we descended by a mountain road to Powder river, on an old bed of which we encamped. Descending from the summit, we enjoyed a picturesque view of high rocky mountains on the right, illuminated by the setting sun.

From the heights we had looked in vain for a well-known landmark on Powder river, which had been described to me by Mr. Payette as l'arbre seul, (the lone tree;) and, on arriving at the river, we found a fine tall pine stretched on the ground, which had been felled by some inconsiderate emigrant axe.

It had been a beacon on the road for many years past. Our

Cayuses had become impatient to reach their homes, and traveled on ahead to day; and this afternoon we were visited by several Indians who belonged to the tribes on the Columbia.

They were on horseback, and were out on a hunting excursion, but had obtained no better game than a large gray hare, of which each had some six or seven hanging to his saddle.

We were also visited by an Indian who had his lodge and family in the mountain to the left. He was in want 6f ammunition, and brought with him a beaverskin to exchange, and which he valued at six charges of powder and ball. I learned from him that there are very few of these animals remaining in this part of the country.

The temperature at sunset was 61o, and the evening clear obtained, with other observations, an immersion and emersion of the third satellite. Elevation 3,100 feet.

16th. For several weeks the weather in the daytime has been very beautiful, clear, and warm; but the nights, in comparison, are very cold. During the night there was ice a quarter of an inch thick in the lodge; and at daylight the thermometer was at 16o, and the same at sunrise, the weather being calm and clear. The annual vegetation now is nearly gone, Tamest all the plants being out of bloom.

Last night two of our horses had run off again, which delayed us until noon, and we made today but a short journey of 13 miles, the road being very good, and encamped in a fine bottom of Powder river.

The thermometer at sunset was at 61°, with an easterly wind, and partially clear sky; and the day has been quite pleasant and warm, though more cloudy than yesterday and the sun was frequently faint, but it grew finer and clearer towards evening.

17th.—Thermometer at sunrise 25°. The weather at daylight was fine, and the sky without a cloud; but these came up, or were formed by the sun, and at seven were thick over all the sky. Just now, this appears to be the regular course—clear and brilliant during the night, and cloudy during the lay. There is snow yet visible in the neighboring mountains, which yesterday extended along our route to the left, in a lofty and dark blue range, having much the appearance of the Wind River mountains. It is probable that they have received their name of the Blue mountains from the dark blue appearance given to them by the pines. We traveled this morning across the affluents to Powder river, the road being good, firm, and level, and the country became constantly more pleasant and interesting. The soil appeared to be very deep, and is black and extremely good, as well among the hollows of the hills on the elevated plats, as on the river bottoms, the vegetation being such as is usually found in good ground.

From the waters of this stream, the road ascended by a good and moderate ascent to a dividing ridge, but immediately entered upon ground covered with fragments of an altered silidons slate, which are in many places large, and render the road racking to a carriage. In this rock the planes of deposition are distinctly preserved, and the metamorphism is evidently due to the proximity of volcanic rocks. On either side, the mountains here are densely covered with tall and handsome trees; and, mingled with the green of a variety of pines, is the yellow of the European larch, (pinus larix,) which loses its leaves in the fall. From its present color, we were enabled to see that it forms a large proportion of the forests on the mountains, and is here a magnificent tree, attaining sometimes the height of 200 feet, which I believe is elsewhere unknown. About two in the afternoon we reached a high point of the dividing ridge, from which we obtained a good view of the Grand Rond—a beautiful level basin, or mountain valley, covered with good grass, on a rich soil, abundantly watered, and surrounded by high and well-timbered mountains—and its name descriptive of its form—the great circle. It is a place—one of the few we have seen on our journey so far—where a farmer would delight to establish himself, if he were content to live in the seclusion which it imposes. It is about 20 miles in diameter, and may, in time, form a superb county. Probably with the view of avoiding a circuit, the wagons had directly descended into the Rond by the face of a hill so very rocky and continuously steep as to be apparently impracticable, and, following down on their trail, we encamped on one of the branches of the Grand Rond river, immediately at the foot of the hill. I had remarked, in descending, some very white spots glistening on the plain, and, going out in that direction after we had encamped, I found them to be the bed of a dry salt lake, or marsh, very firm and bare, which was covered thickly with a fine white powder, containing a large quantity of carbonate of soda, (thirty-three in one hundred parts.)

The old grass had been lately burnt off from the surrounding hills, and, wherever the fire had passed, there was a recent growth of strong, green, and vigorous grass; and the soil of the level prairie, which sweeps directly up to the root of the surrounding mountains, appears to be very rich, produce spontaneously and luxuriantly in various places.

Analysis of Grand Rond soil.

Silica,   70/1

Alumina,   1017

Lime and magnesia,   138

Oxide of iron,   2/1

Vegetable matter, partly decomposed, . 816

Water and loss,   5.46

Phosphate of lime,   1/1

100.00

The elevation of this encampment is 2,940 feet ,,love the sea.

18th.—It began to rain an hour before sunrise, and continued until ten o'clock; the sky entirely overcast, and the temperature at sunrise 48°.

We resumed our journey somewhat later than usual; traveling in a nearly north direction across the beautiful valley; and about noon reached a place on one of the principal streams, where I had determined to leave the emigrant trail, in the expectation of finding a more direct and better road across the Blue mountains. At this place the emigrants appeared to have held some consultation as to their further route, gradually turned directly off to the left; reaching the foot of the hills in about three miles, which they mended by a hill as steep and difficult as that by which we had yesterday descended to the Rond. Quitting, therefore, this road, which, after a very rough crossing, issues from the mountains by the heads of the Umatilah river, we continued our Lei them course across the valley, following an Indian trail which had been indicated to me by Mr. Payette, and encamped at the northern extremity of the Grand Rond, on a sloughlike stream of very deep water, without any apparent current. There are some pines here on the low hills at the creek; awl in the northwest corner of the Rond is a very heavy body of timber, which descends into the plain. The clouds, which had rested very low along the mountain sides during the day, rose gradually up in the afternoon; and in the evening the sky was almost entirely clear, with a temperature at sunset of 470. Some indifferent observations placed the camp in longitude 117° 28' 26", latitude 450 26' 47"; and the elevation was 2,600 feet above the sea.

19th.—This morning the mountains were hidden by fog; there was a heavy dew during the night, in which the exposed thermometer at daylight stood at 32°, and at sunrise the temperature was 350.

We passed out of the Grand Rond by a fine road along the creek, which, for a short distance, runs in a kind of rocky chasm. Crossing a low point, which was a little rocky, the trail conducted into the open valley of the stream—a handsome place fez forms; the soil, even of the hills, being rich, and black. Passing through a point of pines, which bore evidences of being very much frequented by the Indians, and in which the trees were sometimes apparently 200 feet high, and three to seen feet in diameter, we halted for a few minutes in the afternoon at the: foot of the Blue mountains, on a branch of the Grand Rond river, at an elevation of 2,700 feet. Resuming our journey, we commenced the ascent of the mountains through an open pine forest of large and stately trees, among which the balsam pine made its appearance; the road being good, with the exception of one steep ascent, with a corresponding which might both have been easily avoided by opening the way for a short distance through the timber. It would have been well had we encamped on the stream where we had halted below, as the night overtook us on the mountain, and we were obliged to enter without water, and tie up the animals to the trees for the night. We halted on a smooth open place of a narrow descended very rapidly to a ravine or piny hollow, at a considerable distance below; and it was quite a pretty spot, had there been water near. But the fires at night look very cheerless after a day's march, when there is no preparation for supper going; and, after sitting some time around the blazing logs, Mr. Preuss and Carson, with several others, volunteered to take the India rubber buckets and go down into the ravine in search of water It is as a very difficult way in the darkness down the slipper side of the steep mountain, and harder still to climb about half a mile up again; but they found the water, and the cup of coffee (which it enabled us to make) and bread were only enjoyed with greater pleasure.

At sunset the temperature was 46°; the evening remarkably clear; and I obtained an emersion of the first satellite, which does not give a good result, although the observation was a very good one. The chronometric longitude was 1170 28' 34", latitude 450 38' 07", and we had ascended to an elevation of 3,830 feet. It appeared to have snowed yesterday on the mountains, their summits showing very white today.

20th.—There was a heavy white frost during the night, and at sunrise the temperature was 370.

The animals had eaten nothing during the night; and we made an early start, continuing our route among the pines, which were more dense than yesterday, and still retained their magnificent size. The larches cluster together in masses on the side of the mountains, and their yellow foliage contrasts handsomely with the green of the balsam and other pines. After a few miles we ceased to see any pines, and the timber consisted of "several varieties of spruce, larch, and balsam pine, which have a regularly conical figure. These trees appeared from GO to nearly 200 feet in height; the usual circumference being 10 to 12 feet, and in the pines sometimes 21 feet. In open places near the summit, these trees became less high and more branching, the conical form having a greater base. The instrument carriage occasioned much delay, it being frequently necessary to fell trees and remove the fallen timber. The trail we were following led up a long spur, with a very gradual and gentle rise. At the end of three miles, we halted at an open place near the summit, from which we enjoyed a fine view over the mountainous country where we had lately traveled, to take a barometrical observation at the height of 4,460 feet.

After traveling occasionally through open places in the forest, we were obliged to cut a way through a dense body of timber, from which we emerged on an open mountainside, where we found a number of small springs, and encamped after a day's journey of ten miles. Our elevation her was 5,000 feet.

21st.—There was a very heavy white frost during the//night, and the thermometer at sunrise was 300.

We continued to travel through the forest, in which the road was rendered difficult by fallen trunks, and obstructed by many small trees, which it was necessary to cut down. But these are only accidental difficulties, which could easily be removed, and a very excellent road may be had through this pass, with no other than very moderate ascents or declivities. A laborious day, which had advanced us only six miles on the road, brought us in the afternoon to an opening in the forest, in which there was a fine mountain meadow, with good grass, and a large clearwater stream—one of the head branches of the Umatilah river. During this day's journey, the barometer was broken; and the elevations above the sea, hereafter given, depend upon the temperature of boiling water. Some of the white spruces which I measured today were twelve feet in circumference, arid one of the larches ten; but eight feet was the average circumference of those measured along the road. I held in my hand a tape line as I walked along, in order to form some correct idea of the size of the timber. Their height appeared to be from 100 to 180, and perhaps 200 feet, and the trunks of the larches were sometimes 100 feet without a limb; but the white spruces were generally covered with branches nearly to the root. All these trees have their branches, particularly the lower ones, declining.

22d.—The white frost this morning was like snow on the ground; the ice was a quarter of an inch thick on the creek, and the thermometer at sunrise was at 200. But, in a few hours, the day became warm and pleasant, and our road over the mountains was delightful and full of enjoyment.

The trail passed sometimes through very thick young timber, in which there was much cutting to be done; but, after traveling a few miles, the mountains became more bald, and we reached a point from which there was a very extensive view in the northwest. We were on the western verge of the Blue mountains, long spurs of which, very precipitous on either side extended down into the valley, the waters of the mountain roaring between them. On our right was a mountain plateau, covered with a dense forest; and to the westward, immediately below us, was the great Nez Perce (pierced nose) prairie, in which dark lines of timber indicated the course of many affluents to a considerable stream that was pursuing its way across the plain towards what appeared to be the Columbia river. This I knew to be the Walahwalah river, and occasional spots along its banks, which resembled clearings, were supposed to be the mission or Indian settlements; but the weather was smoky and unfavorable to far views with the glass. The rock displayed here in the escarpments is a compact amorphous trap, which appears to constitute the mass of the Blue mountains in this latitude; and all the region of country through which we have traveled since leaving the Snake river has been the seat of violent and extensive igneous action. Along the Burnt River valley, the strata are evidently sedimentary rocks, altered by the intrusion_ of volcanic products, which in some instances nave penetrated and essentially changed their original condition. Along our line of route from this point to the California mountains, there seems but little essential change. All our specimens of sedimentary rocks show them much altered, and volcanic productions appear to prevail throughout the whole intervening distance.

The road now led along the mountain side, around heads of the precipitous ravines; and keeping men ahead to clear the road, we passed alternately through bodies of timber and small open prairies, and encamped in a large meadow, in view of the great prairie below.

At sunset the thermometer was at 400, and the night was very clear and bright. Water was only to be had here by descending a bad ravine, into which we drove our animals, and had much trouble with them in a very close growth of small pines. Mr. Preuss had walked ahead and did not get into the camp this evening. The trees here maintained their size, and one of the black spruces measured 15 feet in circumference. In the neighborhood of the camp, pines have reappeared here among the timber.

23d.—The morning was very clear; there had been a white frost during the night, and at sunrise the thermometer was at 310.

After cutting through two thick bodies of timber, in which I noticed some small trees of hemlock spruce, (peruse,) the forest became more open, and we had no longer any trouble to clear a way. The pines here were 11 or 12 feet in circumference, and about 110 feet high, and appeared to love the open grounds. The trail now led along one of the long spurs of the mountain, descending gradually towards the plain; and after a few miles traveling, we emerged finally from the forest, in full view of the plain below, and saw the snowy mass of Mount Hood, standing high out above the surrounding country at the distance of 180 miles. The road along the ridge was excellent, and the grass very green and good; the old grass having been burnt off early in the autumn. About 4 o'clock in the afternoon we reached a little bottom of the Walahwalah river, where we found Mr. Preuss, who yesterday had reached this place, and found himself too far in advance of the camp to return. The stream here has just issued from the narrow ravines, which are walled with precipices, in which the rock has a brown and more burnt appearance than above.

At sunset the thermometer was at 48o, and our position was in longitude 118o oo' 39", and in latitude 45o 53' 35".

The morning was clear, with a temperature at sunrise of 24o. Crossing the river, we traveled over a hilly country with a good bunchgrass; the river bottom, which generally contains the best soil in other countries being here a sterile level of rocks and pebbles. We had found the soil in the Blue mountains to be of excellent quality, and it appeared also to be good here among the lower hills. Reaching a little eminence over which the trail passed, we had an extensive view along the course of the river, which was divided and spread over its bottom in a network of water, receiving several other tributaries from the mountains. There was a band of several hundred horses grazing on the hills about two miles ahead; and as we advanced on the road we met other bands, which Indians were driving out to pasture also on the hills. True to its general character, the reverse of other countries, the hills and mountains here were rich in grass, the bottoms barren and sterile.

In six miles we crossed a principal fork, below which the scattered waters of the river were gathered into one channel; and, passing' on the way several unfinished houses, and some cleared patches, were corn and potatoes were cultivated, we reached, in about eight miles further, the missionary establishment of Dr. Whitman, which consisted at this time of one adobe house—i e., built of unburnt bricks as in Mexico.

I found Dr. Whitman absent on a: visit to the Dalles of the Columbia; but had the pleasure to see a fine-looking family of emigrants, men, women, and children, in robust health, all indemnifying themselves for previous scanty fare, in a hearty consumption of potatoes, which are produced here of a remarkably good quality. We were disappointed in our expectation of obtaining cornmeal or flour at this station, the mill belonging to the mission having been lately burned down; but an abundant supply of excellent potatoes banished regrets, and furnished a grateful substitute for bread. A small town of Nez Perce Indians gave an inhabited and even a populous appearance to the station; and, after remaining about an hour, we continued our route and encamped on the river about four miles below, passing on the way an emigrant encampment.

Temperature at sunset, 49o.

25th.—The weather was pleasant, with a sunrise, temperature of 36°. Our road today had nothing in it of interest; and the country offered to the eye only a sandy, undulating plain, through which a scantily timbered river takes its course. We halted about three miles above the mouth, on account of grass; and the next morning arrived at the Nez Perce fort, one of the trading establishments of the Hudson Bay Company, a few hundred yards above the junction of the Walahwalah with the Columbia river. Here we had the first view of this river, and found it about 1,200 yards wide, and presenting the appearance of a fine, navigable stream. We made our camp in a little grove of willows on the Walahwalah, which are the only trees to be seen in the neighborhood; but were obliged to send the animals back to the encampment we had left, as there was scarcely a blade of glass to be found. The post is on the bank of the Columbia, on a plain of bare sands, from which the air was literally filled with clouds of dust and sand, during one of the few days we remained here; this place being one of the several points on the river which are distinguished for prevailing high winds, that come from the sea. The appearance of the post and country was without interest, except that we here saw, for the first time, the great river on which the course of events for the last half century has been directing attention and conferring historical fame. The river is, indeed, a noble object, and has here attained its full magnitude. About nine miles above, and in sight from the heights about this post, is the junction of the two great forks which constitute the main stream—that on which we had been traveling from Fort Hall, and known by the names of Lewis's fork, Shoshonee, and Snake river; and the North fork, which has retained the name of Columbia, as being the main stream.

We did not go up to the junction, being pressed for time; but the union of two large streams, coming one from the southeast, and the other from the northeast, and meeting in what may be treated as the geographical centre of the Oregon valley, thence doubling the volume of water to the ocean, while opening two great lines of communication with the interior continent, constitutes a feature in the map of the country which cannot be overlooked; and it was probably in reference to this junction of waters, and these lines of communication, that this post was established. They are important lines, and, from the structure of the country, must forever remain so, —one of them leading to the South Pass and to the valley of the Mississippi, the other to the pass at the head of the Athabasca river, and to the countries drained by the waters of the Hudson Bay. The British fur companies now use both lines; the Americans, in their emigration to Oregon, have begun to follow the one which leads towards the United States. Bateaux from tidewater ascend to the junction, and thence high up the North fork, or Columbia. Land conveyance only is used upon the line of Lewis's fork. To the emigrants to Oregon, the Nez Perce is a point of great interest, as being, to those who choose it, the termination of their overland journey. The road expanse of the river here invites them to embark on its bosom; and the lofty trees of the forest furnish the means of doing so.

From the South Pass to this place is about 1,000 miles; and as it is about the same distance from that pass to the Missouri river at the mouth of the Kansas, it may be assumed that 2,000 miles is the necessary land travel, in crossing from the United States to the Pacific ocean on this line. From the mouth of the Great Platte it would be about 100 miles less.

Mr. McKinley, the commander of the post, received us with great civility; and both to myself, and the heads of the emigrants who were there at the time, extended the rights of hospitality in a comfortable dinner to which he invited us.

By a meridional altitude of the sun, the only observation that the weather permitted us to obtain, the mouth of the Walahwalah river is in latitude 46° 03' 46"; and, by the road we had traveled, 612 miles from Fort Hall. At the time of our arrival, a considerable body of emigrants, under the direction of Mr. Applegate, a man of considerable resolution and energy, had nearly completed the building of a number of Mackinaw boats, in which they proposed to continue their further voyage down the Columbia. I had seen, in descending the Walahwalah river, a fine drove of several hundred cattle, which they had exchanged for California cattle, to be received at Vancouver, and which are considered a very inferior breed. The other portion of the emigration had preferred to complete their journey by land along the banks of the Columbia, taking their stock and wagons with them.

Having reinforced our animals with eight fresh horses, hired from the post, and increased our stock of provisions with dried salmon, potatoes, and a little beef, we resumed our journey down the left bank of the Columbia, being guided on our road by an intelligent Indian boy, whom I had engaged to accompany us as far as the Dalles.

From an elevated point over which the road led, we obtained another far view of Mount Hood 150 miles distant. We obtained on the river bank an observation of the sun at noon which gave for the latitude 45° 58' 08". The country today was very unprepossessing, and our road bad; and as we toiled slowly along through deep loose sands, and over fragments of black volcanic rock, our laborious traveling was strongly contrasted with the rapid progress of Mr. Applegate's fleet of boats, which suddenly came gliding swiftly down the broad river, which here chanced to be tranquil and smooth. At evening we encamped on the river bank, where there was very little grass, and less timber. We frequently met Indians on the road, and they were, collected at every favorable spot along the river.

29th.—The road continued along the river, and in the course of the day Mount St. Helens, another snowy peak of the Cascade range, was visible. We crossed the Umatilah river at a fall near ifs mouth. This stream is of the same class as the Walahwalah river, with a bed of volcanic rock, in places split into fissures. Our encampment was similar to that of yesterday; there was very little grass, and no wood. The Indians brought us some pieces for sale, which were purchased to make our fires.

31st.—By observation, our camp is in latitude 45° 50' 05", and longitude 119° 22' 18". The night has been cold, and we have white frost this morning, with a temperature at daylight of 25°, and at sunrise of 24°. The early morning was very clear, and the stars bright; but, as usual since we are on the Columbia, clouds formed immediately with the rising sun. The day continued fine, the east being covered with scattered clouds, but the west remaining clear, showing the remarkable cone like peak of Mount Hood brightly drawn against the sky. This was in view all day in the southwest, but no other peaks of the range were visible. Our road was a bad one, of very loose, deep sand. We met on the way a party of Indians unusually well-dressed. They appeared intelligent, and, in our slight intercourse, impressed me with the belief that they possessed some aptitude for acquiring languages.

We continued to travel along the river, the stream being interspersed with many sandbars (it being the season of low water) and with many islands, and an apparently good navigation. Small willows were the only wood; rock and sand the prominent geological feature. The rock of this section is a very compact and tough basalt, occurring in strata which nave the appearance of being broken into fragments, assuming the form of columnar hills, and appearing always in escarpments, with the broken fragments strewed at the base and over the adjoining country.

We made a late encampment on the river, and used tonight the purshia tridentata for firewood. Among the rocks which formed the bank, was very good green grass. Latitude 450 44"23", longitude 1190 45' 09".

NOVEMBER.

1st.—Mount Hood is glowing in the sunlight this morning, and the air is pleasant, with a temperature of 390. We continued down the river, and, passing through a pretty green valley, bounded by high precipitous rocks, encamped at the lower end.

On the right shore, the banks of the Columbia are very high and steep; the river is 1,690 feet broad, and dark bluffs of rock give i t a picturesque appearance.

2d.—The river here entered among bluffs, leaving no longer room for a road; and we accordingly left it, and took a more inland way among the river hills—on which we had no sooner entered than we found a great improvement in the country. The sand had disappeared, and the soil was good, and covered with excellent grass, although the surface was broken into high hills, with uncommonly deep valleys. At noon we crossed John Day's river, a clear and beautiful stream, with a swift current and a bed of rolled stones. It is sunk in a deep valley, which is characteristic of all the streams in this region; and the hill we descended to reach it well deserves the name of mountain. Some of the emigrants had encamped on the river, and others at the summit of the farther hill, the ascent)f which had probably cost their wagons a day's labor; and others again had halted for the night a few miles beyond, where they had slept without water. We also encamped in a grassy hollow without water; but, as we had been forewarned of this privation by the guide, the animals had all been watered at the river, and we had brought with us a sufficient ratantity for the night.

3d.—After two hours' ride through a fertile, hilly country, covered, as all the upland here appears to be, with good green grass, we descended again into the river bottom, along which we resumed our sterile road, and in about four miles reached the ford of the Fsil river, (Riviere aux Chutes,) a considerable tributary to the Columbia. We had heard, on reaching the Nez Perce fort, a repetition of the account in regard to the unsettled character of the Columbia Indians at the present time; and to our little party they had at various points manifested a not very friendly disposition, in several attempts to steal our horses. At this place I expected to find a badly disposed band, who had plundered a party of 14 emigrant men a few days before, and taken away their horses; and accordingly we made the necessary preparation for our security, but happily met with no difficulty.

The river was high, divided into several arms, with a rocky island at its outlet into the Columbia, which at this place, it rivalled in size, and apparently derived its highly characteristic name, which is received from one of its many falls some forty miles up the river. It entered the Columbia with a roar of falls and rapids, and is probably a favorite fishing station among the Indians, with whom both banks of the river were populous; but they scarcely paid any attention to us. The ford was very difficult at this time, and, had they entertained any bad intentions, they were offered a good opportunity to carry them out, as I drove directly into the river, and during the crossing the howitzer was occasionally several feet under water, and a number of the men appeared to be more often be low than above. o_7r guide was well acquainted with the ford, ana we succeeded in getting every thing safe over to the left bank. We delayed here only a short time to put the gun in order, and, ascending a long mountain hill, resumed our route again among the interior hills.

The roar of the Falls of the Columbia is heard from the heights, where we halted a few moments enjoy a fine view of the river below. In the season of high water, it would be a very interesting object to visit, in order to witness what is related of the annual submerging of the fall under the, waters which back up from the basin below, constituting a great natural lock at this place. But time had become an object of serious consideration; and the Falls, in their present state, had been seen and described by many.

After a day's journey of 17 miles, we encamped among the hills on a little clear stream, where, as usual, the Indians immediately gathered round us. Among them was a very old man, almost blind from age, with long and very white hair. I happened of my own accord to give this old man a present of tobacco, and was struck with the impression which my unpropitiated notice made on the Indians, who appeared in a remarkable manner acquainted with the real value of goods, and to understand the equivalents of trade. At evening, one of them spoke a few words to his people, and, telling me that we need entertain no uneasiness in regard to our animals, as none of them would be disturbed, they went all quietly away. In the morning, when they again came to the camp, I expressed to them the gratification we felt at their reasonable conduct, making them a present of some large knives and a few smaller articles.

4th.—The road continued among the hills, and, reaching an eminence, we saw before us, watered by a clear stream, a tolerably large valley, through which the trail passed.

In comparison with the Indians of the Rocky mountains and the great eastern plain, these are disagreeably dirty in their habits. Their huts were crowded with half naked women and children, and the atmosphere within was any thing but pleasant to persons who had just been riding in the fresh morning air. We were somewhat amused with the scanty dress of a woman; who, in common with the others, rushed out of the huts or our arrival, and who, in default of other covering, used a child lb; a qgleaf.

The road in about half an hour passed near an elevated point, from which we overlooked the valley of the Columbia for many miles, and saw in the distance several houses surrounded by fields, which a chief, who had accompanied us from the village, pointed out to us as the Methodist missionary station.

In a few miles we descended to the river, which we reached at one of its remarkably interesting features, known as the Dalles of the Columbia. The whole volume of the river at this place passed between the walls of a chasm, which has the appearance of having been rent through the basaltic strata which form the valley rock of the region. At the narrowest place we found the breadth, by measurement, 58 yards, and the average height of the walls above the water 25 feet; forming a trough between the rocks—whence the name, probably applied by a Canadian voyageur. The mass of water, in the present low state of the river, passed swiftly between, deep and black, and curled into many small whirlpools and counter currents, but unbroken by foam, and so still that scarcely the sound of a ripple was heard. The rock, for a considerable distance from the river, was worn over a large portion of its surface into circular holes and well like cavities, by the abrasion of the river, which, at the season of high waters, is spread out over the adjoining bottoms.

In the recent passage through this chasm, an unfortunate event had occurred to Mr. Applegate's party, in the loss of one of their boats, which had been carried under water in the midst of the Dalles, and two of Mr. Applegate's children and one man drowned. This misfortune was attributed only to want of skill in the steersman, as at this season there was no impediment to navigation; although the place is entirely impassable at high, water, when boats pass safely over the great falls above, in the submerged state in which they then find themselves.

The basalt here is precisely the same as that which constitutes the rock of the valley higher up the Columbia, being very compact, with a few round cavities.

We passed rapidly three or four miles down the level valley and encamped near the mission. The character of the forest growth here changes, and we found ourselves, with pleasure, again among oaks and other forest trees of the east, to which we had long been strangers; and the hospitable and kind reception with which we were welcomed among our country people at the mission, aided the momentary illusion of home

Two good-looking wooden dwelling houses, and a large schoolhouse, with stables, barn, and garden, and large cleared fields between the houses and the river bank, on which were scattered the wooden huts of an Indian village, gave to the valley the cheerful and busy air of civilization,' and had in our eyes an appearance of abundant and enviable comfort.

Our land journey found here its western termination. The delay involved in getting our camp to the right bank of the Columbia, and in opening a road through the continuous forest to Vancouver, rendered a journey along the river impracticable; and on this side the usual road across the mountain required strong and fresh animals, there being an interval of three days in which they could obtain no food. I therefore wrote immediately to Mr. Fitzpatrick, directing him to abandon the carts at the Walahwalah missionary station, and, as soon as the necessary packsaddles could be made, which his party required, meet me at the Dalles, from which point I proposed to commence our homeward journey. The day after our arrival being Sunday, no business could be done at the mission; but on Monday, Mr. Perkins assisted me in procuring from the Indians a large canoe, in which I designed to complete our journey to Vancouver, where I expected to obtain the necessary supply of provisions and stores for bur winter journey. Three Indians, from the family to whom the canoe belonged, were engaged to assist in working her during the voyage, and, with them, our water party consisted of Mr. Preuss and myself, with Bernier and Jacob Dodson. In charge of the party which was to remain at the Dalles I left Carson, with instructions to occupy the people in making packsaddles and refitting their equipage. The village from which we were to take the carve was on the right bank of the river, about ten miles below, a Lake mouth of the Tinanens creek; and while Mr. Preuss proceeded down the river with the instruments, in a little canoe paddled by two Indians, Mr. Perkins accompanied me with the remainder of the party by land. The last of the emigrants had just left the Dalles at the time of our arrival, traveling some by water and others by land, making arklike rafts, on which they had embarked their families and households, with their large wagons and other furniture, while their stock were driven along the shore.

For about five miles below the Dalles, the river is narrow, and probably very deep; but during this distance it is somewhat open, with grassy bottoms on the left. Entering, then, among the lower mountains of the Cascade range, it assumes a general character, and high and steep rocky hills shut it in on either side, rising abruptly in places to the height of fifteen hundred feet above the water, and gradually acquiring a more mountainous character as the river approaches the Cascades.

After an hour's travel, when the sun was nearly down, we searched along the shore for a pleasant place, and halted to prepare supper. We had been well supplied by our friends at the mission with delicious salted salmon, which had been taken at the fattest season; also, with potatoes, bread, coffee, and sugar. We were delighted at a change in our mode of traveling and living. The canoe sailed smoothly down the river; at night we encamped upon the shore, and a plentiful supply of comfortable provisions supplied the first of wants. We enjoyed the contrast which it presented to our late toilsome marchings, our night watchings, and our frequent privation of food. We were a motley group, but all happy: three unknown Indians; Jacob, a colored man; Mr. Preuss, a German; Bernier, creole French; and myself.

Being now upon the ground explored by the South Sea expedition under Captain Wilkes, and having accomplished the object of uniting my survey with his, and thus presenting a connected exploration from the Mississippi to the Pacific, and the winter being at hand, I deemed it necessary to economize time by voyaging in the night, as is customary here, to avoid the high winds, which rise with the morning, and decline with the day.

Accordingly, after an hour's halt, we again embarked, and resumed our pleasant voyage down the river. The wind rose to a gale after several hours; but the moon was very bright, and the wind was fair, and the canoe glanced rapidly down the stream, the waves breaking into foam alongside; and our night voyage, as the wind bore us rapidly along between the dark mountains, was wild and interesting. About midnight we put to the shore on a rocky beach, behind which was a dark looking pine forest. We built up large fires among the rocks, which were in large masses round about; and, arranging out blankets on the most sheltered places we could find, passed a delightful night.

After an early breakfast, at daylight we resumed our journey, the weather being clear and beautiful, and the river smooth and still. On either side the mountains are all pine timbered, rocky, and high. We were now approaching one of the marked features of the lower Columbia where the river forms a great cascade, with a series of rapids, in breaking through the range of mountains to which the lofty peaks of Mount Hood and St. Helens belong, and which rise as great pillars of snow on either side of the passage. The main, branch of the Sacramento river, and the Tlamath, issue in cascades from this range; and the Columbia, breaking through it in a succession of cascades, gives the idea of 'cascades to the whole range; and hence the name of CASCADE RANGE, which it bears, and distinguishes it from the Coast Range lower down. In making a short turn to the south, the river forms the cascades in breaking over a point of agglomerated masses of rock, leaving a handsome bay to the right, 'with several rocky, pine covered islands, and the mountains sweep at a distance around a cove where several small streams enter the bay. In less than an hour we halted on the left bank, about five minutes' walk above the cascades, where there were several Indian huts, and where our guides signified it was customary to hire Indians to assist in making the portage. When traveling with a boat as light, as a canoe, which may easily be car tied on the shoulders of the Indians, this is much the better side of the river for the portage, as the ground here is very good and level, being a handsome bottom, which I remarked was covered (as was now always the case along the river) with a growth of green and fresh-looking grass. It was long before we could come to an understanding with the Indians; but to length, when they had first received the price of their assistance in goods, they went vigorously to work; and, in a shorter time than had been occupied in making our arrangements, the canoe, instruments, and baggage, were carried through (a distance of about half a mile) to the bank below the main cascade, where we again embarked, the water being white with foam among ugly rocks, and boiling into a thousand whirlpools. The boat passed with great rapidity, crossing and recrossing in the eddies of the current. After passing through about two miles of broken water, we ran some wilt looking rapids, which are called the Lower Rapids, being the last on, the river, which below is tranquil and smooth—a broad, magnificent stream. On a low broad point on the right bank of the river, at the lower end of these rapids, were pitched many tents of the emigrants, who were waiting here for their friends from above, or for boats and provisions which were expected from Vancouver. In our passage down the rapids, I had noticed their camps along the shore, or transporting their goods across the portage. This portage makes a head of navigation, ascending the, river. It is about two miles in length; and above, to the Dalles, is 45 miles of smooth and good navigation.

We glided on without further interruption between very rocky and high steep mountains, which sweep along the river valley at a little distance, covered with forests of pine, and showing occasionally lofty escarpments of red rock. Nearer, the shore is bordered by steep escarped hills and huge vertical rocks, from which the waters of the mountain reach the river in a variety of beautiful falls, sometimes several hundred feet in height. Occasionally along the river occurred pretty bottoms, covered with the greenest verdure of the spring. To a professional farmer, however, it does not offer many places a sufficient extent to be valuable for agriculture; and after passing a few miles below the Dalles, I had scarcely seen a place on the south shore where wagons could get to the river. The beauty of the scenery was heightened by the continuance of very delightful weather, resembling the Indian summer of the Atlantic. A few miles below the cascades we passed a singular isolated hall; and in the course of the next six miles occurred five vary pretty falls from the heights on the left bank, one of them being of a very picturesque character; aaa towards sunset we reached a remarkable point of rocks, distinguished, on account of prevailing high winds, and the delay it frequently occasions to the canoe navigation, by the name of Caps Horn. It borders the river in a high wall of rock, which comes boldly down into deep water; and in violent gales down the river, and from the opposite shore, which is the prevailing direction of strong winds, the water is dashed against it with considerable violence. It appears to form a serious obstacle to canoe traveling; and I was informed by Mr. Perkins, that in a voyage up the river he had been detained two weeks at this place, and was finally obliged to return to Vancouver.

The winds of this region deserve a particular study. They blow in currents, which show them to be governed by fixed laws; and it is a problem how far they may come from the mountains, or from the ocean through the breaks in the mountains which let out the river.

The hills here had lost something of their rocky appearance, and had already begun to decline. As the sun went down, we searched along the river for an inviting spot; and, finding a clean rocky beach, where some large dry trees were lying an the ground, we ran our boat to the shore; and, after another comfortable supper, ploughed our way along the river in darkness. Heavy clouds covered the sky this evening, and the wind began to sweep in gusts among the trees, as if bad weather were coining. As we advanced, the hills on both sides grew constantly lower; on the right, retreating from the shore, and coming a somewhat extensive bottom of intermingled prairie and wooded land. In the course of a few hours, and opposite to a small stream coming in from the north, called the Tea Prairie river, the highlands on the left declined to the plains, and three or four miles more disappeared entirely on both sides, and the river entered the low country. The river had gradually expanded; and when we emerged from the highlands, the opposite shores were so distant as to appear indistinct in the uncertainty of the light. About ten o'clock our pilots halted, apparently to confer about the course; and, after a little hesitation, pulled directly across an open expansion of the river, where the waves were somewhat rough for a canoe, the wind blowing very fresh. Much to cur surprise, a few minutes afterwards we ran aground. Backing off our boat, we made repeated trials at various places to cross what appeared to be a point of shifting sandbars, where we had attempted to shorten the way by a cutoff. Finally, one of our Indians got into the water, and waded about until he found a channel sufficiently deep, through which we wound along after him, and in a few minutes again entered the deep water below. As we paddled rapidly down the river, we heard the noise of a sawmill at work on the right bank; and, letting our boat float quietly down, we listened with pleasure to the unusual sounds, and before midnight, encamped on the bank of the river, about a mile above Fort Vancouver. Our fine dry weather had given place to a dark cloudy night. At midnight it, began to rain; and we found ourselves suddenly in the gloomy and humid season, which, in the narrow region lying between the Pacific and the Cascade mountains, and for a considerable distance along the coast, supplies the place of winter.

In the morning, the first object that attracted my attention was the barque Columbia, lying at anchor near the landing. She was about to start on a voyage to England, and was now ready for sea; being detained only in waiting the arrival of the express bateaux, which descend the Columbia and its north fork with the overland mail from Canada and Hudson's Bay, which had been delayed beyond the usual time. I immediately waited upon Dr. McLaughlin, the executive officer of the Hudson Bay Company, in the territory west of the Rocky mountains, who received me with the courtesy an, hospitality for which he has been eminently distinguished, and which make: a forcible and delightful impression on a traveler from the long wilderness from which we had issued. I was immediately supplied by him with the necessary stores and provisions to refit and support my party in our contemplated winter journey to the States; and also with a Mackinaw boat and canoes, manned with Canadian and Iroquois voyageurs and Indians, for their transportation to the Dalles of the Columbia. In addition to this efficient kindness in furnishing me with these necessary supplies, I received from him a warm and gratifying sympathy in the suffering which his great experience led him to anticipate for us in our homeward journey, and a letter of recommendation and credit for any officers of the Hudson Bay Company into whose posts we might be driven by unexpected misfortune.

Of course, the future supplies for my party were paid for, bills on the Government of the United States being readily taken; but every hospitable attention was extended to me, and I accepted an invitation to take a room in the fort, " and to make myself at home while I stayed."

I found many American emigrants at the fort; others had already crossed the river into their land of promise—the Walahmette valley.. Others were daily arriving; and all of them have been furnished with shelter, so far as it could be afforded by the buildings connected with the establishment. Necessary clothing and provisions (the latter to be returned in kind from the produce of their labor) were also furnished. This friendly assistance was of very great value to the emigrants, whose families were otherwise exposed to much suffering in the winter rains, which had now commenced; at the same time they were in want of all the common necessaries of life. Thok who had taken a water conveyance at the Nez Perce fort continued to arrive safely, with no other accident than has been already mentioned. The party which had crossed over the Cascade mountains were reported to have lost a number of their animals; and those who had driven their stock down the Columbia had brought them safely in, and found for them a ready and very profitable market, and were already proposing to return to the States in the spring for another supply.

In the space of two days our preparations had been completed, and we were ready to set out on our return. It would have been very gratifying to have gone down to the Pacific, and, solely in the interest and love of geography, to have seen the ocean on the western as well as on the eastern side of the continent, so as to give a satisfactory completeness to the geographical picture which had been formed in our minds; but the rainy season had now regularly set in, and the air was filled with fogs and rain, which left no beauty in any scenery, and obstructed observations. The object, of my instructions had been entirely fulfilled in having connected our reconnoissance with the surveys of Captain Wilkes; and although it would have been agreeable and satisfactory to terminate here also our ruder astronomical observations, I was not, for such a reason, justified to make a delay in waiting for favorable weather.

Near sunset of the 10th, the boats left the fort, and encamped after making only a few miles. Our flotilla consisted of a Mackinaw barge and three canoes—one of them that in which we had descended the river; and a party in all of twenty men. One of the emigrants, Mr. Burnet, of Missouri, who had left his family and property at the Dalles, availed himself of the opportunity afforded by the return of our boats to bring them down to Vancouver. This gentleman, as well as the Messrs. Applegate, and others of the emigrants whom I saw, possessed intelligence and character, with the moral and intellectual stamina, as well as the enterprise, which give solidity and respectability to the foundation of colonies.

11th.—The morning was rainy and misty. We did not move with the practised celerity of my own camp; and it was nearly nine o'clock when our motley crew had finished 'their breakfast and were ready to start. Once afloat, however, they worked steadily and well, and we advanced at a good rate up the river; and in the afternoon a breeze sprung up, which enabled us to add a sail to the oars. At evening we encamped on a warm looking beach, on the right bank, at the foot of the high river hill, immediately at the lower end of Cape Horn. On the opposite shore is said to be a singular hole in the mountain, from which the Indians believe comes the wind producing these gales. It is called the Devil's hole; and the Indians, I was told, had been resolving to send down one of their slaves to explore the region below. At dark, the wind shifted into its stormy quarter, gradually increasing to a gale from the southwest; and the sky becoming clear, I obtained a good observation of an emersion of the first satellite; the result of which being an absolute observation, I have adopted for the longitude of the place.

12th.—The wind during the night had increased to so much violence, that the broad river this morning was angry and white; the waves breaking with considerable force against this rocky wall of the cape. Our old Iroquois pilot was unwilling to risk the boats around the point, and I was not disposed to hazard the stores of our voyage for the delay of a day. Further observations were obtained during the day, giving for the latitude of the place 45o 33' 09"; and the longitude obtained from the satellite is 122° 6' 15".

13th.—We had a day of disagreeable and cold rain, and, late in the afternoon, began to approach the rapids of the cascades. There is here a high timbered island on the left shore, below which, in descending, I had remarked, in a bluff of the river, the extremities of trunks of trees, appearing to be imbedded in the rock. Landing here this afternoon, I found, in the lower part of the escarpment, a stratum of coal and forest trees, imbedded between strata of altered clay, containing the remains of vegetables, the leaves of which indicate that the plants were dicotyledonous. Among these, the stems of some of the ferns are not mineralized, but merely charred, retaining still their vegetable structure and substance; and in this condition a portion also of the trees remain. The indurated appearance and compactness of the strata, as well, perhaps, as the mineralized condition of the coal, are probably due to igneous action. Some portions of the coal precisely resemble in aspect the canal coal of England, and, with the accompanying fossils, have been referred to the tertiary formation.

These strata appear to rest upon a mass of agglomerated rock, being but a few feet above the water of the river; and over them is the escarpment of perhaps 80 feet, rising gradually in the rear towards the mountains. The wet and cold evening, and near approach of night, prevented me from making any other than a slight examination.

The current was now very swift, and we were obliged to cordelle the boat along the left shore, where the bank was covered with large masses of rocks. Night overtook us at the upper end of the island, a short distance below the cascades and we halted on the open point. In the mean time, the lighter canoes, paddled altogether by Indians, had passed ahead, and were out of sight. With them was the lodge, which was the only shelter we had, with most of the bedding and provisions. We shouted, and fired guns; but all to no purpose, as it was impossible for them to hear above the roar of the river; and we remained all night without shelter, the rain pouring down all the time. The old voyageurs did not appear to mind it much, but covered themselves up as well as they could, and lay down on the sandbeach, where they remained quiet until morning. The rest of us spent a rather miserable night; and, to add to our discomfort, the incessant rain extinguished our fires; and we were glad when at last daylight appeared, and we again embarked.

Crossing to the right bank, we cordelled the boat along the shore, there being no longer any use of the paddles, and put into a little bay below the upper rapids. Here we found a lodge pitched, and about 20 Indians sitting around a blazing fire within, making a luxurious breakfast with salmon, bread, butter, sugar, coffee, and other provisions. In the forest, on the edge of the high bluff overlooking the river, is an Indian graveyard, consisting of a collection of tombs, in each of which were the scattered bones of many skeletons. The tombs were made of boards, which were ornamented with many figures of men and animals of the natural size—from their appearance, constituting the armorial device by which,. among Indians, the chiefs are usually known.

The masses of rock displayed along the shores of the ravine in the neighborhood of the cascades, are clearly volcanic products. Between this cove, which t called Graveyard bay, ram another spot of smooth water above. , on the right, called Luders bay, sheltered by a jutting point of huge rocky masses at the foot of the cascades, the shore along the intervening rapids is lined with precipices of distinct strata of red and variously colored lavas, in inclined positions.

The masses of rock forming the point at Luders bay consist of a porous trap, or basalt—a volcanic product of a modern period. The rocks belong to agglomerated masses, which form the immediate ground of the cascades, and have been already mentioned as constituting a bed of cemented conglomerate rocks, appearing at various places along the river. Here they are scattered along the shores, and through the bed of the river, wearing the character of convulsion, which forms the impressive and prominent feature of the river at this place.

Wherever we came in contact with the rocks of these mountains, we found them volcanic, which is probably the character of the range; and at this time, two of the great snowy cones, Mount Regnier [Rainier] and St. Helens, were in action. On the 23d of the preceding November, St. Helens had scattered its ashes, like a white fall of snow, over the Dalles of the Columbia, 50 miles distant. A specimen of these ashes was given to me by Mr. Brewer, one of the clergymen at the Dalles.

The lofty range of the Cascade mountains forms a distinct boundary between the opposite climates of the regions along its western and eastern bases. On the west, they present a barrier to the clouds of fog and rain which roll up from the Pacific ocean and beat against their rugged sides, forming the rainy season of the winter in the country along the coast. Into the brighter skies of the region along their eastern base, this rainy winter never penetrates; and at the Dalles of the Columbia the rainy season is unknown, the brief winter being limited to a period of about two months, during which the earth is covered with the slight snows of a climate remarkably mild for so high a latitude. The Cascade range has an average distance of about 130 miles from the seacoast. It extends fat both north and south of the Columbia; and is indicated to the distant observer, both in course and position, by the lofty volcanic peaks which rise out of it, and which are visible to an immense distance.

During several dayS of constant rain, it kept our whole force laboriously employed in getting our barge and canoes to the upper end of the Cascades. The portage ground was occupied by emigrant families; their thin and insufficient clothing, bareheaded and barefooted children, attesting the length of their journey, and showing that they had, in many instances, set out without a due preparation of what was indispensable.

A gentleman named Luders, a botanist from the city of Hamburg, arrived at the bay I have called by his name while we were occupied in bringing up the boats. I was delighted to meet at such a place a man of kindred pursuits; but we had only the pleasure of a brief conversation, as his canoe, under the guidance of two Indians, was about to run the rapids; and I could not enjoy the satisfaction of regaling him with a breakfast, which, after his recent journey, would have been an extraordinary luxury. All of his few instruments and baggage were in the canoe, and he hurried around by land to meet it at the Graveyard bay; but he was scarcely out of sight, when, by the carelessness of the Indians, the boat was drawn into the midst of the rapids, and glanced down the river, bottom up, with a loss of every thing it contained. In the nature' concern I felt for his misfortune, I gave to the little cove the name of Luders bay.

15th.—We continued today our work at the portage.

About noon, the two barges of the express from Montreal arrived at the upper portage landing, which, for large boats, is on the right bank of the river. They were a fine-looking crew, and among them I remarked a fresh-looking woman and her daughter, emigrants from Canada. It was satisfactory to see the order and speed with which these experienced watermen effected the portage, and passed their boats over the cascades. They had arrived at noon, and in the evening they expected to reach Vancouver. These bateaux carry the express of the Hudson Bay Company to the highest navigable point of the North Fork of the Columbia, whence it is carried by an overland party to Lake Winipec, where it is divided; part going to Montreal, and part to Hudson Bay. Thus a regular communication is kept up between three very remote points.

The Canadian emigrants were much chagrined at the change of climate, and informed me that, only a few miles above, they had left a country of bright blue sky and a shining sun. The next morning the upper parts of the mountains which directly overlook the cascades, were white with the freshly fallen snow, while it continued to rain steadily below.

Late in the afternoon we finished the portage, and, embarking again, moved a little distance up the right bank, in order to clear the smaller rapids of the cascades, and have a smooth river for the next morning. Though we made but a few miles, the weather improved immediately; and though the rainy country and the cloudy mountains were close behind, before us was the bright sky; so distinctly is climate here marked by a mountain boundary.

17th.—We had today an opportunity to complete the sketch of that portion of the river down Which we had come by night.

Many places occur along the river, where the stumps, or rather portions of the trunks of pinetrees, are standing along the shore, and in the water, where they may be seen at a considerable depth below the surface, in the beautifully clear water. These collections of dead trees are called on the Columbia the submerged forest, and are supposed to have been created by the effects of some convulsion which formed the cascades, and which, by damming up the river, placed these trees under water and destroyed them. But I venture to presume that the cascades are older than the trees; and as these submerged forests occur at five or six places along the river, I had an opportunity to satisfy myself that they have been formed by immense landslides from the mountains, which here closely shut in the river, and which brought down with them into till; river the pines of the mountain. At one place, on the right bank, I remarked a place where a portion of one of these slides seemed to have planted itself, with all the evergreen foliage, and the vegetation of the neighboring hill, directly amidst the falling and yellow leaves of the river trees. It occurred to me that this would have been a beautiful illustration to the eye of a botanist.

Following the course of a slide, which was very plainly marked along the mountain, I found that in the interior parts she trees were in their usual erect position; but at the extremity of the slide they were rocked about, and thrown into a confusion of inclinations.

About 4 o'clock in the afternoon we passed a sandy bar in the river, whence we had an unexpected view of Mount Hood, bearing directly south by compass.

During the day we used oar and sail, and at night had again a delightful camping ground, and a dry place to sleep upon.

18th.—The day again was pleasant and bright. At 10 o'clock we passed a rock island, on the right shore of the river, which the Indians use as a burial ground; and halting for a short time, about an hour afterwards, at the village of our Indian friends, early in the afternoon we arrived again at the Dalles.

Carson had removed the camp up the river a little nearer the hills, where the animals had better grass. We found every thing in good order, and arrived just in time to partake of an excellent roast of California beef. My friend, Mr. Gilpin, had arrived in advance of the party. His object in visiting this country had been to obtain correct information of the Walahmette [Willamette] settlements; and he had reached this point in his journey, highly pleased with the country over which he had traveled, and with invigorated health. On the following day he continued his journey, in our returning boats, to Vancouver.

The camp was now occupied in making the necessary preparations for our homeward journey, which, though homeward, contemplated a new route, and a great circuit to the south and southeast, and the exploration of the Great Basin between the Rocky mountains and the Sierra Nevada. Three principal objects were indicated, by report or by maps, as being on this route; the character or existence of which I wished to ascertain, and which I assumed as landmarks, or leading points, on the projected line of return. The first of these points was the Klamathlake, on the tableland between the head of Fall river, which comes to the Columbia, and the Sacramento, which goes to the Bay of San Francisco; and from which lake a river of the same name makes its way westwardly direct to the ocean. This lake and river are often called Klamet, but I have chosen to write its name according to the Indian pronunciation. The position of this lake, on the line of inland communication between Oregon and California; its proximity to the demarcation boundary of latitude 42°; its imputed double character of lake, or meadow, according to the season of the year; and the hostile and warlike character attributed to the Indians about it—all made it a desirable object to visit and examine From this lake our course was intended to be about southeast to a reported lake called Mary's, at some days' journey in the Great Basin; and thence, still on southeast, to the reputed Buenaventura river, which has had a place in so many maps, and countenanced the belief of the existence of a great river flowing from the Rocky mountains to the Bay of San Francisco. From the Buenaventura the next point was intended to be in that section of the Rocky mountains which includes the heads of Arkansas river, and of the opposite waters of the Californian gulf; and thence down the Arkansas to Bent's fort, and home. This was our projected line of return—a great part of it absolutely new to geographical, botanical, and geological science—and the subject of reports in relation to lakes, rivers, deserts, and savages hardly above the condition of mere _wild animals, which inflamed desire to know what this terra incognita really contained.

It was a serious enterprise, at the commencement of winter, to undertake the traverse of such a region, and with a party consisting only of twenty-five persons, and they of many nations—American, French, German, Canadian, Indian, and colored and most of them young, several being under twenty-one years of age. All knew that a strange country was to be explored and dangers and hardships to be encountered; tut no one clenched at the prospect. On the contrary, course! and confidence animated the whole party. Cheerfulness, readiness, subordination, prompt obedience, characterized all; nor did any extremity of peril and privation, to which we were afterwards exposed, ever belie, or derogate from, the fine spirit of this brave and generous commencement. The course of the narrative will show at what point, and for what reasons, we were prevented from the complete execution of this plan, after having made considerable progress upon it, and how we were forced by desert plains and mountain ranges, and deep snows, far to the south, and near to the Pacific ocean, and along the western base of the Sierra Nevada, where, indeed, a new and ample field of exploration opened itself before us. For the present, we must follow the narrative, which will first lead . s south along the valley of Fall river, and the eastern base of the Cascade range, to the Klamath lake, from which, or its margin, three rivers go in three directions—on" west, to the ocean; another north, to the Columbia; the third south, to California.

For the support of the party, I had provided at Vancouver a supply of provisions for not less than three months, consisting principally of flour, peas, and tallow—the latter being used in cooking; and, in addition to this, I had purchased at the mission some California cattle, which were to be driven on the hoof. We had 104 mules and horses—part of the latter procured from the Indians about the mission; and for the sustenance of which, our reliance was upon the grass which we should find, and the soft porous wood which was to be substituted when there was none.

Mr. Fitzpatrick, with Mr. Talbat and the remainder of the party, arrived on the 21st; and the camp was now closely engaged in the labor of preparation. Mr. Perkins succeeded in obtaining as a guide to the Klamath lake two Indians—one of whom had been there, and bore the marks of several wounds he had received from some of the Indians in the neighborhood , and the other went along for company. In order to enable us to obtain horses, he dispatched messengers to the various Indian villages in the neighborhood, informing them that we were desirous to purchase, and appointing a day for them to bring them in.

We made, in the mean time, several excursions in the vicinity. Mr. Perkins walked with Mr. Preuss and myself to the heights, about nine miles distant, on the opposite side of the river, whence, in fine weather, an extensive view may be had over the mountains, including seven great peaks of the Cascade range; but clouds, on this occasion, destroyed the anticipated pleasure, and we obtained bearings only to three that were visible—Mount Regnier, St. Helens, and Mount Hood. On the heights, about one mile south of the mission, a very fine view may be had of Mount Hood and St. Helens. In order to determine their position with as much accuracy as possible, the angular distances of the peaks were measured with the sextant, at different fixed points from which they could be seen.

The Indians brought in their horses at the appointed time, and we succeeded in obtaining a number in exchange foi goods; but they were relatively much higher here, where goods are plenty and at moderate prices, than we had found them in the more eastern part of our voyage. Several of the Indians inquired very anxiously to know if we had any dollars; and the horses we procured were much fewer in number than I had desired, and of thin, inferior quality; the oldest and poorest being those that were sold to us. These horses, as ever in our journey you will have occasion to remark, are valuable for hardihood and great endurance.

24th.—At this place one of the men was discharged; and at the request of Mr. Perkins, a Chinook Indian, a lad of nineteen, who was extremely desirous to " see the whites," and make some acquaintance with our institutions, was received into the party under my special charge, with the understanding that I would again return him to his friends. He had lived for some time in the household of Mr. Perkins, and spoke a few words of the English language.

25th.—We were all up early, in the excitement of turning towards home. The stars were brilliant, and the morning cold, the thermometer at daylight 26o.

Our preparations had been fully completed, and today we commenced our journey. The little wagon which had hitherto carried the instruments, I judged it necessary to abandon; and it was accordingly, presented to the mission. In all our long traveling, it had never been overturned or injured by any accident of the road; and the only things broken were the glass lamps, and one of the front panels, which had been kicked out by an unruly Indian horse, The howitzer was the only wheeled carriage now remaining. We started about noon, when the weather had become disagreeably cold, with flurries of snow. Our friend Mr. Perkins, whose kindness had been active and efficient during our stay, accompanied us several riles on our road, when he bade us farewell, and consignee is to the care of our guides. Ascending to the uplands beyond the southern fork of the Tznantns creek, we found the snow lying on the ground in frequent patches, although the pasture appeared good, and the new short grass was fresh and green. We traveled over high, hilly land, and encamped on a little branch of Tinanens creek, where there were good grass and timber. The southern bank was covered with snow, which was scattered over the bottom; and the little creek, its borders lined with ice, had a chilly and wintry look. A number of Indians had accompanied us so far on our road, and remained with us during the night. Two bad looking fellows who were detected in stealing, were tied and laid before the fire, and guard mounted over them during the night. The night was cold, and partially clear.

26th.—The morning was cloudy and misty, and but a few stars visible. During the night water froze in the tents, and at sunrise the thermometer was at 200. Left camp at 10 o'clock, the road leading along tributaries of the Tinanens, and being, so far, very good. We turned to the right at the fork of the trail, ascending by a steep ascent along a spur to the dividing grounds between this stream and the waters of Fall river. The creeks we had passed were timbered principally with oak and other deciduous trees. Snow lies everywhere here on the ground, and we had a slight fall during the morning; air; towards noon the bright sky yielded to a bright sun.

This morning we had a grand view of St. Helens and Regnier, the latter appeared of a conical form, and very lofty, leading the eye far up into the sky. The line of the timbered country is very distinctly marked here, the bare hills making with it a remarkable contrast. The summit of the ridge commanded a fine view of the Taih prairie, and the stream running through it, which is a tributary to the Fall river, the chasm of which is visible to the right. A steep descent of a mountain hill brought us down into the valley, and we encamped on the stream after dark, guided by the light of fires, which some naked Indians, belonging to a village on the opposite side, were kindling for us on the bank. This is a large branch of the Fall river. There was a broad band of thick ice some fifteen feet wide on either bank, and the river current is swift and bold. The night was cold and clear, and we made our astronomical observation this evening with the thermometer at 200.

In anticipation of coming hardship, and to spare our horses, there was much walking done today; and Mr. Fitzpatrick and myself made the day's journey on foot. Somewhere near the mouth of this stream are the falls from which the river takes its name.

27th.—A fine view of Mount Hood this morning; a rose colored mass of snow, bearing S. 850 W. by compass. The sky is clear, and the air cold; the thermometer 2.50 below zero, the trees and bushes glittering white, and the raid stream filled with floating ice.

Stiletsi and the White Crane, two Indian chiefs who had accompanied us thus far, took their leave, and we resumed our journey at 10 o'clock. We ascended by a steep hill from the river bottom, which is sandy, to a volcanic plain, around which lofty, hills sweep in a regular form. It is cut up by gullies of basaltic rock, escarpments of which appear everywhere in the hills. This plain is called the Taih prairie, and is sprinkled with some scattered pines. The country is now far more interesting to a traveler than the route along the Snake and Columbia rivers. To our right we had always the mountains, from the midst of whose dark pine forests the isolated snowy peaks were looking nut like giants. They served us for grand boa cons to show the rate at which we advanced in our journey. Mount Hood was already becoming an old acquaintance, and, when we ascended the prairie, we obtained a bearing to Mount Jefferson, S. 230 W. The Indian superstition has peopled these lofty peaks with evil spirits, and they have never yet known the tread of a human foot. Sternly drawn against the sky, they look so high and steep, so snowy and rocky, that it appears almost impossible to climb them; but still a trial would have its attractions for the adventurous traveler. A small trail takes off through the prairie, towards a low point in the range, and perhaps there is here a pass into the Wahlamette valley. Crossing the plain, we descended by a rocky hill into the bed of a tributary of Fall river, and made an early encampment. The water was in holes, and frozen over; and we were obliged to cut through the ice for the animals to drink. An ox, which was rather troublesome to drive, was killed here for food.

The evening was fine, the sky being very clear, and I obtained an immersion of the third satellite, with a good observation of an emersion of the first; the latter of which gives for the longitude, 1210 02' 43"; the latitude, by observation, being 450 06' 45". The night was cold—the thermometer during the observations standing at 90.

28th.—The sky was clear in the morning, but suddenly clouded over, and at sunrise it began to snow, with the thermometer at 180.

We traversed a broken high country, partly timbered with pine, and about noon crossed a mountainous ridge, in which, from the rock occasionally displayed, the formation consists of compact lava. Frequent tracks of elk were visible in the snow. On our right, in the afternoon, a high plain, partially covered with pine, extended about ten miles, to the foot of the Cascade mountains.

At evening we encamped in a basin narrowly surrounded by rocky hills, after a day's journey of twenty-one miles. The surrounding rocks ate either volcanic products, nr highly altered by volcanic action, consisting of quartz and reddish colored silicious masses.

29th. We emerged from the basin, by a narrow pass, upon a considerable branch of Fall river, running to the eastward through a narrow valley. The trail, descending this stream, brought us to a locality of hot springs, which were on either bank. Those on the left, which were formed into deep handsome basins, would have been delightful baths, if the outer air had not been so keen, the thermometer in these being at 890. There were others on the opposite side, at the foot of an escarpment, in which the temperature of the water was 1340. These waters deposited around the spring a brecciated mass of quartz and feldspar, much of it of a reddish color.

We crossed the stream here, and ascended again to a high plain, from an elevated point of which we obtained a view of six of the great peaks—Mount Jefferson, followed to the southward by two others of the same class; and succeeding, at a still greater distance to the southward, were three other lower peaks, clustering together in a branch ridge. These, like the great peaks, were snowy masses, secondary only to them; and, from the best examination our time permitted, we are inclined to believe that the range to which they belong is a branch from the great chain which here bears to the westward. The trail, during the remainder of the day, followed near to the large stream on the left, which was continuously walled in between high rocky banks. We halted for the night on a little by stream.

30th.—Our journey today was short. Passing over a high plain, on which were scattered cedars, with frequent beds of volcanic rock in fragments interspersed among the grassy grounds, we arrived suddenly on the verge of the steep and rocky descent to the valley of the stream we had been following, and which here ran directly across our path, emerging from the mountains on the right. You will remark that the country is abundantly watered with large streams, which pour down from the neighboring range.

These streams are characterized by the narrow and chasm like valleys in which they run, generally sunk a thousand feet below the plain. At the verge of this plain, they frequently commence in vertical precipices of basaltic rock, and which leave only casual places at which they can be entered by horses. The road across the country, which would otherwise be very good, is rendered impracticable for wagons by these streams. There is another trail among the mountains, usually followed in the summer, which the snows now compelled us tc avoid; and I have reason to believe that this, passing nearer the heads of these streams, would afford a much better road.

At such places, the gun carriage was unlimbered, and separately descended by hand. Continuing a few miles up the left bank of the river, we camped early in an open bottom among the pines, a short distance below a lodge of Indians. Here, along the river the bluffs present escarpments seven or eight hundred feet in height, containing strata of a very fine porcelain clay, overlaid, at the height of about five hundred feet, by a massive stratum of compact basalt one hundred feet in thickness, which again is succeeded above by other strata of volcanic rocks. The clay strata are variously colored, some of them very nearly as white as chalk, and very fine-grained. Specimens brought from these have been subjected to microscopical examination by Professor Bailey, of West Point, and are considered by him to constitute one of the most remarkable deposites of fluviatile infusoria on record. While they abound in genera and species which are common in fresh water, but which rarely thrive where the water is even brackish, not one decidedly marine form is to be found among them; and their freshwater origin is therefore beyond a doubt. It is equally certain that they lived and died at the situation where they were found, as they could scarcely have been transported by running waters without an admixture of sandy particles; from which, however, they are remarkably free. Fossil infusoria of a freshwater origin had been previously detected by Mr. Bailey, in specimens brought by Mr. James D. Dana from the tertiary formation of Oregon. Most of the species in those specimens differed so much from those now living and known, that he was led to infer that they might belong to extinct species, and considered them also as affording proof of an alteration, in the formation from which they were obtained, of fresh and saltwater deposites, which, common enough in Europe, had not hitherto been noticed in the United States. Coming evidently from a locality entirely different, our specimens show very few species in common with those brought by Mr. Dana, but bear a much closer resemblance to those inhabiting the northeastern states. It is possible that they are from a more recent deposite; but the presence of a few remarkable forms which are common to the two localities renders it more probable that there is no great difference in their age.

I obtained here a good observation of an emersion of the second satellite; but clouds, which rapidly overspread the sky, prevented the usual number of observations. Those which we succeeded in obtaining, are, however, good; and give for the latitude of the place 440 35' 23", and for the longitude from the satellite 1210 10' 25".

DECEMBER.

1st.—A short distance above our encampment, we crossed the river, which was thickly lined along its banks with ice.. In common with all these mountain streams the water was very clear and the current swift. It was not everywhere fordable, and the water was three or four feet deep at our crossing, and perhaps a hundred feet wide. As was frequently the case at such places, one of the mules got his pack, consisting of sugar, thoroughly wet, and turned into molasses. One of the guides informed me that this was a " salmon water," and pointed out several ingeniously contrived places to catch the fish; among the pines in the bottom I saw an immense one, about twelve feet in diameter. A steep ascent from the opposite bank delayed us again; and as, by the information of our guides, grass would soon become very scarce, we encamped on the height of land, in a marshy place among the pines, where there was an abundance of grass. We found here a single Nez Perce family, who had a very handsome horse in their drove, which we endeavored to obtain in exchange for 6 good cow; but the man " had two hearts," or, rather, he had one and his wife had another: she wanted the cow, but he loved the horse too much to part with it. These people attach great value to cattle, with which they are endeavoring to supply themselves.

2d.—In the first rays of the sun, the mountain peaks this morning presented a beautiful appearance, the snow being entirely covered with a hue of rosy gold. We traveled today over a very stony, elevated plain, about which were scattered cedar and pine, and encamped on another branch of Fall river

We were gradually ascending to a more elevated region, which would have been indicated by the rapidly increasing quantities of snow and ice, had we not known it by other means. A mule, which was packed with our cooking utensils, wandered off among the pines unperceived, and several men were sent back to search for it.

3d.—Leaving Mr. Fitzpatrick with the party, I went ahead with the howitzer and, a few men, in order to gain time, as our progress with the gun was necessarily slower. The country continued the same— very stony, with cedar and pine; and we rode on until dark, when we encamped on a hillside covered with snow, which we used tonight for water, as we were unable to reach any stream.

4th.—Our animals had taken the back track, although a great number were hobbled; and we were consequently de layed until noon. Shortly after we had left this encampment, the mountain trail from the Dalles joined that on which we were traveling. After passing for several miles over an arte misia plain, the trail entered a beautiful pine forest, through which we traveled for several hours;

and about 4 o'clock descended into the valley of another large branch, on the bottom of which were spaces of open pines, with occasional meadows of good grass, in one of which we encamped. The stream is very swift and deep, and about 40 feet wide, and nearly half frozen over. Among the timber here, are larches 140 feet high, and over three feet in diameter. We had tonight the rare sight of a lunar rainbow.

5th.—Today the country was all pine forest, and beautiful weather made our journey delightful. It was ton warm at noon for winter clothes; and the snow, which lay everywhere in patches through the forest, was melting rapidly. After a few hours' ride, we came upon a fine stream in the midst of the forest, which proved to be the principal branch of the Fall river. It was occasionally 200 feet wide— sometimes narrowed to 50 feet—the waters very clear, and frequently deep. We ascended along the river, which sometimes presented sheets _ of foaming cascades—its banks occasionally blackened with masses of scoriated rock—and found a good encampment on the verge of open bottom, which had been an old camping ground of the Cayuse Indians. A great number of deer horns were lying about, indicating game in the neighborhood. The timber was uniformly large, some 3. the pines measuring 22 feet in circumference at the ground, and 12 to 13 feet at six feet above.

In all our journeying, we had never traveled through a country where the rivers were so abounding in falls; and the name of this stream is singularly characteristic. At every place where we come in the neighborhood of the river, is heard the roaring of falls. The rock along the banks of the stream, and the ledge over which it falls, is a scoriated basalt, with a bright metallic fracture. The stream goes over in one clear pitch, succeeded by a foaming cataract of several hundred yards. In a little bottom above the falls, a small stream discharges into an erdonnoir, and disappears below.

We made an early encampment, and in the course of the evening Mr. Fitzpatrick joined us here with the lost mule. Our lodgepoles were nearly worn out, and we found here a handsome set, leaning against one bf the trees, very white and cleanly scraped. Had the owners been here, we would have purchased them; but as they were not, we merely left the old ones in their place, with a small quantity of tobacco.

6th.—The morning was frosty and clear. We continued up the stream on undulating forest ground, over which there was scattered much falling timber. We met here a village of Nez Perce Indians, who appeared to be coming down from the mountains, and had with them fine bands of horses. With them we re a few Snake Indians of the root digging species. Prove the forest we emerged into an open valley ten or twelve miles wide, through which the stream was flowing tranquilly, upwards of two hundred feet broad, with occasional islands, and bordered with fine broad bottoms. Crossing the river, which here issues from a great mountain ridge on the right, we continued up the southern and smaller branch over a level country, consisting of fine meadowland, alternating with pine forests, and encamped on it early in the evening. A warm sunshine made the day pleasant.

7th.—Today we had good traveling ground, the trail leading sometimes over rather sandy soils in the pine forest, and sometimes over meadowland along the stream. The great beauty of the country in summer constantly suggested itself to our imaginations; and even now we found it beautiful, as we rode along these meadows, from half a mile to two miles wide. The rich soil and excellent water, surrounded by noble forests, make a picture that would delight the eye of a farmer.

I observed tonight an occultation of a Geminorum; which, although at the bright limb of the moon, appears to give a very good result, that has been adopted for the longitude. The occultation, observations of satellites, and our position deduced from daily surveys with the compass, agree remarkably well together, and mutually support and strengthen each other. The latitude of the camp is 43° 30′ 36″; and longitude, deduced from the occultation, 121° 33′ 50″.

8th.—Today we crossed the last branch of the Fall river, issuing, like all the others we had crossed, in a southwesterly direction from the mountains. Our direction was a little east of south, the trail leading constantly through pine forests. The soil was generally barei consisting, in greater part, of a yellowish white pumice stone, producing varieties of magnificent pines, but not a blade of grass; and tonight our horses were obliged to do without food, and use snow for water. These pines are remarkable for the red color of the bolls; and among them occurs a species of which the Indians had informed me when leaving the Dalles. The unusual size of the cone (16 or 18 inches long) had attracted their attention; and they pointed it out to me among the curiosities of the country. They are more remarkable for their large diameter than their height, which usually averages only about 120 feet. The leaflets are short—only two or three inches long, and five in a sheath; the bark of a red color.

9th.—The trail leads always through splendid pine forests. Crossing dividing grounds by a very fine road, we descended very gently towards the south. The weather was pleasant, and we halted late. The soil was very much like that of yesterday; and on the surface of a hill near our encampment, were displayed beds of pumice stone; but the soil produced no grass, and again the animals fared badly.

10th.—The country began to improve; and about eleven o'clock we reached a spring of cold water on the edge of a savannah, or grassy meadow, which our guides informed us was an arm of the Klamath lake; and a few miles further we entered upon an extensive meadow, or lake of grass, surrounded by timbered mountains. This was the Klamath lake. It was a picturesque and beautiful spot, and rendered more attractive to us by the abundant and excellent grass, which our animals, after traveling through pine forests, so much needed; but the broad sheet of water which constitutes a lake was not to be seen. Overlooking it, immediately west, were several snowy knobs, belonging to what we have considered a branch of the Cascade range. A low point, covered with pines, made out into the lake, which afforded us a good place for an encampment, and for the security of our horses, which were guarded in view on the open meadow. The character of courage and hostility attributed to the Indians in this quarter induced more than usual precaution; and, seeing smokes rising from the middle of the lake (or savannah) and along the opposite shores, I directed the howitzer to be fired. It was the first time our guides had seen it discharged; and the bursting of the shell at a distance, which was something like the second fire of the gun, amazed and bewildered them with delight. It inspired them with triumphant feelings; but on the camps at a distance the effect was different, for the smokes in the lake and on the shores immediately disappeared.

The point on which we were encamped forms, with the opposite eastern shore, a narrow neck, connecting the body of the lake with a deep cove or bay which receives the principal affluent stream, and over the greater part of which the water (or rather ice) was at this time dispersed in shallow pools. Among the grass, and scattered over the prairie lake, appeared to be similar marshes. It is simply a shallow basin, which, for a short period at the time of melting snows, is covered with water from, the neighboring mountains; but this probably soon runs off, and leaves for the remainder of the year a green savannah, through the midst of which the river Klamath, which flows to the ocean, winds its way to the outlet on the southwestern side.

11th.—No Indians made their appearance, and I determined to pay them a visit. Accordingly the people were gathered together, and we rode out towards the village in the middle of the lake which one of our guide's had previously visited. It could not be directly approached, as a large part of the lake appeared a marsh; and there were sheets of ice among the grass on which our horses could not keep their footing. We therefore followed the guide for a considerable distance along the forest; and then turned off towards the village, which we soon began to see was a few large huts, on the tops of which were collected the Indians. When we had arrived within half a mile of the village, two persons were seen advancing to meet us; and, to please the fancy of our guides, we ranged ourselves into a long line, riding abreast, while they galloped ahead to meet the strangers.

We were surprised, on riding up, to find one of them a woman, having never before known a squaw to take any part in the business of war. They were the village chief and his wife, who, in excitement and alarm at the unusual event and appearance, had come out to meet their fate together. The chief was a very prepossessing Indian, with handsome features, and a singularly soft and agreeable voice—so remarkable as to attract general notice.

The huts were grouped together on the bank of the river which, from being spread out in a shallow marsh at the upper end of the lake, was collected here into a single stream. They were large round huts, perhaps 20 feet in diameter, with rounded tops, on which was the door by which "they descended into the interior. Within, they were supported by poste and beams.

Almost like plants, these people seem to have adapted them, selves to the soil, 'And to be growing on what the immediate locality afforded. Their only subsistence at the time appeared to be a small fish, great quantities of which, that had beer smoked and dried, were suspended on strings about the lodge. Heaps of straw were lying around; and their residence in the midst of grass and rushes had taught them a peculiar skill in converting this material to useful purposes. Their shoes were made of straw or grass, which seemed well adapted for a snowy country; and the women wore on their heads a closely woven basket, which made a very good cap. Among °the] things, were particolored mats about four feet square, which we purchased to lay on the snow under our blankets, and tc use for tablecloths.

Numbers of singular looking dogs, resembling wolves, were sitting on the tops of the huts; and of these we purchased e young one, which, after its birthplace, was named Klamath. The language spoken by these Indians is different from that of the Shoshonee and Columbia River tribes; and otherwise Olen by signs they cannot understand each other. They made us comprehend that they were at war with the people who lived to the southward and to the eastward; but I could obtain from them no certain information. The river on which they live enters the Cascade mountains on the western side of the lake, and breaks through them by a passage impracticable fox travelers; but over the mountains, to the northward, are passes which present no other obstacle than in the almost impenetrable forests. Unlike any Indians we had previously seen, these wore shells in their noses. We returned to our camp, after remaining here an hour or two, accompanied by a number of Indians.

In order to recruit a little the strength of our animals, and obtain some acquaintance with the locality, we remained here for the remainder of the day. By observation, the latitude of the camp was 420 56' 51", and the diameter of the lake, or meadow; as has been intimated, about 20 miles. It is a picturesque and beautiful spot, and, under the hand of cultivation, might become a little paradise. Game is found in the forest, timbered and snowy mountains skirt it, and fertility characterizes it. Situated near the heads of three rivers, and on the line of /inland communication with California, and near to Indians noted for treachery, it will naturally, in, the progress of the settlement of Oregon, become a point for military occupation and settlement.

From Klamathlake, the further continuation of our voyage assumed a character of discovery and exploration, which, from the Indians here, we could obtain no information to direct, and where the imaginary maps of the country, instead of assisting, exposed us to suffering and defeat. In our journey across the desert, Mary's lake, and the famous 'Buenaventura river, were two points on which I relied to recruit the animals and repose the party. Forming, agreeably to the best maps in my possession, a connected waterline from the Rocky mountains tc the Pacific ocean, I felt no other anxiety than to pass safely across the intervening desert to the banks of the Buenaventura, where, in the softer climate of a more southern latitude, out Horses might find grass to sustain them, and ourselves be sheltered from the rigors of winter, and from the inhospitable desert. The guides who had conducted us thus far on our journey were about to return; and I endeavored in vain to obtain others to lead us, even for a few days, in the direction (east) which we wished to go. The chief to whom I applied alleged the want of horses, and the snow on the mountains across which our course would carry us, and the sickness of his family, as reasons for refusing to go with us.

12th.—This morning the camp was thronged with Klamath Indians from the southeastern shore of the lake; but, knowing the treacherous disposition which is a remarkable characteristic of the

Indians south of the Columbia, the camp was kept constantly on its guard. I was not unmindful cf the disasters which Smith and other travelers had met with in this country, and therefore was equally vigilant in guarding against treachery and violence.

According to the best information I had been able to obtain from the Indians, in a few days' traveling we should reach another large water, probably a lake, which they indicated exactly in the course we were about to pursue. We struck our tents at 10 o'clock, and crossed the lake in a nearly east direction, where it has the least extension—the breadth of the arm being here only about a mile and a half. There were ponds of ice, with but little grass, for the greater part of the way, and it was difficult to get the pack animals across, which fell frequently, and could not get up with their loads, unassisted. The morning was very unpleasant, snow falling at intervals in large flakes, and the sky dark. In about two hours we succeeded in getting the animals over; and, after traveling another hour along the eastern shore of the lake, we turned up into a cove where there was a sheltered place among the timber, with good grass, and encamped. The Indians, who had accompanied us so far, returned to their village on the southeastern shore. Among the pines here, I noticed some five or six feet in diameter.

13th.—The night has been cold; the peaks around the lake gleam out brightly in the morning sun, and the thermometer is at zero. We continued up the hollow formed by a small affluent to the lake, and immediately entered an open pine forest on the mountain. The way here was sometimes obstructed by fallen trees, and the snow was four to twelve inches deep. The mules at the gun pulled heavily, and walking was a little laborious. In the midst of the wood, we heard the sound of galloping horses, and were agreeably surprised by the unexpected arrival of our Klamath chief with several Indians. He seemed to have found his conduct inhospitable in letting the strangers depart without a guide through the snow, and had come, with a few others, to pilot us a day or two on the way. After traveling in an easterly direction through the forest fox about four hours, we reached a considerable stream, with an order of good grass; and here, by the advice of our guides; we encamped. It is about thirty feet wide, and two to foul feet deep, the water clear, with some current; and, according to the information of our Indians, is the principal affluent to the lake, and the headwater of the Klamath river.

A very clear sky enabled me to obtain here tonight good observations, including an emersion of the first satellite of Jupiter, which gave for the long. 1210 20' 42", and for the lat. 420 51' 26". This emersion coincides remarkably well with the result obtained from an occultation at the encampment of December 7th to 8th, 1843; from which place, the line of our survey gives an easting of 13 miles. The day's journey was 12 miles.

14th.—Our road was over a broad mountain, and we rode seven hours in a thick snowstorm, always through pine forests, when we came down upon the headwaters of another stream, on which there was grass. The snow lay deep on the ground, and only the high swamp grass appeared above. The Indians were thinly clad, and I had remarked during the day that they suffered from cold. This evening they told me that the snow was getting too deep on the mountain, and I could not induce them to go any farther. The stream we had struck issued from the mountain in an easterly direction, turning to the southward a short distance below; and, drawing its course upon the ground, they made us comprehend that it pursued its way for a long distance in that direction, uniting with many other streams, and gradually becoming a great river. Without the subsequent information, which confirmed the opinion, we became immediately satisfied that this water formed the principal stream of the Sacramento river; and, consequently, that this main affluent of the bay of San Francisco had its source within the limits of the United States, and opposite a tributary to the Columbia, and near the head of the Klamath river, which goes to the ocean north of 420, and within the United States.

15th. A present, consisting of useful goods, afforded much satisfaction to our guides; and, showing them the national flag, I explained that it was a symbol of our nation; and they engaged always to receive it in a friendly manner. The chief pointed out a course, by following which we would arrive at the big water, where no more snow was to be found. Traveling in a direction N. 60o E. by compass, which the Indians informed me would avoid a bad mountain to the right, we crossed the Sacramento where it turned to the southward, and entered a grassy level plain—a smaller Grand Rond; from the lower end of which the river issued into an inviting country of low rolling hills. Crossing a hard frozen swamp on the farther side of the Rond, we entered again the pine forest, in which very deep snow made our traveling slow and laborious. We were slowly but gradually ascending a mountain; and; after a hard journey of seven hours, we came to some naked places among the timber, where a few tufts of grass showed above the snow, on the side of a hollow; and here we encamped. Our cow, which every day got poorer, was killed here, but the meat was rather tough.

16th.—We traveled this morning through snow about three feet deep, which, being crusted, very much cut the feet of our animals. The mountain still gradually rose; we crossed several spring heads covered with quaking asp; otherwise it was all pine forest. The air was dark with falling snow, which everywhere weighed down the trees. The depths of the forest were profoundly still; and below, we scarcely felt a breath of the wind which whirled the snow through their branches. I found that it required some exertion of constancy to adhere steadily to one course through the woods, when we were uncertain how far the forest extended, or what lay beyond; and, on account of our animals, it would be bad to spend another night on the mountain. Towards noon the forest looked clear ahead, appearing suddenly to terminate; and beyond a certain point we could see no trees. Riding rapidly ahead to this spot, we found ourselves on the verge of a vertical and rocky wall of the mountain. At our feet—more than a thousand feet below—we looked into a green prairie country, in which a beautiful lake, some twenty miles in length, was spread along the foot of the mountains, its shores bordered with green grass. Just then the sun broke out among the clouds, and illuminated the country below, while around us the storm raged fiercely_ Not a particle of ice was to be seen en the lake, or snow on its borders, and all was like summer or spring. The glow of the sun in the valley below brightened up our hearts with sudden pleasure; and we made the woods ring with joyful shouts to those behind; and gradually, as each came up, he stopped to enjoy the unexpected scene. Shivering on snow three fee: deep, and stiffening in a cold north wind, we exclaimed at once that the names of Summer Lake and Winter Ridge should be applied to these two proximate places of such sudden and violent contrast.

We were now immediately on the verge of the forest land, in which we had been traveling so many days; and, looking forward to the east, scarce a tree was to be seen. Viewed from our elevation, the face of the country exhibited only rocks and grass, and presented a region in which the artemisia became the principal wood, furnishing to its scattered inhabitants fuel for their fires, building material for their huts, and shelter for the small game which ministers to their hunger and nakedness. Broadly marked by the boundary at the mountain wall, and immediately below us, were the first waters of that Great Interior Basin which has the Wahsatct and Bear River mountains for its eastern, and the Sierra Nevada for its western rim; and the edge of which we had entered upwards of three months before, at the Great Salt Lake.

When we had sufficiently admired the scene below, we began to think about descending, which here was impossible, and we turned towards the north, traveling always along the rocky wall. We continues on for four or five miles, making ineffectual attempts at several places; and at length succeeded in getting down at one which was extremely difficult of descent. Night had closed in 'before the foremost reached the bottom, and it was dark before we all found ourselves together in the valley. There were three or four half dead dry cedar trees on the shore, and those who first arrived kindled bright fires to light on the others. One of the mules rolled over and over two or three hundred feet into a ravine, but recovered himself without any other injury than to his pack; and the howitzer was left midway the mountain until morning. By observation, the latitude of this encampment is 42° 57' 22". It delwed us until near noon the next day to recover ourselves and put every thing in order; and we made only a short camp along the western shore of the lake, which, in the summer temperature we enjoyed today, justified the name we had given it. Our course would have taken us to the other shore, and oyez the highlands beyond; but I distrusted the appearance of the country, and decided to follow a plainly beaten Indian trail leading along this side of the lake. We were now in a country where the scarcity of water and of grass makes traveling dangerous, and great caution was necessary.

18th.—We continued on the trail along the narrow strip of land between the lake and the high rocky wall, from which we had looked down two days before. Almost every half mile we crossed a little spring, or stream of pure cold water, and the grass was certainly as fresh and green as in the early spying. From the white efflorescence along the shore of the lake, we were enabled to judge that the water was impure, like that of lakes we subsequently found, but the mud prevented us from approaching it. We encamped near the eastern point of the lake, where there appeared between the hills a broad and low connecting hollow with the country beyond. From a rocky hill in the rear, I could see, marked out by a line of yellow dried grass, the bed of a stream, which probably connected the lake with other waters in the spring.

The observed latitude of this encampment is 420 42' 37".

19th.—After two hours' ride in an easterly direction, through a low country, the high ridge with pine forest still to our right, and a rocky and bald but lower one on the left, we reached a considerable freshwater stream, which issues from the piny mountains. So far as we had been able to judge, between this stream and the lake we had crossed dividing grounds, and there did not appear to be any connection, as might be inferred from the impure condition of the lake water.

The rapid stream of pure water, roaring along between flanks overhung with aspens and willows, was a refreshing and unexpected sight; and we followed down the course of the stream, which brought us soon into a marsh, or dry lake; farmed by the expanding waters of the stream. It was cover ed with high reeds and rushes, and large patches of ground had been turned up by the squaws in digging for roots, as if a farmer had been preparing the land for grain. I could not succeed in finding the plant for which they had been digging. There were frequent trails, and fresh tracks of Indians;

and, from the abundant signs visible, the black tailed hare appears to be numerous here. It was evident that, in other seasons, this place was a sheet of water. Crossing this marsh towards the eastern hills, and passing over a bordering plain of heavy sands, covered with artemisia, we encamped before sundown on the creek, which here was very small, having lost its water in the marshy grounds. We found here tolerably good grass. The wind tonight was high, and we had no longer our huge pine fires, but were driven to our old resource of small dried willows and artemisia. About 12 miles ahead, the valley ap pears to be closed in by a high, dark looking ridge.

20th.—Traveling for a few hours down the stream this morning, we turned the point of a hill on our left, and came suddenly in sight of another and much larger lake, which, along its eastern shore, was closely bordered by the high black ridge which walled it in by a precipitous face on this side. Throughout this region the face of the country is characterized by these precipices of black volcanic rock, generally enclosing the valleys of streams, and frequently terminating the hills. Often, in the course of our journey, we would be tempted to continue our road up the gentle ascent of a sloping hill, which, at the summit, would terminate abruptly in a black precipice Spread out over a length of 20 miles, the lake, when we first came in view, presented a handsome sheet of water, and I gave to it the name of Lake Albert, in honor of the chief of the corps to which I belonged. The freshwater stream we had followed emptied into the lake by a little fall; and I was doubtful for a moment whether to go on, or encamp at this place. The miry ground in the neighborhood of the lake did not allow us to examine the water conveniently, and, being now on the borders of a desert country, we were moving cautiously. It was, however, still early in the day, and I continued on trusting either that the water would be drinkable or that we should find some little spring from the hillside. We were following an Indian trail which led along the steep rocky precipice—a black ridge along the western shore holding out no prospect whatever. The white efflorescences which lined the shore like a bank of snow, and the disagreeable odor which filled the air as soon as we came near, informed us too plainly that the water belonged to one of those fetid salt lakes which are common in this region. We continued until late in the evening to work along the rocky shore, but, as often afterwards, the dry, inhospitable rock deceived us; and, halting on the lake, we kindled up fires, to guide those who were straggling along behind. We tried the water, but it was impossible to drink it, and most of the people tonight lay down without eating; but some of us, who had always a great reluctance to of)se the day without supper, dug holes along the shore, and obtained water, which, being filtered, was sufficiently palatable to be used, but still retained much of its nauseating taste. There was very little grass for the animals, the shore being lined with a luxuriant growth of chenopodiaceous shrubs, which burned with a quick bright flame, and made our firewood.

The next morning we had scarcely traveled two hours along the shore, when we reached a place where the mountains made a bay, leaving at their feet a low bottom around the lake. Here we found numerous hillocks covered with rushes, in the midst of which were deep holes, or springs, of pure water; and the bottom was covered with grass, which, although of a salt and unwholesome quality, and mixed with saline efflorescences, was still abundant, and made a good halting place to recruit our animals, and we accordingly encamped here for the remainder of the day. I rode ahead several miles to ascertain if there was any appearance of a watercourse entering the lake, but found none, the hills preserving their dry character, and the shore of the lake sprinkled with the same white powdery substance, and covered with the same shrubs. There were flocks of ducks on the lake, and frequent tracks of Indians along the shore, where the grass had been recently burn! by their fires.

We ascended the bordering mountain, in order to obtain a more perfect view of the lake, in sketching its figure: hills sweep entirely around its basin, from which the waters have no outlet.

22d.—Today we left this forbidding lake. Impassable rocky ridges barred our progress to the eastward, and I accordingly bore off towards the south, over an extensive sage plain. At a considerable distance ahead, and a little on our left, was a range of snowy mountains, and the country declined gradually towards the foot of a high and nearer ridge, immediately before us, which presented the feature of black precipices now becoming common to the country. On the summit of the ridge, snow was visible; and there being every indication of a stream at its base, we rode on until after dark, but were unable to reach it, and halted among the sage bushes on the open plain, without either grass or water. The two India rubber bags had been filled with water in the morning, which afforded sufficient for the camp; and rain in the night formed pools, which relieved the thirst of the animals. Where we encamped on the bleak sandy plain, the Indians had made huts or circular enclosures, about four feet high and twelve feet broad, of artemisia bushes. Whether these had been forts or houses, or what they had been doing in such a desert place, we could not ascertain.

23d.—The weather is mild; the thermometer at daylight 38°; the wind having been from the southward for several days. The county has a very forbidding appearance, presenting to the eye nothing but sage, and barren ridges. We rode up towards the mountain, along the foot of which we found a lake, that we could not approach on account of the mud; and, passing around its southern end, ascended the slope at the foot of the ridge, where in some hollows we had discovered bushes and small trees—in such situations, a sure sign of water. We found here several springs, and the hillside was well sprinkled with a species offestuca—a better grass than we had found for many days. Our elevated position gave us a good view over the country, but we discovered nothing very encouraging Southward, about ten miles distant, was another small lake, towards which a broad trail led along the ridge; and this appearing to afford the most practicable route, I determined to continue our journey in that direction.

24th.—We found the water at the lake tolerably putt, ana encamped at the farther end. There were some good grass and canes alcng the shore, and the vegetables at this place consisted principally of chenopodiaceous shrubs.

25th.—We were roused on Christmas morning by a discharge from the small arms and howitzer, with which our people saluted the day; and the name of which we bestowed on the lake. It was the first time, perhaps, in this remote and desolate region, in which it had been so commemorated. Always, on days of religious or national commemoration, our voyageurs expect some unusual allowance; and having nothing else, I gave them each a little brandy, (which was carefully guarded, as one of the most useful articles a traveler can carry,) with some coffee and sugar, which here, where every eatable was a luxury, was sufficient to make them a feast. The day was sunny and warm; and resuming our journey, we crossed some slight dividing grounds into a similar basin, walled in on the right by a lofty mountain ridge. The plainly beaten trail still continued, and occasionally we passed camping grounds of the Indians, which indicated to me that we were on one of the great thoroughfares of the country. In the afternoon I attempted to travel in a more eastern direction; but after a few laborious miles, was beaten back into the basin by an impassable country. There were fresh Indian tracks about the valley, and last night a horse was stolen. We encamped in the valley bottom, where there was some creamlike water in ponds, colored by a clay soil, and frozen over. Chenopodiaceous shrubs constituted the growth, and made again our firewood. The animals were driven to the hill, where there was tolerably good grass.

26th.—Our general course was again south. The country consists of larger or smaller basins, into which the mountain waters run down, forming small lakes: they present a perfect level, from which the mountains rise immediately and abruptly. Between the successive basins, the dividing grounds are usually very slight; and it is probable that in the seasons of high water, many of these basins are in communication. At such times there is evidently an abundance of water, though now we find scarcely more than the dry beds. On either aide, the mountains, though not very high, appear to be rocky and sterile. The basin in which we were traveling declined towards the southwest corner, where the mountains indicated a narrow outlet; and, turning round a rocky point or cape, we continued up a lateral branch valley, in which we encamped at night, on a rapid, pretty little stream of fresh water, which we found unexpectedly among the sage, near the ridge, on the right side of the valley. It was bordered with grassy bottoms and clumps of willows; the water partially frozen. This stream belongs to the basin we had left. By a partial observation tonight, our camp was found to be directly on the 42d parallel. Tonight a horse belonging to Carson, one of the best we had in the camp, was stolen by the Indians.

27th.—We continued up the valley of the stream, the principal branch of which here issues from a bed of high mountains. We turned up a branch to the left, and fell into an Indian trail, which conducted us by a good road over open bottoms along the creek, where the snow was five or six inches deep. Gradually ascending, the trail led through a good broad pass in the mountain, where we found the snow about one foot deep. There were some remarkably large cedars in the pass, which were covered with an unusual quantity of frost, which we supposed might possibly indicate the neighborhood of water; and as, in the arbitrary position of Mary's lake, we were already beginning tc look for it, this circumstance contributed to our hope of finding it near. Descending from the mountain, we reached another basin, on the flat lake bed of which we found no water, and encamped among the sage on the bordering plain, where the snow was still about one foot deep. Among this the grass was remarkably green, and tonight the animals fared tolerably well.

28th.—The snow being deep, I had determined, if any more horses were stolen, to follow the tracks of the Indians into the mountains, and put a temporary check to their sly operations; but it did not occur again.

Our road this morning lay down t level valley, bordered by steep mountainous ridges, rising ry abrupt!), from the plain. Artemisia was the principal plant, mingled with Fremontia and the chenopodiaceous shrubs. The artemisia was here extremely large, being sometimes a foot in diameter, and eight feet high. Riding quietly along over the snow, we came suddenly upon smokes rising among these bushes; and, galloping up, we found two huts, open at the top, and loosely built of sage, which appeared to have been deserted at the instant; and, looking hastily around, we saw several Indians on the crest of the ridge near by, and several others scrambling up the side. We had come upon them so suddenly, that they had been well-nigh surprised in their lodges. A sage fire was burning in the middle; a few baskets made of straw were lying about, with one or two rabbit skins; and there was a little grass scattered about, on which they had been lying. " Tabibo—bo!" they shouted from the hills—a word which, in the Snake language, signifies white—and remained looking at us from behind the rocks. Carson and Godey rode towards the hill, but the men ran off like deer. They had been so much pressed, that a woman with two children had dropped behind a sagebrush near the lodge, and when Carson accidentally stumbled upon her, she immediately began screaming in the extremity of fear, and shut her eyes fast to avoid seeing him. She was brought back to the lodge, and we endeavored in vain to open a communication with the men. By dint of presents, and friendly demonstrations, she was brought to calmness; and we found that they belonged to the Snake nation, speaking the language of that people. Eight or ten appeared to live together, under the same little shelter; and they seemed to have no other subsistence than the roots or seeds they might have stored up, and the hares which live in the sage, and which they are enabled to track through the snow, and are very skilful in killing. Their skins afford them a little scanty covering. Herding together among bushes, and crouching almost naked over a little sage fire, using their instinct only to procure food, these may be considered, among human beings, the nearest approach to the animal creation. We have reason to believe that these had never before seen the face of a white man.

The day la I been pleasant, but about two o'clock it began blow , and crossing a slight dividing ground we encamped on the sheltered side of a hill, where there was good bunchgrass having made a day's journey of 24 miles. The night closed in, threatening snow; but the large sage bushes made bright fires.

29th.—The morning mild, and at 4 o'clock it commenced snowing. We took our way amidst a plain, thickly covered with snow, towards a range of hills in the southeast. The sky soon became so dark with snow, that little could be seer of the surrounding country; and we reached the summit of the hills in a heavy snowstorm.. On the side we had approached, this had appeared to be only a ridge of low bills and we were surprised to find ourselves on the summit of a bed of broken mountains, which, as far as the weather would permit us to see, declined rapidly to some low country ahead, presenting a dreary and savage character; and for a moment I looked around in doubt on the wild and inhospitable prospect, scarcely knowing what road to take which might conduct us to some place of shelter for the night. Noticing among the hills the bead of a grassy hollow, I determined to follow it, in the hope that it would conduct us to a stream. We followed a winding descent for several miles, the hollow gradually broadening into little meadows, and becoming the bed of a stream as we advanced; and towards night we were agreeably surprised by the appearance of a willow grove, where we found a sheltered camp, with water and excellent and abundant grass. The grass, which was covered by the snow on the bottom, was long and green, and the face of the mountain had a more favorable character in its vegetation, being smoother, and covered with good bunchgrass. The snow was deep, and the night very cold. A broad trail had entered the valley from the right, and a short distance below the camp were the tracks where a considerable party of Indians had passed on horseback, who had turned out to the left, apparently with the view of crossing the mountains to the eastward.

30th.—After following the stream for a few hours in a southeasterly direction, it entered a canon where we could not follow; but, determined not to leave the stream, we searched passage below where we could regain it, and entered a narrow valley. The water had now more the appearance of a flowing creek; several times we passed groves of willows and we began to feel ourselves out of all difficulty. From our position, it was reasonable to conclude that this stream would find its outlet in Mary's lake, and conduct us into a bent country. We had descended rapidly, and here we found very little snow. On both sides, the mountains showed often stupendous and curious looking rocks, which at several places so narrowed the valley, that scarcely a pass was left for the camp. It was a singular place to travel through—shut up in the earth, a sort of chasm, the little strip of grass under our feet, the rough walls of bare rock on either hand, and the narrow strip of sky above. The grass tonight was abundant, and we en camped in high spirits.

31st.—After an hour's ride this morning, our hopes were once more destroyed. The valley opened out, and before us again lay one of the dry basins. After some search, we discovered a high-water outlet, which brought us in a few miles, and by a descent of several hundred feet, into a long, broad basin, in which we found the bed of the stream, and obtained sufficient water by cutting the ice. The grass on the bottoms was salt and unpalatable.

Here we concluded the year 1843, and our new year's eve was rather a gloomy one. The result of our journey began to be very uncertain; the country was singularly unfavorable to travel; the grasses being frequently of a very unwholesome character, and the hoofs of our animals were so worn and cut by the rocks, that many of them were lame, and could scarcely be got along.

JANUARY.

NEW YEAR'S DAY, 1844.—We continued down the valley, between a dry looking black ridge on the left, and a more snowy and high one on the right. Our road was bad along the bottom, being broken by gullies and impeded by sage, and sandy on the hills, where there is not a blade of grass, nor does any appear on kite mountains The soil in many places consists of a fine powdery sand, covered with a saline allures.7:once; and the general character of the country is desert. During the day we directed mar course towards a black cape, at the foot of which a column of smoke indicated hot springs.

2d.—We were on the road early. The face of the country was hidden by falling snow. We traveled along the bed of the stream, in some places dry, in others covered with ice; the traveling being very bad, through deep fine sand, rendered tenacious by a mixture of clay. The weather cleared up a at noon, and we reached the hot springs of which we had seen the vapor the day before. There was a large field of the usual salt grass here, peculiar to such places. The country otherwise is a perfect barren, without a blade of grass, the only plant being some dwarf Fremontias. We passed the rocky cape, a jagged broken point, bare and torn. The rocks are volcanic, and the hills here have a burnt appearance—cinders and coal occasionally appearing as at_ a blacksmith's forge. We crossed the large dry bed of a muddy lake in a southeasterly direction, and encamped at night, without water and without grass, among sage bushes covered with snow. The heavy road made several mules give out today; and a horse, which had made the journey from the States successfully, thus far, was left on the trail.

3d.—A fog, so dense that we could not see a hundred yards, covered the country, and the men that were sent out after the horses were bewildered and lost; and we were consequently detained at camp until late in the day. Our situation had now become a serious one. We had reached and run over the position where, according to the best maps in my possession, we should have found Mary's lake or river. We were evidently on the verge of the desert which had been reported to us; and the appearance of the country was so forbidding, that I was afraid to enter it, and determined to bear away to the southward, keeping close along the mountains, in the full expectation of reaching the Buenaventura river. This morning I put every man in the camp on foot—myself, of course, among the rest—and in this manner lightened by distribution the loads of the animals WP traveled seven or eight miles along the ridge bordering the valley, and encamped where there were a few bunches of grass on the bed of a hill torrent, without water. There were some large artemisias; but the principal plants are chenopodiaceous shrubs. The rock composing the mountains is here changed suddenly into white granite. The fog showed the tops of the hills at sunset, and stars enough for observations in the early evening, and then closed over us as before. Latitude by observation, 40o 48' 15".

4th.—The fog today was still more dense, and the people again were bewildered. We traveled a few miles around the western point of the ridge, and encamped where there were a few tufts of grass, but no water. Our animals now were in a very alarming state, and there was increased anxiety in the camp.

5th. Same dense fog continued, and one of the mules died in camp this morning. I have had occasion to remark, on such occasions as these, that animals which are about to die leave the band, and, coming into the camp, lie down about the fires. We moved to a place where there was a little better grass, about two miles distant. Taplin one of our best men, who had gone out on a scouting excursion, ascended a mountain near by, and to his surprise emerged into a region of bright sunshine, in which the upper parts of the mountain were glowing, while below all was obscured in the darkest fog.

6th.—The fog continued the same, and, with Mr. Preuss and Carson, I ascended the mountain, to sketch the leading features of the country as some indication of our future route, while Mr. Fitzpatrick explored the country below. In a very short distance we had ascended above the mist, but the view obtained was not very gratifying. The fog had partially cleared off from below when we reached the summit; and in the southwest corner of a basin communicating with that in which we had encamped, we saw a lofty column of smoke, 16 miles distant, indicating the presence of, hot springs. There, also, appeared to be the outlet of those draining channels of the country; and, as such places afforded always more or less grass, I determined to steer in that direction. The ridge we had ascended appeared to be composed of fragments of white granite. We saw here traces of sheep and antelope.

Entering the neighboring valley, and crossing the bed of another lake, after a hard day's travel over ground of yielding mud and sand, we reached the springs, where we found an abundance of grass, which, though only tolerably good, made this plain, with reference to the past, a refreshing and agreeable spot.

This is the most extraordinary locality of hot springs we had met during the journey. The basin of the largest one has a circumference of several hundred feet; but there is at one extremity a circular space of about fifteen feet in diameter, entirely occupied by the boiling water. It boils up at irregular intervals, and with much noise. The water is clear, and the spring deep: a pole about sixteen feet long was easily immersed in the centre; but we had no means of forming a good idea of the depth. It was surrounded on the margin with a border of, green grass, and near the shore the temperature of the water was 206o. We had no means of ascertaining that of the centre, where the heat was greatest; but, by dispersing the water with a pole, the temperature at the margin was increased to 208o, and in the centre it was doubtless higher. By driving the pole towards the bottom, the water was made to boil up with increased force and noise. There are several other interesting places, where water and smoke or gas escape; but they would require a long description. The water is impregnated with common salt, but not so much as to render it unfit for general cooking; and a mixture of snow made it pleasant to drink.

In the immediate neighborhood, the valley bottom is covered almost exclusively with chenopolaceous shrubs, of greater luxuriance, and larger growth, than we have seen them in any preceding part of the journey.

I obtained this evening some astronomical observations.

Our situation now required caution. Including those which gave out from the injured condition el their feet, and those stolen by Indians, we had lost, since leaving the Dalles of the Columbia fifteen animals, and of these line had been left in the last few days. I therefore determined, until we should reach a country of water and vegetation, to feel our way ahead, by navigating the line of route explored some fifteen or twenty miles in advance, and only to leave a present encampment when the succeeding one was known.

Taking with me Godey and Carson, I made today a thorough exploration of the neighboring valleys, and found in a ravine, in the bordering mountains, a good encamping place, where was water in springs, and a sufficient quantity of grass for a night. Overshadowing the springs were some trees of the sweet cottonwood, which, after a long interval of absence, we saw again with pleasure; regarding them as harbingers of a better country. To us, they were eloquent of green prairies and buffalo. We found here a broad and plainly marked trail, on which there were tracks of horses, and we appeared to have regained one of the thoroughfares which pass by the watering places of the country. On the western mountains of the valley, with which this of the boiling spring communicates, we remarked scattered cedars—probably indicating that we were on the borders of the timbered region extending to the Pacific. We reached the camp at sunset, after a day's ride of about 40 miles. The horses we rode were in good order, being of some that were kept for emergencies, and rarely used.

Mr. Preuss had ascended one of the mountains, and occupied the day in sketching the country; and Mr. Fitzpatrick had found, a few miles distant, a hollow of excellent grass and pure water, to which the animals were driven, as I remained another day to give them an opportunity to recruit their strength. Indians appear to be everywhere prowling about like wild animals, and there is a fresh trail across the snow in the valley near. Latitude of the boiling springs, 40° 39' 46".

On the 9th we crossed over to the cottonwood camp. Among the shrubs on the hills were a few bushes of ephedra occidentals, which afterwards occurred frequently along the road and, as usual, the lowlands were occupied with artemisia. While the party proceeded to this place, Carson and myself reconnoitred the road in advance, and found another good encampment for the following day.

10th.—We continued our reconnoissance ahead, pursued a south direction in the basin along the ridge; the camp following slowly after. On a large trail there is never any doubt of finding suitable places for encampments. We reached the end of the basin, where we found, in a hollow of the mountain which enclosed it, an abundance of good bunchgrass. Leaving a signal for the party to encamp, we continued our way up the hollow, intending to see what lay beyond the mountain. The hollow was several miles long, forming a good pass; the snow deepening to about a foot as we neared the summit. Beyond, a defile between the mountains descended rapidly about two thousand feet; and, filling up all the lower space, was a sheet of green water, some twenty miles broad. It broke upon our eyes like the ocean. The neighboring peaks rose high above us, and we ascended one of them to obtain a better view. The waves were curling in the breeze, and their dark green color showed it to be a body of deep water. For a long time we sat enjoying the view, for we had become fatigued with mountains, and the free expanse of moving waves was very grateful. It was set like a gem in the mountains, which, from our position, seemed to enclose it almost entirely. At the western end it communicated with the line of basins we had left a few days since; and on the opposite side it swept a ridge of snowy mountains, the foot of the great Sierra. Its position inclined us to believe it Mary's lake, but the rugged mountains were so entirely discordant with descriptions of its low rushy shores and open country, that we concluded it some unknown body of water, which it afterwards proved to be.

On our road down, the next day, we saw herds of mountain sheep and encamped on a little stream at the mouth of the defile, about a mile from the margin of the water, to which we hurried down immediately. The water is so slightly salt, that, at first, we thought it fresh, and would be pleasant to drink when no other could be had. The shore was rocky—a handsome beach, which reminded us of the sea. On some large granite boulders that were scattered about the shore, I remark ad a coating of calcareous substance, in some places a few inches and in others a foot in thickness Near our camp, the hills, which were of primitive rock, were also covered with this substance, which was in too great quantity on the mountains along the shore of the lake to have been deposited by water, and has the appearance of having been spread over the rocks in mass.*

Where we had halted appeared to be a favorite camping place for Indians.

13th.—We followed again a broad Indian trail along the shore of the lake to the southward. For a short space we had room enough in the bottom; but, after traveling a short distance, the water swept the foot of the precipitous mountains, the peaks of which are about 3,000 feet above the lake.. The trail wound along the base of these precipices, against which the water dashed below, by a way nearly impracticable for the howitzer. During a greater part of the morning the lake was nearly hid by a snowstorm, and the waves broke on the nar row beach in a long line of foaming serf, five or six feet high. The day was unpleasantly cold, the wind driving the snow sharp against cur faces; and, having advanced only about 12 miles, we encamped in a bottom formed by a ravine, covered with good grass, which was fresh and green.

We did not get the howitzer into camp, but were obliged to leave it on the rocks until morning. We saw several flocks of sheep, but did not succeed in killing any. Ducks were riding on, the waves, and several large fish were seen. The mountain sides were crusted with the calcareous cement previously mentioned. There were chenopodiaceous and other

The label attached to a specimen of this rock was lost; but I append an analysis of that which, from memory, I judge to be the specimen:

Carbonate of lime. . 7711

Carbonate of magnesia. . 515

Oxide of iron. .HO

Alumina .1.05

Silica. . .815

10000 shrubs along the beach; and, at the foot of the rocks, an abundance of ephedra occidentalis, whose dark green color makes them evergreens among the shrubby growth of the lake towards evening the snow began to fall heavily, and the country had a wintry appearance.

The next morning the snow was rapidly melting under a warm sun. Part of the morning was occupied in bringing up the gun; and, making only nine miles, we encamped on the shore, opposite a very remarkable rock in the lake, which had attracted our attention for many miles. It rose, according to our estimate, 600 feet above the water, and, from the point we viewed it, presented a pretty exact outline of the great pyramid of Cheops. Like other rocks along the shore, it seemed to be incrusted with calcareous cement. This striking feature suggested a name for the lake, and I called it Pyramid Lake; and though it may be deemed by some a fanciful resemblance, I can undertake to say that the future traveler will find much more striking resemblance between this rock and the pyramids of Egypt, than there is between them and the object from which they take their name.

The elevation of this lake above the sea is 4,890 feet, being nearly 700 feet higher than the Great Salt lake, from which it Lies nearly west, and distant about eight degrees of longitude. The position and elevation of this lake make it an object of geographical interest. It is the nearest lake to the western rim, as the Great Salt lake is to the eastern rim, of the Great Basin which lies between the base of the Rocky mountains and the Sierra Nevada—and the extent and character of which, its whole circumference and contents, it is so desirable to know.

The last of the cattle which had been driven from the Dalles was killed here for food, and was still in good condition.

15th.—A few poor looking Indians made their appearance this morning, and we succeeded in getting one into the camp. He was naked, with the exception of a tunic of hare skins. He told us that there was a river at the end of the lake, but that he lived in the rocks near by. From the few words our fecrile could understand, he spoke a dialect of the Snake language; but we were not able to understand enough to know whether the river ran in or out, or what was its course; consequently, there still remained a chance that this might be Mary's lake.

Groves of large cottonwood, which we could see at the mouth of the river, indicated that it was a stream of considerable size, and, at all events, we had the pleasure to know that now we were in a country where human, beings could live. Accompanied by the Indian, we resumed our road, passing on the way several caves in the rock where there were baskets and seeds, but the people had disappeared. We saw also horse tracks along the shore

Early in the afternoon, when we were approaching the groves at the mouth of the river, three or four Indians met us on the trail. We had an explanatory conversation in signs, and then we moved on together towards the village, which the chief said was encamped on the bottom.

Reaching the groves, we found the inlet of a large freshwater stream, and all at once were satisfied that it was neither Mary's river nor the waters of the Sacramento, but that we had discovered a large interior lake, which the Indians informed us had no outlet. It is about 35 miles long, and, by the mark of the waterline along the shore, the spring level is about 12 feet above its present waters. The chief commenced speaking in a loud voice as we approached; and parties of Indians, armed with bows and arrows, issued from the thickets. We selected a strong place for our encampment—a grassy bottom, nearly enclosed by the river, and furnished with abundant firewood. The village, a collection of straw huts, was a few hundred yards higher up. An Indian brought in a large fish to trade, which we had the inexpressible satisfaction to find was a salmon trout; we gathered round him eagerly. The Indians were amused with our delight, and immediately brought in numbers, so that the camp was soon stocked. Their flavor was excellent—superior, in fact,, to that of any fish I have ever known. They were of extraordinary size—about as large as the Columbia River salmon—generally from two to four feet in length. From the information of Mr. Walker, who passed among some lakes lying more to the eastward, this fish is common to the streams of the inland lakes. He subsequently informed me that he had obtained them weighing six pounds when cleaned and the head taken off, which corresponds very well with the size of those obtained at this place. They doubtless formed the subsistence of these people, who hold the fishery in exclusive possession.

I remarked that one of them gave a fish to the Indian we had first seen, which he carried off to his family. To them it was probably a feast; being of the Digger tribe, and having no share in the fishery, living generally on seeds and roots. Although this was a time of the year when the fish have not yet become fat, they were excellent, and we could only imagine what they are at the proper season. These Indians were very fat, and appeared to live an easy and happy life. They crowded into the camp more than was consistent with our safety, retaining always their arms; and, as they made some unsatisfactory demonstrations, they were given to understand that they would, not be permitted to come armed into the camp; and strong guards were kept with the horses. Strict vigilance was maintained among the people, and one third at a time were kept on guard during the night. There is no reason to doubt that these dispositions, uniformly preserved, conducted our party securely through Indians famed for treachery.

In the mean time, such a salmon trout feast as is seldom seen was going on in our camp; and every variety of manner in which fish could be prepared—boiled, fried, and roasted in the ashes—was put into requisition; and every few minutes an Indian would be seen running off to Veal a fresh one. Whether these Indians had seen whites before, we could not be certain; but they were evidently in communication with others who had, as one of them had some brass buttons, and we noticed several other articles of civilized manufacture. We could obtain from them but little information respecting the country. They made on the ground a drawing of the river, which they represented as issuing from another lake is the mountains three or four days distant, in a direction a little west of south; beyond which, they drew a mountain; and further still, two rivers; on one of which they told us that people like ourselves traveled. Whether they alluded to the settlements on the Sacramento, or to a party from the United States which had crossed the Sierra about three degrees to the southward, a few years since, I am unable to determine.

I tried unsuccessfully to prevail on some of them to guide us' for a few days on the road, but they only looked at each other and laughed.

The latitude of our encampment, which may be considered the mouth of the inlet, is 390 51' 13" by our observations.

16th.—This morning we continued our journey along this beautiful stream, which we naturally called the Salmon Trout river. Large trails led ap on either side; the stream was handsomely timbered with large cottonwoods; and the waters were very clear and pure. We were traveling along the mountains of the great Sierra, which rose on our right, covered with snow; but below the temperature was mild and pleasant. We saw a number of dams which the Indians had constructed to catch fish. After having made about 18 miles, we encamped under some large cottonwoods on the river bottom, where there was tolerably good grass.

17th.—This morning we left the river, which here issues from the mountains on the west. With every stream I,now expected to see the great Buenaventura; and Carson hurried eagerly to search, on every one we reached, for beaver cuttings, which he always maintained we should find only on waters that ran to the Pacific; and the absence of such signs was to him a sure indication that the water had no outlet from the Great Basin. We followed the Indian trail through a tolerably level country, with small sage bushes, which brought us, after 20 miles' journey, to another large stream, timbered with cottonwood, and flowing also out of the mountains, but running more directly to the eastward.

On the way we surprised a family of Indians in the hills; but one man ran up the mountain with rapidity; and the woman was so terrified, and kept up such a continued scream that we could do nothing with her and were obliged to let her go.

18th.—There were Indian lodges and fish dams on the stream. There were no beaver cuttings on the river; but below, it turned round to the right; and, hoping that it would prove a branch of the Buenaventura, we followed it down for abou three hours, and encamped.

I rode out with Mr. Fitzpatrick and Carson to reconnoitre the country, which had evidently been alarmed by the news of our appearance. This stream joined with the open valley of another to the eastward; but which way the main water ran, it was impossible to tell. Columns of smoke rose over the country at scattered intervals—signals by which the Indians here, as elsewhere, communicate to each other that enemies are in the country. It is a signal of ancient and very universal application among barbarians.

Examining into the condition of the animals when I returned into the camp, I found their feet so much cut up by the rocks, and so many of them lame, that it was evidently impossible that they could cross the country to the Rocky mountains. Every piece of iron that could be used for the purpose had been converted into nails, and we could make no further use of the shoes we had remaining. I therefore determined to abandon my eastern course, and to cross the Sierra Nevada into the valley of the Sacramento, wherever a practicable pass could be found. My decision was heard with joy by the people, and diffused new life throughout the camp.

Latitude, by observation, 39o 24' 16".

19th.—A great number of smokes are still visible this morning, attesting at once the alarm our appearance had spread among these people, and their ignorance of us. If they knew the whites, they would understand that their only object in coming among them was to trade, which required peace and friendship; but they have nothing to trade—consequently, nothing to attract the white man; hence their fear and flight.

At daybreak we had a heavy snow; but set out, and, re turning up the stream, went out of our way in a circuit ove a little mountain; and encamped on the same stream, a few miles above, in latitude 39° 19' 21" by observation.

20th.—Today we continued up the stream, and encamped on it close to the mountains. The freshly fallen snow was covered with the tracks of Indians, who had descended from the upper waters, probably called down by the smokes in the plain.

We ascended a peak of the range, which commanded a view of this stream behind the first ridge, where it was winding its course through a somewhat open valley, and I sometimes regret that I did not make the trial to cross here; but while we had fair weather below, the mountains were darkened with falling snow, and, feeling unwilling to encounter them, we turned away again to the southward. In that direction we traveled the next day over a tolerably level country, having always the high mountains on the west. There was but little snow or rock on the ground; and, after having traveled 24 miles, we encamped again on another large stream, running off to the northward and eastward, to meet that we had left It ran through broad bottoms, having a fine meadowland appearance.

Latitude 39° 01' 53".

22d.—We traveled up the stream about fourteen miles, to the foot of the mountains, from which one branch issued in the southwest, the other flowing S.S.E. along their base. Leaving the camp below, we ascended the range through which the first stream passed, in a canon; on the western side was a circu lar valley about 15 miles long, through which the stream wound its way, issuing from a gorge in the main mountain, which rose abruptly beyond. The valley looked yellow with faded grass; and the trail we had followed was visible, making to wards the gorge, and this was evidently a pass; but again, while all was bright sunshine on the ridge and on the valley where w.: were, the snow was falling heavily in the mountains. I determine, still to the southward, and encamped on the stream near the forks animals being fatigue and the grass tolerably good.

The rock of the ridge we had ascended is a compact lava assuming a granitic appearance and structure, and containing, in some places, small nodules of obsidian. So far as composttion and aspect are concerned, the rock in other parts of the ridge appears to be granite; but it is probable that this is only a compact form of lava of recent origin.

By observation, the elevation of the encampment was 5,020 feet; and the latitude 38° 49' 54".

23.1.—We moved along the course of the other branch towards the southeast, the country affording a fine road; and, passing some slight dividing grounds, descended towards the valley of another stream. There was a somewhat rough looking mountain ahead, which it appeared to issue from, or to enter—we could not tell which; and as the course of the valley and the inclination of the ground had a favorable direction, we were sanguine to find here a branch of the Buenaventura; but were again disappointed, finding it an inland water, on which we encamped after a day's journey of 24 miles. It was evident that, from the time we descended into the plain at Summer lake, we had been flanking the great range of mountains which divided the Great Basin from the waters of the Pacific; and that the continued succession, and almost connection, of lakes and rivers which we encountered, were the drainings of that range. Its rains, springs, and snows, would sufficiently account for these lakes and streams, numerous as they were.

24th.—A man was discovered running towards the camp as we were about to start this morning, who proved to be an Indian of rather advanced age—a sort of forlorn hope, who seemed to have been worked up into the resolution of visiting the strangers who were passing through the country. He seized the hand of the first man he met as he came up, out of breath, and held on, as if to assure himself of protection. He brought with him, in a little skin bag, a few pounds of the seeds of a pinetree, which today we saw for the first time, and which Dr. Torrey has described as a new species, under the name of pinus monophyllus; in popular language it might be called the nut pine. We purchased them all from him. The nut is oily, of very agreeable 'favor, and must be very nutritious, as it constitutes the principal subsistence of the tribes among which we were now traveling. By a present of scarlet cloth, and other striking articles, we prevailed' upon this man to be out guide of two days' journey. As clearly as possible by signs, we made him understand our object; and he engaged to conduct us in sight of a good pass which he knew. Here we ceased to hear the Shoshonee language— that of this man being perfectly unintelligible. Several Indians, who had been waiting to see what reception he would meet with, now came into camp; and, accompanied by the newcomers, we resumed our journey.

The road led us up the creek, which here becomes a rather rapid mountain stream, fifty feet wide, between dark looking hills without snow; but immediately beyond them rose snowy mountains on either side, timbered principally with the nut pine. On the lower grounds, the general height of this tree is twelve to twenty feet, and eight inches the greatest diameter; it is rather branching, and has a peculiar and singular, but pleasant odor. We followed the river for only a short distance along a rocky trail,, and crossed it at a dam which the Indians made us comprehend had been built to catch salmon trout. The snow and ice were heaped up against it three or four feet deep entirely across the stream.

Leaving here the stream, which runs through impassable canons, we continued our road over a very broken country, passing through a low gap between the snowy mountains. The rock which occurs immediately in the pass has the appearance of impure sandstone, containing scales of black mica. This may be only a stratified lava. On issuing from the gap, the compact lava, and other volcanic products usual in the country, again occurred. We descended from the gap into a wide valley, or rather basin, and encamped on a small tributary to the last stream, on which there was very good grass. It was covered with such thick ice, that it required some labor with pickaxes to make holes for the Animals to drink. The banks are lightly wooded with willow, and on the upper bottoms are sage and Fremontia, with ephedra occidentalis; which begins to occur more frequently. The day has been a summer one, warm and pleasant; no snow on the trail, which, as we are all on foot, makes traveling more agreeable. The hunters went into a neighboring mountain, but found no game. We have five Indians in camp tonight.

25th.—The morning was cold and bright, and as the sun rose the day became beautiful. A party of twelve Indians came down from the mountains to trade pine nuts, of which each one carried a little bag. These seemed now to be the staple of the country; and whenever we met an Indian, his friendly salutation consisted in offering a few nuts to eat and to trade; their only arms were bows and flint pointed arrows. It appeared that in almost all the valleys the neighboring bandy were at war with each other; and we had some difficulty in prevailing on our guides to accompany us on this day's journey, being at war with the people on the other side of a large snowy mountain which lay before us.

The general level of the country appeared to be getting higher, and we were gradually entering the heart of the mountains. Accompanied by all the Indians, we ascended a long ridge, and reached a pure spring at the edge of the timber, where the Indians had waylaid and killed an antelope, and where the greater part of them left us. Our pacific conduct had quieted their alarms; and though at war among each other, yet all confided in us—thanks to the combined effects of power and kindness—for our arms inspired respect, and our little presents and good treatment conciliated their confidence. Here we suddenly entered snow six inches deep, and the ground was a little rocky, with volcanic fragments, the mountain appearing to be composed of such rock. The timber consists principally of nut pines, (pinus monophyllus,) which here are of larger size 12 to 15 inches in diameter; heaps of cones lying on the ground, where the Indians have gathered the seeds.

The snow deepened gradually as we advanced. Our guides wore out their moccasins; and putting one of them on a horse, we enjoyed the unusual sight of an Indian who could not ride. He could not even guide the animal, and appeared to have ns knowledge of horses. The snow was three or four feet deep on the summit of the pass; and from this point the guide pointed out our future road, declining to go any further. Below us was a little valley; and beyond this the mountains rose higher still, one ridge above another, presenting a rude and rocky outline. We descended rapidly to the valley: the snow impeded us but little; yet it was dark when we reached the foot of the mountain.

The day had been so warm that our moccasins were we with melting snow; but here, as soon as the sun begins to decline, the air gets suddenly cold, and we had great difficulty to keep our feet from freezing—our moccasins being frozen perfectly stiff. After a hard day's march of 27 miles, we reached the river some time after, dark, and found the snow about a foot deep on the bottom—the river being entirely frozen over. We found a comfortable camp, where there were dry willows abundant, and we soon had blazing fires. A little brandy, which I husbanded with great care, remained, and I do not know any medicine more salutary, or any drink (except coffee) more agreeable, than this in a cold night and after a hard day's march. Mr. Preuss questioned whether the famed nectar ever possessed so exquisite a flavor. All felt it to be a reviving cordial.

The next morning, when the sun had not yet risen over the mountains, the thermometer was at 20 below zero but the sky was bright and pure, and the weather changer rapidly into a pleasant day of summer. I remained encamped in order to examine the country, and allow the animals a day of rest, the grass being good and abundant under the snow.

The river is fifty or eighty feet wide, with a lively current, and very clew water. It forked a little above our camp, one of its branches coming directly from the south. At its head appeared to be a handsome pass; and from the neighboring heights we could see, beyond, a comparatively low and open country, which was supposed to form the valley of the Buenaventura. The other branch issued from a nearer pass, in a direction S. 75o W., forking at the foot of the mountain, and receiving a part of its waters from a little lake. I was in advance of the camp when our last guides had left us; but, so far could be understood, this was the pass which they had indicated, and, in company with Carson, today I set out to explore it. Entering the range, we continued in a north westerly direction up the valley, which here bent to the right.

It was a pretty open bottom, locked between lofty mountains, which supplied frequent streams as we advanced. On the lower part they were covered with nutpine trees, and above with masses of pine, which we easily recognised, from the darker color of the foliage. From the fresh trails which occurred frequently during the morning, deer appeared to be remarkably numerous in the mountain.

We had now entirely left the desert country, and were on the verge of a region which, extending westward to the shores of the Pacific, abounds in large game, and is covered with a singular luxuriance of vegetable life.

The little stream grew rapidly smaller, and in about twelve miles we had reached its head, the last water coming immediately out of the mountain on the right; and this spot was selected for our next encampment. The grass showed well in sunny places; but in colder situations the snow was deep, and began to occur in banks through which the horses found some difficulty in breaking a way.

To the left, the open valley continued in a southwesterly direction, with a scarcely perceptible ascent, forming a beautiful pass, the exploration of which we deferred until the next day, and returned to the camp.

Today an Indian passed through the valley, on his way into the mountains, where he showed us was his lodge. We comprehended nothing of his language; and, though he appeared to have no fear, passing along in full view of the camp he was indisposed to hold any communication with us, but showed the way he was going, and pointed for us to go on our road.

By observation, the latitude of this encampment was 38° 18' 01", and the elevation above the sea 6,310 feet.

27th.—Leaving the camp to follow slowly, with directions to Carson to encamp at the place agreed on, Mr. Fitzpatrick and myself continued the reconnoissance. Arriving at the heap of the at ream, we began to enter the pass—passing occasionally through open groves of large pine trees, on the warm side of the defile, where the snow had melted away, occasionally exposing a large Indian trail. Continuing, along a narrow meadow, we reached, in a few miles, the gate of the pass, where there was a narrow strip of prairie, about 50 yards wide, between walls of granite rock. On either side rose the mountains, forming on the left a rugged mass, or nucleus, wholly covered with deep snow, presenting a glittering and icy surface. At the time, we supposed this to be the point, into which they were gathered between the two great rivers, and from which the waters flowed off to the bay. This was the icy and cold side of the pass, and the rays of the sun hardly touched the snow. On the left, the mountains rose into peaks, but they were lower and secondary, and the country had a somewhat more open and lighter character. On the right were several hot springs, which appeared remarkable in such a place. In going through, we felt impressed by the majesty of the mountain, along the huge wall of which we were riding. Here there was no snow; but immediately beyond was a deep bank, through which we dragged our horses with considerable effort. We then immediately struck upon a stream, which gathered itself rapidly, and descended quick; and the valley did not preserve the open character of the other side, appearing below to form a canon. We therefore climbed one of the peaks on the right, leaving our horses below; but we were so much shut up that we did not obtain an extensive view, and what we saw was not very satisfactory, and awakened considerable doubt. The valley of the stream pursued a northwesterly direction, appearing below to turn sharply to the right, beyond which further view was cut off. It was, nevertheless, resolved to continue our road the next day town this valley, which we trusted still would prove that of the middle stream between the two great rivers. Towards the summit of this peak, the fields f snow were four or five feet deep on the northern side; and Are saw several large bares, which had on their winter color, being white as the snow around them.

The winter day is short in the mountains, the sun having but a small space of sky to travel over in the visible par above our horizon; and the moment his rays are gone, the air is keenly cold. The interest of our work had detained us long, and it was after nightfall when we reached the camp

29th.—Today we went through the pass with all the camp, and, after a hard day's journey of twelve miles, encamped on a high point where the snow had been blown off, and the ex posed grass afforded a scanty pasture for the animals. Snow and broken country together made our traveling difficult; we were often compelled to make large circuits, and ascend the highest and most exposed ridges, in order to avoid snow, which in other places was banked up to a great depth.

During the day a few Indians were seen circling around us on snowshoes, and skimming along like birds; but we could not bring them within speaking distance. Godey, who was little distance from the camp, had sat down to tie his moccasins when he heard a low whistle near, and, looking up, saw two Indians half hiding behind a rock about forty yards distant they would not allow him to approach, but breaking into laugh, skimmed off over the snow, seeming to have no idea of the power of firearms, and thinking themselves perfectly safe when beyond arm's length.

Tonight we did not succeed in getting the howitzer into camp. This was the most laborious day we had yet passed through, the steep ascents and deep snow exhausting both men and animals. Our single chronometer had stopped during the day, and its error in time occasioned the loss of an eclipse of a satellite this evening. It had not preserved the rate with which we started from the Dalles, and this will account for the absence of longitudes along this interval of our journey.

29th.—From this height we could see, at a considerable distance below, yellow spots in the valley, which indicated that there was not much snow. One of these places we expected to reach tonight; and some time being required to bring up the gun, I went ahead with Mr.

Fitzpatrick and a few men, leaving the camp to follow, in charge of Mr. Preuss. We followed a trail down a hollow where the Indians had descended, the snow being so deep that we never came near the ground, bui

his only made our descent the easier, and, when we reached a Hale affluent to the river, at the bottom, we suddenly found ourselves in presence of eight or ten Indians. They seemed to be watching our motions, and, like the others, at first were indisposed to let us approach, ranging themselves like birds on a fallen log, on the hillside above our heads, where, being out of our reach, they thought themselves safe. Our friendly demeanor reconciled them, and, when we got near enough, they immediately stretched out to us handfuls of pinenuts, which seemed an exercise of hospitality. We made them a few presents, and, telling us that their village was a few miles below, they went on to let their people know what we were. The principal stream still running through an impracticable canon, we ascended a very steep hill, which proved afterwards the last and fatal obstacle to our little howitzer, which was finally abandoned at this place. We passed through a small meadow a few miles below, crossing the river, which depth, swift current, and rock, made it difficult to ford; and, after a few more miles of very difficult trail, issued into a larger prairie bottom, at the farther end of which we encamped, in a position rendered strong by rocks and trees. The lower parts of the mountain were covered with the nutpine. Several Indians appeared on the hillside, reconnoitring the camp, and were induced to com in; others came in during the afternoon; and in the evening we held a council. The Indians immediately made it clear that the waters on which we were also belonged to the Great Basin, in the edge of which we had been since the 17th of December; and it became evident that we had still the great ridge on the left to cross before we could reach the Pacific waters.

We explained to the Indians that we were endeavoring to find a passage across the mountains into the country of the whites, whom we were going to see; and told them that we wished them to bring us a guide, to whom we would give presents of scarlet cloth, and other articles, which were shown to them. They looked at the reward we offered, and conferred with each other, but pointed to the snow on the mountain, and with their hands across their necks, and raised them above their heads, o show the depth; and signified that it was impossible for us to get through. They made signs that we must go to the southward, over a pass through a lower range, which they pointed out: there, they said, at the end of one day's travel, we would find people who lived near a pass in the great mountain; and to that point they engaged to furnish us a guide. They appeared to have a confused idea, from report, of whites who lived on the other side of the mountain; and once, they told us, about two years ago, a party of twelve men like ourselves had ascended their river, and crossed to the other waters. They pointed out to us where they had crossed; but then, they said, it was summer time; but now it would be impossible. I believe that this was a party led by Mr. Chiles, one or the only two men whom I know to have passed through the California mountains from the interior of the Basin—Walker being the other; and both were engaged upwards of twenty days, in the summer time, in getting over. Chiles's destination was the bay of San Francisco, to which he descended by the Stanislaus river; and Walker subsequently informed me that, like myself, descending to the southward on a more eastern line, day after day he was searching for the Buenaventura, thinking that he had found it with every new stream, until, like me, he abandoned all idea of its existence, and, turning abruptly to the right, crossed the great chain. These were both western men, animated with the spirit of exploratory enterprise which characterizes that people.

The Indians brought in during the evening an abundant supply of pinenuts, which we traded from them. When roasted, their pleasant flavor made them an agreeable addition to ur now scanty store of provisions, which were reduced to a very low ebb. Our principal stock was in peas, which it is not necessary to say contain scarcely any nutriment. We had still a little flour left, some coffee, and a quantity of sugar, which I reserved as a defence against starvation.

The Indians informed us that at certain seasons they have fish in their waters, which we supposed to be salmon trout: for the remainder of the year they live upon the pinenuts, which form their great winter subsistence—a portion being always at hand, shut up in the natural storehouse of the cones. At present, they were presented to us as a whole people living upon this simple vegetable.

The other division of the party did not come in tonight, but encamped in the upper meadow, and arrived the next morning. They had not succeeded in getting the howitzer beyond the place mentioned, and where it 1.'d been left by Mr. Preuss, in obedience to my orders; and, in anticipation of the snowbank:. and snowfields still ahead, foreseeing the inevitable detention to which it would subject us, I reluctantly determined to leave it there for the time. It was of the kind invented by the French for the mountain part of their war in Algiers; and the distance it had come with us proved how well it was adapted to its pur pose. We left it, to the great sorrow of the whole party, who were grieved to part with a companion which had made the whole distance from St. Louis, and commanded respect for 1.1 on some critical occasions, and which might be needed for the same purpose again.

30th.—Our guide, who was a young man, joined us this morning; and, leaving our encampment late in the day, we descended the river, which immediately opened out into a broad valley, furnishing good traveling ground. In a short distance we passed the village, a collection of 'straw huts; and a few miles below, the guide pointed out the place where the whites had been encamped, before they entered the mountain. With our late start we made but ten miles, and encamped on the low river bottom, where there was no snow, but a great deal of ice; and we cut piles of long grass to lay under our blankets, and fires were made of large dry willows, groves of which wooded the stream. The river took here a northeasterly direction, and through a spur from the mountains on the left was the gap where we were to pass the next day.

31st.—We took our way over a gently rising ground, the dividing ridge being tolerably low; and traveling easily along a broad trail, in twelve or fourteen miles reached the upper part of the pass, when it began to snow thickly, with very cold weather. The Indians had only the usual scanty covering, and appeared to suffer greatly from the cold. All left us, except our guide. Half hidden by the storm, the mountains looked dreary; and,, as night began to approach, the guide showed great reluctance to go forward. I placed him between two rifles, for the way began to be difficult. Traveling a little farther, we struck a ravine, which the Indian said would conduct us to the river; and as the poor fellow suffered greatly, shivering in the snow which fell upon his naked skin, I would not detain him any longer; and he ran off to the mountain, where he said was a hut near by. He had kept the blue and scarlet cloth I had given him tightly rolled up, preferring rather to endure the cold than to get them wet. In the course of the afternoon, one of the men had his foot frostbitten; and about dark we had the satisfaction to reach the bottoms of a stream timbered with large trees, among which we Found a sheltered camp, with an abundance of such grass as the season afforded for the animals. We saw before us, in descending from the pass, a great continuous range, along which stretched the valley of the river; the lower parts steep, and dark with pines, while above it was hidden in clouds of snow. This we felt instantly satisfied was the central ridge of the Sierra Nevada, the great California mountain, which only now intervened between us and the waters of the bay. We had made a forced march of 26 miles, and three mules had given out on the road. Up to this point, with the exception of two stolen by Indians, we had lost none of the horses which had been brought from the Columbia river, and a number of these were still strong and in tolerably good order. We had now 67 animals in the band.

We had scarcely lighted, our fires, when the camp was crowded with nearly naked Indians; some of them were furnished with long nets in addition to bows, and appeared to nave been out on the sage hills to hunt rabbits. These nets were perhaps 30 to 40 feet long, kept upright in the ground by slight sticks at intervals, and were made from a kind of wild hemp, very much resembling in manufacture those common among the Indians of the Sacramento valley. They came among us without any fear, and scattered themselves about he fires, mainly occupied in gratifying their astonishment. I was struck by the singular appearance of a row of about a dozen, who were Sitting on their haunches perched on a log near one of the fires, with their quick sharp eyes following every motion.

We gathered together a few of the most intelligent of the Indians, and held this evening an interesting council. I explained to them my intentions. I told them that we had come from a very far country, having been traveling now nearly a year, and that we were desirous simply to go across the mountain into the country of the other whites. There were two who appeared particularly intelligent—one, a somewhat old man. He told me that, before the snows fell, it was six sleeps to the place where the whites lived, but that now it was impossible to cross the mountain on account of the deep snow; and showing us, as the others had done, that it was over our heads, he urged us strongly to follow the course of the river, which he said would conduct us to a lake in which there were many large fish. There, he said, were many people; there was no snow on the ground; and we might remain there until the spring. From their descriptions, we were enabled to judge that we had encamped on the upper water of the Salmon Trout river. It is hardly necessary to say that our communication was only by signs, as we understood nothing of their language; but they spoke, notwithstanding, rapidly and vehemently, explaining what they considered the folly of our intentions, and urging us to go down to the lake. Tahve, a word signifying snow, we very soon learned to know, from its frequent repetition. I told him that the men and the horses were strong, that we would break a road through the snow; and spreading before him our bales of scarlet cloth, and trinkets, showed him what we would give for a guide. It was necessary to obtain one, if possible; for I had determined here to attempt the passage of the mountain. Pulling a bunch of grass from the ground, after a short discussion among themselves, the old man made us comprehend, that if we could break through the snow, at the end of three days we would come down upon grass, which he showed us would be about six inches high, and where the ground was entirely free. So far, he said, he had been in hunting for elk; but beyond that (and he closed his eyes) he had seen nothing; but there was one among them who had been to the whites, and, going out ,of the lodge, he returned with a young man of very intelligent appearance. Here, said he, is a young man who has seen the whites with his own eyes; and he swore, first by the sky, and then by the ground, that what he said was true. With a large present of goods, we prevailed upon this young man to be our guide, and he acquired among us the name of Melo—a word signifying friend, which they used very frequently. He was thinly clad, and nearly barefoot; his moccasins being about worn out. We gave him skins to make a new pair, and to enable him to perform his undertaking to us. The Indians remained in the camp during the night, and we kept the guide and two others to sleep in the lodge with us—Carson lying across the door, and having made them comprehend the use of our fire arms.

FEBRUARY. 1st.—The snow, which had intermitted in the evening, commenced falling again in the course of the night, and it snowed steadily all day. In the morning I acquainted the men with my decision, and explained to them that necessity required us to make a great effort to clear the mountains. I reminded them of the beautiful valley of the Sacramento, with which they were familiar from the descriptions of Carson, who had been there some fifteen years ago, and who, in our late privations, had delighted us in speaking of its rich pastures and abounding game, and drew a vivid contrast between its summer climate, less than a hundred miles distant, and the falling snow around us. I informed them (and long experience had given them confidence in my observations and good instruments) that almost directly west, and only about 70 miles distant, was the great farming establishment of Captain Sutter—a gentleman who had formerly lived in Missouri, and, emigrating to this country, had become the possessor of a principality. I assured them that, from the heights of the mountain before us, we should doubtless see the valley of the Sacramento river, and with one effort place ourselves again in the midst of plenty. The people received this decision with the cheerful obedience which had always characterized them, and the day was immediately devoted to the preparations necessary to enable 1€ to carry it into effect. Leggins, moccasins, clothing—al were put into the best state to resist the cold. Our guide was not neglected. Extremity of suffering might make him desert; we therefore did the best we could for him. Leggins, moccasins, some articles of clothing, and a large green Blanket, in addition to the blue and scarlet cloth, were lavished upon him, and to his great and evident contentment. He arrayed himself in all his colors, and, clad in green, blue, and scarlet, he made a gay looking Indian; and, with his various presents, was probably richer and better clothed than any 9f his tribe had ever been before.

I have already said that our provisions were very low; we had neither tallow nor grease of any kind remaining, and the want of salt became one of our greatest privations. The poor dog which had been found in the Bear River valley, and which had been a compagnon de voyage ever since, had now become fat, and the mess to which it belonged, requested permission to kill it. Leave was granted. Spread out on the snow, the meat looked very good; and it made a strengthening meal for the greater part of the camp. Indians brought in two or three rabbits during the day, which were purchased from them.

The river was 40 to 70 feet wide, and now entirely frozen over. It was wooded with large cottonwood, willow, and grain de boeuf. By observation, the latitude of this encampment was 08° 37' 18".

2d.—It had ceased snowing, and this morning the lower aim was clear and frosty; and six or seven thousand feet above, the peaks of the Sierra now and then appeared among the rolling clouds, which were rapidly dispersing before the sun. Our Indian shook his head as he pointed to the icy pinnacles shooting high up into the sky, and seeming almost immediately above us. Crossing the river on the ice, and leaving it immediately, we commenced the ascent of the mountain along the valley of a tributary stream. The people were unusually lent, for every man knew that our enterprise was hazardous, and the issue doubtful.

The snow deepened rapidly, and it soon became necessary to break a road. For this service, a party of ten was formed; mounted on the strongest horses, each man in succession opening the road on foot, or on horseback, until himself and his horse became fatigued, when he stepped aside, and, the remaining number passing ahead, he took his station in the rear. Leaving this stream, and pursuing a very direct course, we passed over an intervening ridge to the river we had left, On the way we passed two low huts entirely covered with snow, which might very easily have escaped observation. A family was living in each; and the only trail I saw in the neighborhood was from the door hole to a not pine tree near, which supplied them with food and fuel. We found two similar huts on the creek where we next arrived; and, traveling a little higher up, en camped on its banks in about four feet depth of snow. Carson found near, an open hillside, where the wind and the sun had melted the snow, leaving exposed sufficient bunchgrass for the animals tonight.

The nutpines were now giving way to heavy timber, and there were some immense pines on the bottom, around the roots of which the sun had melted away the snow; and here we made our camp and built huge fires. Today we had traveled 16 miles, and our elevation above the sea was 6,760 feet.

3d.—Turning our faces directly towards the main chain, we ascended an open hollow along a small tributary to the river which, according to the Indians, issues from a mountain to the south. The snow was so deep in the hollow, that we were obliged to travel along the steep hillsides, and over spurs, where the wind and sun had in places lessened the snow, and where the grass, which appeared to be in good quality along the sides of the mountains, was exposed. We opened our road in the same way as yesterday, but made only seven miles, and encamped by some springs at the foot of a high and steep hill, by which the hollow ascended to another basin in the mountain. The little stream below was entirely buried in snow. The springs were shaded by the boughs of a lofty cedar, which here made its first appearance; the usual height was 120 to 130 feet, and one that was measured near by was six feet in diameter.

There being no grass exposed here, the horses were sent back to that which we had seen a few miles below. We occupied the remainder of the day in beating down a road to the toot of the hill, a mile or two distant; the snow being beater down when moist, in the warm part of the day, and then han1 frozen at night, made a foundation that would bear the weight of the animals next morning. During the day several Indians joined us on snowshoes. These were made of a circular hoop, about a foot in diameter, the interior space being filled with an open network of bark.

4th.—I went ahead early with two or three men, each with a led horse to break the road. We were obliged to abandon the hollow entirely, and work along the mountainside, which was very steep, and the snow covered with an icy crust. We cut a footing as we advanced, and trampled a road through for the animals; but occasionally one plunged outside the trail, and slid along the field to the bottom, a hundred yards below. Late in the day we reached another bench in the hollow, where, in summer, the stream passed over a small precipice. Here was a short distance of dividing ground between the two ridges, and beyond an open basin, some ten miles across, whose bottom presented a field of snow. At the further or western side rose the middle crest of the mountain, a dark looking ridge of volcanic rock.

The summit line presented a range of naked peaks, apparently destitute of snow and vegetation; but below, the face of the whole country was covered with timber of extraordinary size.

Towards a pass which the guide indicated here, we attempted in the afternoon to force a road; but after a laborious plunging through two or three hundred yards, our best horses gave out, entirely refusing to make any further effort, and, for the time, we were brought to a stand. The guide informed us that we were entering the deep snow, and here began the difficulties of the mountain; and to him, and almost to all, our enterprise seemed hopeless. I returned a short distance back, to the break in the hollow, where I met Mr. Fitzpatrick.

The camp had been occupied all the day in endeavoring to ascend the hill, but only the best horses had succeeded; the animals, generally, not having sufficient strength to bring themselves up without the packs; and all the line of road between this and the springs was strewed with camp stores and equipage, and horses floundering in snow. I therefore immediately encamped on the ground with my own mess, which was in advance, and directed Mr. Fitzpatrick to encamp at the springs, and send all the animals, in charge of Tabeau, with a strong guard, back to the place where they had been pastured the night before. Here was a small spot of level ground, protected on one side by the mountain, and on the other sheltered by a little ridge of rock. It was an open grove of pines, which assimilated in size to the grandeur of the mountain, being frequently six feet in diameter.

Tonight we had no shelter, but we made a large fire around the trunk of one of the huge pines; and covering the snow with small boughs, on which we spread our blankets, soon made ourselves comfortable. The night was very bright and clear, though the thermometer was only at 10o. A strong wind, which sprang up at sundown, made it intensely cold; and this was one of the bitterest nights during the journey.

Two Indians joined our party here; and one of them, an old man, immediately began to harangue us, saying that ourselves and animals would perish in the snow; and that if we would go back, he would show us another and a better way across the mountain. He spoke in a very loud voice, and there was a singular repetition of phrases and arrangement of words which rendered his speech striking and not unmusical.

We had now begun to understand some words, and, with the aid of signs, easily comprehended the old man's simple ideas,

"Rock upon rock—rock upon rock—snow upon snow," said he; " even if you get over the snow, you will not be able to get down from the mountains." He made us the sign of precipices, and showed us how the feet of the horses would slip, and brow them off from the narrow trails that led along, their sides. Our Chinook, who comprehended even more readily than ourselves, and believed our situation hopeless, covered his head with his blanket, and began to weep and lament. "I wanted to see the whites," said he; " I came away from my own people to see the whites, and I wouldn't care to die among them, but here"—and he looked around into the cold night and gloomy forest, and, drawing his blanket over his head, began again to lament.

Seated around the tree, the fire illuminating the rocks and the tall bolls of the pines round about, and the old Indian haranguing, we presented a group of very serious faces.

5th.—The night had been too cold to sleep, and we were up very early. Our guide was standing by the fire with all finery on; and seeing him shiver in the cold, I threw on his shoulders one of my blankets. We missed him a few minutes afterwards, and never saw him again. He had deserted. His bad faith and treachery were in perfect keeping with the estimate of Indian character, which a long intercourse with this people had gradually forced upon my mind.

While a portion of the camp were occupied in bringing up the baggage to this point, the remainder were busied in making sledges and snowshoes. I had determined to explore the mountain ahead, and the sledges were to be used in transporting the baggage.

The mountains here consisted wholly of a white micaceous granite. The day was perfectly clear, and, while the sun was in the sky, warm and pleasant.

By observation our latitude was 380 42' 26"; and elevation oy the boiling point, 7,400 feet.

6th.—Accompanied by Mr. Fitzpatrick, I set out today with a reconnoitring party on snowshoes. We marched al in single file, trampling the snow as heavily as we could Crossing the open basin, in a march of about ten miles we reached the top of one of the peaks, to the left of the pass indicated by our guide. Far below us, dimmed by the distance, was a large snowless valley, bounded on the western side, at the distance of about a hundred miles, by a low range of mountains, Which Carson recognised with delight as the mountains bordering the coast. " There," said he, "is the little mountain—it is fifteen years since I saw it; but I am just as sure as if I had seen it yesterday." Between us, then, and this low coast range was the valley of the Sacramento; and no one who had not accompanies us through the incidents of our life for the last few months could realize the delight with which at last we looked down upon it. At the distance of apparently 30 miles beyond us wore distinguished spots of prairie; and a dark line which could be traced with the glass, was imagined to be the course of the river; but we were evidently at a great height above the valley, and between us and the plains extended miles of snowy fields and broken ridges of pine covered mountains.

It was late in the day when we turned towards the camp; and it grew rapidly cold as it drew towards night. One of the men became fatigued, and his feet began to freeze, and building a fire in the trunk of a dry old cedar, Mr. Fitzpatrick remained with him until his clothes could be dried, and he was in a condition to come on. After a day's march of 20 miles, we straggled into the camp one after another, at nightfall; the greater number excessively fatigued, only two of the party having ever traveled on snowshoes before.

All our energies are now directed to getting our animals across the snow; and it was supposed that after all the baggage had been drawn with the sleighs over the trail we had made, it would be sufficiently hard to bear our animals. A several places between this point and the ridge, we had discovered some grassy spots, where the wind and sun had dispersed the snow from the sides of the hills, and these were to form resting places to support the animals for a night in their passage across. On our way across we had set on fire several woken stumps, and dried trees, to melt places in the snow for camps. Its general depth was five feet; but we passed over places where it was 20 feet deep, as shown by the trees.

With one party drawing sleighs loaded with baggage, I advanced today about four miles along the trail, and encamped at the first grassy spot, where we expected to bring our horses. Mr. Fitzpatrick, with another party, remained behind, to form an intermediate station between us and the animals.

8th.—The night has been extremely cold; but perfectly still, and beautifully clear. Before the sun appeared this morning, the thermometer was 30 below zero; 1° higher, when his rays struck the lofty peaks; and 00 when they reached our camp.

Scenery and weather, combined, must render these mountains beautiful in summer; the purity and deep blue color of the sky are singularly beautiful; the days are sunny and bright, and even warm in the noon hours; and if we could be free from the many anxieties that oppress us, even now we would be delighted here; but our provisions are getting fear.. fully scant. Sleighs arrived with baggage about ten o'clock; and leaving a portion of it here, we continued on for a mile and a half, and encamped at the foot of a long hill on this side of the open bottom.

Bernier and Godey, who yesterday morning had been sent to ascend a higher peak, got in, hungry and fatigued. They confirmed what we had already seen. Two other sleighs ar rived in the afternoon; and the men being fatigued, I gave them all tea and sugar. Snow clouds began to rise in the

S.S.W.; and, apprehensive of a storm, which would destroy our road, I sent the people back to Mr. Fitzpatrick, with directions to send for the animals in the morning. With me remained Mr. Preuss, Mr. Talbot, and Carson, with Jacob.

Elevation of the camp, by the boiling point, is 7,920 feet.

9th.—During the night the weather changed, the wind rising to a gale, and commencing to snow before daylight; be fore morning the trail was covered. We remained quiet in camp all day, in the course of which the weather Improved. Four sleighs arrived towards evening, with the bedding of the men. We suffer much from the want of salt; and all the men are becoming weak from insufficient food.

10th.—Taplin was sent back with a few men to assist Mr Fitzpatrick; and continuing on with three sleighs carrying a part of the baggage, we had the satisfaction to encamp within two and a half miles of the head of the hollow, and at the foot of the last mountain ridge. Here two large trees had been set on fire, and in the holes, where the snow had been melted away, we found a comfortable camp.

The wind kept the air filled with snow during the day; the sky was very dark in the southwest, though elsewhere very clear. The forest here has a noble appearance; and tall cedar is abundant; its greatest height being 130 feet, and circumference 20, three or four feet above the ground; and here I see for the, first time the white pine, of which there are some magnificent trees. Hemlock spruce is among the timber, occasionally as large as eight feet in diameter, four feet above the ground; but, in ascending, it tapers rapidly to less than one foot at the height of eighty feet. I have not seen any higher than 130 feet, and the slight upper part is frequently broken off by the wind. The white spruce is frequent; and the red pine (pinus colorado of the Mexicans) which constitutes the beautiful forest along the banks of the Sierra Nevada to the northward, is here the principal tree, not attaining a greater 'height than 140 feet, though with sometimes a diameter of 10. Most of these trees appeared to differ slightly from those of the same kind on the other side of the continent.

The elevation of the camp by the boiling point, is 8,050 feet. We are now 1,000 feet above the level of the South Pass in the Rocky mountains; and still we are not done ascending. The top of a flat ridge near was bare of snow, and very well sprinkled with bunchgrass, sufficient to pasture the animals two or three days; and this was to be their main point of support. This ridge is composed of a compact trap, or basalt of a columnar structure; over the surface are scattered large boulders of porous trap. The hills are in many places entirely covered with small fragments of volcanic rock.

Putting on our snowshoes, we spent the afternoon in exploring a road ahead. The glare of the snow, combined with great fatigue, had rendered many of the people earl blind but we were fortunate in having some black silken kerchiefs, which, worn as veils, very much relieved the eye.

11th.—High wind continued, and our trail this morning was nearly invisible—here and there indicated by a little ridge of snow. Our situation became tiresome and dreary, requiring a strong exercise of patience and resolution.

In the evening I received a message from Mr. Fitzpatrick, acquainting me with the utter failure of his attempt to get our mules and horses over the snow—the half hidden trail had proved entirely too slight to support them, and they had broken through, and were plunging about or lying half buried in snow. He was occupied in endeavoring to get them back to his camp; and in the mean time sent to me for further instructions. I wrote to him to send the animals immediately back to their old pastures; and, after having made mauls and shovels, turn in all the strength of his party to open and beat a road through the snow, strengthening it with branches and boughs of the pines.

12th.—We made mauls, and worked hard at our end of the road all day. The wind was high, but the sun bright, and the snow thawing. We worked down the face of the hill, to meet the people at the other end. Towards sundown it began to grow cold, and we shouldered our mauls and trudged back to camp.

13th.—We continued to labor on the road; and in the course of the day had the satisfaction to see the people working down the face of the opposite hill, about three miles distant. During the morning we had the pleasure of a visit from Mr. Fitzpatrick, with the information that all was going on well. A party of Indians had passed on snowshoes, who said they were going to the western side of the mountain after fish. This was an indication that the salmon were coming up the streams; and we could hardly restrain our impatience as we thought of them, and worked with increased vigor.

The meat train did not arrive this evening, and I gave Godey leave to kill our little dog, (Klamath,) which he prepared in Indian fashion; scorching off the hair, and washing the skin with soap and snow, And then cutting it up into pieces, which were laid on the snow. Shortly afterwards, the sleigh arrived with a supply of horsemeat; and we had tonight an extraordinary dinner—peasoup, mule, and dog.

14th.—The di!ding ridge of the Sierra is in sight from this encampment. Accompanied by Mr. Preuss, I ascended today the highest peak to the right; from which we had a beautiful view of a mountain lake at our feet, about fifteen miles in length, and so entirely surrounded by mountains that we could not discover an outlet. We had taken with us a glass; but though we enjoyed an extended view, the valley was half hidden in mist, as when we had seen it before. Snow could be distinguished on the higher parts of the coast mountains; eastward, as far as the eye could extend, it ranged over a terrible mass of broken snowy mountains, fading off blue in the distance. The rock composing the summit consists of a very coarse, dark, volcanic conglomerate; the lower parts appeared to be of a slaty structure. The highest trees were a few scattering cedars and aspens. From the immediate foot of the peak, we were two hours reaching the summit, and one hour and a quarter in descending. The day had been very bright, still, and clear, and spring seems to be advancing rapidly. While the sun is in the sky, the snow melts rapidly, and gushing springs cover the face of the mountain in all the exposed places; but their surface freezes instantly with the disappearance of the sun.

I obtained tonight some observations; and the result from these, and others made during our stay, gives for the latitude 38° 41' 57", longitude 120° 25' 57", and rate of the chronometer 25.82".

16th.—We had succeeded in getting our animals safely to the first grassy hill; and this morning I started with Jacob on a reconnoitring expedition beyond the mountain. We traveled along the crests of narrow ridges, extending down from the mountain in the direction of the valley, from which the snow was fast melting away. On the open spots was tolerably good grass; and I judged we should succeed in getting the camp down by way of these. Towards sundown we discovered some icy spots in a deep hollow; and, descending the mountain, we encamped on the headwater of a little creek, where at last the mater found its way to the Pacific.

The night was clear and very long. We heard the cries of some wild animals, which had been attracted by our fire, and a flock of geese passed over during the night. Even these strange sounds had something pleasant to our senses in this region of silence and desolation.

We started again early in the morning. The creek acquired a regular breadth of about 20 feet, and we soon began to hear the rushing of the water below the icy surface, over which we traveled to avoid the snow; a few miles below we broke through, where the water was several feet deep, and halted to make a fire and dry our clothes. We continued a few miles farther, walking being very laborious without snowshoes.

I was now perfectly satisfied that we had struck the stream on which Mr. Sutter lived; and, turning about, made a hard push, and reached the camp at dark. Here we had the pleasure to find all the remaining animals, 57 in number, safely arrived at the grassy hill near the camp; and here, also, we were agreeably surprised with the sight of an abundance of salt. Some of the horse guard had gone to a neighboring hut for pine nuts, and discovered unexpectedly a large cake of very white fine-grained salt, which the Indians told them they had brought from the other side of the mountain; they used it to eat with their pine nuts, and readily sold it for goods.

On the 19th, the people were occupied in making a road and bringing up the baggage; and, on the afternoon of the next day, February 20, 1844, we encamped, with the animals and all the materiel of the camp, on the summit of the PASS in the dividing ridge, 1,000 miles by our traveled road from the Dalles to the Columbia.

The people, who had not yet been to this point, climbed the neighboring peak to enjoy a look at the valley.

The temperature of boiling water gave for the elevation of the encampment, 9,338 feet above the sea.

This was 2,000 feet higher than the South Pass in the Rocky mountains, and several peaks in view rose several thousand feet still higher. Thus, at the extremity of the continent, and near the coast, the phenomenon was seen of a range of mums tains stil_ higher than the great Rocky mountains themselves. This extraordinary fact accounts for the Great Basin, and shows that there must be a system of small lakes and rivers here scattered over a flat country, and which the extended and lofty range of the Sierra Nevada prevents from escaping to the Pacific ocean. Latitude 38° 44'; longitude 1200 28'.

Thus the Pass in the Sierra Nevada, which so well deserves its name of Snowy mountain, is eleven degrees west and about four degrees south of the South Pass.

21st.—We now considered ourselves victorious over the mountain; having only the descent before us, and the valley under our eyes, we felt strong hope that we should force our way down. But this was a case in which the descent was not facile. Still deep fields of snow lay between them, and there was a large intervening space of rough looking mountains, through which we had yet to wind our way. Carson roused me this morning with an early fire, and we were all up long before day, in order to pass the snowfields before the sun should render the crust soft. We enjoyed this morning a scene at sunrise, which even here was unusually glorious and beautiful. Immediately above the eastern mountains was repeated a cloud formed mass of purple ranges, bordered with bright yellow gold; the peaks shot up into a narrow line of crimson cloud, above which the air was filled with a greenish orange; and over all was the singular beauty of the blue sky. Passing along a ridge which commanded the lake on our right, of which we began to discover an outlet through a chasm on the west, we passed over alternating open ground and hard crusted snowfields which supported the animals, and encamped on the ridge, after a journey of six miles. The grass was better than we had yet seen, and we were encamped in a clump of trees 20 or 30 feet high, resembling white pine. With the exception of these small clumps, the ridges were bare; and, where the snow found the support of the trees, the wind bad blown it up into banks 10 or 15 feet high. It required much care to hunt out a practicable way, as the most ones places frequently led to impassable banks.

We had hard and doubtful labor yet before us, as the snow appeared to be heavier where the timber began further down, with few open spots. Ascending a height, we traced out the best line we could discover for the next day's march, 'and had at least the consolation to see that the mountain descended rapidly. The day had been one of April—gusty, with a few occasional flakes of snow— which, in the afternoon, enveloped the upper mountain in clouds. We watched them anxiously, as now we dreaded a snowstorm. Shortly afterwards we heard the roll of thunder, and, looking towards the valley, found it enveloped in a thunderstorm. For us, as connected with the idea of summer, it had a singular charm, and we watched its progress with excited feelings until nearly sunset, when the sky cleared off brightly, and we saw a shining line of water directing its course towards another, a broader and larger sheet. We knew that these could be no other than the= Sacramento and the Bay of San Francisco; but, after our long wandering in rugged mountains, where so frequently we had met with disappointments, and where the crossing of every ridge displayed some unknown lake or river, we were yet almost afraid to believe that we were at last to escape into the genial country of which we had heard so many glowing descriptions, and dreaded to find some vast interior lake, whose bitter waters would bring us disappointment. On the southern shore of what appeared to be the bay could be traced the gleaming line where entered another large stream; and again the Buenaventura rose up in our minds.

Carson had entered the valley along the southern side of the bay, and remembered perfectly to have crossed the mouth of a very large stream, which they had been obliged to raft; but the country then was so entirely covered with water from snow and rain, that he had been Ole to form no correct impressions of watercourses.

We had the satisfaction to know that at least there were people below. Fires were lit up in the valley just at night, appearing to be in answer to ours; and these signs of life renewed, in some measure, the gayety of the camp. They appeared so near, that we judged them to be among the timber of some of the neighboring ridges; but, having them instantly in view day after day, and night after night, we afterwards found them to be fires that had been kindled by the Indians among the tulares, on the shore of the bay, 80 miles distant.

Among the very few plants that appeared here, was the common blue flax. Tonight a mule was killed for food.

22d.—Our breakfast was over long before day. We took advantage of the coolness of the early morning to get over the snow, which today occurred in very deep banks among the timber; but we searched out the coldest places, and the animals passed successfully with their loads over the hard crust. Now and then the delay of making a road occasioned much labor and loss of time. In the after part of the day, we saw before us a handsome grassy ridge point; and, making a desperate push over a snow field 10 to 15 feet deep, we happily succeeded in getting the camp across, and encamped on the ridge, after a march of three miles. We had again the prospect of a thunderstorm below, and tonight we killed another mule—now our only resource from starvation.

We satisfied ourselves during the day that the lake had an outlet between two ranges on the right; and with this, the creek on which I had encamped probably effected a junction below. Between these, we were descending.

We continued to enjoy the same delightful weather; the sky of the same beautiful blue, and such a sunset and sunrise as on our Atlantic coast we could scarcely imagine. And here among the mountains, 9,000 feet above the sea, we have the deep blue sky and sunny climate of Smyrna and Palermo, which a little map before me shows are in the same latitude.

The elevation above the sea, by the boiling point, is 8,565 feet.

23d.—This was our most difficult day; we were forced off the ridges by the quantity of snow among the timber, and obliged to take to the mountain sides, where occasionally rocks and a southern exposure afforded us a chance to scramble along. But these were steep, and slippery with snow and ice and the tough evergreens of the mountain impede our way, tore our skins, and exhausted our patience. Some of us had the misfortune to wear moccasins with padliche soles, so slippery that we could not keep our feet, and generally crawled across the snow beds. Axes and mauls were necessary today, to make a road through the snow. Going ahead with Carson to reconnoitre the road, we reached in the afternoon the rivet which made the outlet of the lake. Carson sprang over, clear across a place where the stream was compressed among rocks, but the sole of my moccasin glanced from the icy rock, and precipitated me into the river. It was some few seconds before I could recover myself in the current, and Carson, thinking me hurt, jumped in after me, and we both had an icy bath. We tried to search awhile for my gun, which had been lost in the fall, but the cold drove us out; and making a large fire on the bank, after we had partially dried ourselves we went back to meet the camp. We afterwards found that the gun had been slung under the ice which lined the banks of the creek.

Using our old plan of breaking roads with alternate horses, we reached the creek in the evening, and encamped on a dry open place in the ravine.

Another branch, which we had followed, here comes in on the left; and from this point the mountain wall, on which we had traveled today, faces to the south along the right bank of the river, where the sun appears to have melted the snow; but the opposite ridge is entirely covered. Here, among the pines, the hillside produces but little grass—barely sufficient to keep life in the animals. We had the pleasure to be rained upon this afternoon; and grass was now our greatest solicitude. Many of the men looked badly; and some this evening were giving out.

24th.—We rose at three in the morning, for an astronomical observation, and obtained for the place a lat of 38o 46' 58"; long. 120o 34' 20" The sky was clear and pure, with a sharp wind from the northeast, and the thermometer 20 below the freezing point.

We continued down the south face of the mountain; our road leading over dry ground, we were able to avoid the snow al most entirely. In the course of the morning, we struck a foot path, which we were generally able to keep; and the ground was soft to our animals' feet, being sandy or covered with mould. Green grass began to make its appearance, and occasionally we passed a hill scatteringly covered with it. The character of the forest continued the same; and, among the trees, the pine with sharp leaves and very large cones was abundant, some of them being noble trees. We measured one that had 10 feet diameter, though the height was not more than 130 feet. All along, the river was a roaring torrent, its fall very great; and, descending with a rapidity to which we had long been strangers, to our great pleasure oaktrees appeared on the ridge, and soon became very frequent; on these I remarked great quantities of mistletoe. Rushes began to make their appearance; and at a small creek where they were abundant one of the messes was left with the weakest horses, while we continued on.

The opposite mountainside was very steep and continuous— unbroken by ravines, and covered with pines and snow on the side we were traveling, innumerable rivulets poured down from the ridge. Continuing on, we halted a moment at one of these rivulets, to admire some beautiful evergreen trees, resembling live oak, which shaded the little stream. They were forty to fifty feet high, and two in diameter, with a uniform tufted top; and the summer green of their beautiful foliage, with the singing birds, and the sweet summer wind which was whirling about the dry oak leaves, nearly intoxicated us with delight; and we hurried on, filled with excitement, to escape entirely from the horrid region of inhospitable snow, to the perpetual spring of the Sacramento.

When we had traveled about tell miles, the valley opened a tittle to an oak and pine bottom, through which ran rivulets closely bordered with rushes, on which our half-starved horses fell with avidity; and here we made our encampment. Here the roaring torrent has already become a river, and we had descended to an elevation of 3,864 feet.

Along or r road today the rock was a white granite, wince appears to constitute the upper part of the mountains on both the eastern and western slopes; while between, the central is a volcanic rock.

Another horse was killed tonight, for foot,

25th.—Believing that the difficulties of the road were passed, and leaving Mr. Fitzpatrick to follow slowly, as the condition of the animals required, I started ahead this morning with a °arty of eight, consisting of myself, Mr. Preuss and Mr. Talbo4 Carson, Derosier, Towns, Prone, and Jacob. We took with us some of the nest animals, and my intention was to proceed as rapidly as possible to the house of Mr. Sutter, and return to meet the party with a supply of provisions and fresh animals.

Continuing down the river, which pursued a very direct westerly course through a narrow valley, with only a very slight and narrow bottomland, we made twelve miles, and encamped at some old Indian huts, apparently a fishing place on the river. The bottom was covered with trees of deciduous foliage, and overgrown with vines and rushes. On a bench of the hill near by, was a hill of fresh green grass, six inches long in some of the tufts which I had the curiosity to measure. The animals were driven here; and I spent part of the afternoon sitting on a large rock among them, enjoying the pauseless rapidity with which they luxuriated on the unaccustomed food.

The forest was imposing today in the magnificence of the trees; some of the pines, bearing large cones, were 10 feet in diameter. Cedars also abounded, and we measured one 281 feet in circumference, four feet from the ground. This noble tree seemed here to be in its proper soil and climate. We found it on both sides of the Sierra, but most abundant on the west.

26th.—We continued to follow the stream, the mountains on either hand increasing in height as we descended, and shutting up the river narrowly in precipices, along which we had grew difficulty to get our horses.

It rained heavily during the afternoon, and we were forced 41* the river to the heights above; whence we descended, at nightfall, the point of a spur between the river and a fork of nearly equal size, coming in from the right. Here we saw, on the lower hills, the first flowers in bloom, which occurred suddenly, and in considerable quantity—one of them a species of gilia.

The current in both streams (rather torrents than rivers) was broken by large boulders. It was late, and the animals fatigued; and not succeeding to find a ford immediately, we encamped, although the hillside afforded but a few stray bunches of grass, and the horses, standing about in the rain, looked very miserable.

27th.—We succeeded in fording the stream, and made a trail by which we crossed the point of the opposite hill, which, on the southern exposure, was prettily covered with green grass, and we halted a mile from our last encampment. The river was only about 60 feet wide, but rapid, and occasionally deep, foaming among boulders, and the water beautifully clear. We encamped on the hill slope, as there was no bottom level, and the opposite ridge is continuous, affording no streams.

We had with us a large kettle; and a mule being killed here, his head was boiled in it for several hours, and made a passable soup for famished people.

Below, precipices on the river forced us to the heights, which we ascended by a steep spur 2,000 feet high. My favorite horse, Proveau, had become very weak, and was scarcely able to bring himself to the top. Traveling here was good, except in crossing the ravines, which were narrow, steep, and frequent. We caught a glimpse of a deer, the first animal we had seen; but did not succeed in approaching him. Proveau could not keep up, and I left Jacob to bring him on, being obliged to press forward with the party, as there was no grass in the forest. We grew very anxious as the day advanced and no grass appeared, for the lives of our animals depended on finding tonight. They were in just such a condition that grass and repose for the night enabled them to get on the next day. Every hour we had been expecting to see open out before us the valley, which, from the mountain above, seemed almost at our feet. A new and singular shrub, which had made its appearance since crossing the mountain, was very frequent today. It branched out near the ground, forming a clump eight to ten feet high, with pale green leaves, of an oval form; and the body and blanches had a naked appearance, as if stripped of the bark, which is very smooth and thin, of a chocolate color, contrasting well with the pale green of the leaves. The day was nearly gone; we had made a hard day's march, and found no grass. Towns became lightheaded, wandering off into the woods without knowing where he was going, and Jacob brought him back.

Neal nightfall we descended into the steep ravine of a handsome creek 30 feet wide, and I was engaged in getting the horses up the opposite hill, when I heard a shout from Carson, who bad gone ahead a few hundred yards—" Life yet," said he, as he came up, " life yet; I have found a hillside sprinkled with grass enough for the night." We drove along our horses, and encamped at the place about dark, and there was just room enough to make a place for shelter on the edge of the stream, Three horses were lost today—Proveau; a fine young horse from the Columbia, belonging to Charles Towns; and another Indian horse, which carried our cooking utensils. The two former gave out, and the latter strayed off into the woods as we reached the camp.

29th.—We lay shut up in the narrow ravine, and gave the animals a necessary day; and men were sent back after the others. Derosier volunteered to bring up Proveau, to whom he knew I was greatly attached, as he had been my favorite horse on both expeditions. Carson and I climbed one of the nearest mountains; the forest land still extended ahead, and the valley appeared as far as ever. The packhorse was found near the camp; but Derosier did not get in.

MARCH.

1st.—Derosier did not get in during the night, and leaving him to follow, as no grass remained here, we continued on over the uplands, crossing many small streams, and camped near, on the river, having made six miles. Here we found the hillside covered (although lightly) with fresh green grass; and from this time forward we found it always improving and abundant.

We made a pleasant camp on the river hill, where were some beautiful specimens of the chocolate colored shrub, which were a foot in diameter near the ground, and fifteen to twenty feet high. The opposite ridge runs continuously along, unbroken by streams. We are rapidly descending into the spring, and we are leaving our snowy region far behind; every thing is getting green; butterflies are swarming; numerous bugs are creeping out, wakened from their winter's sleep; and the forest flowers are coming into bloom. Among those which appeared most numerously today was dodecatheon dentatum.

We began to be uneasy at Derosier's absence, fearing he might have been bewildered in the woods. Charles Towns, who had not yet recovered his mind, went to swim in the river, as if it were summer, and the stream placid, when it was a cold mountain torrent foaming among the rocks. We were happy to see Derosier appear in the evening. He came in, and, sitting down by the fire, began to tell us where he had been. He imagined he had been gone several days, and thought we were still at the camp where he had left us; and we were pained to see that his mind was deranged. It appeared that he had been lost in the mountain, and hunger and fatigue, joined to weakness of body and fear of perishing in the mountains, had crazed him. The times were severe when stout men lost their minds from extremity of suffering—when horses died—and when mules and horses, ready to die of starvation, were killed for food. Yet there was no murmuring or hesitation.

A short distance below our encampment the river mountains terminated in precipices, and, after a fatiguing march of only a few miles, we encamped on a bench where there were springs, and an abundance of the freshest grass. In the mean time, Mr. Preuss continued on down the river, and, unaware that we had encamped so early in the day, was lost. When night arrived, and he did not come in, we began to understand what Lad happened to him; but it was too late to make any search.

3d.—We followed Mr. Preuss' trail for a considerable distance along the river, until we reached a place where he had descended to the stream below and encamped. Here we shouted and fired guns, but received no answer; and we concluded that he had pushed on down the stream. I determined o keep out from the river, along which it was nearly impracticable to travel with animals, until it should form a valley. At every step the country improved in beauty; the pines were rapidly disappearing, and oaks became the principal trees of the forest. Among these, the prevailing tree was the evergreen oak, (which, by way of distinction, we call the live oak;) and with these occurred frequently a new species of oak bearing a long slender acorn, from an inch to an inch and a half in length, which we now began to see formed the principal vegetable food of the inhabitants of this region. In a short distance we crossed a little rivulet, where were two old huts, and near by were heaps of acorn hulls. The ground round about was very rich, covered with an exuberant sward of grass; and we sat down for a while in the shade of the oaks, to let the animals feed. We repeated our shouts for Mr. Preuss; ana this time were gratified with an answer. The voice grew rapidly nearer, ascending from the river; but when we expected to see him emerge, it ceased entirely. We had called up some straggling Indian—the first we had met, although for two days back we had seen tracks—who, mistaking us for his fellows, had been only undeceived on getting close up. It would have been pleasant to witness his astonishment; he would not have been more frightened had some of the old mountain spirits they are so much afraid of suddenly appeared in his path. Ignorant of the character of these people, we had now an additional cause of uneasiness in regard to Mr. Preuss; he had no arms with him, and we began to think his chance doubtful. We followed on a trail, still keeping out from the river, and descended to a very large creek, dashing with great velocity over a preeminently rocky bed, and among large boulders. The bed had sudden breaks, formed by deep holes and ledges of rock running across. Even here, it deserves the name of Rock creek, which we gave to it. We succeeded in fording it, and toiled about three thousand feet up the opposite hill. The mountains now were getting sensibly lower; but still there is no valley on the river, which presents steep and rocky banks; but here, several miles from the river, the country is smooth and grassy; the forest has no undergrowth; and in the open valleys of rivulets, or around springheads, the low groves of live oak give the appearance of orchards in an old cultivated country. Occasionally we met deer, but had not the necessary time for hunting. At one of these orchard grounds, we encamped about noon to make an effort for Mr. Preuss. One man took his way along a spur leading into the river, in hope to cross his trail; and another took our own back. Both were volunteers; and to the successful man was promised a pair of pistols—not as a reward, but as a token of gratitude for a service which would free us all from much anxiety.

We had among our few animals a horse which was so much reduced, that, with traveling, even the good grass could not save him; and, having nothing to eat, he was killed this afternoon. He was a good animal, and had made the journey round from Fort Hall.

Dodecatheon dentatum continued the characteristic plant in flower; and the naked looking shrub already mentioned continued characteristic, beginning to put forth a small white blossom. At evening the men returned, having seen or heard nothing of Mr. Preuss; and I determined to make a hard push down the river the next morning and get a hold of him.

4th.—We continued rapidly along on a broad plainly beaten trail, the mere traveling and breathing the delightful air being a positive enjoyment. Our road led along a ridge inclining to the river, and the air and the open grounds were fragrant with flowering shrubs; and in the course of the morning we issued on an open spur; by which we descended directly to the stream. Here the river issues suddenly from the mountains, which hitherto had hemmed it closely in; these now become softer, and change sensibly their character; and at this point commences the most beautiful valley in which we had ever traveled. We hurried to the river, on which we noticed a small sand beach, to which Mr. Preuss would naturally have gone. We found no trace of him, but, instead, were recent tracks of bare footed Indians, and little piles of muscle shells, and old fire where they had roasted the fish. We traveled on over th river grounds, which were undulating, and covered with grass to the river brink. We halted to noon a few miles beyond, always under the shade of the evergreen oaks, which formed open groves on the bottoms.

Continuing our road in the afternoon, we ascended to the uplands, where the river passes round a point of great beauty, and goes through very remarkable dalles, in character resembling those of the Columbia. Beyond, we again descended to the bottoms, where we found an Indian village, consisting of two or three huts; we had come upon them suddenly, and the people had evidently just run off. The huts were low and slight, made like beehives in a picture, five or six feet high, and near each was a crate, formed of interlaced branches and grass, in size and shape like a very large hogshead. Each of these contained from six to nine bushels. These were filled with the long acorns already mentioned, and in the huts were several neatly Made baskets, containing quantities of the acorns roasted. They were sweet and agreeably flavored, and we supplied ourselves with about half a bushel, leaving one of our shirts, a handkerchief, and some smaller articles, in exchange. The river again entered for a space among the hills, and we followed a trail leading across a bend through a handsome hollow behind. Here, while engaged in trying to circumvent a deer, we discovered some Indians on a hill several hundred yards ahead, and gave them a shout, to which they responded by loud and rapid talking and vehement gesticulation, but made no stop, hurrying up the mountain as fast as their legs could carry them. We passed on, and again encamped in a grassy grove.

The absence of Mr. Preuss gave me great concern; and for a large reward, Derosier volunteered to go back on the trail I directed him to search along the river, traveling upward for the space of a day and a half, at which time I expected he would meet Mr. Fitzpatrick, whom I requested to aid in the search; at all events, he was to go no farther, but return to this camp, where a cache of provisions was made for him.

Continuing the next day down the river, we discovered three squaws in a little bottom, and surrounded them before they could make their escape. They had large conical baskets, which they were engaged in filling with a small leafy plant (erodium cicutarium) just now beginning to bloom, and covering the ground like a sward of grass. These did not make any lamentations, but appeared very much impressed with our appearance, speaking to us only in a whisper, and offering us smaller baskets of the plant, which they signified to us was good to eat, making signs also that it was to be cooked by the fire. We drew out a little cold horsemeat, and the squaws made signs to us that the men had gone out after deer, and that we could have some by waiting till they came in. We observed that the horses ate with great avidity the herb which they had been gathering; and here also, for the first time, we saw Indians eat the common grass—one of the squaws pulling several tufts, and eating it with apparent relish. Seeing our surprise, she pointed to the horses; but we could not well understand what she meant, except, perhaps, that what was good for the one was good for the other.

We encamped in the evening on the shore of the river, at a place where the associated beauties of scenery made so strong an impression on us that we gave it the name of the Beautiful Camp. The undulating river shore was shaded with the live oaks, which formed a continuous grove over the country, and the same grassy sward extended to the edge of the water, and we made our fires near some large granite masses which were lying among the trees. We seen several of the acorn caches during the day, and here there were two which were very large, containing each, probably, ten bushels. Towards evening we heard a weak shout among the hills behind, and had the pleasure to see Mr. Preuss descending towards the camp. Like ourselves, he had traveled today 25 miles, but had seen nothing of Derosier. Knowing, on the day he was lost that I was determined to keep the river as much as possible, he had not thought it necessary to follow the trail very closely, but walked on, right and left, certain to find it somewhere along the river, searching places to obtain good views of the country. Towards sunset he climbed down towards the river to look for the camp; but, finding no trail, concluded that we were behind, and walked back till night came on, when, being very much fatigued, he collected driftwood and made a large fire among the rocks. The next day it became more serious and he encamped again alone, thinking that we must have taken some other course. To go back would have been mad ness in his weak and starved condition, and onward towards the valley was his only hope, always in expectation of reaching it soon. His principal means of subsistence were a few roots, which the hunters call sweet onions, having very little taste, but a good deal, of nutriment, growing generally in rocky ground, and requiring a good deal of labor to get, as he had only a pocketknife. Searching for these, he found a nest of big ants, which he let run on his hand, and stripped them off in his mouth; these had an agreeable acid taste. One of his greatest privations was the want of tobacco; and a pleasant smoke at evening would have been a relief which only a voyageur could appreciate. He tried the dried leaves of the live oak, knowing that those of other oaks were sometimes used as a substitute; but these were too thick, and would not do. On the 4th he made seven or eight miles, walking slowly along the river, avoiding as much as possible to climb the hills. In little pools he caught some of the smallest kind of frogs; which he swallowed, not so much in the gratification of hunger, as in the hope of obtaining some strength.. Scattered along the river were old fireplaces, where the Indians had roasted muscles and acorns; but though he searched diligently, he did not there succeed in finding either. He had collected firewood for the night, when he heard, at some distance from the river the barking of what he thought were two dogs, and walked it that direction as quickly as he was able, hoping to find then, some Indian hut, but met only two wolves; and, in his disappointment, the gloom of the forest was doubled.

Traveling the next day feebly down the river, he found five or six Indians at the huts of which we save spoken: some were Fainting themselves black, and others roasting acorns.

Being only one man, they did not run off, but received him kindly, and gave him a welcome supply of roasted acorns.

He gave them his pocketknife in return, and stretched out tis hand to one of the Indians, who did not appear to comprehend the motion, but jumped back, as if he thought he was about to lay hold of him. They seemed afraid of him, not certain as to what he was.

Traveling on, he came to the place where we had found the squaws. Here he found our fire still burning, and the tracks of the horses. The sight gave him sudden hope and courage; and, following as fast as he could, joined us at evening.

6th.—We continued on our road through the same surpassingly beautiful country; entirely unequalled for the pasturage of stock by any thing we had ever seen. Our horses had now become so strong that they were able to carry us, and we traveled rapidly—over four miles an hour; four of us riding every alternate hour. Every few hundred yards we came upon a little band of deer; but we were too eager to reach the settlement, which we momentarily expected to discover, to halt for any other than a passing shot. In a few hours we reached a large fork, the northern branch of the river, and equal in size to that which we had descended. Together they formed a beautiful stream, 60 to 100 yards wide; which at first, ignorant of the nature of the country through which that river ran, we took to be the Sacramento.

We continued down the right bank of the river, traveling for a while over a wooded upland, where we had the delight to discover tracks of cattle. To the southwest was visible a black column of smoke, which we had frequently noticed in descending, arising from the fires we had sees from the top of the

Sierra. From the upland we descended into broad groves on the river, consisting of the evergreen, and a new species of a white oak, with a large tufted top, and three to six feet in diameter. Among these was no brushwood; and the grassy surface gave to it the appearance of parks in an old settled country. Following the tracks of the horses and cattle, in search of people, we discovered a small village of Indians. Some of these had on shirts of civilized manufacture, but were other wise naked, and we could understand nothing from them: they appeared entirely astonished at seeing us.

We made an acorn meal at noon, and hurried on; the valley being gay with flowers, and some of the banks being absolutely golden with the Californian poppy, (eschescholtzia crocea.) Here the grass was smooth and green, and the groves very open; the large oaks throwing a broad shade among sunny spots. Shortly afterwards we gave a shout at the appearance, on a little bluff, of a neatly built adobe house, with glass windows. We rode up, but, to our disappointment, found only Indians. There was no appearance of cultivation, and we could see no cattle; and we supposed the place had been abandoned. We now pressed on more eagerly than ever: the river swept round a large bend to the right; the hills lowered down entirely; and, gradually entering a broad valley, we came unexpectedly into a large Indian village, where the people looked clean, and wore cotton shirts and various other articles of dress. They immediately crowded around us, and we had the inexpressible delight to find one who spoke a little indifferent Spanish, but who at first confounded us by saying there were no whites in the country; but just then a well-dressed Indian came up, and made his salutations in very well-spoken Spanish. In answer to our inquiries, he informed us that we were upon the Rio de los Americans, (the river of the Americans,) and that it joined The Sacramento river about ten miles below. Never did a name sound more sweetly! We felt ourselves among our country men; for the name of American, in these distant parts, is applied to the citizens of the United States. To our eager inquiries he answered, "I am a vaquero (cowherd) in the service of Capt. Sutter, and the people of this ranchena work for him." Our evident satisfaction made him communicative; and he went on to say that Capt. Sutter was a very rich man, and always glad to see his country people. We asked for his house.

He answered, that it was just over the hill before us; and offered, if we would wait a moment, to take his horse and conduct us to it. We readily accepted this civil offer. In a short distance we came in sight of the fort; and, passing on the way the house at a settler on the opposite side, (a Mr. Sinclair, we forded the river; and in a few miles were met, a short distance from the fort, by Capt. Sutter himself. He gave us a most frank and cordial reception—conducted us immediately to his residence—and under his hospitable roof we had a night of rest, enjoyment, and refreshment, which none but ourselves could appreciate. But the party left in the mountains, with Mr. Fitzpatrick, were to be attended to; and the next morning, supplied with fresh horses and provisions, I hurried off to meet them. On the second day we met, a few miles below the forks of the Rio de los Americanos; and a more forlorn and pitiable sight than they presented, cannot well be imagined. They were all on foot— each man, weak and emaciated, leading a horse or mule as weak and emaciated as themselves. They had experienced great difficulty in descending the mountains, made slippery by rains and melting snows, and many horses fell over precipices, and were killed; and with some were lost the packs they carried. Among these, was a mule with the plants which we had collected since leaving Fort Hall, along a line of 2,000 miles' travel. Out of 67 horses and mules, with which we commenced crossing the Sierra, only 33 reached the valley of the Sacramento, and they only in a condition to be led along. Mr. Fitzpatrick and his party, traveling more slowly, had been able to make some little exertion at hunting and had killed a few deer. The scanty supply was a great relief to them; for several had been made sick by the strange and unwholesome food which the preservation of life compelled them to use. We stopped and encamped as soon as we met and a repast of good beef, excellent bread, and delicious salmon, which I had brought along, was their first relief from the sufferings of the Sierra, and their first introduction to the luxuries of the Sacramento. It required all our philosophy and forbearance to prevent plenty from becoming as hurtful to us now as scarcity had been before.

The next day, March 8th, we encamped at the junction of the two rivers, the Sacramento and Americanos; and thus found the whole party in the beautiful valley of the Sacramento. It was a convenient place for the camp; and, among other things, was within reach of the wood necessary to make the packsaddles, which we should need on our long journey home, from which we were farther distant now than we were four months before, when from the Dalles of the Columbia we so cheerfully took up the homeward line of march.

Captain Sutter emigrated to this country from the western part of Missouri in 1838-39, and formed the first settlement in the valley, on a large grant of land which he obtained from the Mexican Government. He had, at first, some trouble with the Indians; but, by the occasional exercise of well-timed authority, he has succeeded in converting them into a peaceable and industrious people. The ditches around his extensive wheat fields; the making of the sundried bricks, of which his fort is constructed; the ploughing, harrowing, and other agricultural operations, are entirely the work of these Indians, for which they receive a very moderate compensation—principal in shirts, blankets, and other articles of clothing. In the same manner, on application to the chief of a village, he readily obtains as many boys and girls as he has any use for. There were at this time a number of girls at the fort, in training for a future woolen factory; but they were now all busily engaged in constantly watering the gardens, which the unfavorable dryness of the season rendered necessary. The occasional dryness of some seasons, I understood to be the only complain 3f the settlers in this fertile valley, as it sometimes renders the 3rops uncertain. Mr. Sutter was about making arrangements o irrigate his lands by means of the Rio de los Americanos. He had this year sown, and altogether by Indian labor, three hundred fingers of wheat.

A few years since, the neighboring Russian establishment of Ross, being about to withdraw from the country, sold to him a large number of stock, with agricultural and other stores with a number of pieces of artillery and other munitions o ear; for those, a regular yearly payment is made in grain

The fort is a quadrangular adobe structure, mounting twelve pieces of artillery, (two of them brass,) and capable of a mitting a garrison of a thousand men; this, at present, consists of forty Indians in uniform—one of whom was always found on duty at the gate. As might naturally be expect the pieces are not in very good order. The whites in the employment of Capt. Sutter, American, French, and Germs amount, perhaps, to thirty men. The inner wall is form into buildings, comprising the common quarters, with blacksmith and otter workshops; the dwelling house, with a large distillery house, and other buildings, occupying more the cent of the area.

It is built upon a pond like stream, at times a running cm communicating with the Rio de los Americanos, which enters the Sacramento about two miles below. The latter is here noble river, about three hundred yards broad, deep and tranquil, with several fathoms of water in the channel, and banks continuously timbered. There were two vessels I longing to Capt. Sutter at anchor near the landing—one large two-masted lighter, and the other a schooner, which w shortly to proceed on a voyage to Fort Vancouver for a cat) of goods.

Since his arrival, several other persons, principally Americans, have established themselves in the valley. Mr. Sinclair: from whom I experienced much kindness during my stay, settled a few miles distant, on the Rio de los Americanos. N Coudrois, a gentleman from Germany, has established himself on Feather river, and is associated with Capt. Sutter in ag] cultural pursuits. Among other improvements, they are abo to introduce the cultivation of rapeseed, (brassica rapes,) which there is every reason to believe is admirably adapted to t] climate and soil. The lowest average produce of wheat, far as we can at present know, is thirty-five fingers for or sown; but, as an instance of its fertility, it may be mention(that Señor Valejo obtained, on a piece of ground where she had been pastured, 800 fanegas for eight sown. The product being different in various places, a very correct idea cannot be formed.

An impetus was given to the active little population by out arrival, as we were in want of every thing. Mules, horses and cattle, were to be collected; the horse mill was at work day and night, to make sufficient flour; the blacksmith's shop was put in requisition for horseshoes and bridle bits; and packsaddles, ropes, and bridles, and all the other little equipments of the camp, were again to be provided.

The delay thus occasioned was one of repose and enjoyment; which our situation required, and, anxious as we were to resume our homeward journey, was regretted by no one. In the mean time, I had the pleasure to meet with Mr. Chiles, who was residing at a farm on the other side of the river Sacramento, while engaged in the selection of a place for a settlement, for which he had received the necessary grant of land from the Mexican government.

It will be remembered that we had parted near the frontier of the states, and that he had subsequently descended the val ley of Lewis's fork, with a party of ten or twelve men, with the intention of crossing the intermediate mountains to the waters of the Bay of San Francisco. In the execution of this design, and aided by subsequent information, he left the Columbia at the mouth of Malheur river, and, making his way to the headwaters of the Sacramento with a part of his company, traveled down that river to the settlements of Nueva Helvetia,. The other party, to whom he had committed his wagons, and mill irons, and saws, took a course further to the south, and the wagons and their contents were lost.

On the 22d we made a preparatory move, and encamped near the settlement of Mr. Sinclair, on the left bank of the Rio de los Americanos. I had discharged five of the party; Neal the blacksmith, (an excellent workman, and an unmarried man, who had done his duty faithfully, and had been of very great service to me,) desired to remain, as strong inducements were offered here to mechanics.

Although at considerable inconvenience to myself, his good conduct induced me to comply with his request; and I obtained for him from Capt. Sutter, a present compensation of two dollars and a half per diem, with a promise that it should be increased to five, if he proved as good a workman as had been represented. He was more particularly an agricultural blacksmith. The other men were discharged with their own consent.

While we remained at this place, Derosier, one of our best men, whose steady good conduct had won my regard, wandered off from the camp, and never returned to it again, nor has he since been heard of.

24th.—We resumed our journey with an ample stock of provisions and a large cavalcade of animals, consisting of 130 horses and mules, and about 30 head of cattle, five of which were milk cows. Mr. Sutter furnished us also with an Indian boy, who had been trained as a vaquero, and who Would be serviceable in managing our cavalcade, great part of which were nearly as wild as buffalo, and who was, besides, very anxious to go along with us. Our direct course home was east, but the Sierra would force us south, above 500 miles of traveling, to a pass at the head of the San Joaquin river. This pass, reported to be good, was discovered by Mr. Joseph Walker, of whom I have already spoken, and whose name it might therefore appropriately bear. To reach it, our course lay along the valley of the San Joaquin—the river on our right, and the lofty wall of the impassable Sierra on the left. From that pass we were to move southeastwardly, having the Sierra then on the right, and reach the "Spanish trail," deviously traced from one watering place to another, which constituted the route of the caravans from Puebla de los Angelos, near the coast of the Pacific, to Santa Fe of New Mexico. From the pass to this trail was 150 miles. Following that trail through a desert, relieved by some fertile plains indicated by the recurrence of the term vegas, until it turned to the right to cross the Colorado, our course would be northeast until we regained the latitude we had lost in arriving at Utah lake, and thence to the Rocky mountains at the head of the Arkansas. This course of traveling, forced upon us by the structure of the country, would occupy a computed distance of 2,000 miles before we reached the head of the Arkansas—not a settlement to be seen upon it—and the names of places along it, all being Spanish or In.

Alan, indicated that it had been but little trod by American feet. Though long, and not free from hardships, this route presented some points of attraction, in tracing the Sierra Nevada—turning the Great Basin, perhaps crossing its rim on the south—completely solving the problem of any river, except the Colorado, from the Rocky mountains on that part of our continent —and setting the southern extremity of the Great Salt lake, of which the northern part had been examined the year before.

Taking leave of Mr. Sutter, who, with several gentlemen, accompanied us a few miles on our way, we traveled about 18 miles, and encamped on the Rio de los Cosumnes, a stream receiving its name from the Indians who live in its valley. Our road was through a level country, admirably suited to cultivation, and covered with groves of oak trees, principally the evergreen oak, and large oak already mentioned, in form like those of the white oak. The weather, which here, at this season, can easily be changed from the summer heat of the valley to the frosty mornings and bright days nearer the mountains,, continued delightful for travelers, but unfavorable to the agriculturists, whose crops of wheat began to wear a yellow tinge from want of rain.

25th.—We traveled for 28 miles over the same delightful country as yesterday, and halted in a beautiful bottom at the ford of the Rio de los Mukelemnes, receiving its name from another Indian tribe living on the river. The bottoms on the stream are broad, rich, and extremely fertile, and the uplands are shaded with oak groves. A showy lupinus, of extraordinary beauty, growing four to five feet in height, and covered with spikes in bloom, adorned the banks of the river, and filled the air with a light and grateful perfume.

On the 26th we halted at the Arroyo de las Calaveras, (Skull creek,) a tributary to the San Joaquin — the previous two streams entering the bay between the San Joaquin and Sacramento rivers. This place is beautiful, with open groves of oak, and a grassy sward beneath, with many plants in bloom, some varieties of which seem to love the shade of the trees, and grow there in close small fields. Near the river, and relacing the grass, are great quantities of ammole, (soap plant,) the leaves of which are used in California for making, among other things, mats for saddlecloths. A vine with a small white flower, (meloihria I) called here la yerba buena, and which, from its abundance, gives name to an island and town in the bay, was today very frequent on our road—sometimes running on the ground or climbing the trees.

27th—Today we traveled steadily and rapidly up the valley; for, with our wild animals, any other gait was impossible, and making about five miles an hour. During the earlier part of the day, our ride had been over a very level prairie, or rather a succession of long stretches of prairie, separated by lines and groves of oak timber, growing along dry gullies, which are filled with water in seasons of rain; and, perhaps, also, by the melting snows. Over much of this extent, the vegetation was sparse; the surface showing plainly the action of water, which, in the season of flood, the Joaquin spreads over the valley., About one o'clock we came again among innumerable flowers; and a few miles further, fields of the beautiful blue flowering lupine, which seems to love the neighborhood of water, indicated that we were approaching a stream. We here found this beautiful shrub in thickets, some of them being 12 feet in height. Occasionally three or four plants were clustered together, forming a grand bouquet, about 90 feet in circumference, and 10 feet high; the whole summit covered with spikes of flowers, the perfume of which is very sweet and grateful. A lover of natural beauty can imagine with what pleasure we rode among these flowering groves, which filled the air with a light and delicate fragrance. We continued our road for about a half a mile, interspersed through an open grove of live oaks, which, in form, were the most symmetrical and beautiful we had yet seen in this country. The ends of their branches rested on the ground, forming somewhat more than a half sphere of very full and regular figure, with leaves apparently smaller than usual.

The Californian poppy, of a rich orange color, was numerous today. Elk and several bands of antelope made their appearance. Our road was now one continued enjoyment; and it was pleasant riding among this assemblage of green pastures with varied flowers 4nd scattered groves, and out of the warm green spring to look at the rocky and snowy peaks where lately we had suffered so much. Emerging from the timber, we came suddenly upon the Stanislaus river, where we hoped to find a ford, but the stream was flowing by, dark and deep, swollen by the mountain snows; its general breadth was about 50 yards.

We traveled about five miles up the river, and encamped without being able to find a ford. Here we made a large coral, in order to be able to catch a sufficient number of our wild animals to relieve those previously packed.

Under the shade of the oaks, along the river, I noticed erodium cicutarium in bloom, eight or ten inches high. This is the plant which we had seen the squaws gathering on the Rio de los Americanos. By the inhabitants of the valley it is highly esteemed for fattening cattle, which appear to be very fond of it. Here, where the soil begins to be sandy, it supplies to a considerable extent the want of grass.

Desirous, as far as possible, without delay, to include in our examination the San Joaquin river, I returned this morning down the Stanislaus for 17 miles, and again encamped without having found a fording place. After following it for eight miles further the next morning, and finding ' ourselves in the vicinity of the San Joaquin, encamped in a handsome oak grove, and, several cattle being killed, we ferried over our baggage in their skins. Here our Indian boy, who probably had not much" idea of where he was going, and began to be alarmed at the many streams which we were rapidly putting between him and the village, deserted.

Thirteen head of cattle took a sudden fright, while we were driving them across the river, and galloped off. I remained a day in the endeavor to recover them; but, finding they has taken the trail back to the fort, let them go without further effort. Here we had several days of warm and pleasant rain, which doubtless saved the crops below.

APRIL.

On the 1st of April, we made 10 miles across a prairie without timber, when we were stopped again by another large river, which is called the Rio de la Merced, (river of our Lady of Mercy.) Here the country had lest its character of extreme fertility, the soil having become more sandy and light; but, for several days past, its beauty had been increased by the additional animation of animal life; and now, it is crowded with bands of elk and wild horses; and along the rivers are frequent fresh tracks of grizzly bear, which are unusually numerous in this country:

Our route had been along the timber of the San Joaquin, generally about eight miles distant, over a high prairie.

In one of the bands of elk seen today, there were about 200; but the larger bands, both of these and wild horses, are generally found on the other side of the river, which, Tor that reason, I avoided crossing. I had been informed below, that the droves of wild horses were almost invariably found on the western bank of the river; and the danger of losing our animals among them, together with the wish of adding to our reconnoissance the numerous streams which run down from the Sierra, decided me to travel up the eastern bank.

2d.—The day was occupied in building a boat, and ferrying our baggage across the river; and we encamped on the bank. A large fishing eagle was slowly sailing along, looking after salmon; and there were some pretty birds in the timber, with partridges, ducks and geese innumerable in the neighborhood. We were struck with the tameness of the latter bird at Helvetia, scattered about in flocks near the wheatfields, and eating grass on the prairie; a horseman would ride by within 30 yards, without disturbing them.

3d.—Today we touched several times the San Joaquin river—here a finelooking tranquil stream, with a slight current, and apparently deep It resembled the Missouri in color, with occasional points of white sand; and itsbanks, where steep, were a kind of sandy clay; its average width appeared to be about eighty yards. In the bottoms are frequent ponds, where our approach disturbed multitudes of wild fowl, principally geese. Skirting along the timber, we frequently started elk; and large bands were seen during the day, with antelope and wild horses. The low country and the timber rendered it difficult to keep the main line of the river; and this evening we encamped on a tributary stream, about five miles from its mouth. On the prairie bordering the San Joaquin bottoms, there occurred during the day but little grass, and in its place was a sparse and dwarf growth of plants; the soil being sandy, with small bare places and hillocks, reminded me much of the Platte bottoms; but, on approaching the timber, we found a more luxuriant vegetation, and at our camp was an abundance of grass and pea vines.

The foliage of the oak is getting darker; and every thing, except that the weather is a little cool, shows that spring is rapidly advancing; and today we had quite a summer rain.

4th.—Commenced to rain at daylight, but cleared off brightly at sunrise. We ferried the river without any difficulty, and continued up the San Joaquin. Elk were running in bands over the prairie and in the skirt of the timber. We reached the river at the mouth of a large slough, which we were unable to ford, and wade a circuit of several miles around. Here the country appears very flat; oak trees have entirely disappeared, and are replaced by a large willow, nearly equal to it in size. The river is about a hundred yards in breadth, branching into sloughs, and interspersed with islands. At this time it appears sufficiently deep for a small steamer, but its navigation would be broken by shallows at low water. Bearing in towards the river, we were again forced off by another slough; and passing around, steered towards a clump of trees on the river, and finding there good grass, encamped. The prairies along the left bank are alive with immense droves of wild horses; and they had been seen during the day at every opening through the woods which afforded us a view across the river. Latitude, by observation, 37° 08' 00"; longitude 120° 45' 22".

5th —During the earlier part of the day's ride, the country presented a lacustrine appearance; the river was deep, and nearly on a level with the surrounding country; its banks raised like a levee, and fringed with willows. Over the bordering plain were interspersed spots of prairie among fields of tale, (bulrushes,) which in this country are called tulares, and little ponds. On the opposite side, a line of timber was visible, which, according to information, points out the course of the slough, which at times of high water connects with the San Joaquin river—a large body of water in the upper part of the valley, called the Tule lakes. The river and all its sloughs are very' full, and it is probable that the lake is now discharging. Here elk were frequently started, and one was shot out of a band which ran around us. On our left, the Sierra maintains its snowy height, and masses of snow appear to descend very low towards the plains; probably the late rains in the valley were snow on the mountains. We traveled 37 miles, and encamped on the river. Longitude of the camp, 1200 28' 34", and latitude, 360 49' 12".

6th.—After having traveled fifteen miles along the river we made an early halt, under the shade of sycamore trees Here we found the San Joaquin coming down from the Sierra with a westerly course, and checking our way, as all its tributaries had previously done. We had expected to raft the river; but found a good ford, and encamped on the opposite bank, where droves of wild horses were raising clouds of dust on the prairie. Columns of smoke were visible in the direction of the Tule lakes to the southward—probably kindled in the tulares by the Indians, as signals that there were strangers in the valley.

We made, on the 7th, a hard march in a cold chilly rain from morning until night—the weather so thick that we traveled by compass. This was a traverse from the San Joaquin to the waters of the Tule lakes, and our road was over a very level prairie country. We saw wolves frequently during the day, prowling about after the young antelope, which cannot run very fast. These were numerous during the day, and they were caught by the people.

Late in the afternoon we discovered timber, which was found to be groves of oak trees on a dry arroyo. The rain, which had fallen in frequent showers, poured down in a storm at sunset, with a strong wind, which swept off the clouds, and left a clear sky. Riding on through the timber, about dark we found abundant water in small ponds, 20 to 30 yards in diameter, with clear deep water and sandy beds, bordered with bog rushes, (juncus effusus,) and a tall rush (scirpus lacustris) twelve feet high, and surrounded near the margin with willow trees in bloom; among them one which resembled salix myricoides. The oak of the groves was the same already mentioned, with Small leaves, in form like those of the white oak, and forming, with the evergreen oak, the characteristic trees of the valley

8th.—After a ride of two miles through brush and open groves, we reached a large stream, called the River of the Lake, resembling in size the San Joaquin, and being about 100 yards broad. This is the principal tributary to the Tule lakes, which collect all the waters in the upper part of the valley. While we were searching for a ford, some Indians appeared on the opposite bank, and having discovered that we were not Spanish soldiers, showed us the way to a good ford several mike above.

The Indians of the Sierra make frequent descents upon the settlements west of the Coast Range, which they keep constantly swept of horses; among them are many who are called Christian Indians, being refugees from Spanish missions. Several of these incursions occurred while we were at Helvetia. Occasionally parties of soldiers follow them across the Coast Range, but never enter the Sierra.

On the opposite side we found some forty or fifty Indians, who had come to meet us from the village below. We made them some small presents, and invited them to our encampment, which, after about three miles through fine oak groves, we made on the river. We made a fort, principally on account of our animals. The Indians brought otter skins, and several kinds of fish, and bread made of acorns, to trade. Among them were several who had come to live among these Indians when the missions were broken up, and who spoke Spanish fluently. They informed us that they were called by the

Spaniards mansaos, (tame,) in distinction from the wilder tribes of the mountains. They, however, think themselves very insecure, not knowing at what unforeseen moment the sins of the latter may be visited upon them. They are dark-skinned, but handsome and intelligent Indians, and live principally on acorns and the roots of the tule, of which also their huts are made.

By observation, the latitude of the encampment is 360 24' 50", and longitude 1190 41' 40".

9th.—For several miles we had very bad traveling over what is called rotten ground, in which the horses were frequently up to their knees. Making towards a line of timber, we found a small fordable stream, beyond which the county improved, and the grass became excellent; and crossing a number of dry and timbered arroyos, we traveled until late through open oak groves, and encamped among a collection of streams. These were running among rushes and willows; and, as usual, flocks of blackbirds announced our approach to water. We have here approached considerably nearer to the eastern Sierra, which shows very plainly, still covered with masses of snow, which yesterday and today has also appeared abundant on the Coast Range.

10th.—Today we made another long journey of about forty miles, through a country uninteresting and flat, with very little grass and a sandy soil, in which several branches we crossed had lost their water. In the evening the face of the country became hilly; and, turning a few miles up towards the mountains, we found a good encampment on a pretty stream hidden among the hills, and handsomely timbered, principally with large cottonwoods, (populus, differing from any in Michaux's Sylva.) The seed vessels of this tree were now just about bursting.

Several Indians came down the river to see us in the even ing; we gave them supper, and cautioned them against steal mg our horses; which they promised not to attempt.

11th.—A broad trail along the river here takes out arrimg the hills. "Buen camino," (good road,) said one of the Indians, of whom we had inured about the pass; and, following it accordingly, it conducted us beautifully through a very broken country, by an excellent way, which, otherwise, we should have found extremely bad. Taken separately, the hills present smooth and graceful outlines, but, together, make bad traveling ground. Instead of grass, the whole face of the country it closely covered with erodium cicutarium, here only two or three inches high. Its height and beauty varied in a remarkable manner with the locality, being, in many low places which we passed during the day, around streams and springs, two and three feet high. The country had now assumed a character of aridity; and the luxuriant green ot these little streams, wooded with willow, oak, or sycamore, looked very refreshing among the sandy hills.

In the evening we encamped on a large creek, with abundant water. I noticed here in bloom, for the first time since leaving the Arkansas waters, the Miribilis Jalapa.

12th.—Along our road today the country was altogether sandy, and vegetation meager. Ephedra occidentalis, which we had first seen in the neighborhood of the Pyramid lake, made its appearance here, and in the course of the day became very abundant, and in large bushes. Towards the close of the afternoon, we reached a tolerably large river, which empties into a small lake at the head of the valley; it is about thirty five yards wide, with a stony and gravelly bed, and the swiftest stream we have crossed since leaving the bay. The bottoms produced no grass, though well timbered with willow and cottonwood; and, after ascending several miles, we made a late encampment on a little bottom, with scanty grass In greater part, the vegetation along our road consisted now of rare and unusual plants, among which many were entirely new.

Along the bottoms were thickets consisting of several varieties of shrubs, which made here their first appearance; and among these was Garrya elliptica, (Lindley,) a small tree belonging to a very peculiar natural order, and, in its general appearance, (growing in thickets,) resembling willow. It now became common along the streams, frequently supplying the place of salix longtfolia.

13th.—The water was low, and a few miles above we forded the river at a rapid, and marched in a southeasterly direction over a less broken country. The mountains were now very near, occasionally looming out through fog. In a few hours we reached the bottom of a creek without water, over which the sandy beds were dispersed in many branches. Immediately where we struck it, the timber terminated; and below, to the right, it was a broad bed of dry and bare sands. There were many tracks of Indians and horses imprinted in the sans, which, with other indications, informed us was the creek issuing from the pass, and which we have called Pass creek. We ascended a trail for a few miles along the creek, and suddenly found a stream of water five feet wide, running with a lively current, but losing itself almost immediately. This little stream showed plainly the manner in which the mountain "eaters lose themselves in sand at the eastern foot of the Sierra, leaving only a parched desert and arid plains beyond. The stream enlarged rapidly, and the timber became abundant as we ascended.

A new species of pine made its appearance, with several kinds of oaks, and a variety of trees; and the country changing its appearance suddenly and entirely, we found ourselves again traveling among the old orchard like places. Here we selected a delightful encampment in a handsome green oak hollow, where among' the open bolls of the trees was an abundant sward of grass and pea vines. In the evening a Christian Indian rode into the camp, well dressed, with long spurs, and a sombreo, and speaking Spanish fluently. It was an unexpected apparition, and a strange and pleasant sight in this desolate gorge of a mountain—an Indian face, Spanish costume, jingling spurs, and horse equipped after the Spanish manner. He informed me that he belonged to one of the Spanish missions to the south, distant two or three days' ride, and that he had obtained from the priests leave to spend a few days with his relations in the Sierra. Having seen us enter the pass, he had come down to visit us. He appeared familiarly acquainted with the country, and gave me definite and clear information in regard to the desert region east of the mountains. I had entered the pass with a strong disposition to vary my loafs, and to travel directly across towards the Great Salt lake, in the view of obtaining some at pittance with the interior of the Great Basin, while pursuit; a direct course for the frontier; but his representation, which described it as an arid and barren desert, the.. had repulsed by its sterility all the attempts of the Indians to penetrate it, determined me for the present to relinquish the plan, and agreeably to his advice, after crossing the Sierra, continue our intended route along its eastern base to the Spanish trail. By this route, a party of six Indians, who had come from a great river in the eastern part of the desert to trade with his people, had, just started on their return. He would himself return the next day to San Fernando, and as our roads would be the same for two days, he offered his services to conduct us so far on our way. His offer was gladly accepted. The fog which had somewhat interfered with views in the valley, had entirely passed off, and left a clear sky. That which had enveloped us in the neighborhood of the pass proceeded evidently from fires kindled among the tulares by Indians living near the lakes, and which were intended to warn those in the mountains that there were strangers in the valley. Our position was in latitude 35° 17' 12", and longitude 118° 35' 03"

14th.—Our guide joined us this morning on the trail; and, arriving in a short distance at an open bottom where the creek forked, we continued up the right-hand branch, which was enriched by a profusion of flowers, and handsomely wooded with sycamore, oaks, cottonwood, and willow, with other trees, and some shrubby plants. In its long strings of balls, this sycamore differs from that of the United States, and is the platanus occidentalus of Hooker—a new species recently described among the plants collected in the voyage of the Sulphur. The cottonwood varied its foliage with white tufts; and the feathery seeds were flying plentifully through the air. Gooseberries, nearly ripe, were very abundant in the mountains; and as we passed the dividing grounds, which were not very easy to ascertain, the air was filled with perfume, as if we were entering a highly cultivated garden; and, instead of green, our pathway and the mountain sides were covered with fields of yellow flowers, which here was the prevailing color. Our journey today was in the midst of an advanced spring, whose green and floral beauty offered a delightful contrast to the sandy valley we had just left. All the day, snow was in sight on the butte of the mountain, which frowned down upon us on the right; but we beheld it now with feelings of pleasant security, as, we rode along between green trees, and on flowers, with hummingbirds and other feathered friends of the traveler enlivening the serene spring air. As we reached the summit of this beautiful pass, and obtained a view into the eastern country, we saw at once that here was the place to take leave of all such pleasant scenes as those around us. The distant mountains were now bald rocks again, and below the land had any color but green. Taking into consideration the nature of the Sierra Nevada, we found this pass an excellent one for horses; and with a little labor, or perhaps with a more perfect examination of the localities, it might be made sufficiently practicable for wagons. Its latitude and longitude may be considered that of our last encampment, only a few miles distant. The elevation was not taken—our half wild cavalcade making it troublesome to halt before night, when once started.

We here left the waters of the bay of San Francisco, and, though forced upon them contrary to my intentions, I cannot regret the necessity which occasioned the deviation. It made me well acquainted with the great range of the Sierra Nevada of the Alta California, and showed that this broad and elevated snowy ridge was a continuation of the Cascade Range of Oregon, between which and the ocean there is still another and a lower range, parallel to the former and to the coast, and which may be called the Coast Range. It also made me well acquainted with the basin of the San Francisco bay, and with the two pretty rivers and their valleys (the Sacramento and San Joaquin) which are tributary to that bay, and cleared up some points in geography on which error had long prevailed. It had been constantly represented, as I have already stated, that the bay of S tit Francisco opened far into the interior, b some river coming: down from the base of the Rocky mountains and upon which supposed stream the name of Rio Buenaventura had been bestowed. Our observations of the Sierra Nevada, in the long distance from the head of the Sacramento, to the head of the San Joaquin, and of the valley below it, which collects all the waters of the San Francisco bay, show that this neither is nor can be the case. No river from the interior does, or can, cross the Sierra Nevada—itself more lofty than the Rocky mountains; and as to the Buenaventura, the mouth of which seen on the coast gave the idea and the name of the reputed great river, it is, in fact, a small stream of no consequence, not only below the Sierra Nevada, but actually below the Coast Range— taking its rise within half a degree of the ocean, running parallel to it for about two degrees, and then falling into the Pacific near Monterey. There is no opening from the bay of San Francisco into the interior of the continent. The two rivers which flow into it are comparatively short, and not perpendicular to the coast, but lateral to it, and having their heads towards Oregon and southern California. They open lines of communication north and south, and not eastwardly; and thus this want of interior communication from the Sarr Francisco bay, now fully ascertained, gives great additional value to the Columbia, which stands alone as the only great river on the Pacific slope of our continent which leads from the ocean to the Rocky mountains, and opens a line of communication from the sea to the valley of the Mississippi.

Four companeros joined our guide at the pass; and two going back at noon, the others continued on in company. Descending from the hills, we reached a country of fine grass, where the erodium cicularium finally disappeared, giving place to an excellent quality of bunchgrass. Passing by some springs where there was a rich sward of grass among groves of large black oak, we rode over a plain on which the guide pointed out a spot where a refugee Christian Indian had been killed by a party of soldiers which had unexpectedly penetrated into the mountains. Crossing a low sierra, and descending a hollow where a spring gushed out, we were struck by the sudden appearance of yucca trees, which gave a sumpuous and southern character to the country, and suited well with the dry and desert region we were approaching. Associated with the idea of barren sands, their stiff and ungraceful form makes them to the traveler the most repulsive tree in the vegetable kingdom. Following the hollow, we shortly came upon a creek timbered with large black oak, which yet had not put forth a leaf. There was a small rivulet of running water, with good grass.

15th.—The Indians who had accompanied the guide returned this morning, and I purchased from them a Spanish saddle and long spurs, as reminiscences of the time; and for a few yards of scarlet cloth they gave me a horse, which afterwards became food for other Indians.

We continued a short distance down the creek, in which our guide informed us that the water very soon disappeared, and turned directly to the southward along the foot of the mountain; the trail on which we rode appearing to describe the eastern limit of travel, where water and grass terminated. Crossing a low spur, which bordered the creek, we descended to a kind of plain among the lower spurs, the desert being in full view on our left, apparently illimitable. A hot mist lay over it today, through which it had a white and glistening appearance; here and there a few dry looking buttes and isolated black ridges rose suddenly upon it. "There," said our guide., stretching out his hand towards it "there are the great news. (plains,) no hay aqua; no hay zaca.'e—nada: there is neither water nor grass—nothing; every animal that goes upon them, dies." It was indeed dismal to look upon, and to conceive so great a change in so short a distance. One might travel the world over, without finding a valley more fresh and verdant—more floral and sylvan—more alive with birds and animals—more bounteously watered—than we had left in the San Joaquin: here, within a few miles' ride, a vast desert plain spread before us, from which the boldest traveler turned away in despair.

Directly in front of us, at some distance to the southward, and running out in an easterly direction from the mountains, stretched a sierra, having at the eastern end (perhaps 50 miles distant) some snowy peaks, on which, by the information of out guide, snow rested all the year.

Our cavalcade made a strange and grotesque appearance; and it was impossible to avoid reflecting upon our position and composition in this remote solitude. Within two degrees of the Pacific ocean—already far south of the latitude of Monterey—and still forced on south by a desert on one hand, and a mountain range on the other—guided by a civilized Indian, attended by two wild ones from the Sierra—a Chinook from the Columbia, and our mixture of American, French, German —all armed—four or five languages heard at once—above a hundred horses and mules, half wild—American, Spanish, and Indian dresses and equipments intermingled—such was our composition. Our march was a sort of procession. Scouts ahead and on the flanks; a front and rear division; the pack animals, baggage, and horned cattle in the centre; and the whole stretching a quarter of a mile along our dreary path. In this form we journeyed, looking more as if we belonged to Asia than to the United States of America.

We continued in a southerly direction across the plain, to which, as well as to all the country, so far as we could see, he yucca trees gave a strange and singular character. Several new plants appeared, among which was a zygophyllaceous shrub, (zygophyllum Californicum, Torr and Frem.,) sometimes ten feet in height; in form, and in the pliancy of its branches, it is rather a graceful plant. Its leaves are small, covered with a resinous substance; and, particularly when bruised and crushed, exhale a singular but very agreeable and refreshing odor. This shrub and the yucca, with many varieties of cactus, make the characteristic features in the vegetation for a long distance to the eastward. Along the foot of the mountain, 20 miles to the southward, red stripes of flowers were visible during the morning, which we supposed to be variegated sandstones. We rode rapidly during the day, and in the afternoon emerged from the yucca forest at the foot of an outlier of the Sierra before us, and came among the fields of flowers we had seen in the morning, which consisted primarily of the rich orange colored California poppy, mingled with other flowers of brighter tints. Reaching the top of the sloth, which was covered with fine bunchgrass, and where the hills were very green, our guide pointed to a small hollow in the mountain before us, saying, " a este piedra hay aqua." He appeared to know every nook in the country. We continued our beautiful road, and reached a spring in the slope at the foot of the ridge, running in a green ravine, among granite boulders; here nightshade, and borders of buckwheat, with their white blossoms around the granite rocks, attracted our notice as familiar plants. Several antelopes were seen among the hills, and some large hares. Men were sent back this evening in search of a wild mule with a valuable pack, which had managed (as they frequently do) to hide itself along the road.

By observation, the latitude of the camp is 340 41° 42", and longitude 1180 20' 00". The next day the men returned with the mule.

17th.—Crossing the ridge by a beautiful pass of hollows, where several deer broke out of the thickets, we emerged at a small salt lake in a valley lying nearly east and west, where a trail from the mission of San Buenaventura comes in. The lake is about 1,200 yards in diameter; surrounded on the margin by a white salty border, which, by the smell, reminded us slightly of Lake Albert. There are some cottonwoods, with willow and elder, around the lake; and the water is a little salt, although not entirely unfit for drinking. Here we turned directly to the eastward along the trail, which, from being seldom used, is almost imperceptible; and, after traveling a few miles, our guide halted, and, pointing to the hardly visible trail, "aqui es camino," said he, " no se pierde—va siempre."

He pointed out a black butte on the plain at the foot of the mountain, where we would find water to encamp at night; and, giving him a present of knives and scarlet cloth, we shook hands and parted. He bore off south, and in a day's ride would arrive at San Fernando, one of several missions in this part of California, where the country is so beautiful that it is considered a paradise, and the name of its principal town (Puebla Gig los Angeles) wr ald make it angelic tinned on through a succession of valleys, and came into a most beautiful spot of flower fields; instead of green, the hills were purple and orange, with unbroken beds, into which each color was separately gathered. A pale straw color, with a bright yellow, the rich red orange of the poppy mingled with fields of purple, covered the spot with a floral beauty; and, on the border of the sandy deserts, seemed to invite the traveler to go no farther. Riding along through the perfumed air, we soon after entered a defile overgrown with the ominous artemisia tridentata, which conducted us into a sandy plain covered more or less densely with forests of yucca.

Having now the snowy ridge on our right, we continued out way towards a dark butte, belonging to a low sierra on the plain, and which our guide had pointed out for a landmark. Late in the day, the familiar growth of cottonwood, a line of which was visible ahead, indicated our approach to a creek, which we reached where the water spread out into sands, and a little below sank entirely. Here our guide had intended we should pass the night; but there was not a blade of grass, and, hoping to find nearer the mountain a little for the night, we turned up the stream. A hundred yards above, we found the creek a fine stream, sixteen feet wide, with a swift current. A dark night overtook us when we reached the hills at the foot of the ridge, and we were obliged to encamp without grass; tying up what animals we could secure in the darkness, the greater part of the wild ones having free range fin the night. Here the stream was two feet deep, swift and clear, issuing from a neighboring snow peak. A few miles before reaching this creek, we had crossed a broad dry riverbed, which, nearer the hills, the hunters had found a bold and handsome stream.

18th.—Some parties were engaged in hunting up the scattered horses, and others in searching for grass above; both were successful, and late in the day we encamped among some springheads of the river, in a hollow which was covered with only tolerably good grasses, the lower ground being entirely overgrown will large bunches of the coarse stiff grass, (carts ratchensis.)

Our latitude, by observation, was 34° 27' 03", and longitude 117° 13' 00'

Traveling close along the mountain, we followed up, in the afternoon of the 19th, another stream, in hopes to find a grass patch like that of the previous day, but were deceived; except some scattered bunchgrass, there was nothing but sand; and even the fertility of the mountain seemed withered by the air of the desert. Among the few trees was the nut pine, (pinus monophyllus.)

Our road the next day was still in an easterly direction along the ridge, over very bad traveling ground, broken and confounded with crippled trees and shrubs; and, after a difficult march of eighteen miles, a general shout announced that we had struck the great object of our search—THE SPANISH TRAIL —which here was running directly north. The road itself, and its course, were equally happy discoveries to us. Since the middle of December we had continually been forced south by mountains and by deserts, and now would have to make six degrees of northing, to regain the latitude on which we wished to cross the Rocky mountains. The course of the road, therefore, was what we wanted; and, once more, we felt like going homewards. A road: to travel on, and the right course to go, were joyful consolations to us; and our animals enjoyed the beaten track like ourselves. Relieved from the rocks and brush, our wild mules started off at a rapid rate, and in fifteen miles we reached a considerable river, timbered with cottonwood and willow, where we found a bottom of tolerable grass. As the animals had suffered a great deal in the last few days, I remained here all next day, to allow them the necessary repose; and it was now necessary, at every favorable place, to make a little halt. Between us and the Colorado river we were aware that the country was extremely poor in grass, and scarce for water, there being many jornadas, (days' journey,) or long stretches of forty to sixty miles, without water, where the road was marked by bones of animals.

Although in California we had met with people who had passed over this trail, we had been able to obtain no correct information about it; and the li 'eater part of what we had heard was found to be only a tissue of falsehoods. The rivers that Is a found an it were never mentioned, and others, described in name and locality, were subsequently seen in another part of the country. It was described as a tolerably good sandy road, with so little rock as scarcely to require the animals to be shod; and we found it the roughest and rockiest road we had ever seen in the country, and which nearly destroyed our band of fine mules and horses. Many animals are destroyed on it every year by a disease called the foot evil; and a traveler should never venture on it without having his animals well shod, and also carrying extra shoes.

Latitude 34° 34' 11"; and longitude 117° 13' 00".

The morning of the 22d was clear and bright, and a snowy peak to the southward shone out high and sharply defined. As has been usual since we crossed the mountains and descended into the hot plains, we had a gale of wind. We traveled down the right bank of the stream, over sands which are somewhat [close, and have no verdure, but are occupied by various shrubs. A. clear bold stream, 60 feet wide, and several feet deep, had a strange appearance, running between perfectly naked banks of sand. The eye, however, is somewhat relieved by willows, and the beautiful green of the sweet cottonwoods with which it is well wooded. As we followed along its course, the river, instead of growing constantly larger, gradually dwindled away, as it was absorbed by the sand. We were now careful to take the old camping places of the annual Santa Fe caravans, which, luckily for us, had not yet made their yearly passage. A drove of several thousand horses and mules would entirely have swept away the scanty grass at the watering places, and we should have been obliged to leave the road to obtain subsistence for our animals. After riding 20 miles in a northeasterly direction, we found an old encampment, where we halted.

By observation, the elevation of this encampment is 2,250 feet.

23d.—The trail followed still along the river, which, in the course of the morning, entirely disappeared. We continued along the dry bed, in which, after an interval of about 10 miles, the water reappeared in some low places, well timbers.' with cottonwood and willow, where was another of the customary camping grounds. Here a party of six Indians came into camp, poor and hungry, and quite in keeping with the character of the country. Their arms were bows of unusual length, and each had a large gourd, strengthened with meshes of cord, in which he carried water. They proved to be the Mohahve Indians mentioned by our recent guide; and from one of them, who spoke Spanish fluently, I obtained some interesting information, which I would be glad to introduce here. An account of the people inhabiting this region would undoubtedly possess interest for the civilized world. Our journey homewards was fruitful in incident; and the country through which we traveled, although a desert, afforded much to excite the curiosity of the botanist; but limited time, and the rapidly advancing season for active operations, oblige me to omit all extended descriptions, and hurry briefly to the conclusion of this report.

The Indian who spoke Spanish had been educated for a number of years at one of the Spanish missions, and, at the breaking up of those establishments, had returned to the mountains, where he hid been found by a party of Mohahve (sometimes called Amuchaba) Indians, among whom he had ever since resided.

He spoke of the leader of the present party as "mes amo," (my master.) He said they lived upon a large river in the southeast, which the "soldiers called the Rio Colorado;" but that, formerly, a portion of them lived upon this river, and among the mountains which had bounded the river valley to the northward during i he day, and that here along the river they had raised various kinds of melons. They sometimes came over to trade with the Indians of the Sierra, bringing with them blankets and goods manufactured by the Monquis and other Colorado Indians. They rarely carried home horses, on account of the difficulty of getting them across the desert, and of guarding them afterwards from the Pautah Indians who inhabit the Sierra, at the head of the Rio Virgen, (river if the Virgin.

He informed us that, a short distance below, this rivet finally disappeared. The two different portions in which water is found had received from the two different names; and subsequently I heard it called by the Spaniards the Rew de las Animas, but on the map we have called it the Mohahve river.

24th.—We continued down the stream (or rather its bed) for about eight miles, where there was water still in several holes, and encamped. The caravans sometimes continued below, to the end of the river, from which there is a very long jornada of perhaps 60 miles, without water. Here a singular and new species of acacia, with spiral pods or seed vessels, made its first appearance; becoming henceforward, for a considerable distance, the characteristic tree. It was here comparatively large, being about 20 feet in height, with a full and spreading top, the lower branches declining towards tha ground. It afterwards occurred of smaller size, frequently in groves, and is very fragrant. It has been called by Dr. Torrey, spirolobium odoratum. The zygophyllaceous shrub had been constantly characteristic of the plains along the river; and here, among many new plants, a new and very remarkable species of eriogonum (eriogonum inflatum, Tor. & Frem.) made its first appearance.

Our cattle had become so tired and poor by this fatiguing traveling, that three of them were killed here, and the meat dried. The Indians had now an occasion for a great feast, and were occupied the remainder of the day and all night in cooking and eating. There was no part of the animal for which they did not find some use, except the bones. In the afternoon we were surprised by the sudden appearance in the camp of two Mexicans—a man and a boy. The name of the man was Andreas Fuentes; and that of the boy, (a handsome lad, 11 years old,) Pablo Hernandez. They belonged to a party consisting of six persons, the remaining four being the wife of Fuentes, and the father and mother of Pablo, and Santiago Giacome, a resident of New Mexico. With a cavalcade of about thirty horses, they had come out from Peubla de los Angeles, near the coast, under the guidance of Giacome, advance of the great caravan, in order to travel more at leisure, and obtain better grass. Having advanced as far into the desert as was considered consistent with their safety, they halted at the Archilette, one of the customary camping grounds, about 80 miles from our encampment, where there is a spring of good water, with sufficient grass; and concluded to await there the arrival of the great caravan. Several Indians were soon discovered lurking about the camp, who, in a day or two after, came in, and, after behaving in a very friendly manner, took their leave, without awakening any, suspicions. Their deportment begat a security which proved fatal. In a few days afterwards, suddenly a party of about one hundred Indians appeared in sight, advancing towards the camp. It was too late, or they seemed not to have presence of mind to take proper measures of safety; and the Indians charged down into their camp, shouting as they advanced, and discharging flights of arrows. Pablo and Fuentes were on horse guard at the time, and mounted according to the custom of the country. One of the principal objects of the Indians was to get possession of the horses, and part of them immediately surrounded the band; but, in obedience to the shouts of Giacome, Feuntes drove the animals over and through the assailants, in spite of their arrows; and, abandoning the rest to their fate, carried them off at speed across the plain. Knowing that they would be pursued by the Indians, without making any halt except to shift their saddles to other horses, they drove them on for about sixty miles, and this morning left them at a watering place on the trail, called Agua de Tomaso. Without giving themselves any time for rest, they hurried on, hoping to meet the Spanish caravan, when they discovered my camp. I received them kindly, taking them into my own mess, and promised them such aid as circumstances might put it in my power to give.

25th.—We left the river abruptly, and, turning to the north, regained in a few miles the main trail, (which had left the river sooner than ourselves,) and continued our way across a lower ridge of the mountain, through a miserable tract of sand and gravel. We crossed at intervals the broad beds of dry gullies, where in the seasons of rains and melting snows there would be brooks or rivulets: and at one of these, where there was no indication of water, were several freshly dug holes, in which there was water at the depth of two feet. These holes had been dug by the wolves, whose keen sense of smell had scented the water under the dry sand. They were nice little wells, narrow, and dug straight down; and we got 'pleasant water out of them.

The country had now assumed the character of an elevated and mountainous desert; its general features being black, rocky ridges, bald, and destitute of timber, with sandy basins between. Where the sides of these ridges are washed by gullies, the plains below are strewed with beds of large pebbles or rolled stones, destructive to cur soft footed animals, accustomed to the soft plains of the Sacramento valley. Through these sandy basins sometimes struggled a scanty stream, or occurred a hole of water, which furnished camping grounds for travelers. Frequently in our journey across, snow was visible on the surrounding mountains; but their waters rarely reached the sandy plain below, where we toiled along, oppressed with thirst and a burning sun. But, throughout this nakedness of sand and gravel, were many beautiful plants and flowering shrubs, which occurred in many new species, and with greater variety than we had been accustomed to see in the most luxuriant prairie countries; this was a peculiarity of this desert. Even where no grass would take root, the naked sand would bloom with some rich and rare flower, which found its appropriate home in the arid and barren spot.

Scattered over the plain, and tolerably abundant, was a handsome leguminous shrub, three or four feet high; with fine bright purple flowers. It is a new psoralea, and occurred frequently henceforward along our road.

Beyond the first ridge, our road bore a little to the east of north, towards a gap in a higher line of mountains; and, after traveling about 25 miles, we arrived at the Agua de Tomaso—the spring where the horses had been left; but, as we expected they were gone. A brief examination of the ground convinced us that they had been driven off by the Indians. Carson and

Godey volunteered, with the Mexican, to pursue them; and well mounted, the three set off on the trail. At this stopping place there are a few bushes, and a very little grass. Its water was a pool; but near by was a spring, which had been dug out by Indians or travelers. Its water was cool—a great refreshment to us under a burning sun.

In the evening Fuentes returned, his horse having failed; but Carson and Godey had continued the pursuit.

I observed tonight an occultation of a Cancri, at the dark limb of the moon, which gives for the longitude of the place 116° 23' 28"; the latitude, by observation, is 35° 13' 08". from Helvetia to this place, the positions along the intervening are laid down, with the longitudes obtained from the chronometer, which appears to have retained its rate remarkably wt. II; but henceforward, to the end of our journey, the few longitudes given are absolute, depending upon a subsequent or cultation and eclipses of the satellites.

In the afternoon of the next day, a war whoop was heard, such as Indians make when returning from a victorious enterprise; and soon Carson and Godey appeared, driving before Clem a band of horses, recognised by Fuentes to be part of fiose they had lost. Two bloody scalps, dangling from the end of Godey's gun, announced that they had overtaken the Indians as well as the horses. They informed us, that after Fuentes left them, from the failure of his horse, they continued the pursuit alone, and towards nightfall entered the mountains, into which the trail led. After sunset the moon gave light, and they followed the trail by moonshine until late in the night, when it entered a narrow defile, and was difficult to follow. Afraid of losing it in the darkness of the defile, they tied up their horses, struck no fire, and lay down to sleep, in silence and in darkness. Here they lay from midnight until morning. At daylight they resumed the pursuit, and about sunrise discovered the horses; and, immediately dismounting and tying up their own, they crept cautiously to a rising ground which intervened, from the crest of which they perceived the encampment of four lodges close by. They proceeded quietly, and had got within 30 or 40 yards of their object, when a move ant among the horses discovered them to the Indians. Giving he war shout, they instantly charged into the camp, regardless of the number which the four lodges would imply. The Indians received them with a flight of arrows shot from their long bows, one of which passed through Godey's shirt collar, barely missing the neck: our men fired their rifles upon a steady aim, and rushed in. Two Indians were stretched upon the ground, fatally pierced with bullets: the rest fled, except a little lad that was captured. The scalps of the fallen were instantly stripped off; but in the process, one of them, who had two balls through his body, sprang to his feet, the blood streaming from his skinned head, and uttering a hideous howl. An old squaw, possibly his mother, stopped and looked back from the mountainsides she was climbing, threatening and lamenting. The frightful spectacle appalled the stout hearts of our men; but they did what humanity required, and quickly terminated the agonies 4f the gory savage. They were now masters of the camp, which was a pretty little recess in the mountain, with a fine spring, and apparently safe from all invasion. Great preparations had been made to feast a large party, for it was a very proper place to rendezvous, and for the celebration of such orgies as robbers of the desert would delight in. Several of the best horses had been killed, skinned, and cut up; for the Indians living in mountains, and only coming into the plains to rob and murder, make no other use of horses than to eat them. Large earthen vessels were on the ,fire, boiling and stewing the horse beef; and several baskets, containing 50 or 60 pairs of moccasins, indicated the presence, or expectation, of a considerable party. They released the boy, who had given strong evidence of stoicism, or something else, of the savage character, in commencing his breakfast upon a horse's head, as soon as he found he was not to be aided, but only tied as a prisoner. Their object accomplished, our men gathered up all the surviving horses, fifteen in number, returned upon their trail, and rejoined us, at our camp, in the afternoon of the same day. They had rode about 100 miles, in the pursuit and return, and all in 30 hours. The time, place, object, and numbers considered, this expedition of Carson and Godey may be considered among the boldest and most disinterested which the annals of western adventure, so full of daring deeds, can present. Two men, in a savage desert, pursue day and night an unknown body of Indians, into the defile of an unknown mountain—attack them on sight, without counting numbers—and defeat them in an instant—and for what? To punish the robbers of the desert, and to avenge the wrongs of Mexicans whom they din not know. I repeat: it was Otterson and Godey who did this—the former an American, born in the Boonslick bounty of Missouri; the latter a Frenchman, born in St. Louis,—and both trained to western enterprise from early life.

By the information of Fuentes, we had now to make a long, stretch of 40 or 50 miles across a plain which lay between us and the next possible camp; and we resumed our journey late in the afternoon, with the intention of traveling through the night, and avoiding the excessive heat of the day, which was oppressive to our animals. For several hours we traveled across a high plain, passing, at the opposite side, through a canon by the bed of a creek, running northwardly into a small lake beyond, and both of them being dry. We had a warm, moon shiny night; and, traveling directly towards the north star, we journeyed now across an open plain, between mountain ridges—that on the left being broken, rocky, and bald, according to Carson and Godey, who had entered here in pursuit of the horses. The plain appeared covered principally with the zygcrphyllum Californicuntr already mentioned; and the line of our road was marked by the skeletons of horses, which were strewed to considerable breadth over the plain. We were always warned on entering one of these long stretches, by the bones of these animals, which had perished before they could reach the water. About midnight we reached a considerable streambed, now dry—the discharge of the waters of this basin, (when it collected any)—down which we descended, in a northwesterly direction. The creek bed was overgrown with shrubbery, and several hours before day it brought us to the entrance of a canon, where we found water, and encamped. This word canon is used by the Spaniards to signify a defile or gorge in a creek or river, where high rocks press in close, and make a narrow way, usually difficult, and often impossible to be passed.

In the morning we found that we had a very poor camping ground—a swampy, salty spot, with a little long, unwholesome grass; and the water, which rose in springs, being useful only to wet the mouth, but entirely too salt to drink. All around was sand and rocks, and skeletons of horses which had not been able to find support for their lives. As we were about to start, we found, at the distance of a few hundred yards, among the hills to the southward, a spring of tolerably good water, which was a relief to ourselves; but the place was too poorto remain long, and therefore we continued on this morning. On the creek were thickets of spzrolobium odoratum (acacia) in bloom, and very fragrant.

Passing through the canon, we entered another sandy basin, through which the dry streambed continued its northwesterly course, in which direction appeared a high snowy mountain.

We traveled through a barren district, where a heavy gale was blowing about the loose sand, and, after a ride of eight miles, reached a large creek of salt and bitter water, running in a westerly direction, to receive the streambed we had left. It is called by the Spaniards Amargosathe bitterwater of the desert. Where we struck it, the stream bends; and we continued in a northerly course up the ravine of its valley passing on the way a fork from the right, near which occurred a bed of plants, consisting of a remarkable new genus of cruciferm.

Gradually ascending, the ravine opened into a green valley, where, at the foot of the mountain, were springs of excellent water. We encamped among groves of the new acacia, and there was an abundance of good grass for the animals.

This was the best camping ground we had seen since we struck the Spanish trail. The day's journey was about twelve miles.

29th.—Today we had to reach the Archilette, distant seven miles, where the Mexican party had been attacked, and, leaving our encampment early, we traversed a part of the desert the moat sterile and repulsive we had yet seen. Its prominent features were dark sierras, naked and dry; on the plains a few straggling shrubs— among them, cactus of several types. Fuentes pointed out one called by the Spaniards bisnada, which has a juicy pulp, slightly acid, and is eaten by the traveler to allay thirst. Our course was generally north; and, after crossing an intervening ridge, we descended into a sandy plain, or basin, in the middle of which was the grassy spot, with its springs and willow bushes, which constitutes a camping place in the desert, and is called the Archilette. The dead silence of the place was ominous; and, galloping rapidly up, we found only the corpses of the two men: every thing else was gone. They were naked, mutilated, and pierced with arrows. Hernandez had evidently fought, and with desperation. He lay in advance of the willow half faced tent, which sheltered his family, as if he had come out to meet danger, and to repulse it from that asylum One of his hands, and both his legs, had been cut off. Giacome, who was a large and strong looking man, was lying in one of the willow shelters, pierced with arrows.

Of the women no trace could be found, and it was evident they had been carried off captive. A little lapdog, which had belonged to Pablo's mother, remained with the dead bodies, and was frantic with joy at seeing Pablo; he, poor child, was fran—tic with grief, and filled the air with lamentations for his father and mother. Mi Padre! Mi Madre!was his incessant cry. When we beheld this pitiable sight, and pictured to ourselves the fate of the two women, carried off by savages so brutal and so loathsome, all compunction for the scalped alive Indian ceased; and we rejoiced that Carson and Godey had been able to give so useful a lesson to these American Arabs who lie in wait to murder and plunder the innocent traveler.

We were all too much affected by the sad feelings which the place inspired, to remain an unnecessary moment. The night we were obliged to pass there. Early in the morning we left it, having first written a brief account of what had happened, and put it in the cleft of a pole planted at the spring, that the approaching caravan might learn the fate of their friends. In commemoration of the event, we called the place Ague de Hernandez—Hernandez's spring. By observation, its latitude was 35o 51' 21".

30th.—We continued our journey over a district similar to that of the day before. From the sandy basin, in which was the spring, we entered another basin of the same character, surrounded everywhere by mountains. Before us stretched a high range, rising still higher to the left, and terminating in a snowy mountain.

After a day's march of 24 miles, we reached at evening the bed of a stream from which the water had disappeared, a little only remaining in holes, which we increased by digging; and about a mile above, the stream, not yet entirely sunk, was spread out over the sands, affording a little water for the animals. The stream came out of the mountains on the left, very slightly wooded with cottonwood, willow, and acacia, and a few dwarf oaks; and grass was nearly as scarce as water. A plant with showy yellow flowers (Stanleya integrifolia) occurred abundantly at intervals for the last two days, and triogo sum infiatum was among the characteristic plants.

MAY. lst.—The air is rough, and overcoats pleasant. The sky, 4s blue, and the day bright. Our road was over a plain, towards the foot of the mountain; zygophyllum Californicum, now in bloom, with a small yellow flower, is characteristic of the country; and cacti were very abundant, and in rich fresh bloom, which wonderfully ornaments this poor country. We encamped at a spring in the pass, which had been the site of an old village. Here we found excellent grass, but very little water. We dug out the old spring, and watered some of our animals. The mountain here was wooded very slightly with the nutpine, cedars, and a dwarf species of oak; and among the shrubs were Purshia tridentata, Artemisia, and ephedra edentaliz. The numerous shr abs which constitute the vege ration of the plains are now in bloom, with flowers of white yellow, red, and purple. The continual rocks, and want of water and grass, began to be very hard on our mules ant horses; but the principal loss is occasioned by their crippled feet, the greater part of those left being in excellent order, and scarcely a day passes without some loss; and, one by one, Fuentes' horses are constantly dropping behind. Whenever they give out, he dismounts and cuts off their tails and manes, to make saddle girths—the last advantage one can gain from them.

The next day, in a short but rough ride of 12 miles, we crossed the mountain; and, descending to a small valley plain, encamped at the foot of the ridge, on the bed of a creek, and found good grass in sufficient quantity, and abundance of water in holes. The ridge is extremely rugged and broken, presenting on this side a continued precipice, and probably affords very few passes. Many digger tracks were seen around us, but no Indians were visible.

3d,—After a day's journey of 18 miles, in a northeasterly direction, we encamped in the midst of another very large basin, at a camping ground called las Vegas—a term which the Spaniards use to signify fertile or marshy plains, in contradistinction to lianas, which they apply to dry and sterile plains. Two narrow streams of clear water, four or five feet deep, gush suddenly, with a quick current, from two singularly large springs; these, and other waters of the basin, pass out in a gap to the eastward. The taste of the water is good, but rather too warm to be agreeable; the temperature being 71o in the one, and 73o in the other. They, however, afford a delightful bathing place.

4th.—We started this morning earlier than usual, traveling in a northeasterly direction across the plain. The new acacia (spirolobium odoratum) has now become the characteristic tree of the country; it is in bloom, and its blossoms are very fragrant. The day was still, and the heat, which soon became very oppressive, appeared to bring out strongly the refreshing scent of the zygophyllaceous shrubs and the sweet perfume of the acacia. The snowy ridge we bad just crossed looked out conspicuously in the northwest. In about five hours ride, we crossed a gap in the surrounding ridge, and the appearance of skeletons of horses very soon warned us that we were engaged in another dry jornad,a, which proved the longest we had made in all our journey—between fifty and sixty miles without a drop of water.

Travelers through countries Affording water and timber can have no conception of our intolerable thirst while journeying over the hot yellow sands of this elevated country, where the heated air seems to be entirely deprived of moisture. We ate occasionally the bisnada, and moistened our mouths with the acid of the sour dock, (rumex venoms.) Hourly expecting to find water, we continued to press on until towards midnight, when, after a hard and uninterrupted march of 10 hours, our wild mules began running ahead; and in a mile or two we came to a bold running stream—so keen is the sense of that animal, in these desert regions, in scenting at a distance this necessary of life,

According to the information we had received, Sevier river was a tributary of the Colorado; and this, accordingly, should have been one of its affluents. It proved to be the Rio de los Angeles, (river of the Angels)—a branch of the Rio Virgen. (river of the Virgin.)

5th.—On account of our animals, it was necessary to remain today at this place. Indians crowded numerously around us in the morning; and we were obliged to keep arms in hand all day, to keep them out of the camp. They began to surround the horses, which, for the convenience of grass, we were guarding a little above, on the river. These were immediately driven in, and kept close to the camp.

In the darkness of the night we had made a very bad encampment, our fires being commanded by a rocky bluff within 50 yards; but, notwithstanding, we had the river and small thickets of willows on the other side. Several times during the day the camp was insulted by the Indians; but, peace being our object, I kept simply on the defensive. Some of the Indians were on the bottom, and others haranguing us from the bluffs; and they were scattered in every direction over the hills. Their language bring probably a dialect of the Utak with the aid of signs some of our people could comprehend them very well. They were the same people w1,1 had murdered the Mexicans; and towards us their disposition was evidently hostile, nor were we well disposed towards them. They were barefooted, and nearly naked; their hair gathered up into a knot behind; and with his bow, each man carried a quiver with thirty or forty arrows partially drawn out. Besides these, each held in his hand two or three arrows for instant service. Their arrows are barbed with a very clear translucent stone, a species of opal, nearly as hard as the diamond; and, shot from their long bow, are almost as effective as a gunshot. In these Indians, I was forcibly struck by an expression of countenance resembling that in a beast of prey; and all their actions are those of wild animals. Joined to the restless motion of the eye, there is a want of mind—an absence of thought—and an action wholly by impulse, strongly expressed, and which constantly recalls the similarity.

A man who appeared to be a chief, with two or three others forced himself into the camp, bringing with him his arms, in spite of my orders to the contrary. When shown our weapons, he bored his ear with his fingers, and said he could not hear. " Why," said he, " there are none of you." Counting the people around the camp, and including in the number a mule that was being shod, he made out 22. " So many," said he, showing the number, " and we—we are a great many;" and he pointed to the hills and mountains round about. " If you have your arms," said he, twanging his bow, " we have these." I had some difficulty in restraining the people, particularly Carson, who felt an insult of this kind as much as if it had been given by a more responsible being. " Don't say that, old man," said he; " don't you say that—your life's in danger" —speaking in good English; and probably the old man was nearer to his end than he will be before he meets it.

Several animals had been necessarily left behind near the vamp last night; and early in the morning, before the Indians made their appearance, several men were sent to bring them In. When I was beginning to be uneasy at their absence, they returned with information that they had been driven off from the trail by Indians; and, having followed the tracks in a short distance, they found the animals cut up and spread out upon bushes. In the evening I gave a fatigued horse to some of the Indians for a feast; and the village which carried him off refused to share with the others, who made loud complaints from the rocks of the partial distribution. Many of these Indians had long sticks, hooked at the end, which they use in hauling out lizards, and other small animals, from their holes. During the day they occasionally roasted and ate lizards at our fires. These belong to the people who are generally known under the name of Diggers; and to these I have more particularly had reference when occasionally speaking of a people whose sole occupation is to procure food sufficient to support existence. The formation here consists of fine yellow sandstone, alternating with a coarse conglomerate, in which the stones are from the size of ordinary gravel to six or eight inches in diameter. This is the formation which renders the surface of the country so rocky, and gives us now a road alternately of loose heavy sands and rolled stones, which cripple the animals in a most extraordinary manner.

On the following morning we left the Rio de los Angeles, and continued our way through the same desolate and revolting country, where lizards were the only animal, and the tracks of the lizard eaters the principal sign of human beings. After twenty miles' march through a road of hills and heavy sands, we reached the most dreary river I have ever seen—a deep rapid stream, almost a torrent, passing swiftly by, and roaring against obstructions. The banks were wooded with willow, acacia, and a frequent plant of 'he country already mentioned, (Garrya elliptica,) growing in thickets, resembling willow, and bearing a small pink flower. Crossing it we encamped on the left bank, where we found a very little grass. Our three remaining steers, being entirely given out, were killed here. B y the boiling point, the elevation of the river here is 4,060 feet; and latitude, by observation, 360 41' 33". The stream was running towards the southwest, and appeared to come from a snowy mountain in the north. It proved to be the Rio Virgen—a tributary to the Colorado. Indians appeared in banns or the hills, but did not come into camp. For several days we continued our journey up the river, the bottoms of which were thickly overgrown with various kinds of brush; and the sandy soil was absolutely covered with the tracks of Diggers, who followed us stealthily, like a band of wolves; and we had no opportunity to leave behind, even for a few hours, the tired animals, in order that they might be brought into camp after a little reprieve. A horse or mule, left behind, was taken (ATM a moment, On the evening of the 8th, having traveled 28 miles up the river from our first encampment on it, we encamped at a little grassplot, where a spring of cool water issued from the bluff. On the opposite side was a grove of cottonwoods at the mouth of t fork, which here enters the river. On either side the valley is bounded by ranges of mountains, everywhere high, rocky, and broken. The caravan road was lost and scattered is the sandy country, and we had been following an Indian trail up the river. The hunters the next day were sent out to reconoitre, and in the mean time we moved about a mile farther up, where we found a good little patch of grass. There being only sufficient grass for the night, the horses were sent with a strong guard in charge of Tabeau to a neighboring hollow, where, they might pasture during the day; and, to be ready in case the Indians should make any attempt on the animals, several of the best horses were picketed at the camp. In a few hours the hunters returned, having found a convenient ford in the river, and discovered the Spanish trail on the other side.

I had been engaged in arranging plants; and, fatigued with the heat of the day, I fell asleep in the afternoon, and did not awake until sundown. Presently Carson came to me, and retorted that Tabeau, who early in the day had left his post, and, without my knowledge, rode back to the camp we had left, in search of a lame mule, had not returned. While we were speaking, a smoke rose suddenly from the cottonwood grove below, which plainly told us what had befallen him; it was raised to inform the surrounding Indians that a blow had been struck, and to tell them to be on their guard. Carson, with several men well mounted, was instantly sent down the river, but returned in the night without tidings of the missing man. They went to the camp we had left, but neither he nor the mule was there. Searching down the river, they found the tracks of the mule, evidently driven along by Indians, whose tracks were on each side of those made by the animal. After going several miles, they came to the mule itself, standing in some bushes, Mortally wounded in the side by an arrow, and left to die, that it might be afterwards butchered for food. They also found, in another place, as they were hunting about on the ground for Tabeau's tracks, something that looked like a little puddle of blood, but which the darkness prevented them from verifying. With these details they returned to our camp, and their report saddened all our hearts.

10th.—This morning, as soon as there was light enough to follow tracks, I set out myself, with Mr. Fitzpatrick and several men, in search of Tabeau. We went to the spot where the appearance of puddled blood had been seen; and this, we saw at once, had been the place where he fell and died. Blood upon the leaves, and beaten down bushes, showed that he had got his wound about twenty paces from where he fell, and that he had struggled for his life. He had probably been shot through the lungs with an arrow. From the place where he lay and bled, it could be seen that he had been dragged to the river bank, and thrown into it. No vestige of what had belonged to him could be found, except a fragment of his horse equipment. Horse, gun, clothes—all became the prey of these Arabs of the New World.

Tabeau had been one of our best men, and his unhappy death spread a gloom over our party. Men, who have gone through such dangers and sufferings as we had seen, become tike brothers, and feel each other's loss. To defend and avenge each other, is the deep feeling of all. We wished to avenge his death; but the condition of our horses, languishing for grass and repose, forbade an expedition into unknown mountains. We knew the tribe who had done the mischief—the same which had been insulting our camp. They knew what they deserved, and had the discretion to show themselves to us no more. The day before, they infested camp; now, not one appeared; nor did we ever afterwards see but one who even belonged to the same tribe, and he at a distance.

Our camp was in a basin below a deep canon—a gap of two thousand feet deep in the mountain—through which the Rio Virgen passes, and where no man or beast could follow it. The Spanish trail, which we had lost in the sands of the basin, was on the opposite side of the river. We crossed over to it, and followed it northwardly towards a gap which was visible in the mountain. We approached it by a defile, rendered difficult for our barefooted animals by the rocks strewed along it; and here the country changed its character. From the time we entered the desert, the mountains had been bald and rocky; here they began to be wooded with cedar and pine, and clusters of trees gave shelter to birds—a new and welcome sight—which could not have lived in the desert we had passed.

Descending a long hollow, towards the narrow valley of a stream, we saw before us a snowy mountain, far beyond which appeared another more lofty still. Good bunchgrass began to appear on the hillsides, and here we found a singular variety of interesting shrubs. The changed appearance of the country infused among our people a more lively spirit, which was heightened by finding at evening a halting place of very good grass on the clear waters of the Santa Clara fork of the Rio Virgen.

11th.—The morning was cloudy and quite cool, with a shower of rain—the first we have had since entering the desert, a period of 27 days—and we seem to have entered a different climate, with the usual weather of the Rocky mountains. Our march today was very laborious, over very broken ground, along the Santa Clara river; but then the country is no longer so distressingly desolate. The stream is prettily wooded with sweet cottonwood trees—some of them of large size; and on the hills, where the nutpine is often seen, a good and wholesome grass occurs frequently. This cottonwood, which is am in fruit, is of a different species from any in Michaux's Sylva. Heavy dark clouds covered the sky in the evening and a cold wind sprang up, making fires and overcoats corn Portable.

12th.—A little above our encampment the river forked, and we continued up the right-hand branch, gradually ascending towards the summit of the mountain. As we rose towards the head of the creek, the snowy mountains on our right showed out handsomely—high and rugged, with precipices, and covered with snow for about two thousand feet from their summits down. Our animals were somewhat repaid for their hard marches by an excellent camping ground on the summit of the ridge, which forms here the dividing chain between the waters of the Rio Virgen, which goes south to the Colorado, and those of Sevier river, flowing northwardly, and belonging to the Great Basin. We considered ourselves as crossing the rim of the basin; and, entering it at this point, we found here an extensive mountain meadow, rich in bunchgrass, and fresh with numerous springs of clear water, all refreshing and delightful to look upon. It was, in fact, that las Vegas de Santa Clara, which had been so long presented to us as the terminating point of the desert, and where the annual caravan from California to New Mexico halted and recruited for some weeks. It was a very suitable place to recover from the fatigue and exhaustion of a month's suffering in the hot and sterile desert. The meadow was about a mile wide, some ten miles long, bordered by grassy hills and mountains—some of the latter rising two thousand feet, and white with snow down to the level of the vegas. Its elevation above the sea was 5,280 feet; latitude, by observation, 370 28' 28"; and its distance from where we first struck the Spanish trail about 400 miles. Counting from the time we reached the desert, and began to skirt, at our descent from Walker's Pass in the Sierra Nevada, we had traveled 550 miles, occupying 27 days, in that inhospitable region. In passing before the Great Caravan, we had the advantage of finding more grass, but the disadvantage of finding also the marauding savages, who had gathered down upon the trail, waiting the approach of that prey. This greatly increased our labors, besides costing us the life of an excellent man. We had to move all day in a state of watch, and prepared for combat—scouts and flankers out, a front and rear division of our men, and baggage animals in the centre. At night, camp duty was severe. Those who had toiled all day, had to guard, by turns, the camp and the horses, all night. Frequently one third of the whole party were on guard at once; and nothing but this vigilance saved us from attack. We were constantly dogged by bands, and even whole tribes of marauders; and although Tabeau was killed, and our camp infested and insulted by some, while swarms of them remained on the hills and mountainsides, there was manifestly a consultation and calculation going, on, to decide the question of attacking us. Having reached the resting place of the Vegas de Santa Clara, we had complete relief from the heat and privations of the desert, and some relaxation from the severity of camp duty. Some relaxation, and relaxation only—for camp guards, horse guards, and scouts, are indispensable from the time of leaving the frontiers of Missouri until we return h them.

After we left the Vegas, we had the gratification to be joined by the famous hunter and trapper, Mr. Joseph Walker, whom have before mentioned, and who now became our guide. He had left California with the great caravan; and perceiving, from the signs along the trail, that there was a party of whites ahead, which he judged to be mine, he detached himself from the caravan, with eight men, (Americans,) and ran the gauntlet of the desert robbers, killing two, and getting some of the horses wounded, and succeeded in overtaking us. Nothing but his great knowledge of the country, great courage and presence of mind, and good rifles, could have brought him safe from such a perilous enterprise.

13th.—We remained one day at this noted place of rest and refreshment; and, resuming our progress in a northwestwardly direction, we descended into a broad valley, the water of which is tributary to Sevier lake. The next day we came in sight of the Wasatch range of mountains on the right, white with Snow, and here forming the southeast part of the Great Basin. Sevier Jake, upon the waters of which we now know belong to the system of lakes in the eastern part of the Basin —of which, the Great Salt lake, and its southern limb, the Utah lake, were the principal—towards the region of which we were now approaching. We traveled for several days in this direction, within the rim of the Great Basin, crossing little streams which bore to the left for Sevier lake; and plainly seeing, by the changed aspect of the country, that we were entirely clear of the desert, and approaching the regions which appertained to the system of the Rocky mountains. We met, in this traverse, a few mounted Utah Indians, in advance of their main body, watching the approach of the great caravan.

16th.—We reached a small salt lake, about seven miles long and one broad, at the northern extremity of which we encamped for the night. This little lake, which well merits its characteristic name, lies immediately at the base of the Wasatch range, and nearly opposite a gap in that chain of mountains through which the Spanish trail passes; and which, again falling upon the waters of the Colorado, and crossing that river, proceeds over a mountainous country to Santa Fe.

17th.—After 440 miles of traveling on a trail, which served for a road, we again found ourselves under the necessity of exploring a track through the wilderness. The Spanish trail had borne off to the southeast, crossing the Wasatch range. Our course led to the northeast, along the foot of that range, and leaving it on the right. The mountain presented itself to us under the form of several ridges, rising one above the other, rocky, and wooded with pine and cedar; the 'ast ridge covered with snow. Sevier river, flowing northwardly to the lake of the same name, collects its principal waters from this section of the Wasatch chain. We had now entered a region of great pastoral promise, abounding with fine streams, the rich bunchgrass, soil that would produce wheat, and indigenous flax growing as if it had been sown. Consistent with the general character of its bordering mountains, this fertility of soil and vegetation does not extend far into the Great Basin. Mr. Joseph Walker, our guide, and who has more knowledge of these parts than any man I know, informed me hat all the country to the left was unknown to him, and that even the Digger tribes, which frequented Lake Sevier, could tell him nothing about it.

20th.—We met a band of Utah Indians, headed by a well-known chief, who had obtained the American or English name of Walker, by which he is quoted and well known. They were all mounted, armed with rifles, and used their rifles well. The chief had a fusee, which he carried slung, in addition to his rifle. They were journeying slowly towards the Spanish trail, to levy their usual tribute upon the great California caravan. They were robbers of a higher order than those of the desert. They conducted their depredations with form, and under the color of trade and toll, for passing through their country. Instead of attacking and killing, they affect to purchase—taking the horses they like, and giving something nominal in return. The chief was quite civil to me. He was personally acquainted with his namesake, our guide, who made my name known to him. He knew of my expedition of 1842; and, as tokens of friendship, and proof that we had met, proposed an interchange of presents. We had no great store to choose out of; so he gave me a Mexican blanket, and I gave him a very fine one which I had obtained at Vancouver.

23d.—We reached Sevier river—the main tributary of the lake of the same name—which, deflecting from its northern course, here breaks from the mountains to enter the lake. It was really a fine river, from eight to twelve feet deep; and after searching in vain for a fordable place, we made little boats (or rather rafts) out of bulrushes, and ferried across. These rafts are readily made, and give a good conveyance across a river. The rushes are bound in bundles, and tied hard; the bundles are tied down upon poles, as close as they can be pressed, and fashioned like a boat, in being broader in the middle and pointed at the ends. The rushes, being tubular and jointed, are light and strong. The raft swims well, and is shoved along by poles, or paddled, or pushed and pulled by swimmers, or drawn by ropes. On this occasion, we used ropes—one at each end—and rapidly drew our little float backwards and forwards from shore to shore. The, horses swam. At our place of crossing, which was the most northern point of its bend, the latitude was 39° 22' 19". The banks sustained the character for fertility and vegetation which we had seen for some days. The name of this river and lake was an indication of our approach to regions of which our people had been the explorers. It was probably named after some American trapper or hunter, and was the first American name we had met with since leaving the Columbia river. From the Dalles to the point where we turned across the Sierra Nevada, near 1,000 miles, we heard Indian names, and the greater part of the distance none; from Nueva Helvetia (Sacramento) to las Vegas de Santa Clara, about 1,000 more, all were Spanish; from the Mississippi to the Pacific, French and American or English were intermixed; and this prevalence of names indicates the national character of the first explorers.

We had here the misfortune to lose one of our people, Francois Badeau, who had been with me on both expeditions; during which he had always been one of my most faithful and efficient men. He was killed in drawing towards him a gun by the muzzle; the hammer being caught, discharged the gun, driving the ball through his head. We buried him on the banks of the river.

Crossing the next day a slight ridge along the river, we entered a handsome mountain valley covered with fine grass, and directed our course towards a high snowy peak, at the top of which lay the Utah lake. On our right was a bed of high mountains, their summits covered with snow, constituting the dividing ridge between the Basin waters and those of the Colorado. At noon we fell in with a party of Utah Indians coming out of the mountain, and in the afternoon encamped on a tributary to the lake, which is separated from the waters of the Sevier by very slight dividing grounds.

Early the next day we came in sight of the lake; and, as we descended to the broad bottoms of the Spanish fork, three horsemen were seen galloping, towards us, who proved to be Utah Indians—scouts from a village, which was encamped near the mouth of the river. They were armed with rifles, and their horses were in good condition. We encamped near them, on the Spanish fork, which is one of the principal tributaries to the lake. Finding the Indians troublesome, and desirous to remain here a day, we removed the next morning farther down the lake and encamped on a fertile bottom near the foot of the same mountainous ridge which borders the Great Salt lake, and along which we had journeyed the previous September. Here the principal plants in bloom were two, which were remarkable as affording to the Snake Indians —the one an abundant supply of food, and the other the most useful among the applications which they use for wounds. These were the kooyah plant, growing in fields of extraordinary luxuriance, and convollaria stellata, which, from the experience of Mr. Walker, is the best remedial plant known among these Indians. A few miles below us was another village of Indians, from which we obtained some fish—among them a few salmon tiopt, which were very much inferior in size to those along the Californian mountains. The season for taking them had not yet arrived; but the Indians were daily expecting them to come up out of the lake.

We had now accomplished an object we had in view when leaving the Dalles of the Columbia in November last: we had reached the Utah lake; but by a route very different from the one we had intended, and without sufficient time remaining to make the examinations which we desired. It is a lake of note in this country, under the dominion of the Utahs, who resort to it for fish. Its greatest breadth is about fifteen miles, stretching far to the north, narrowing as it goes, and connecting with the Great Salt lake. This is the report, which I believe to be correct; but it is fresh water, while the other is not only salt, but a saturated solution of salt; and here is a problem which requires to be solved. It is almost entirely surrounded by mountains, walled on the north and east by a high and snowy range, which supplies to it a fan of tributary streams. Among these, the principal river is the Timpanogo—signifying Rock river—a name which the rocky grandeur of its scenery, recognizable even in this country of rugged mountains, has obtained for it from the Indians. In the Utah language, ogwallbe, tae term for river, when coupled with other words in common conversation, is usually abbreviated to ogo; fiimpan signifying rock. It is probable that this river furnished the name which on the older maps has been generally applied to the Great Salt lake; but for this I have preferred a name which will be regarded as highly characteristic, restricting to the river the descriptive term Timpanogo, and leaving for the lake into which it flows the name of the people who reside, on its shores, and by which it is known 'throughout the country.

The volume of water afforded by the Timpanogo is probably equal to that of the Sevier river; and, at the time of our 7isit, there was only one place in the lake valley at which the Spanish fork was fordable. In the cove of the mountains along its eastern shore, the lake is bordered by a plain, where the soil is generally good, and in greater part fertile; watered by a delta of prettily timbered streams. This would be an excellent locality for stock farms; it is generally covered with good bunchgrass, and would abundantly produce the ordinary grains.

In arriving at the Utah lake, we had completed an immense circuit of twelve degrees diameter north and south, and ten degrees east and west; and found ourselves, in May, 1844, on the same sheet of water which we had left in September, 1843. The Utah is the southern limb of the Great Salt lake; and thus we had seen that remarkable sheet of water both at its northern and southern extremity, and were able to fix its position at these two points. The circuit which we had made, and which had cost us eight months of time, and 3,500 miles of traveling, had given us a view of Oregon and of North California from the Rocky mountains to the Pacific ocean, and of the two principal streams which form bays or harbors on the coast of that sea. Having completed this circuit, and being now about to turn the back upon the Pacific slope of our continent, and to recross the Rocky mountains, it is natural to look back upon our footsteps, and take some brief view of the leading features and general structure of the country we had traversed. These are peculiar and striking, and differ essentially from the Atlantic side of the country. The mountains all are higher, more numerous, and more distinctly defined in their ranges and directions; and, what is so contrary to the natural order of formations, one of these ranges, which is near the coast, (the Sierra Nevada and the Coast Range,) presents higher elevations and peaks than any which are to be found in the Rocky mountains themselves. In our eight months' circuit, we were never out of sight of snow; and the Sierra Nevada, where we crossed it, was near 2,000 feet higher than the South Pass in the Rocky mountains. In height, these mountains greatly exceed those of the Atlantic side, constantly presenting peaks which enter the region of eternal snow; and some of them volcanic, and in a frequent state of activity. They are seen at great distances, and guide the traveler in his course.

The course and elevation of these ranges give direction to the rivers and character to the coast. No great river does, or can, take its rise below the Cascade and Sierra Nevada range; the distance to the sea is too short to admit of it. The rivers of the San Francisco bay, which are the largest after the Columbia, are local to that bay, and lateral to the coast, having their sources about on a line with the Dalles of the Columbia, and running each in a valley of its own, between the Coast range and the Cascade and Sierra Nevada range. The Columbia is the only river which traverses the whole breadth of the country, breaking through all the ranges, and entering the sea. Drawing its waters from a section of ten degrees of latitude in the Rocky mountains, which are collected into one stream by three main forks (Lewis's, Clark's, and the North fork) near the centre of the Oregon valley, this great river thence proceeds by a single channel to the sea, while its three forks lead each to a pass in the mountains, which opens the way into the interior of the continent. This fact in relation to the rivers of this region, gives an immense value to the Columbia. Its mouth is the only inlet and outlet to and from the sea: Its three forks the passes in the mountains: it is, therefore, the only line of communication between the Pacific and the interior of

North America; and all operations of war or commerce, of national or social intercourse, must be conducted upon it.

This gives it a value beyond estimation, and would involve irreparable, injury if los., In this unity and concentration of its waters, the Pacific side of our continent differs entirely from the Atlantic side, where the waters of the Allegheny mountains are dispersed into many rivers, having their different en,. trances into the sea, and opening many lines of communication with the interior.

The Pacific coast is equally different from that of the At. 'antic. The coast of the Atlantic is low and open, indented with numerous bays, sounds, and river estuaries, accessible everywhere, and opening by many channels into the heart of the country. The Pacific coast, on the contrary, is high and compact, with few bays, and but one that opens into the hart of the country. The immediate coast is what the seamen call ironbound. A little within, it is skirted by two successive ranges of mountains, standing as ramparts between the see and the interior of the country; and to get through which there is but one gate, and that narrow and easily defended. This strut Lure of the coast, backed by these two ranges of mountains, with its concentration and unity of waters, gives to the country in immense military strength, and will probably render Oregon the most impregnable country in the world.

Differing so much from the Atlantic side of our continent, in toast, mountains, and rivers, the Pacific side differs from it in another most rare and singular feature—that of the Great

Interior Basin, of which I have so often spoken, and the whole form and character of which I was so anxious to ascertain.

Its existence is vouched for by such of the American traders and hunters as have some knowledge of that region; the structure of the Sierra Nevada range of mountains requires it to be there; and my own observations confirm it. Mr. Joseph

Walker, who is so well acquainted in those parts, informed me that, from the Great Salt lake west, there was a succession of lakes and rivers which have no outlet to the sea, nor any connection with the Columbia, or with the Colorado of the Gulf of California. He described some of these lakes as being large, with numerous streams, and even considerable rivers falling, into them. In fact, all concur in the general report of them interior rivers and lakes; and, for want of understanding the force and power of evaporation, which so soon establishes an equilibrium between the loss and supply of waters, the fable of whirlpools and subterraneous outlets has gained belief, as the only imaginable way of carrying off the waters which have no visible discharge. The structure of the country would require this formation of interior lakes; for the waters which would collect between the Rocky mountains and the Sierra Nevada, not being able to cross this formidable barrier, nor to get to the Columbia or the Colorado, must naturally collect into reservoirs, each of which would have its little system of streams and rivers to supply it. This would be the natural effect; and what I saw went to confirm it. The Great Salt lake is a formation of this kind, and quite a large one; and having many streams, and one considerable river, 400 or 500 miles long, falling into it. This lake and river I saw and examined myself; and also saw the Wasatch and Bear River mountains, which enclose the waters of the lake on the east, and constitute, in that quarter, the rim of the Great Basin. Afterwards, along the eastern base of the Sierra Nevada, where we traveled for 42 days, I saw the line of lakes and rivers which lie at the foot of that Sierra; and which Sierra is the western rim of the Basin. In going down Lewis's fork and the main Columbia, I crossed only inferior streams coming in from the left, such as could draw their water from a short distante only; and I often saw the mountains at their heads white with snow,—which, all accounts said, divided the waters of the desert from those of the Columbia, and which could be no other than the range of mountains which form the rim of the Basin on its northern side. And in returning from California along the Spanish trail, as far as the head of the Santa Clara fork of the Rio Virgen, I crossed only small streams making their way south to the Colorado, or lost in sand, (as the Mohahve;) while to the left, lofty mountains, their summits white witn snow, were often visible, and which must have turned water to the north as well as 'o the south, and thus constituted, on this part the southern rim of the Basin. At the head of the Santa Clara fork, and in the Vegas de Santa Clara, we crossed the ridge which parted the two systems of waters. We entered the Basin at that point, and have traveled in it ever since; having its southeastern rim (the Wasatch mountain) op the right, and crossing the streams which flow down into it. The existence of the Basin is, therefore, an established fact in my mind: its extent and contents are yet to be better ascertained. It cannot be less than 400 or 500 miles each way, and must lie principally in the Alta California; the demarcation latitude of 42° probably cutting a segment from the north part of the rim. Of its interior, but little is known. It is called a desert, and, from what I saw of it, sterility may be its prominent characteristic; but where there is so much water, there must be some oasis. The great river, and the great lake, reported, may not be equal to the report; but where there is so much mow, there must be streams; and where there is no outlet, here must be lakes to hold the accumulated waters, or sands o swallow them up. In this eastern part of the, Basin, containing Sevier, Utah, and the Great Salt lake, and the rivers and creeks falling into them, we know there is good soil and good grass, adapted to civilized settlements. In the western part, on Salmon Trout river, and some other streams, the same remark may be made.

The contents of this great Basin are yet to be examined. That it is peopled, we know; but miserably and sparsely. From all that I heard and saw, I should say that humanity here appeared in its lowest form, and in its most elementary state. Dispersed in single families; without firearms; eating seeds and insects; digging roots, (and hence their name,)—such is the condition of the greater part. Others are a degree higher, and live in communities upon some lake or river that supplies fish, and from which they repulse the miserable Digger. The rabbit is the largest animal known in this desert; its flesh affords Is little meat; and their baglike covering is made of its skins. The wild sage is their only wood, and here it is of extraordinary size— sometimes a foot in diameter, and six or eight feet high, It serves for fuel, for building material/ for shelter to the rabbits, and for some sort of covering for the feet and legs in cold weather. Such are the accounts of the inhabitants and productions of the Great Basin; and which, though imperfect, must have some foundation, and excite out desire to know the whole.

The whole idea of such a desert, and such a people, is a novelty in our country, and excites Asiatic, not American ideas. Interior basins, with their own systems of lakes and rivers, and often sterile, are common enough in Asia; people still in the elementary state of families, living in deserts, with no other occupation than the mere animal search for food, may still be seen in that ancient quarter of the globe; but in America such things are new and strange, unknown and unsuspected, and discredited when related. But I flatter myself that what is discovered, though not enough to satisfy curiosity, is sufficient to excite it, and that subsequent explorations will complete what has been commenced.

This account of the Great Basin, it will be remembered, belongs to the Alta California, and has no application to Oregon, whose capabilities may justify a separate remark. Referring to my journal for particular descriptions, and for sectional boundaries between good and bad districts, I can only say, in general and comparative terms, that, in that branch of agriculture which implies the cultivation of grains and staple crops, it would be inferior to the Atlantic States, though many parts are superior for wheat; while in the rearing of flocks and herds it would claim a high place. Its grazing capabilities are great; and even in the indigenous grass now there, an element of individual and national wealth may be found. In fact, the valuable grasses begin within one hundred and fifty miles of the Missouri frontier, and extend to the Pacific ocean. East of the Rocky mountains, it is the short curly grass, on which the buffalo delights to feed, (whence its name of buffalo,) and which is still good when dry and apparently dead. West of those mountains it is a larger growth, in clusters, and hence called bunchgrass, and which has a second or fall growth. Plains and mountains both exhibit them; and I have seen good pasturage at an elevation of ten thousand feet. In this spontaneous product the trading or traveling caravans can find subsistence for their animals; and in military operations any number of cavalry may be moved, and any number of cattle may be driven; and thus men and horses be supported on long expeditions, and even in winter, in the sheltered situations.

Commercially, the value of the Oregon country must be great, washed as it is by the North Pacific ocean—fronting Asia—producing many of the elements of commerce—mild and healthy in its climate—and becoming, as it naturally will a thoroughfare for the East India and China trade.

Turning our faces once more eastward, on the morning of the 27th we left the Utah lake, and continued for two days to ascend the Spanish fork, which is dispersed in numerous branches among very rugged mountains, which afford few passes, and render a familiar acquaintance with them necessary to the traveler. The stream can scarcely be said to have a valley, the mountains rising often abruptly from the water's edge; but a good trail facilitated our traveling, and there were frequent bottoms, covered with excellent grass. The streams are prettily and variously wooded; and everywhere the mountain shows grass and timber.

At our encampment on the evening of the 28th, near the head of one of the branches we had ascended, strata of bituminous limestone were displayed in an escarpment on the rivet bluffs, in which were contained a variety of fossil shells of new species.

It will be remembered, that in crossing this ridge about 120 miles to the northward in August last, strata of fossiliferous rock were discovered, which have been referred to the oolitic period; it is probable that these rocks also belong to the same formation.

A few miles from this encampment we reached the bed of the stream, and crossing, by an open and easy pass, the di viding ridge which separates the waters of the Great Basin from those of the Colorado, we reached the head branches of one of its larger tributaries, which, from the decided color of its waters, has received the name of White river. The snows of the mountains were now beginning to melt, and all the little rivulets were running by in rivers, and rapidly becoming difficult to ford. Continuing a few miles up a branch of White river, we crossed a dividing ridge between its waters and those of Uintah. The approach to the pass, which is the best known to Mr. Walker, was somewhat difficult for packs, and impracticable for wagons—all the streams being shut in by narrow ravines, and the narrow trail along the steep hillsides allowing the passage of only one animal at a time. From the summit we had a fine view of the snowy Bear River range, and there were still remaining beds of snow on the cold sides of the hills near the pass. We descended by a narrow ravine, in which was rapidly gathered a little branch of the Uintah, and halted to noon about 1,500 feet below the pass, at an elevation, by the boiling point, of 6,900 feet above the sea.

The next day we descended along the river, and about noon reached a point where three forks come together. Fording one of these with some difficulty, we continued up the middle branch, which, from the color of its waters, is named the Red river. The few passes, and extremely rugged nature of the country, give to it great strength, and secure the Utahs from the intrusion of their enemies. Crossing in the afternoon a somewhat broken highland, covered in places with fine grasses, and with cedar on the hillsides, we encamped at evening on another tributary to the Uintah, called the Dnchesne fork. The water was very clear, the stream not being yet swollen by the melting snows, and we forded it without any difficulty. It is a considerable branch, being spread out by islands, the largest arm being about a hundred feet wide, 4nd the name it bears is probably that of some old French trapper.

The next day we continued down the river, which we were twice obliged to cross; and, the water having risen during the night, it was almost everywhere too deep to be forded. After traveling about sixteen miles, we encamped again on the left bank.

I obtained here an occultation of Scorpii at the irk limb of the moon, which gives for the longitude of the place 112° 18 30' and the latitude 40° 19' 53".

JUNE.

1st.—We left today the Duchesne fork, and, after traversing a broken country for about sixteen miles, arrived at noon at another considerable branch, a river of great velocity, to which the trappers have improperly given the name of Lake fork. The name applied to it by the Indians signifies great swiftness, and is the same which they use to express the speed of a racehorse. It is spread out in various channels over several hundred yards, and is everywhere too deep and swift to be forded. At this season of the year, there is an uninterrupted noise from the large rocks which are rolled along the bed. After infinite difficulty, and the delay of a day, we succeeded in getting the stream bridged, and got over with the loss of one of our animals. Continuing our route across a broken country, of which the higher parts were rocky and timbered with cedar, and the lower parts covered with good grass, we reached, on the afternoon of the 3d, the Uintah fort, a trading post belonging to Mr. A. Roubideau, on the principal fork of the Uintah river. We found the stream nearly as rapid and difficult as the Lake fork, divided into several cyannels, which were too broad to be bridged. With the aid of guides from the fort, we succeeded, with very great difficulty, in fording it, and encamped near the fort, which is situated a short distance above the junction of two branched which make the river.

By an immersion of the first satellite, (agreeing well with the result of the occultation observed at the Duchesne fork,) the, longitude of the post is 109° 56' 42", the latitude 40° 27' 45".

It has a motley garrison of Canadian and Spanish engages and hunters, with the usual number of Indian women. We obtained a small supply of sugar and coffee, with some dried meat and a cow, which was a very acceptable change from the pinoh on which we had subsisted for some weeks past. I strengthened my party at this place by the addition of Augusto

Arcnarabeau, an excellent voyageur and hunter, belonging to the class of Carson and Godey.

On the morning of the 5th we left the fort* and the Uintah river, and continued our road over a broken country, which afforded, however, a rich addition to our botanical collection; and, after a march of 25 miles, were again checked by another stream, called Ashley's fork, where we were detained until noon of the next day.

An immersion of the second satellite gave for this place a longitude of 1090 27' 07", the latitude, by observation, being 400 28' 07".

In the afternoon of the next day we succeeded in finding a ford; and, after traveling 15 miles, encamped high up on the mountainside, where we found excellent and abundant grass, which we had not hitherto seen.. A new species of elymus, which had a purgative and weakening effect upon the animals, had occurred abundantly since leaving the fort. From this point, by observation

7,300 feet above the sea, we had a view of the Colorado below, shut up amongst rugged mountains, and which is the recipient of all the streams we had been crossing since we passed the rim of the Great Basin at the head of the Spanish fork.

On the 7th we had a pleasant but long day's journey, through beautiful little valleys and a high mountain country, arriving about evening at the verge of a steep and rocky ravine, by which we descended to " Brown's hole." This is a place well known to trappers in the country, where the canons through which the Colorado runs expand into a narrow bu pretty valley, about 16 miles in length. The river was sev eral hundred yards in breadth, swollen to the top of its banks, near to which it was in many places 15 to 20 feet deep. We repaired a skin boat which had been purchased at the fort, and, after a delay of a day, reached the opposite banks with much less delay than had been encountered on the Uintah waters. According to information, the lower end of the valley is the most eastern part of the Colorado; and the latitude of our encampment, which was opposite to the remains of an old fort on the left bank of the river, was 40° 46' 27", and, by observation, the elevation above the sea 5,150 feet. The bearing to the entrance of the canon below was south 20° east. Here the river enters between lofty precipices of red rock, and the country below is said to assume a very rugged character, the river and its affluents passing through canons which forbid all access to the water. This sheltered little valley was formerly a favorite wintering ground for the trappers, as it afforded them sufficient pasturage for their animals, and the surrounding mountains are well stocked with game.

We surprised a flock of mountain sheep as we descended to the river, and our hunters killed several. The bottoms of a small stream called Vermilion creek, which enters the left bank of the river a short distance below our encampment, were covered abundantly with F. vermicularis, and other chenopodiaceous shrubs. From the lower end of Brown's hole we issued by a remarkably dry canon, fifty or sixty yards wide, and rising, as we advanced, to the height of six or eight hundred feet. Issuing from this, and crossing a small green valley, we entered another rent of the same nature, still narrower than the other, the rocks on either side rising in nearly vertical precipices perhaps 1,500 feet in height. These places are mentioned, to give some idea of the country lower down on the Colorado, to which the trappers usually apply the name of a canon country. The canon opened upon a pond of water, where we halted to noon. Several flocks of mountain sheep were here among the rocks, which rung with volleys of small arms. In the afternoon we entered upon an ugly, barren, and broken country, corresponding well with that we had traversed a few degrees north, an the same side of the Colorado. The Vermilion creek afforded us brackish water and indifferent grass for the night.

A few scattered cedar trees were the only improvement of the country on the following day; and at a little spring of bad water, where we halted at noon, we had not even the shelter of these from the hot rays e' the sun. At night we encamped in a fine grove of cottonwood trees, on the banks of the Elk Head river, the principal fork of the Yampah river, commonly called by the trappers the Bear river. We made here a very strong fort, and formed the camp into vigilant guards. The country we were now entering was constantly infested by war parties of the Sioux and other Indians, and is among the most dangerous war grounds in the Rocky mountains; parties of whites having been repeatedly defeated on this river.

On the 11th we continued up the river, which is a considerable stream, fifty to a hundred yards in width, handsomely and continuously wooded with groves of the narrow leaved cottonwood, populus angusttfolia; with these were thickets of willow, and grain du bceuf. The characteristic plant along the river is F. vermicularis, which generally covers the bottoms; mingled with this are saline shrubs and artemisia. The new variety of grass which we had seen on leaving the Uintah fort had now disappeared. The country on either side was sandy and poor, scantily wooded with cedars, but the river bottoms afforded good pasture. Three antelopes were killed in the afternoon, and we encamped a little below a branch of tilt river, called St. Vrain's fork. A few miles above was the fort at which Frapp's party had been defeated two years since; and we passed during the day a place where Carson had been fired upon so close that one of the men had five bullets through his body. Leaving this river the next morning, we took our way across the hills, where every hollow had a spring of running water with good grass.

Yesterday and today we had before our eyes the high mountains which divide the Pacific from the Mississippi waters; and entering here among the lower spurs or foothills of the range, the face of the country began to improve with a magical rapidity. Not only the river bottoms, but the hills were covered with grass; and among the usual varied flora of the mountain region, these were occasionally blue with the showy bloom of a lupinus. In the course of the morning we had the first glad view of buffalo, and welcomed the appearance of two old bulls with as much joy as if they had been messengers from home; and when we descended to noon on St. Vrain's fork, an affluent of Green river, the hunters brought in mountain sheep and the meat of two fat bulls. Fresh entrails in the river showed us that there were Indians above, and at evening, judging it unsafe to encamp in the bottoms, which were wooded only with willow thickets, we ascended to the spurs above, and forted strongly in a small aspen grove, near to which was a spring of cold water. The hunters killed two fine cows near the camp. A band of elk broke out of a neighboring grove; antelopes were running over the hills; and on the opposite river plains herds of buffalo were raising clouds of dust. The country here appeared more variously stocked with game than any part of the Rocky mountains we had visited; and its abundance is owing to the excellent pasturage, and its dangerous character as a war ground.

13th.—There was snow here near our mountain camp, and the morning was beautiful and cool. Leaving St. Vrain's fork, we took our way directly towards the summit of the dividing ridge. The bottoms of the streams and level places were wooded with aspens; and as we neared the summit, we entered again the piny region. We had a delightful morning's ride, the ground affording us an excellent bridle path, and reached the summit towards midday, at an elevation of 8,000 feet. With joy and exultation we saw ourselves once more on the top of the Rocky mountains, and beheld a little stream taking its course towards the rising sun. It was an affluent of the Platte, called Pullam's fork, and we descended to noon upon it. It is a pretty stream, twenty yards broad, and bears the name of a trapper who, some years since, was killed here by the Gros Ventre Indians.

Issuing from the pines in the afternoon we saw spread out before us the valley of the Platte, with the pass of the Medicine Butte beyond, and some of the Sweet Water mountains; but a smoky haziness in the air entirely obscured the Wind River chain.

We were now about two degrees south of the South Pass; and our course home would have been eastwardly; but that would have taken us over ground already examined, and therefore without the interest that would excite curiosity. Southwardly there were objects worthy to be explored, to wit the approximation of the headwaters of three different rivers—the Platte, the Arkansas, and the Grand River fork of the Rio Colorado of the Gulf of California; the passages at the heads of these rivers; and the three remarkable mountain coves, called Parks, in which they took their rise. One of these Parks was, of course, on the western side of the dividing ridge; and a visit to it would once more require us to cross the summit of the Rocky mountains to the west, and then to recross to the east, making in all, with the transit we had just accomplished, three crossings of that mountain in this section of its course. But no matter. The coves, the heads of the rivers, the approximation of their waters, the practicability of the mountain passes and the locality of the three Parks, were all objects of interest and, although well known to hunters and trappers, were unknown to science and to history. We therefore changed our course and turned up the valley of the Platte instead of going down it

We crossed several small affluents, and again made a fortified camp in a grove. The country had now became very beautiful—rich in water, grass, and game; and to these were added the charm of scenery and pleasant weather._

14th.—Our route this morning lay along the foot of the mountain, over the long low spurs which sloped gradually down to the river, forming the broad valley of the Platte The country is beautifully watered. In almost every hollow ran a clear, cool, mountain stream;

and in the course of that morning we crossed seventeen, several of them being large creeks, forty to fifty feet wide, with a swift current, and tolerably deep. These were variously wooded with groves of aspen and cottonwood, with willow, cherry, and other shrubby trees. Buffalo, antelope, and elk, were frequent during the day; and, in their abundance, the latter sometimes reminded us slightly of the Sacramento valley.

We halted at noon on Potter's fork—a clear and swift stream, forty yards wide, and in many places deep enough to swim our animals; and in the evening encamped on a pretty stream, where there were several beaver dams, and many trees recently cut down by the beaver. We gave to this the name of Beaver Dam creek, as now they are becoming sufficiently rare to distinguish by their names the streams on which they are found. In this mountain they occurred more abundantly than elsewhere in all our journey, in which their vestiges had been scarcely seen.

The next day we continued our journey up the valley, the country presenting much the same appearance, except that the grass was more scanty on the ridges, over which was spread a scrubby growth of sage; but still the bottoms of the creeks were broad, and afforded good pasture grounds. We had an animated chase after a grizzly bear this morning, which we tried to lasso. Fuentes threw the lasso upon his neck, but it slipped off, and he escaped into the dense thickets of the creek, into which we did not like to venture. Our course in the afternoon brought us to the main Platte river, here a handsome stream, with a uniform breadth of seventy yards, except where widened by frequent islands. It was apparently deep, with a moderate current, and wooded with groves of large willow.

The valley narrowed as we ascended, and presently degenerated into a gorge, through which the river passed as through a gate. We entered it, and found ourselves in the New Park —a beautiful circular valley of thirty miles diameter, walled in all round with snowy mountains, rich with water and with grass, fringed with pine on the mountain sides below the snow line, and a paradise to all grazing animals. The Indian name for it signifies " cow lodge," of which our own may be considered a translation; the enclosure, the grass, the water, and the herds of buffalo roaming over it, naturally presenting the idea of a park. We halted for the night just within the gate, and expected, as usual, to see herds of buffalo; but an Arapahoe village had been before us, and not one was to be seen. Latitude of the encampment 40o 52' 44". Elevation by the boiling point 7,720 feet.

It is from this elevated cove, and from the gorges of the surrounding mountains, and some lakes within their bosoms, that the Great Platte river collects its first waters, and assumes its first form; and certainly no river could ask a more beau& fill origin.

16th.—In the morning we pursued our way through the Park, following a principal branch of the. Platte, and crossing, among many smaller ones, a bold stream, scarcely fordable, called Lodge Pole fork, and which issues from a lake in the mountains on the right, ten miles long. In the evening we encamped on a small stream near the upper end of the Park. Latitude of the camp 40o 3e 22"

17th.—We continued our way among the waters of the Park over the foothills of the bordering mountains, where we found good pasturage, and surprised and killed some buffalo. We fell into a broad and excellent trail, made by buffalo, where a wagon would pass with ease; and, in the course of the morning we crossed the summit of the Rocky mountains, through a pass which was one of the most beautiful we had ever seen. The trail led among the aspens, through open grounds, richly covered with grass, and carried us over an elevation of about 9,000 feet above the level of the sea.

The country appeared to great advantage in the delightful summer weather of the mountains, which we still continued to enjoy. Descending from the pass, we found ourselves again on the western waters; and halted to noon on the edge of another mountain valley, called the Old Park, in which is formed

Grand river, one of the principal branches of the Colorado of California. We were now moving with some caution, as, from the trail, we found the Arapahoe village had also passed this way; as we were coming out of their enemy's country, and this was a war ground, we were desirous to avoid them. After a long afternoon's march, we halted at night on a small creek; tributary to a main fork of Grand river, which ran through this portion of the valley. The appearance of the country in the Old Park is interesting, though of a different character from the New; instead of being a comparative plain, it is more or less broken into hills, and surrounded by the high mountains, timbered on the lower parts with quaking asp and pines.

18th.—Our scouts who were as usual ahead, made from a butte this morning the signal of Indians, and we rode up in time to meet a party of about 30 Arapahoes. They were men and women going into the hills—the men for game, the women for roots—and informed us that the village was encamped a few miles above, on the main fork of Grand river which passes through the midst of the valley. I made then the usual presents; but they appeared disposed to be unfriendly and galloped back at speed to the village. Knowing that we had trouble to expect, I descended immediately into the bottoms of Grand river, which were overflowed in places, the river being up, and made the best encampment the ground afforded. We had no time to build a fort, but found an open place among the willows, which was defended by the river on one side and the overflowed bottoms on the other. We had scarcely made our few preparations, when about 200 of them appeared on the verge of the bottom, mounted, painted, and armed for war. We planted the American flag between us; and a short parley ended in a truce, with something more than the usual amount of presents. About 20 Sioux were with them—one of them an old chief, who had always been friendly to the whites. He informed me that, before coming down, a council had been held at the village, in which the greater part had declared for attacking us—we had come from their enemies, to whom we had doubtless been carrying assistance in arms and ammunition; but his own party, with some few of the Arapahoes who had seen us the previous year in the plains, opposed it. It will be remembered that it is customary for this people to attack the trading parties which they meet in this region, considering all whom they meet on the western side of the mountains to be their enemies. They deceived me into the belief that I should find a ford at their village, and I could not avoid accompanying them; but put several sloughs between us and their village, and forted strongly on the banks of the river, which was everywhere rapid and deep, and over a hundred yards in breadth. The camp was generally crowded with Indians; and though the baggage was carefully watched and covered, a number of things were stolen.

The next morning we descended the river for about eight miles, and halted a short distance above a canon, through which Grand river issues from the Park. Here it was smooth and deep, 150 yards in breadth, and its elevation at this point 6,700 feet. A frame for the boat being very soon made, our baggage was ferried across; the horses, in the mean time, awimming over. A southern fork of Grand river here makes its junction, nearly opposite to the branch by which we had entered the valley, and up this we continued for about eight miles in the afternoon and encamped in a bottom on the left bank, which afforded good grass. At our encampment it was 70 to 90 yards in breadth, sometimes widened by islands, and separated into several channels, with a very swift current and bed of rolled rocks.

On the 20th we traveled up the left bank, with the prospect of a bad road, the trail here taking the opposite side; but the stream was up, and nowhere fordable. A piny ridge of Mountains, with bare rocky peaks, was on our right all the day, and a snowy mountain appeared ahead. We crossed many foaming torrents with rocky beds, rushing down the river; and in the evening made a strong fort in an aspen grove. The valley had already become very narrow, shut up more closely in densely timbered mountains, the pines sweeping down the verge of the bottoms. The coq de prairie (tetrad europhasianus) was occasionally seen among the sage.

We saw today the returning trail of an Arapahoe party which had been sent from the village to look for Utahs in the Bayou Salade, (South Park;) and it being probable that they would visit our camp with the desire to return on horseback, we were more than usually on the alert.

Here the river diminished to 35 yards, and, notwithstanding the number of affluents we had crossed, was still a large stream, dashing swiftly by, with a great continuous fall, and not yet fordable. We had a delightful ride along a good trail among the fragrant pines; and the appearance of buffalo in great numbers indicated that there were

Indians in the Bayou Salade, (South Park,) by whom they were driven out. We halted to noon under the shade of the pines, and the weather was most delightful. The country was literally alive with buffalo; ani the continued echo of the hunters' rifles on the other side of the river for a moment made me uneasy, thinking perhaps they were engaged with Indians; but in a short time they came into camp with the meat of seven fat cows.

During the earlier part of the day's ride, the river had been merely a narrow ravine between high piny mountains, backed on both sides, but particularly on the west, by a line of snowy ridges; but, after several hours' ride, the stream opened out into a valley with pleasant bottoms. In the afternoon the river forked into three apparently equal streams; broad buffalo trails leading up the left hand, and the middle branch, indicating good passes over the mountains; but up the right-hand branch, (which, in the object of descending from the mountain by the main head of the Arkansas, I was most desirous tc follow,) there was no sign of a buffalo trace. Apprehending from this reason, and the character of the mountains, which are known to be extremely rugged, that the right-hand branch led to no pass, I proceeded up the middle branch, which formed a flat valley bottom between timbered ridges on the left and snowy mountains on the right, terminating in large buttes of naked rock. The trail was good, and the country interesting; and at nightfall we encamped in an open place among the pines, where we built a strong fort. The mountains exhibit their usual varied growth of flowers, and at this place I noticed, among others, thermopsis montana, whose bright yellow calor makes it a showy plant. This has been a characteristic in many parts of the country since reaching the Uintah waters. With fields of iris were aquilegia mrulea, violets, esparcette, and strawberries.

At dark we perceived a fire in the edge of the pines, on the opposite side of the valley. We had evidently not been discovered, and, at the report of a gun, and the blaze of fresh fuel which was heaped on our fires, those of the strangers were instantly extinguished. In the morning, they were found to be a party of six trappers, who had ventured out among the mountains after beaver.

They informed us that two of the number with which they had started had been already killed by the

Indians—one of them but a few days since—by the Arapahos we had lately seen, who had found him alone at a camp on this river, and carried off his traps and animals. As they were desirous to join us, the hunters returned with them to the encampment, and we continued up the valley, in which the stream rapidly diminished, breaking into small tributaries—every hollow affording water. At our noon halt, the hunters joined us with the trappers. While preparing to start from their encampment, they found themselves suddenly surrounded by a party of Arapahoes, who informed them that their scouts had discovered a large Utah village in the Bayou Salade, (South Park,) and that a large war party, consisting of almost every man in the village, except those who were too old to go to war, were going over to attack them. The main body had ascended the left fork of the river, which afforded a better pass than the branch we were on, and this party had followed our trail, in order that we might add our force to theirs. Carson informed them that we were too far ahead to turn back, but would join them in the bayou; and the Indians went off apparently satisfied. By the temperature of boiling water, our elevation here was 10,430 feet, and still the pine forest continued, and grass was good.

In the afternoon we continued our road occasionally through open pines, with a very gradual ascent. We surprised a herd of buffalo, enjoying the shade at a small lake among the pines, and they made the dry branches crack, as they brake through the woods. In a ride of about three-quarters of an hour, and having ascended perhaps 800 feet, we reached the summit of the dividing rage, which would thus have an estimated height of 11,200 feet. Here the river spreads itself into small branches and springs, heading nearly in the summit of the ridge, which is very narrow. Immediately below us was a green valley, through which ran a stream; and a short distance opposite rose snowy mountains, whose summits were formed into peaks of naked rock. We soon afterwards satisfied ourselves that immediately beyond these mountains was the main branch of the Arkansas river—most probably heading directly with the hue stream below us, which gathered its waters in the snowy mountains near by. Descriptions of the rugged character of the mountains around the head of the Arkansas, which their appearance amply justified, deterred me from making any attempt to reach it, which would have involved a greater length of time than now remained at my disposal.

In about a quarter of an hour, we descended from the summit of the Pass into the creek below, our road having been very much controlled and interrupted by the pines and springs on the mountainside. Turning up the stream, we encamped on a bottom of good grass near its head, which gathers its waters in the dividing crest of the Rocky mountains, and, according to the best, information we could obtain, separated only by the rocky wall of the ridge from the head of the main Arkansas river. By the observations of the evening, 'the latitude of our encampment was 39° 20' 24", and south of which, therefore, is the head of the Arkansas river. The stream on which we bad encamped is the head of either the Fontainequibouit, branch of the Arkansas, or the remotest head of the south fork of the Platte, as which you will find it laid down on the map. But descending it only through a portion of its course, we have not been able to settle this point satisfactorily. In the evening a band of buffalo furnished a little excitement, by charging through the camp.

On the following day we descended the stream by an excel lent buffalo trail, along the open grassy bottom of the river

On our right, the bayou was bordered by a mountainous range, crested with rocky and naked peaks; and below, it had a beautiful park like character of pretty level prairies, interspersed among low spurs, wooded openly with pine and quaking asp, contrasting well with the denser pines which swept around on the mountain sides. Descending always the valley of the stream, towards noon we descried a mounted party descending the point)f a spur, and, fudging them to be Arapahoes—who, defeated Dr victorious, were equally dangerous to us, and with whom a fight would be inevitable—we hurried to post ourselves as strongly as possible on some willow islands in the river. We bad scarcely halted when they arrived, proving to be a party of Utah women who told us that on the other side of the ridge their village was fighting with the Arapahoes. As soon as they had given us this information, they filled the air with cries and lamentations, which made us understand that some of their chiefs had been killed.

Extending along the river, directly ahem/ of us, was a low piny ridge, leaving between it and the stream a small open bottom, on which the Utahs had very injudiciously placed their village, which, according to the women, numbered about 300 warriors. Advancing in the cover of the pines, the Arapahoes, about daylight, charged into the village, driving off a great number of their horses, and killing four men; among them, the principal chief of the village. They drove the horses perhaps a mile beyond the village, to the end of a hollow, where they had previously forted, at the edge of the pines. Here the Utahs had instantly attacked them in turn, and, according to the report of the women, were getting rather the best of the day. The women pressed us eagerly to join with their people, and would immediately have provided us with the best, horses at the village; but it was not for us to interfere in such a conflict. Neither party were our friends, or under our protection; and each was ready to prey upon us that could. But we could not help feeling an unusual excitement at being within a few hundred yards of a fight, in which 500 men were closely engaged, and hearing the sharp cracks of their rifles. We were in a bad position, and subject to be attacked in it. Either party which we might meet, victorious or defeated, was certain to fall upon us; and, gearing up immediately, we kept close along the pines of the ridge, having it between us and the village, and keeping the scouts on the summit, to give us notice f the approach of Indians. As we passed by the village, which was immediately below us, horsemen were galloping to and fro, and groups of people were gathered around those who were wounded and dead, and who were being brought in from the field. We continued to press on, and, crossing another fork, which came in from the right, after having made fifteen miles from the village, fortified ourselves strongly in the pines, a short distance from the river.

During the afternoon, Pike's Peals had been plainly in view before us, and, from our encampment, bore N. 870 E. by compass. This was a familiar object, and it had for us the face of an old friend. At its foot were the springs, where we had spent a pleasant day in coming out. , Near it were the habitations of civilized men; and it overlooked the broad smooth plains, which promised us an easy journey to our home.

The next day we left the river, which continued its course towards Pike's Peak; and taking a southeasterly direction, in about ten miles we crossed a gentle ridge, and, issuing from the South Park, found ourselves involved among the broken spurs of the mountains which border the great prairie plains. Although broken and extremely rugged, the country was very interesting, being well watered by numerous affluents to the Arkansas river, and covered with grass and a variety of trees. The streams, which, in the upper part of their course, ran through grassy and open hollows, after a few miles all descended into deep and impracticable canons, tilt)ugh which they found their way to the Arkansas valley. Here the buffalo trails we had followed were dispersed among the hills, or crossed over into the, more open valleys of other streams.

During the day our road was fatiguing and difficult, reminding us much, by its steep and rocky character, of our traveling the year before among the Wind River mountains; but always at night we found some grassy bottom, which afforded us a pleasant camp. In the deep seclusion of these little streams, we found always an abundant pasturage, and a wild luxuriance of plants and trees. Aspens and pines were the prevailing timber: on the creeks oak was frequent; but the narrow leaved cottonwood, (populus angusiffolia,) of unusually large size, and seven or eight feet in circumference, was the principal tree. With these were mingled a variety of shrubby trees, which aided to make the ravines almost impenetrable.

After several days' laborious traveling, we succeeded in extricating ourselves from the mountains, and on the morning of the, 28th encamped immediately at their foot, on a handsome tributary to the Arkansas river. In the afternoon we descended the stream, winding our way along the bottoms, which were densely wooded with oak, and in the evening encamped near the main river. Continuing the next day our road along the Arkansas, and meeting on the way a war party of Arapahoe Indians, (who had recently been committing some outrages at Bent's fort, kitting stock and driving off horses,) we arrived before sunset at the Pueblo, near the mouth of the Fontainequibouit river, where we had the pleasure to find a number of our old acquaintances. The little settlement appeared in a thriving condition; and in the interval of our absence another had been established on the river,, some thirty, miles above.

On the 30th of June our cavalcade moved rapidly down the Arkansas, along the broad road which follows the river.

JULY.

On the let of July we arrived at Bent's fort, about 70 miles below the mouth of the Fontainequibouit. As we emerged into view from the groves on the river, we were saluted with a display of the national flag, and repeated discharges from the guns of the fort, where we were received by Mr. George Bent with a cordial welcome and a friendly hospitality, in the enjoyment of which we spent several very agreeable days. We were now in the region where our mountaineers were accustomed to live'; and all the dangers and difficulties of the road being considered past, four of them, including Carson and Walker, remained at the fort.

On the 5th we resumed our journey down the Arkansas traveling along a broad wagon road, and encamped about 20 miles below the fort. On the way we met a very large village of Sioux and Cheyenne Indians, who, with the Arapahoes, were returning from the crossing of the Arkansas, where they had been to meet the Kioway and Camanche Indians. A few days previous they had massacred a party of fifteen Delawares, whom they had discovered in a fort on the Smoke Hill river, losing in the affair several of their own people. They were desirous that we should bear a pacific message to the

Delawares on the frontier, from whom they expected retaliation; and we passed through them without any difficulty of delay. Dispersed over the plain in scattered bodies of horsemen, and family groups of women and children, with dog trains carrying baggage, and long lines of packhorses, their appearance was picturesque and imposing.

Agreeably to your instructions, which required me to complete, as far as practicable, our examinations of the Kansas, I left at this encampment the Arkansas river, taking a northeasterly direction across the elevated dividing grounds which separate that river from the waters of the Platte. On the 7th

We crossed a large stream, about forty yards wide, and one or two feet deep, flowing with a lively current on a sandy bed. The discolored and muddy appearance of the water indicated that it proceeded from recent rains; and we are inclined to consider this a branch of the Smoky Hill river, although, possibly, it may be the Pawnee fork of the Arkansas. Beyond this stream we traveled over high and level prairies, halting at small ponds and holes of water, and using for our fires the bois de vache, the country being without timber. On the evening of the 8th we encamped in a cottonwood grove on the banks of a sandy streambed, where there was water in holes sufficient for the camp. Here several hollows, or dry creeks with sandy beds, met together, forming the head of a stream which afterwards proved to be the Smoky Hill fork of the Kansas river.

The next morning, as we were leaving our encampment, a number of Arapahoe Indians were discovered. They belonged to a war party which had scattered over the prairie in returning from an expedition against the Pawnees.

As we traveled down the valley, water gathered rapidly in the sandy bed from many little tributaries; and at evening it bad become a handsome stream, fifty to eighty feet in width, with a lively current in small channels, the water being principally dispersed among quicksands.

Gradually enlarging, in a few days' march it became a river eighty yards in breadth, wooded with occasional groves of cottonwood. Our road was generally over level upland bordering the river, which were closely covered with a sward of buffalo grass.

On the 10th we entered again the buffalo range, where we had found these animals so abundant on our outward journey, and halted for a day among numerous herds, in order to make a provision of meat sufficient to carry us to the frontier.

A few days afterwards, we encamped, in a pleasant evening, on a high river prairie, the stream being less than a hundred yards broad. During the night we had a succession of thunderstorms, with heavy and continuous rain, and towards morning the water suddenly burst over the banks, flooding the bottoms and becoming a large river, five or six hundred yards in breadth. The darkness of the night and incessant rain had concealed from the guard the rise of the water; and the river broke into the camp so suddenly, that the baggage was instantly covered, and all our perishable collections almost entirely ruined, and the hard labor of many months destroyed in a moment.

On the 17th we discovered a large village of Indians encamped at the mouth of a handsomely wooded stream on the right bank of the river. Readily inferring, from the nature of the encampment, that they were Pawnee Indians, and confidently expecting good treatment from a people who receive regularly an annuity from the government, we proceeded directly to the village, where we found assembled nearly all the Pawnee tribe, who were now returning from the crossing of the Arkansas, where they had met the Kioway and Comanche Indians. We were received by them with the unfriendly rudeness and characteristic insolence which they never fail to display whenever they find an occasion for doing so with impunity. The little that remained of our goods was distributed among them, but proved entirely insufficient to satisfy their greedy rapacity; and, after some delay, and considerable difficulty, we succeeded in extricating ourselves from the village, and encamped on the river about 15 miles below.

The country through which we had been traveling since leaving the Arkansas river, for a distance of 260 miles, presented to the eye only a succession of far stretching green prairies, covered with the unbroken verdure of the buffalo grass, and sparingly wooded along the streams with straggling trees and occasional groves of cottonwood; but here the country began perceptibly to change its character, becoming a more fertile, wooded, and beautiful region, covered with a profusion of grasses, and watered with innumerable little streams, which were wooded with oak, large elms, and the usual varieties of timber common to the lower course of the Kansas river.

As we advanced, the country steadily improved, gradually assimilating itself in appearance to the northwestern part of the state of Missouri. The beautiful sward of the buffalo grass, which is regarded as the best and most nutritious found on the prairies, appeared now only in patches, being replaced by a longer and coarser grass, which covered the face of the country luxuriantly. The difference in the character of the grasses became suddenly evident in the weakened condition of our animals, which began sensibly to fail as soon as we quitted the buffalo grass.

The river preserved a uniform breadth of eighty or a hundred yards, with broad bottoms continuously timbered with large cottonwood trees, among which were interspersed a few other varieties.

While engaged in crossing one of the numerous creeks which frequently impeded and checked our way, sometimes obliging us to ascend them for several miles, one of the people (Alexis Ayot) was shot through the leg by the accidental discharge of a rifle—a mortifying and painful mischance, to be crippled for life by an accident, after having nearly accomplished in safety a long and eventful journey. He was a young man of remarkably good and cheerful temper, and had been among the useful and efficient men of the party.

After having traveled directly along its banks for 290 miles, we left the river, where it bore suddenly off in a northwesterly direction, towards its junction with the Republican fork of the Kansas, distant about 63 miles; and, continuing our easterly course, in about 20 miles we entered the wagon road from Santa Fe to Independence, and on the last day of July encamped again at the little town of Kansas, on the banks of the Missouri river.

During our protracted absence of 14 months, in the course of which we had necessarily been exposed to great varieties of weather and of climate, not one case of sickness had ever occurred among us.

Here ended our land journey; and the day following our arrival, we found ourselves on board a steamboat rapidly gliding down the broad Missouri. Our travel worn animals had not been sold and dispersed over the country to renewed labor, but were placed at good pasturage on the frontier, and are now ready to do their part in the coming expedition.

On the 6th of August we arrived at St. Louis, where the party was finally disbanded, a great number of the men having their homes in the neighborhood.

Andreas Fuentes also remained here, having readily found employment for the winter, and is one of the men engaged to accompany me the present year.

Pablo Hernandez remains in the family of Senator Benton, where he is well taken care of, and conciliates goodwill by his docility, intelligence, and amiability. General Almonte, the Mexican minister at Washington, to whom he was of course made known, kindly offered to take charge of him, and to carry him back to Mexico; but the boy preferred to remain where he was until he got an education, for which he shows equal ardor and aptitude.

Our Chinook Indian had his wish to see the whites fully gratified. He accompanied me to Washington, and, after remaining several months at the Columbia College, was sent by tile Indian department to Philadelphia, where, among other things, he learned to read and write well, and speak the English language with some fluency. He will accompany me in a few days to the frontier of Missouri, where he will be sent with some one of the emigrant companies to the village at the Dalles of the Columbia.

Very respectfully, your obedient servant,

J. C. FREMONT

> Get your FREE EBOOK—join our mailing list to get notified of great new (old) books and the latest blog posts.
>
> BIG BYTE BOOKS is your source for great lost history!

Made in the USA
Middletown, DE
19 September 2022